# DICKENS STUDIES ANNUAL
## Essays on Victorian Fiction

EDITORS

Michael Timko
Fred Kaplan
Edward Guiliano

# DICKENS STUDIES ANNUAL

## Essays on Victorian Fiction

VOLUME
17

*Edited by*
Michael Timko, Fred Kaplan,
and Edward Guiliano

**AMS PRESS**
NEW YORK

DICKENS STUDIES ANNUAL

ISSN 0084-9812

*Dickens Studies Annual: Essays on Victorian Fiction* is published in cooperation with the Victorian Committee of the City University of New York and in association with Queens College and the Graduate Center, CUNY.

**International Standard Book Number**
**Series: 0-404-18520-7**
**Vol. 17: 0-404-18537-1**

*Dickens Studies Annual: Essays on Victorian Fiction* welcomes essay and monograph-length contributions on Dickens as well as on other Victorian novelists and on the history or aesthetics of Victorian fiction. All manuscripts should be double-spaced, including footnotes, which should be grouped at the end of the submission, and should be prepared according to the format used in this journal. An editorial decision can usually be reached more quickly if two copies are submitted. The preferred editions for citations from Dickens' works are the Clarendon and the Norton Critical when available, otherwise the Oxford Illustrated Dickens or the Penguin.

Please send submission to the Editors, *Dickens Studies Annual*, Room 1522, Graduate School and University Center, City University of New York, 33 West 42nd Street, New York, N.Y. 10036; please send subscription inquiries to AMS Press, Inc., 56 East 13th Street, New York, N.Y. 10003.

Manufactured in the United States of America

# Contents

# Preface

"Round up the usuals," is no glib response to the writing of a preface and acknowledgments to the seventeenth volume in a continuing series. Rather, it is an affirmation that behind each appearance of *Dickens Studies Annual: Essays on Victorian Fiction,* and behind the quality of each new volume, is an establishment the editors have come to rely upon.

Naturally, the members of the editorial and advisory boards and the many outside manuscript readers form a large part of the support system for the *Annual.* The good counsel, and especially the detailed reader's reports, which these good people submit is deeply appreciated and a service to our profession and to our understanding of the history, criticism, and aesthetics of Victorian fiction. For undertaking the arduous task of writing comprehensive review essays for this volume, we wish to thank Frederick R. Karl (Biography), Dale Kramer (Hardy), and David Paroissien (Dickens). For especially notably "silent" (or at least unwritten) contributions to this volume we thank professors Murray Baumgarten, Edwin Eigner, John Jordan, and Gerhardt Joseph, and add special commendation to the two C.U.N.Y. Ph.D. candidates in English who served as our editorial assistants: Debra Ann Suarez and Bansie Kotwal.

We continue to enjoy and to offer our thanks for the generous support of President Shirley Strum Kenny, Dean John Reilly, and Chair of English Charles Molesworth of Queens College; Senior Vice President for Academic Affairs Theodore S. Steele and Dean of Humanities Michael Spitzer of The New York Institute of Technology; President Harold Proshansky, Provost Stephen Kahn, and Executive Director, Ph.D. Program in English, Martin Stevens, the Graduate School and University Center; and finally Chancellor Joseph Murphey of the City University of New York.

Once again we acknowledge our collaborators at AMS Press: Gabriel Hornstein, president, William B. Long, editor, and Robert Harris.

# Notes on Contributors

DANIELA BIELECKA is a professor of English in the Polish university system who specializes in theatre and linguistics.

STANLEY FRIEDMAN, Associate Professor of English at Queens College, CUNY, has previously published articles on Dickens in *Dickens Studies Annual*, *Nineteenth-Century Fiction*, *Dickens Studies Newsletter*, *Dickens Quarterly*, *Victorian Newsletter*, and MLA's *Approaches to Teaching Dickens' "David Copperfield"*.

SARAH GILEAD's teaching and research interests include the Victorian novel, children's literature, and autobiography. She has published articles in *TSLL*, *ELH*, *Criticism*, *Victorian Poetry*, *Children's Literature*, and elsewhere. Currently an assistant professor of English at the University of Haifa, Israel, she is working on a book on the Victorian novel.

RUTH GLANCY teaches English at the University of Alberta. She has published several articles on Dickens, an annotated bibliography of his short-story work, and an edition of the Christmas Books for Oxford University Press. She is currently writing a textbook on *A Tale of Two Cities*.

ROBERT HIGBIE is professor of English at Appalachian State University in Boone, North Carolina. He recently completed a book on British fiction.

FREDERICK R. KARL, Professor of English at New York University, has written extensively about nineteenth-century fiction and about biography. His critical biography of William Faulkner will appear in early 1989.

DALE KRAMER is Professor of English at the University of Illinois at Urbana-Champaign. He is the author of *Thomas Hardy: The Forms of Tragedy* (1975) and the editor of *Critical Approaches to the Fiction of Thomas Hardy* (1979). He has edited critical editions of *The Woodlanders* (1981) and *The Mayor of Casterbridge* (1987); with Simon Gatrell he is attempting to launch a complete critical edition of Hardy's fiction. Other current projects are a collection of the best recent critical essays and chapters on Hardy, and a long-term study of the production of tragedy in Victorian literature.

PATRICK J. McCARTHY, Professor of English at the University of California, Santa Barbara, has written a variety of studies on Victorian subjects, including *Matthew Arnold and the Three Classes* (1964). The essay published here will be part of a longer work on the language of value in Dickens's novels.

SYLVIA MANNING is Professor of English and Vice Provost at the University of Southern California. She is the author of *Dickens as Satirist, Hard Times: an Annotated Bibliography,* and essays on Dickens Thackeray, and Tennyson. Her first writing on film adaptation of Dickens appeared in the *Dickens Quarterly 4* (1987), "Murder in Three Media: Adaptations of *Oliver Twist.*"

JAMES E. MARLOW is a professor of English at Southeastern Massachusetts University. His interest in Victorian cookery and digestion is a natural result of his previous work on the Victorian dread of and fascination with cannibalism.

SYLVERE MONOD is Emeritus Professor of English at the Sorbonne Nouvelle. Having strayed beyond the pale of Dickens studies by editing Conrad in French, and beyond the pale of scholarship by publishing his own first novel in 1988, he may have become a lost soul.

DAVID PAROISSIEN, Professor of English at the University of Massachusetts, Amherst, teaches courses in the Victorian novel, Dickens, and British literature. Since 1983, he has edited *Dickens Quarterly.* He is presently finishing *The Companion to "Oliver Twist."*

ROBERT TRACY. Professor of English at the University of California, Berkeley, teaches courses in nineteenth- and twentieth-century literature, specializing in the literatures of Britain and Ireland. His *Trollope's Later Novels* (1978) is a standard work, and his *Stone* (1981), translations of early poems by the Russian poet Osip Mandelstam, has been well received. He is a recent Guggenheim Fellow and an active participant in the University of California Dickens Project.

GEORGE J. WORTH is Professor of English at the Univeristy of Kansas. He has published extensively on Victorian literature. Among his books are two on Dickens: *Dickensian Melodrama* (1976) and *"Great Expectations": An Annotated Bibliography* (1986). "Mr. Wopsle's Hamlet" marks his first appearance in *DSA*, but his review-essay "Recent Dickens Studies: 1987" is scheduled for publication in *DSA* 18.

# "The Old Story" and Inside Stories: Modish Fiction and Fictional Modes in *Oliver Twist*

## Robert Tracy

Make 'em your models, my dear. Make 'em your models, . . . do everything they bid you, and take their advice in all matters—especially the Dodger's, my dear. He'll be a great man himself, and will make you one too, if you take pattern by him.—Is my handkerchief hanging out of my pocket, my dear?

*Oliver Twist*, chapter 9

When he came to the tree of glory, he was welcomed with an universal shout of the people, who were there assembled in prodigious numbers to behold . . . the proper catastrophe of a great man.

Henry Fielding, *The History of the Life of the Late Mr. Jonathan Wild the Great*

Very early in *Oliver Twist* we meet a connoisseur of stories and a projector of stories. The connoisseur is the workhouse doctor who delivers Oliver. He recognizes the child and his nameless mother as figures from a familiar narrative. " 'The old story,' " he remarks, examining the dead woman's hand; " 'no wedding ring, I see.' "[1] He reads her story in her circumstances and comments on that story's lack of novelty. And, though we must wait until the very end of *Oliver Twist* to hear the story in detail, the doctor is quite right. A young woman trusted a lover too far, found herself pregnant, and ran away with her guilty secret. But when we do hear the story of Oliver's parentage, of Edwin Leeford's loveless marriage and his affair with Agnes Fleming, it does not really seem to have very much to do with the novel we have been reading. Indeed, these revelations even cancel out the novel's title and subtitle: we have, it seems, been reading "Oliver Leeford" or "Oliver

1

Fleming'' all along, and the story moves backward in time, belying the ''Parish Boy's Progress'' we have been promised.

The projector of stories is Mr. Bumble, whose duties include the naming of the parish orphans. Like a novelist who must name a character in a way that will reinforce that character's fictional identity, Bumble names Oliver to become the hero of a certain story. '' 'I inwented' '' his name, Bumble tells Mrs. Mann:

> ''We name our fondlins in alphabetical order. The last was a S,—Swubble, I named him. This was a T,—Twist, I named *him*. The next one as comes will be Unwin, and the next Vilkins. I have got names ready made to the end of the alphabet, and all the way through it again, when we come to Z.''
> ''Why, you're quite a literary character, sir!'' said Mrs. Mann.
> ''Well, well,'' said the beadle, evidently gratified with the compliment; ''perhaps I may be. Perhaps I may be, Mrs. Mann.''                    (2:7)

Like Bumble, Fang, Grimwig, and Bolter, the alias Noah Claypole chooses for himself after he runs away, the names Bumble ''inwents'' predict certain temperaments and fates for their bearers: Swubble rhymes with trouble and Unwin is a loser's name, both probable enough destinies for parish boys, while Vilkins recalls the lugubrious/comic cockney ballad of Villikins and his Dinah. Twist is full of implications. To twist is to eat heartily, and a twister is a very hearty eater, appropriate for the boy who is to ask for more and whose probable appetite makes Mrs. Sowerberry apprehensive. To twist is also to hang, and represents an all-too-likely end for a parish boy. The gentleman in the white waistcoat thrice prophesizes that fate for Oliver (2: 11–12; 3: 19), responding perhaps as much to the implications of his name as to the sociological odds, and a protracted stay with Fagin can have no other ending. Finally, in nineteenth-century naval parlance, a twist is a yarn, a story, as Dickens, son of a naval clerk, would have known—in the January 1838 *Bentley's*, ''Father Prout'' (Francis Sylvester Mahony) praises Boz for ''the yarn you spin concerning Oliver Twist.'' Oliver's true destiny is to feature in a story. In standard English, twist has connotations of perversion, appropriate to the atmosphere of Fagin's gang and to the Monks plot, which would pervert Oliver into a criminal. As for Oliver, it is the highwayman's and the burglar's slang term for the moon: perhaps Bumble, like Dickens, had read Edward Bulwer's *Paul Clifford* (1830) or William Harrison Ainsworth's *Rookwood* (1834), where the term is often employed.[2] Here, combined with the hanging implications of Twist, it helps to suggest a criminal career for Oliver.

The doctor and Bumble both think they can tell the story of Oliver Twist.

But that story evades their categories. Dickens refuses to satisfy their (or our) expectations. The story he tells us also consistently evades its own categories. There are sudden and drastic changes of plot and purpose as the novel develops. It is made up of four different plots, which are not exactly combined—they are, rather, stitched together to create a book-length narrative. It is a tribute to Dickens' extraordinary skill and energy that we can overlook the uncertain progress of the story when we read *Oliver Twist*.

Dickens' subtitle, "The Parish Boy's Progress," suggests that Oliver is to grow and develop, but he does not really do so. Apart from three moments early in the novel, when he asks for more, knocks Noah Claypole down, and runs off to London, Oliver hardly acts at all. On one later occasion he decides to take the initiative by alarming the Maylie family during the burglary, "whether he died in the attempt or not" (22: 145). But he has no chance to do this. Though he passively resists efforts to make him perform criminal acts, he is controlled and manipulated by others throughout the novel.

Nor does the plot of *Oliver Twist* really progress or develop. Instead, on at least three occasions Dickens drastically shifts both the mode and the direction of his story, in such a way as to suggest that he was improvising rather than following a plan already worked out. Oliver's uncertain progress reflects the uncertain process by which he is written. *Oliver Twist* begins as a sardonic account of a child's life as a ward of the Parish, describing Oliver's upbringing, the mean calculations of public charity, his near apprenticeship to Mr. Gamfield as a chimney sweep, and his service with Mr. Sowerberry the undertaker. This section includes the satirically presented figure of Bumble, and the bleak portrayal of a pauper death and funeral. Dickens' tone is ironic, and he often addresses the reader directly, to underline the evils and the parsimony of the workhouse system. But the workhouse theme, and Oliver's specific identity as a Parish Boy and so a victim of a meanly conceived theory of public charity, ends in Part IV (chapters 7–8, May 1837), with Oliver's departure for London.

*Oliver Twist* may not originally have been intended as a novel at all. When the first installment appeared in *Bentley's Miscellany* (February 1837), the opening sentence specified "Mudfog" as the town of Oliver's birth, suggesting that Oliver was not to figure in a novel, but in some of the "Mudfog Papers" that Dickens contributed to *Bentley's* in 1837–38. These were aimed at contemporary abuses and absurdities. Their slightly labored sarcasm is echoed in the novel's early chapters.[3] Dickens' subsequent dispute with Richard Bentley, publisher of the *Miscellany*, over Bentley's unwillingness to accept *Oliver Twist* as the second of two novels for which Dickens had signed a contract (the first, as yet unwritten, was *Barnaby Rudge*), is further evidence that *Oliver Twist* had not originally been planned as a novel; Bentley argued that *Oliver Twist* had already been paid for as a series of papers in the *Miscellany* (Wheeler 44, 49–50; Johnson I: 236–237; *Letters* I: 301n).

Oliver's story veers completely away from the workhouse theme when he meets the Artful Dodger and Fagin in Part IV (chapter 8), and the second plot, with its criminal theme, begins. This is not necessarily at variance with what has gone before—a "Parish Boy's Progress" may very well bring him into the dens of thieves and through them to the gallows. But we hear nothing more about the workhouse as an institution, and when Bumble reappears he is being groomed for another role, as a criminal, albeit an ineffectual and comic one. Dickens' personal comments are more general, as in his remarks about the human passion "for *hunting something*" (10: 59), or more specific, as in his hostile portrayal of the real Magistrate Laing (11) as the impatient Mr. Fang.

Once the Artful Dodger and Fagin appear, *Oliver Twist* becomes a study of criminal life in London at its lowest level, emphasizing its poverty, discomfort, and brutality. This theme persists through Part X (chapters 20–22, January 1838). Dickens records Oliver's first stay with Fagin, his arrest and appearance before Mr. Fang, his rescue by Mr. Brownlow, his recapture, and his enforced participation in Bill Sikes' attempt to burglarize Mrs. Maylie's house. Fagin, at once attractive and repellent, dominates this part of the book.

Early in these criminal chapters, there is an abortive movement toward yet another plot. In Part V (chapters 9–11, July 1837), Oliver, half awake, watches Fagin draw out his treasures from a hole in the floor and examine them, especially a trinket "so small that it lay in the palm of his hand. There seemed to be some very minute inscription on it; for the Jew laid it flat upon the table, and, shading it with his hand, pored over it, long and earnestly. At length he put it down, as if despairing of success" (9: 52). Presumably Dickens at one point intended that this trinket have something to do with Oliver, but we never hear of it again; it is later superseded by the "little gold locket: in which were two locks of hair, and a plain gold wedding-ring" with "Agnes" engraved on the inside and a blank left for the surname, then a date "within a year" before Oliver's birth (38: 254).

The burglary ends Oliver's criminal career, and any active role for him in the novel. He disappears for two whole numbers (XI and XII: chapters 23–27, February and March, 1838), and once he is settled with the Maylies, he becomes a static character; events occur around him, but he has no real part in them.

As the story appeared in *Bentley's*, Dickens headed Part XI (chapters 23–25, February 1838) with the words "Book II," although he had commenced his narrative with no indication that it was to be divided into books, that it was to be a tale of novel length. Part XI also represents another drastic change in direction for the plot, with the intimation that Oliver is no ordinary parish boy but some sort of dispossessed heir. Part XI—or Book II—opens with Mr. Bumble's wooing of Mrs. Corney, interrupted by her interview with old Sally and the first mention of some mysterious gold object which might have gained Oliver better treatment, had Sally not stolen it from his mother's corpse. This episode is clearly an afterthought, a completely new idea. Dickens' initial account of Oliver's birth and his mother's death left no room for her dying speech and the presence of identifying jewelry. It seems clear that Oliver was originally intended to be an ordinary parish boy who undergoes the vicissitudes and neglect of his lot. Dickens decided much later to make him of gentle though illegitimate birth, the hero of a conventional melodramatic plot of dispossession.

The three chapters of Part XI prepare the reader for the new plot concerning Monks, his hatred of Oliver, and his plot to prevent the boy from inheriting the money left to him by Edwin Leeford—their mutual father—both by concealing his identity, and by arranging with Fagin for Oliver's involvement in some criminal act: Edwin Leeford's will stipulated that his second son would inherit only on condition that " 'in his minority he should never have stained his name with any public act of dishonour, meanness, cowardice, or wrong' " (51: 351). The atmosphere of the story changes from the sometimes jolly, sometimes brutal atmosphere of the thieves' den to one of mystery and spying, or to the sentimentality of the Maylie household. We are far from the sardonic treatment of workhouse life and public charity with which the story began, and Fagin's practical motives for making Oliver a criminal have been replaced by Monks' fantastic hatred.

Monks himself appears in the first chapter of Part XII (chapters 26–27, March 1838). Now Oliver is threatened, not by public neglect or the temptations of the criminal life, but by an insane fraternal vindictiveness, which Dickens improvises in a retroactive effort to impose a specific plot and direction upon his novel. He does this at considerable risk to the plausibility of the story, as when Monks allegedly recognized Oliver by sight on the day he went out with Charley Bates and the Dodger (26: 171), and was wrongfully accused of picking Mr. Brownlow's pocket. Monks' " 'suspicions were first awakened by' " Oliver's resemblance to his father (49: 336), according to Mr. Brownlow, but Brownlow also noted the boy's " 'strong resemblance' "

(335) to his mother's portrait, painted by Edwin Leeford, and old Sally recalls that " 'The boy grew so like his mother . . . that I could never forget it when I saw his face' " (24: 155).

Before old Sally's deathbed confession in chapter 24, there is really nothing in *Oliver Twist* to prepare us for the plot involving Monks and Oliver's parentage. Dickens seems to have added this new plot as a way of stretching his story to novel length. In doing so, he abandons the satire of the early chapters, and the realistic drama of the Fagin chapters, for melodrama. Though Monks and Fagin continue to menace Oliver, they are not able to touch him. They are excluded from the Maylie world of calm domesticity, and their adventures essentially diverge from those of Oliver. And Dickens introduces yet another plot, the not very interesting love story of Harry and Rose Maylie, its weakness emphasized by Rose's nearly fatal illness and Harry's nearly thwarted courtship.

With the virtual disappearance of Oliver, Nancy emerges as the principal character in and after Part XII (chapters 26–27, March 1838), a development foreshadowed by her passionate defence of Oliver after his recapture (16: 102–104). "I am glad you like Oliver this month—especially glad that you particularize the first chapter," Dickens wrote to Forster on 3 November 1837, referring to the chapter in which Nancy defends Oliver. "I hope to do great things with Nancy. If I can only work out the idea I have formed of her, and of the female who is to contrast with her" (*Letters* I: 328). She becomes the chief opponent of Monks and Fagin by eavesdropping on them in chapter 26, the very chapter in which the Monks plot begins. Her emergence as heroine and eventually as victim in the second half of the book, coupled with Oliver's disappearance, strongly suggests that she has superseded Oliver as the representative of "the principle of Good surviving through every adverse circumstance" which Dickens later declared to be his subject, in his 1841 preface to the third edition (lxii; Wheeler 41, 52, 57). When he turned her into a heroine, Dickens had to go back and suppress certain references to her vulgarity as he revised his text for book publication—for example, he strips her of the "red gown, green boots, and yellow curl-papers" (13: 79) which she wore when she first appeared in the pages of *Bentley's*.[4]

Nancy's conversion, or the emergence of her suppressed better self, is more interesting and psychologically more believable than Oliver's instinctive virtue and gentlemanly ideals, apparently genetic in origin, spontaneously developed, and preserved throughout his years in the workhouse. Nancy offered Dickens a greater opportunity for sustaining and developing his story. In his

1841 preface, he saves his strongest defence for his treatment of Nancy, and with it concludes that preface:

> It is useless to discuss whether the conduct and character of the girl seems natural or unnatural, probable or improbable, right or wrong. IT IS TRUE . . . From the first introduction of that poor wretch, to her laying her bloody head upon the robber's breast, there is not one word exaggerated or over-wrought. It is emphatically God's truth, for it is the truth He leaves in such depraved and miserable breasts; the hope yet lingering behind; the last fair drop of water at the bottom of the dried-up weed-choked well. . . . I am glad to have had it doubted, for in that circumstance I find a sufficient assurance that it needed to be told. (lxv)

In representing Nancy's devotion to the brutal Sikes, Dickens may be drawing on an actual experience of his own. He is certainly drawing on his own earlier work. One of the most moving of the *Sketches by Boz*, "The Hospital Patient" (*Carlton Chronicle*, August 6, 1836), describes a dying girl, savagely beaten by her lover, who refuses on her deathbed to identify him as her assailant, because she loves him.[5]

Dickens' uncertainty about the way *Oliver Twist* was to develop is understandable when we look at the extraordinary pressures under which he wrote the book. He began writing the novel in January 1837, and publication began in the February *Bentley's*. At this time he was still only half way through the writing and immediate publication of *Pickwick Papers*; when he finished writing *Oliver Twist*, in September 1838, he had already published six numbers of *Nicholas Nickleby*. During this period he also edited *Bentley's Miscellany* for nine months (until Sepember 1837) and edited two books: the memoirs of Grimaldi the clown, and *The Pic Nic Papers* (1841).[6] He experienced the death of his beloved sister-in-law, Mary Hogarth (May 1837), an event that reverberates in Nancy's death and Rose Maylie's illness.

Dickens was also inexperienced. He had learned to write popular newspaper sketches describing odd or touching characters and situations, and he had embarked on *Pickwick Papers*, originally to supply letterpress about cockney sportsmen for the plates which Robert Seymour was to prepare. Strictly speaking, *Pickwick Papers* is not a novel but a brilliant set of improvisations around Pickwick's character. *Oliver Twist* is Dickens' first novel. In writing it he taught himself the art of the novel. Dickens' inability to develop a unified plot becomes, in a sense, the plot of the novel as we have it. As he seeks alternative solutions to the problems his fiction is causing him, he internalizes his own changes of plan: characters within the novel become the embodiments of the different fictional possibilities Dickens discerns in Oliver.

There are two other factors which contribute to the changes of direction which characterize *Oliver Twist*. One of these is Dickens' increasingly strained relationship with George Cruikshank, his illustrator and would-be co-author. The other is his awareness of contemporary modes of fiction, and his simultaneous effort to imitate, parody, and transcend those modes, which led him to begin a grim tale of workhouse life, transform it into an account of petty criminals and their methods, then move into a story of a lost heir and a fiendish brother, to conclude with the genuine horror of Nancy's death and Sikes's self-execution, intermixed with the sentimentality of the Maylie love story and the happy life it seems to initiate. In effect, Dickens explored virtually every aspect of his new profession while writing—or teaching himself to write—*Oliver Twist*. And he also began to examine that uneasiness with the act of fiction, with the novelist's ability to form and manipulate his characters, that is a persistent theme in much of his later work. These factors may further explain the uncertain development of *Oliver Twist*. They also seem to have worked to create the novel's most memorable character, Fagin.

Like Cruikshank, Fagin has his own ideas about how Oliver is to develop, what his story is to be. In Fagin's hands, that story seems initially to be a novel of crime, of the sort that Dickens' contemporaries called "Newgate" novels; later, when Fagin joins forces with Monks, the projected story of Oliver as criminal turns into a story of Oliver as dispossessed heir and as victim of terror, traditional elements in the equally popular Gothic novels of the day. In the role of Fagin, Dickens internalizes Cruikshank's efforts to control the novel. Fagin also internalizes the ways in which Dickens' awareness of popular fictional modes threaten his novel by offering models to which it might conform, and so become an example of a type rather than the highly original work it is. Since Fagin's efforts to shape Oliver's story are criminal efforts, Fagin also represents Dickens' uneasiness about writing fiction.

George Cruikshank was twenty years Dickens' senior, and the most popular illustrator in England, when the two men first met, in November 1835. They had been brought together by the publisher John Macrone, who had engaged Cruikshank to illustrate *Sketches by Boz* for book publication. Dickens was delighted at the prospect of working with Cruikshank, whose work he admired. He even proposed that Cruikshank receive equal billing on the title page, suggesting "Sketches by Boz and Cuts by Cruikshank" or "Etchings by Boz and Wood Cuts by Cruikshank."[7]

Cruikshank was already a student of London's odd corners, and was particularly gifted at picturing scenes of grimness and despair, as his plates for *Oliver Twist* prove. He seems to have had some effect on Dickens' choice of topics for those sketches written after they had met. Dickens begins to write of prisons and prisoners, starting with "The Prisoners' Van," which appeared in *Bell's Life in London* on November 29, 1835, twelve days after his first encounter with Cruikshank; later we have "Gin-shops," "The Pawnbroker's Shop," "Criminal Courts," "A Visit to Newgate," and "The Hospital Patient." Although Cruikshank illustrated only the first, second, and fifth of these, they may well have been chosen at his suggestion as promising subjects for his special skills. Most of them have some later echo in *Oliver Twist*: "The Pawnbroker's Shop" and Cruikshank's plate for that sketch contrast a refined young woman and a prostitute, anticipating the contrasting yet connected roles of Nancy and Rose Maylie; the Artful Dodger's cheeky behavior at his trial is foreshadowed in "Criminal Courts"; "A Visit to Newgate" describes the condemned cell, where Dickens and Cruikshank will place Fagin on the eve of his execution; Nancy, as we have seen, owes something to the victim in "The Hospital Patient," and in Cruikshank's plate to illustrate that sketch, "A Pickpocket in Custody," we can spot the first appearance of Bill Sikes. The artist has also added Dickens himself, observing Sikes with great interest.

Despite these tokens of Cruikshank's importance as a partial collaborator for at least some of the later *Sketches*, by October 1836 Dickens was already weary of the artist's constant suggestions and his eagerness to offer "any little alteration to suit the Pencil" for the text of *Sketches*, Second Series. "I have long believed Cruikshank to be mad," Dickens told Macrone. "If you have any further communication with him, you will greatly oblige me by saying *from me* that I am very much amused at the notion of his altering my Manuscript, and that had it fallen into his hands, I should have preserved his emendations as 'curiosities of Literature.' Most decidedly am I of opinion that he may just go to the Devil; and so far as I have any interest in the book, I positively object to his touching it." Dickens was angry enough to propose substituting "Phiz"—Hablot Browne—as illustrator (*Letters* I: 183).

Nevertheless, Cruikshank apparently offered suggestions about the development of *Oliver Twist*, and was rebellious about the subjects to be illustrated, throughout the writing and publishing of the novel. The time needed to prepare a plate, and Dickens' inability to provide the completed text of a number before the printer's deadline, made it impossible for Cruikshank to read what Dickens had written and then illustrate it appropriately. Since Cruikshank disliked written instructions from an author, he preferred to meet with Dickens, be told what was to occur in the next number, and then negotiate about the subject of each plate. Well aware at each meeting that Oliver's next adventure had not yet been written, he seems to have been full of ideas about how the story should develop.

Because of these meetings, we have few written records about the way the novelist and the illustrator worked together. At first, Dickens was enthusiastic. "I think I have hit on a capital notion for myself, and one which will bring Cruikshank out," he wrote Bentley, while preparing the first installment of *Oliver Twist*—as indeed it did, in the famous plate "Oliver asking for More" (*Letters* I: 224). But Cruikshank's frequent suggestions, and his apparent wish to control the enterprise, eventually annoyed Dickens. William Harrison Ainsworth, whose novels were also illustrated by Cruikshank, later described the artist as "excessively troublesome and obtrusive in his suggestions. Mr. Dickens declared to me that he could not stand it, and should send him printed matter in future" (Jerrold I: 264). Dickens' declaration must refer to the period of *Oliver Twist*, since he never worked with Cruikshank again. There were frequent disputes about the subjects for plates, the direction of the story, and even about Oliver's name—Cruikshank wanted him to be called "Frank Foundling or Frank Steadfast." He forced Dickens, "with the greatest difficulty," to provide a scene in the condemned cell at Newgate.[8] Dickens insisted that "the scene of Sikes's escape will not do for illustration. It is so very complicated, with such a multitude of figures, such violent action, and torch-light to boot, that a small plate could not take in the slightest idea of it" (*Letters* I: 440). But Cruikshank proved him wrong by brilliantly depicting the scene in "The Last Chance." A final crisis occurred when Dickens returned to London on November 8, 1838, and saw for the first time Cruikshank's last plates for *Oliver Twist*, which had already been engraved and bound. He apparently objected to several of them, notably "Sikes attempting to destroy his dog" and the last plate, the so-called "Fireside Plate," which showed a comfortable parlor with Oliver, Rose, Harry Maylie, and Mrs. Maylie seated around the fire. Forster immediately notified Bentley that both plates constituted "a vile and disgusting interpolation of the sense and bearing of the tale" and claimed that he had "had some difficulty in prevailing with Mr. Dickens to restrict the omissions to these two"—an intimation that Dickens did not like "The Meeting" (Nancy with Mr. Brownlow and Rose Maylie, while Noah Claypole eavesdrops) nor the extremely effective "Fagin in the condemned cell." Dickens wrote more mildly to Cruikshank the next day, objecting only to the "Fireside" plate and asking for a new design. Though Cruikshank tried to improve the plate, Dickens insisted on a substitution, the drawing of "Rose Maylie and Oliver" which all subsequent editions have contained. "But when done, what was it?" Cruikshank later exclaimed bitterly. "Why, merely a lady and a boy standing inside of a church looking at a stone wall!" (*Letters* I: 450–451; CD to Cruikshank, November 9, 1838; Forster to Bentley, November 8; Cruikshank, "Origin").

Cruikshank later claimed to have been the originator of most of the characters and incidents of *Oliver Twist*, and to have shaped several of Ainsworth's novels. E. S. Morgan, Bentley's accountant at the time *Oliver Twist* first appeared, long afterwards remembered that Cruikshank "stated to me emphatically in the course of many conversations I had with him on the subject, in the course of business, that it was to him, Mr. Dickens had been indebted for his introduction to many of the characters that served as prototypes of prominent personages in Oliver Twist: Fagin, the Artful Dodger etc. etc.; as well as for many suggestions as to the incidents that figure conspicuously in that work."[9] In 1847 Cruikshank told a similar story to Robert Shelton Mackenzie, who published a slightly confused account in *The Round Table* (Philadelphia) on November 11, 1865, two years before Dickens' last tour of the United States (November 9, 1867, to April 22, 1868), and five years before Dickens' death. Mackenzie's story, repeated in his *Life of Charles Dickens* (1870), was that he had seen in Cruikshank's house a portfolio of drawings representing the criminal gang in *Oliver Twist*, and that Cruikshank had told him these had originally been intended "to show the life of a London thief by a series of drawings engraved by himself, in which, without a single line of letter-press, the story would be strikingly and clearly told"—that is, a pictorial "Progress" in the tradition of Hogarth's *The Harlot's Progress* (1732) and *The Rake's Progress* (1735), or of Cruikshank's own "The Sailor's Progress" (1819) and "The Progress of a Midshipman exemplified in the career of Master Blockhead" (1835), as well as his later pair of series, *The Bottle* (1847) and *The Drunkard's Children* (1848). According to Cruikshank, Dickens had "ferreted out that bundle of drawings" and decided to change the plan of *Oliver Twist* to bring Oliver among a band of London thieves (Forster I: 100–101).

Forster denied this story in the first volume of his *Life of Charles Dickens* (1871). Cruikshank replied with a letter to the *Times*, which appeared on December 30, 1871, in which he took full responsibility for the substance of Mackenzie's story—"I am the originator of 'Oliver Twist,' and . . . all the principal characters are mine"—but indicated that the story about the portfolio of pictures was not quite right. In a separate letter to Mackenzie he reminded him that what he had seen was a "*list* . . . of the proposed illustrations for 'The Life of a London Thief'—with some of the sketches—all of which were done when Charles Dickens was a little boy—some 15 years before I ever saw or heard of him.'' Cruikshank later repeated his claim at greater length in a pamphlet, *The Artist and the Author* (1872), in which he also took credit for many of Ainsworth's characters and scenes. This provoked a sharp denial from Ainsworth and another denial from Forster in the second volume of the *Life of Charles Dickens* (1872). Nevertheless, Cruikshank's assertions about his contributions to some of Ainsworth's novels have been to a considerable extent substantiated by recent scholarship.[10]

Cruikshank claims that after the appearance of ''Oliver asking for more'' (Plate 1), he drew Dickens' attention to the deaths of some workhouse children in London, and urged him to write about workhouse abuses of children; ''and I earnestly begged of him to let me make Oliver a nice pretty little boy, and if we so represented him the public—and particularly the ladies—would be sure to take a greater interest in him.'' Cruikshank points out that Oliver's ''appearance . . . is altered after the two first illustrations.'' The Oliver of ''Oliver plucks up a spirit'' (Plate 3) is very different from the Oliver of ''Oliver asking for more,'' in which he is portrayed as what Cruikshank called ''rather a queer kind of chap.'' We can see the beginnings of the change to ''a nice pretty little boy'' in ''Oliver escapes being bound apprentice to the Sweep'' (Plate 2).[11]

This change certainly anticipates shifts in the direction of the story. Oliver's sad appearance moves the old gentleman in the tortoise-shell spectacles to pity him and save him from becoming one of Mr. Gamfield's sweeps (3: 18); a little later, Mr. Sowerberry, the undertaker, is struck by the '' 'very interesting' . . . 'expression of melancholy in his face' '' and decides to make Oliver a mute (5: 29). Whether he was partially agreeing with Cruikshank's advice or not, Dickens does seem to be changing his concept of Oliver and of his story, presumably changing him from the limited role of parochial victim to a larger role as an honest boy fallen among the colorful thieves of London, allegedly the objects of Cruikshank's special studies.

Cruikshank may well have suggested the shift of the story to London, though Dickens himself had clearly exhausted the workhouse theme, and a change was necessary if he was to go on. Dickens hardly needed Cruikshank's advice. The departure to London to seek one's fortune was an obvious move. But he may well have received that advice, a commodity that the artist seldom spared. As for the introduction of the criminal gang, Dickens had plenty of precedents in Newgate fiction. Nevertheless, Cruikshank's long-cherished project for a series of plates, ''The Life of a London Thief,'' was a reality and did predate his relationship with Dickens. Furthermore, long before he met Dickens, Cruikshank had published drawings which contain figures who seem to be the prototypes for Fagin, Bumble, and many other characters from *Oliver Twist*. Apparently he simply redrew these figures, with some variations, when illustrating *Oliver Twist*, but they were already part of his repertory. We cannot be sure that Dickens knew these earlier drawings, or that they played any role in the literary—as opposed to the pictorial—development of his novel. But in view of the great popularity of Cruikshank's work, and Dickens' long admiration for it, he probably did know at least some of them.[12]

Cruikshank's own statement of his role in the development of the criminal theme in *Oliver Twist* is as follows:

> I suggested to Mr. Dickens that he should write the life of a London boy, and strongly advised him to do this, assuring him that I would furnish him with the subject and supply him with all the characters, which my large experience of London life would enable me to do. My idea was to raise a boy from a most humble position up to a high and respectable one—in fact, to illustrate one of those cases of common occurrence, where men of humble origin by natural ability, industry, honest and honourable conduct, raise themelves to first-class positions in society. And as I wished particularly to bring the habits and manners of the thieves of London before the public (and this for a most important purpose, which I shall explain one of these days), I suggested that the poor boy should fall among thieves, but that his honesty and natural good disposition should enable him to pass through this ordeal without contamination, and after I had fully described the full-grown thieves (the "Bill Sikes") and their female companions, also the young thieves (the "Artful Dodgers") and the receivers of stolen goods, Mr. Dickens agreed to act on my suggestion, and the work was commenced, but we differed as to what sort of boy the hero should be. Mr. Dickens wanted rather a queer kind of chap. . . . Cruikshank, "Origin"

Cruikshank then refers to the workhouse abuses to which he drew Dickens' attention, and the resulting change in Oliver's appearance by Plate 3. He also claims "to have described and performed the character" of one of the Holborn Hill "Jew receivers, whom I had long had my eye upon" for Dickens and Ainsworth; "and this was the origin of 'Fagan' " (sic). We can doubt Cruikshank's estimation about the importance of his own role but not his eagerness to control the story's development. One piece of evidence that suggests that Dickens at one point intended to follow Cruikshank's plan is the last sentence of chapter 7, as it appeared in *Bentley's Miscellany*: when Oliver says goodbye to little Dick, and the child blesses him, Dickens comments, "through all the struggles and sufferings of his after life, through all the troubles and changes of many weary years, he never once forgot it" (7: 43–44).[13] Dickens altered this for book publication, since Oliver is still a boy when we leave him. But the "many weary years," like the earlier uncertainty—removed for book publication—as to whether Oliver's life "will be a long or a short piece of biography'' (2: 12), argue that at some point Dickens intended to bring Oliver to manhood, probably to have him avoid the temptation to crime and raise himself to a "first-class position in society."

To suggest that Fagin, who creates criminals and controls their stories by informing on them, is partly based on Cruikshank's efforts to control Dickens' novel, is not necessarily to endorse Cruikshank's claims about his role in the composition of *Oliver Twist*. According to the illustrator's own account, Dickens did not really follow Cruikshank's suggestions, or did not follow them very far. The differences between *Oliver Twist* as Cruikshank wanted it written and the novel Dickens actually wrote are in fact evidence that Cruikshank's story is essentially true. Had Cruikshank been lying or hallucinating, he presumably would have claimed to have suggested the existing plot of *Oliver Twist*, not the plot as it might have been. What we can believe is that Cruikshank made frequent suggestions about the development of the story; that Dickens sometimes followed these, but more often ignored or drastically altered them; and that they contributed to the character and behavior of Fagin, who tried to shape Oliver's destiny as a novelist shapes the destiny of a fictional character.

Like Cruikshank, Fagin recognizes the commercial possibilities in "a nice pretty little boy" as opposed to ordinary boys, whose " 'looks convict 'em when they get into trouble. . . . With this boy, properly managed, my dears, I could do what I couldn't with twenty of them' " (19: 126). He is determined to make Oliver's life that "Life of a London Thief" which Cruikshank urged Dickens to make the plot of *Oliver Twist*, though Fagin's version would have a grimmer ending. Something of Fagin's eagerness to shape and control Oliver's destiny seems to reflect Cruikshank's efforts to control Dickens' book, an irritation which Dickens has brilliantly transformed into his novel's chief source of energy. To hint at this, Dickens, near the end of his tale, has Fagin become absorbed in an artist—Cruikshank?—"sketching his face in a little notebook" during his trial. "He wondered whether it was like, and looked on when the artist broke his pencil-point, and made another with his knife" (52: 359). As for Cruikshank, he had partly modelled Fagin's features on his own, and when he came to draw the penultimate plate, "Fagin in the condemned cell," he posed himself before a mirror and copied what he saw (Jerrold I: 227–230). Chesterton sensed Cruikshank's identification with Fagin when he remarked that "In the doubled-up figure and frightful eyes of Fagin in the condemned cell there is not only a baseness of subject; there is a kind of baseness in the very technique of it. It is not drawn with the free lines of a free man; it has the half-witted secrecies of a hunted thief. It does not look merely like a picture of Fagin; it looks like a picture by Fagin'' (Chesterton 112). In later life, various witnesses report, Cruikshank often imitated Fagin's speech and movements as a kind of performance, and in self-caricatures exaggerated his own features into Fagin's (Jerrold I: 227; Cohen 23).[14]

Even without Cruikshank, contemporary literature offered Dickens an abundance of hints and models for continuing Oliver's adventures among the criminal classes, and once he had made the decision to shift the story to London, Dickens immediately began to imitate and yet repudiate these models. With the appearance of the Artful Dodger, Dickens brings us, not quite yet into the world of criminals, but into the world of the dandy who prided himself on his knowledge of London low life and on his ability to converse in the "flash" language of the underworld. Here his literary prototype was Pierce Egan's enormously popular *Tom and Jerry* (1821), or, in full, *Life in London; or, The Day and Night Scenes of Jerry Hawthorn, Esq., and his elegant friend Corinthian Tom, accompanied by Bob Logic, the Oxonian, in their Rambles and Sprees through the Metropolis.* Egan's book is a kind of light-hearted guide to the fashionable pleasures available in London, which are about equally divided between excursions into high society and slumming expeditions. It was, incidentally, illustrated by Cruikshank and his brother, Isaac Robert Cruikshank. Egan, as author, was properly deferential to his artist collaborators. Each episode leads up to a culminating moment which a plate depicts, and Egan's text carefully points out the beauties and details of the plate. He even describes one plate as "equal to anything in HOGARTH's collection; it may be examined again and again with delight: and the author thinks, that his readers will agree with him, that he has not travelled out of his way to thank the artist for the powerful talents he has displayed in portraying such a scene."[15] It is not surprising that Cruikshank, accustomed to this sort of treatment from the writers he worked with, should have resented Dickens' assumption that the artist's role was subordinate to the author's.

*Tom and Jerry* was popular in parts, as a book, and especially on the stage. It made low life and flash language fashionable, as did Edward Bulwer's *Pelham, or the Adventures of a Gentleman* (1828).[16] Dickens drew the Dodger to represent and to parody the heroes of these works. The Dodger prides himself on his knowledge of flash language and his constant use of it. He is eager to be Oliver's guide, as Tom is Jerry's guide to the low life of the metropolis. The Dodger has also adopted the clothing and manner of the lounging dandy: "he had about him all the airs and manners of a man. . . . His hat was stuck on the top of his head so lightly, that it threatened to fall off every moment: and would have done so, very often, if the wearer had not had a knack of every now and then giving his head a sudden twitch: which brought it back to its old place again.'' He wears a man's coat, and lounges with his hands in his pockets—''as roystering and swaggering a young gentle-man as ever stood four feet six [three feet six in *Bentley's*], or something less, in his bluchers'' (8: 46–47). The Dodger's language, stance, his later temporary ''anxiety regarding the decoration of his person'' (18: 115) and his ''dissipated and careless turn'' (8: 48) all identify him as a ''flash swell,'' a man about town who models himself on Tom and Jerry. He represents all that is essentially a dandy, while his dirt and rags simultaneously mock the very type—literary and social—that he represents.

There was a particularly close connection between literature and crime at the period when Dickens was writing *Oliver Twist*. A criminal career of any notoriety was almost certain to culminate not only in hanging but in a literary text. In the seventeenth century, and well into the eighteenth, the Ordi-nary—the chaplain—of Newgate prison had the privilege of preparing and publishing the confessions of criminals who were executed; these included the details of the crime or crimes, the criminal's last words, his demeanor on the way to public execution, and an estimate of how large and demonstrative the crowd had been. These confessions were published as pamphlets, and often republished in collections. The more or less definitive collection was *The Newgate Calendar* in five volumes (1773), which was often reprinted and augmented with accounts of new criminal exploits. The *Calendar* was particularly popular during the 1820s and '30s, when Andrew Knapp and William Baldwin prepared an elaborate edition (1824–26), while George Borrow compiled *Celebrated Trials* (1825) and ''Camden Pelham'' his *Chron-icles of Crime* (1841). Among many others, the *Calendar* contains accounts of Jack Sheppard, Jonathan Wild, Dick Turpin, and Eugene Aram, all of them destined to reappear as the heroes of Newgate novels by Ainsworth or Bulwer in the 1830s, and of Catherine Hayes, the heroine of Thackeray's anti-Newgate novel *Catherine*. Bulwer's highwayman hero Paul Clifford ea-gerly reads the *Newgate Calendar* as a child, and later imitates criminal deeds and techniques he has discovered in its pages (Bulwer-Lytton I: 13–14; 17; 25; 30–31; 37). Fagin, who has certainly read the *Newgate Calendar*, and possibly *Paul Clifford* as well, gives Oliver the *Calendar*—''a history of the lives and trials of great criminals . . . the pages . . . soiled and thumbed with use'' (20: 129–130); he hopes that this reading matter will weaken Oliver's resistance to a criminal career. When the Artful Dodger is arrested, Charley Bates is less concerned with the Dodger's plight than with the likelihood that he has lost his chance to figure in the *Newgate Calendar*: '' 'nobody will never know half of what he was. How will he stand in the Newgate Calendar? P'raps not be there at all' " (43: 295).

Though Cruikshank may well have noted and imitated a Holborn Hill receiver of stolen goods, Fagin also comes out of the *Newgate Calendar*. There we can read of one Ikey Solomon, who was transported in 1831 for receiving stolen goods. Solomon was a thief and pickpocket by the age of fourteen, and later became a receiver of stolen goods in London. "His purchases were, for the most part, confined to small articles, such as jewellery, plate, &c., and in his house, under his bed, he had a receptacle for them, closed by a trap-door, so nicely fitted, that it escaped every examination which was made. In the space between the flooring and the ceiling of the lower room, there were abundant means to conceal an extent of valuable property which was quite astonishing." Solomon also dealt in cloth, especially stolen handkerchiefs, and was particularly expert at removing from them all identifying marks. Cruikshank, incidentally, seems to have drawn the frontispiece for a chapbook about Solomon's career (Pelham II: 235–241).[17]

A notorious criminal, then, could look forward to an account of his crimes, his capture and trial, his confession, if any, his behavior as he was led to execution—a breezy unconcerned manner was much appreciated—and perhaps, at the end of the account, a few lines of verse which he had allegedly composed while awaiting death—all of which might well make him an object of envy and emulation for criminals to come. He could also expect a more immediate literary apotheosis. His alleged confession and last works would probably be available as a printed broadside sold to the crowd at his execution, and very likely there would be a rude ballad as well, commemorating his exploits. In his younger days, the ubiquitous Cruikshank had drawn and engraved some of these broadsides. The ballads were usually supplied by the enterprising Jemmy Catnach of Seven Dials, who retired in 1838.[18]

Fagin himself has a copy of what appears to be a Catnach broadside, depicting three hanging bodies with the caption "LAST DYING SPEECHES," on the wall above his fireplace in the plate entitled "Oliver introduced to the respectable Old Gentleman"—an appropriate piece of decor for one who trains thieves so that they will eventually figure in such a broadside. Shades of the printing-house, as well as of the prison-house, are destined to close round Fagin's growing boys. He informs upon them when he decides their usefulness to him is ended, and even profits from their executions. " 'What a fine thing capital punishment is!' " he muses, as he examines his hidden hoard. " 'Ah, it's a fine thing for the trade! Five of 'em strung up in a row. . . .' " On Oliver's first morning with Fagin, the Dodger and Bates are sent to attend at an execution—presumably of Fagin's five ex-colleagues—to pick pockets (9: 52–54). The lives which he has directed, and the dramatic spectacle with which he has caused them to end, become the opportunity for further criminal activity.

Though Fagin himself fails to make the jaunty or the pious exit expected of a *Newgate Calendar* or execution broadside hero, the death of Bill Sikes does conform, more or less, to the Newgate convention, although by accident. The huge crowd, their wolfish eagerness, the sudden drop, the silence, and the hanging body are all part of the convention, and in dying publicly by hanging, Sikes fulfills both his criminal and his literary destiny.

The Newgate novel was a much more sophisticated and developed version of the execution broadside, and could claim a dual literary ancestry: the *Newgate Calendar* and contemporary newspaper accounts of famous crimes and criminals, which usually supplied the plots, and works of the *Tom and Jerry* school, which nourished the fashionable interest in low and criminal life. Edward Bulwer, who can plausibly claim to have invented the Newgate novel in 1830 with *Paul Clifford*, had used thieves' slang and scenes of low life two years earlier in *Pelham*, and part of his plot centers on his hero's investigation of a murder very similar to the 1823 murder of William Weare by Thurtell and Hunt (Hollingsworth 39–40). Bulwer himself suggested a slightly different lineage for the new form by describing John Gay's *Beggar's Opera* (1728) as his model, an argument Dickens accepts, for polemic purposes, in his 1841 preface to *Oliver Twist*. The classic Newgate novels—Bulwer's *Paul Clifford* and *Eugene Aram* (1832), Ainsworth's *Rookwood* and *Jack Sheppard*—were historical novels set in the eighteenth century, the age of highwaymen and *The Beggar's Opera*. Except for Paul Clifford, their heroes were real criminals whose exploits had been recorded in the *Newgate Calendar*.

*Paul Clifford* begins with the immortal sentence, ''It was a dark and stormy night.'' Despite his political and satiric intentions, Bulwer is primarily writing a romantic melodrama. His highwaymen are glamorous figures. He emphasizes their wealth, generosity, wit, gentility, and the dash and excitement of their nocturnal escapades. When he occasionally remembers to satirize the political world, the picture he draws seems to justify or excuse a life of crime rather than to indict society. Bulwer's touch is unsure, and his message muted, or perverted into making his criminals attractive: here we find those ''canterings upon moonlit heaths, . . . merry-makings in the snuggest of all possible caverns, . . . the attractions of dress, . . . embroidery, . . . lace, . . . jackboots, . . . crimson coats and ruffles'' to which Dickens objected in his 1841 preface, and to which he contrasted the "foul and frowsy dens" and "shabby rags" which characterize Fagin and his gang (lxiii).

But Dickens also found some useful material in *Paul Clifford*. The novel begins with a dying woman, who tries to indicate that there is an important secret about her little Paul's identity. Paul grows up in a tavern, cared for by Mrs. Lobkins, a kind of retired Moll Flanders. One of his favorite childhood games is stealing handkerchiefs from people's pockets, which he does with great dexterity, though he always gives them back. He learns to read and write, and the *Newgate Calendar* becomes his favorite book; he is especially interested in the exploits of Dick Turpin. Later he uses a cavern as a hide-out, as Turpin had done (I: 13–14, 25, 37; II: 103, 107).

Paul is arrested for picking pockets, although the real criminal is his friend Long Ned, and his unjust imprisonment determines him to be a criminal and to prey on society for its treatment of him. Paul's aliases include "Solomons, alias Devil" (I: 295; II: 135), a foreshadowing of Fagin's prototype, and even of his diabolic role. Paul's identity, like Oliver's, can be proved by several trinkets, among them "an old ring, which was inscribed with letters, and circled a heart containing hair. The inscription was simply 'W. B. to Julia' " (I: 344). These items were stolen from Paul's mother on her deathbed and pawned. There is a criminal named Bill Fang. Paul's true identity is only revealed late in the book, after he has been a successful highwayman.

It is clear from these parallels that Dickens read *Paul Clifford* with considerable care—he mentions the book in his 1841 preface—and borrowed from it freely (there seem to be no parallels with Bulwer's other well-known Newgate novel, *Eugene Aram*). As a beginning novelist, Dickens naturally studied the work of the most popular novelist of the day, and simultaneously imitated and resisted what he found. He resisted because the Newgate novelist's habit of celebrating criminals threatened the integrity of his own novel and, as he discovered, to write about criminals in such company was to run the risk of being branded as a writer whose works could corrupt. Dickens does catch something of the cheer and warmth of Newgate novel thieves' dens when Oliver spends his first night with Fagin—the cheery mood is considerably increased in the musical *Oliver!*—and Fagin and the Dodger have a dangerous attractiveness. As a model, the Newgate novel offered Dickens certain temptations which in his own novel he struggled to overcome, and which he internalized, as he internalized the struggle with Cruikshank, by introducing characters who are attractive enough to offer Oliver plausible reasons for joining them. Dickens resists the temptation to write a novel making the thief's life attractive, but allows his thieves to argue for their way of life. Oliver resists the temptation to yield to their attractions. If Fagin is partly a version of Cruikshank, he is also a generalized Newgate novelist, continually presenting the criminal life as dashing and well paid. He prepares his pupils to figure in Newgate novels as well as in the *Newgate Calendar*. The struggle for Oliver is the struggle about which kind of novel he is to figure in, whose literary property he is to be. Dickens' simultaneous imitation and repudiation of prevailing fictional modes becomes the alternating current which powers his novel.

Fagin himself is a creator of fiction in a variety of ways. Apart from planning the literary destinies of his gang, he is a gifted story-teller, able to tell "stories of robberies he had committed in his younger days: mixed up with so much that was droll and curious, that Oliver could not help laughing heartily, and showing that he was amused in spite of all his better feelings" (18: 120). He can act an absent-minded old gentleman to perfection (9: 54–55), and endow Nancy with the props to turn her into a respectable girl (13: 80). Fagin seems to have read Fielding's *Jonathan Wild*, and to have savored its ironies, when he urges Oliver to make the members of the gang, and especially the Dodger, his models. " 'He'll be a GREAT MAN himself; and will make you one too, if you take pattern by him. Is my handkerchief HANGING out of my pocket, my dear?' " (9: 55; caps added). In *Jonathan Wild*, Fielding uses GREAT MAN, usually in caps, when he refers to Wild, well aware that in contemporary usage GREAT MAN almost invariably meant Sir Robert Walpole. Fielding considered the corrupt Walpole to be as great a rogue as Wild, a thief and informer. But Walpole is honored, Wild is hung. Fagin's apparently accidental shift from "great man" to hanging suggests his subconscious awareness that a great man, in the sense he is using the term, will end on the gallows.

At once the thieves' former and informer, Fagin both contributes to and derives from the *Newgate Calendar*. He can also be identified with the devil. He has red hair (8: 50) and a red beard, which were then popularly believed to be traditionally Jewish characteristics—in the eighteenth and early nineteenth centuries, Shylock was always played with red hair.[19] But red hair is also associated with the devil. Fagin's touch reminds Sikes of " 'being nabbed by the devil. . . . There never was another man with such a face as yours, unless it was your father, and I suppose *he* is singeing his grizzled red beard by this time, unless you came straight from the old 'un without any father at all betwixt you; which I shouldn't wonder at, a bit' " (44: 302). Fagin first appears as a kind of shabby devil, with a cooking fire for the fires of hell and a toasting fork for the traditional pitchfork, but he is truly diabolic in his efforts to corrupt and pervert (Lane). Dickens also endows him with something of his own creative energy. After all, Fagin too is a contriver of stories, of plots, and in depicting him, Dickens—who would have known that his own name was a euphemism for the devil—perhaps exorcises some of his own persistent guilt about creating characters in rivalry with God, and then determining their fates.

With the robbery, and Oliver's acceptance among the Maylies, Dickens shifts away from the Newgate novel mode, although he returns to it from time to time as the story reverts to the doings of Fagin's gang. He even introduces a miniature Newgate novel in Mr. Blathers' account of Conkey Chickweed (31: 200–202). In his treatment of criminal life, and his simultaneous use of and parody of some of the Newgate conventions, Dickens may almost be credited with the destruction of the Newgate novel as a literary form, though he himself may not have realized this—he returns to the charge, at least symbolically, in *Barnaby Rudge* (1841), a novel in gestation during the writing of *Oliver Twist*. *Barnaby Rudge* is, in a sense, the Newgate novel to end all Newgate novels, for in it Dickens destroys Newgate itself. "I have just burnt into Newgate, and am going in the next number to tear the prisoners out by the hair of their heads," he exultantly wrote Forster of the scene in which the jail is destroyed, and a week later, "I have let all the prisoners out of Newgate, burnt down Lord Mansfield's, and played the very devil. . . . I feel quite smoky when I am at work" (*Letters* I: 377, 385).

For the remainder of *Oliver Twist*, Dickens shifts primarily to another popular mode, the Gothic novel, a shift signalized by the advent of Monks in chapter 26. In combining the Newgate mode with the Gothic, or developing one out of the other—and thus concocting that romance which he wished Mrs. Fry, the prison reformer, had written as a substitute for one of Mrs. Radcliffe's Gothic novels (*Sketches* 197)—Dickens had been anticipated by Ainsworth, who had merged the two forms in *Rookwood*. In his preface, Ainsworth describes himself as the heir of Horace Walpole, Monk Lewis, Mrs. Radcliffe, and Maturin—the major Gothic novelists—but suggests that he has improved on their imperfections and inharmonies by adding "a warmer and more genial current"—presumably the vigor of Dick Turpin and his friends (Ainsworth xxxiii, xxxviii).

*Rookwood* opens in a funeral vault and is rich in crypts, a ruined friary, secret passageways, supernatural portents, a sinister Jesuit, and a real ghost. There is even a band of gypsies. Secret passages and half-ruined buildings, often of a monastic nature, are the characteristic settings of the Gothic novel, from the half-ruined castle of Otranto in Walpole's novel of that name (1764) and the half-ruined abbey of Mrs. Radcliffe's *Romance of the Forest* (1791) through the labyrinthine monasteries of her *The Mysteries of Udolpho* (1794) and "Monk" Lewis's *The Monk* (1796) to those described in Charles Robert Maturin's *Melmoth the Wanderer* (1820). Among the other components of the Gothic are ghosts and demons (real in most Gothic novels, elaborate contrivances in Mrs. Radcliffe's); a dark protagonist, who is ultimately both doomed and damned; a passive heroine-victim, threatened sometimes by rape, sometimes by death, but always by the loss of her rightful fortune and estate. *Rookwood* showed Dickens how these elements could be combined with the Newgate mode, and so gave him the basic recipe for the second half of *Oliver Twist.*

The ruinous and labyrinthine settings of Gothic novels and of *Rookwood* are metaphors for the elaborate plots and deceits which the evil forces in these books use to accomplish their aims. They reappear, diminished, in *Oliver Twist*, in the half-ruined tenements where Fagin and his gang lurk, and in the labyrinthine streets surrounding those tenements—metaphors for the schemes and the twisting minds of Fagin and Monks. Those tenements and streets begin as sordid but eventually—with the advent of Monks—become evil and haunted, as the criminal theme gives way to the demonic malevolence that directs Monks's efforts at moral fratricide.

Monks's name, his malevolent nature, and even his appearance indicate his origins in Gothic fiction. Gothic novels were almost always set in the Catholic countries of southern Europe, and their villains were often monks or priests. Such villains were invariably dark, pale, and haggard. Walpole's Manfred, Mrs. Radcliffe's Montoni and Schedoni, "Monk" Lewis's Ambrosio, and Maturin's Melmoth all share these physical traits, as do their Byronic cousins, Manfred and Childe Harold, and such later descendants as Dracula. Monks comes with the appropriate black cloak, pale face, dark hair and eyes, gnashing teeth, " 'lurking walk' " (33: 217; 46: 314–315). He even has a peculiar scar or mark round his throat, " 'A broad red mark, like a burn or scald' " (46: 315), suggesting that he has somehow survived hanging or is the ghost of a hanged man.

Monks's association with Fagin recalls the association of villain and demon or tempter often found in Gothic novels, especially in Monk Lewis's *The Monk*, where Ambrosio is tempted and then destroyed by a demon, and in *Melmoth the Wanderer*, where Melmoth has sold himself to the devil. Though Fagin is identified with the devil, Dickens blurs the role of tempter and tempted after Monks's appearance in the story: Fagin describes himself as " 'bound . . . to a born devil' " (26: 167), and he becomes less a scheming criminal and more a kind of supernatural terror once he is allied with Monks. When he appears with Monks outside of the room at the Maylies in which Oliver has fallen asleep—the subject of one of Cruikshank's most striking plates—and Oliver wakes and raises the alarm, Monks and Fagin escape, leaving no footprints or any other sign of physical presence. No one in the neighborhood has seen them (34–35: 227–231).

Monks's supernatural aura brings about a distinct change in the atmosphere of the novel; the sordid world of the thieves becomes one of hauntings and terror. Monks's black-cloaked figure establishes a new mood of nocturnal meetings, portents, apparitions, that eventually pervades the book and touches most of the characters: Nancy thinks of death and shrouds and coffins before her meeting with Mr. Brownlow and Rose Maylie, and a ghostly coffin passes her in the street (46: 312); Sikes is pursued by Nancy's eyes after he has murdered her. Even Mr. Brownlow's rhetoric is affected: " 'Shadows on the wall have caught your whispers, and brought them to my ear' " (49: 336), he tells the thwarted Monks.

When Fagin and Monks gaze into that window, Oliver has become a different kind of victim—not a social victim of the workhouse, nor of the poverty which can lead to a life of crime, but the object of a specific individual malevolence very different from society's general indifference and scorn. That malevolence governs through terror, and the Gothic novel is about terror. Its villains terrorize their intended victims, and its authors tried to terrify their readers. The victim, usually female and passive, is physically and often sexually threatened. She is to be frightened into surrendering herself and her fortune—the Gothic novel is almost invariably about the exploitation or in- timidation of a woman through fear. Oliver's role as Gothic victim conforms to this tradition. Monks and Fagin want to possess him, in order to corrupt his very soul, to mark him with that "poison which . . . would blacken it" (18: 120), a metaphor for both moral and sexual possession. Ambrosio in *The Monk* and the hero of *Melmoth* are both possessed and corrupted in that way, by tempting demons; Monks would turn Oliver into a criminal, not merely for gain, as Fagin would do, but to destroy him. Oliver's passivity, his captive state, his youth and prettiness associate him with the Gothic heroine (Oliver has often been played by an actress on the stage). Like her, he is a potential victim of sexual exploitation, though Dickens cannot say so—Humphry House comments on the use of prostitutes in recruiting for such gangs as Fagin's, and adds that "the whole atmosphere in which Oliver lived in London would have been drenched in sex" (House 217). The introduction of Rose Maylie and her nearly fatal illness, and Rose's association with and contrast to Nancy, seem to suggest Dickens' partial recognition of these aspects of his tale. Like Gothic heroines, Oliver is also heir to an estate, and for Monks, to destroy Oliver morally is to gain that estate under the terms of Edwin Leeford's will.

Dickens does interestingly vary the formulae he had inherited in his final explanation about Oliver's identity. In *Paul Clifford, Rookwood*, and many Gothic novels, the identifying tokens—those lockets and rings and documents—not only identify an heir or heiress but prove legitimacy. As Dickens manipulated the conventions, his readers could reasonably have expected that Oliver too will prove to be legitimate, and that his mother's reputation will be rehabilitated. Instead, Dickens excuses her fall—a serious business for nineteenth-century readers—by stressing the loveless nature of Edwin Leeford's marriage to Monks's mother, and the vindictiveness of that woman and her son. The liaison with Agnes Fleming is not exactly justified, and Agnes suffers the traditional punishment of a fallen woman, but she is not condemned. Dickens, as he exploits the conventions of the Newgate and Gothic novels, also deliberately thwarts them. He uses these forms as models, but is determined to transcend them and create a novel that defies easy categorization.

Here again he has internalized his own problems as a novice writer whose enterprise is threatened by the attractive modes of popular successes. If Fagin wished to write Oliver's story by making him the hero of a Newgate romance, Monks is eager to make him the protagonist-victim of a Gothic thriller. Dickens' novel develops out of this clash or mixture of novel types, and these internal efforts by characters in the novel to write Oliver's story comprise the story of Oliver Twist.

Oliver's true destiny is to be the subject of a written story, to be scripted—externally by Charles Dickens, internally by Fagin, Monks, and eventually Mr. Brownlow, who uses him to write a happy ending to the story of Edwin Leeford and Agnes Fleming. Leeford himself has already scripted this story, and Oliver unconsciously lives it by adhering to the requirement written into Leeford's will, that Oliver " 'should never have stained his name' " (51: 351). Even his fortunate encounter with Brownlow comes about because Brownlow has been reading a book. When Brownlow asks him if he would like to write books, Oliver replies that he would rather read them, or better yet, sell them (14: 85).[20]

Fagin is the victim of his own plotting after one of his creatures, Nancy, rebels and alters the plot—the novelist's nightmare. Fagin himself contrived for her the role of Oliver's respectable and caring older sister. Nancy performs the role so convincingly that she begins to live her part, and continues to play it in defiance of Fagin's scenario, protecting Oliver and betraying Fagin. When we last see him, in the condemned cell, he has lost control of Oliver's story and, despite his effort to contrive a Newgate novel escape, of his own. The law has taken over, and written an ending for his story, a point neatly made by the Sheriff's warrant—presumably for Fagin's execution—which Cruikshank has placed on the wall of the condemned cell, an ironic contrast to that broadside celebrating an execution Fagin himself contrived, which we see over the fireplace in the first plate depicting him.

But when Fagin loses control over Oliver, Oliver himself ceases to be a character in the novel. Separated from Fagin's creative energy, he loses whatever animation he has possessed. Dickens seems to anticipate the inevitable cancellation of a fictional character once the last page of the story is written, and even to incorporate this cancellation into his story.

Dickens ends *Oliver Twist* with a series of brief summaries recording the future lives of the characters. Charley Bates has worked hard and becomes a grazier, Rose Maylie is a mother surrounded by "joyous little faces." But we hear nothing of Oliver's future life, and Dickens refers to him only as a child—Rose's "dead sister's child," Mr. Brownlow's "adopted child" (367–368). We never learn of him looking back on his childhood adventures and adversities from adulthood, as Pip and David Copperfield look back. They not only grow up, they also become the authors of their own stories. Dickens ends "in the old village church" where he shows us "a white marble tablet, which bears as yet but one word,—'AGNES'. There is no coffin in that tomb; and may it be many, many years, before another name is placed above it!" (53: 368). Here Agnes' shade may sometimes hover, evoked by love.

Dickens rejected Cruikshank's "Fireside" plate, which showed Oliver happy in a warm and contented family circle, and demanded instead the present last plate, which Cruikshank so unwillingly substituted, showing Rose Maylie and Oliver contemplating that marble tablet. Dickens may have wanted to insist on the unity of his book, by ending with a verbal and visual reminder of the young woman who dies in the opening pages, or he may have felt that a tomb was more in harmony with the over-all atmosphere of the tale than a scene of domestic bliss.

But there is an ominous and chilling quality about those last words and the plate depicting them. The tablet bears only one word *as yet*, and Dickens prays that many years will pass before "another name is placed above" the empty tomb. But, as on that ring that bore the one word "Agnes" and space for a surname, so here there is a space for another name. Even at the last, Oliver is waiting to be written, inscribed; his true destiny is to be the other name, again without surname, on that tablet. A space on a wall waits for Oliver, as a space on our bookshelves waits for *Oliver Twist*. No longer an object of competition or speculation as a fictional character, shut in a book, a box, he is to return to that void whence fictional characters come, and into which they vanish when the book is closed. In his first novel, Dickens has made his subject the processes and the metaphysic of fiction itself. The subject of *Oliver Twist* is the writing of Oliver Twist.

## APPENDIX
### "The Origin of *Oliver Twist*"
### To the Editor of *The Times*

Sir,—As my name is mentioned in the second notice of Mr. John Forster's *Life of Charles Dickens*, in your paper of the 26th inst., in connexion with a statement made by an American gentleman (Dr. Sheldon Mackenzie) respecting the origin of *Oliver Twist*, I shall be obliged if you will allow me to give some explanation upon this subject. For some time past I have been preparing a work for publication, in which I intend to give an account of the origin of "Oliver Twist," and I now not only deeply regret the sudden and unexpected decease of Mr. Charles Dickens, but regret also that my proposed work was not published during his life time. I should not now have brought this matter forward, but as Dr. Mackenzie states that he got the information from me, and as Mr. Forster declares his statement to be a falsehood, to which, in fact, he could apply a word of three letters, I feel called upon, not only to defend the doctor, but myself also from such a gross imputation. Dr. Mackenzie has confused some circumstances with respect to Mr. Dickens looking over some drawings and sketches in my studio, but there is no doubt whatever that I did tell this gentleman that I was the originator of the story of *Oliver Twist*, as I have told very many others who may have spoken to me on the subject, and which facts I now beg permission to repeat in the columns of The *Times*, for the information of Mr. Forster and the public generally.

When *Bentley's Miscellany* was first started, it was arranged that Mr. Charles Dickens should write a serial in it, and which was to be illustrated by me; and in a conversation with him as to what the subject should be for the first serial, I suggested to Mr. Dickens that he should write the life of a London boy, and strongly advised him to do this, assuring him that I would furnish him with the subject and supply him with all the characters, which my large experience of London life would enable me to do. My idea was to raise a boy from a most humble position up to a high and respectable one—in fact, to illustrate one of those cases of common occurrence, where men of humble origin by natural ability, industry, honest and honourable conduct, raise themselves to first-class positions in society. And as I wished particularly to bring the habits and manners of the thieves of London before the public (and this for a most important purpose, which I shall explain one of these days), I suggested that the poor boy should fall among thieves, but that his honesty and natural good disposition should enable him to pass through this ordeal without contamination, and after I had fully described the full-grown thieves (the "Bill Sikes") and their female companions, also the young thieves (the "Artful Dodgers") and the receivers of stolen goods, Mr. Dickens agreed to act on my suggestion, and the work was commenced, but we differed as to what sort of boy the hero should be. Mr. Dickens wanted rather a queer kind of chap, and although this was contrary to my original idea I complied with his request, feeling that it would not be right to dictate too much to the writer of the story, and then appeared "Oliver asking for more"; but it so happened, just about this time, that an inquiry was being made in the parish of St. James's, Westminster, as to the cause of the death of some of the workhouse children who had been "farmed out," and in which inquiry my late friend Joseph Pettigrew (surgeon to the Dukes of Kent and Sussex) came forward on the part of the poor children, and by his interference was mainly the cause of saving the lives of many of these poor little creatures. I called the attention of Mr. Dickens to this inquiry, and said that if he took up this matter, his doing so might help to save many a poor child from injury and death, and I earnestly begged of him to let me make Oliver a nice pretty little boy, and if we so represented him, the public—and particularly the ladies—would be sure to take a greater interest in him and the work would then be a certain success. Mr. Dickens agreed to that request, and I need not add here that my prophecy was fulfilled; and if any one will take the trouble to look at my representations of "Oliver" they will see that the appearance of the boy is altered after the two first illustrations, and, by a reference to the records of St. James's parish, and to the date of the publication of the *Miscellany*, they will see that both the dates tally, and therefore support my statement. I had a long time previously to this directed Mr. Dickens's attention to "Field-lane," Holborn-hill, wherein resided many thieves and receivers of stolen goods, and it was suggested that one of these receivers, a Jew, should be introduced into the story; and upon one occasion Mr. Dickens and Mr. Harrison Ainsworth called upon me at my house in Myddleton Terrace,

GEORGE CRUIKSHANK

Hampstead-road, December 29.


## NOTES

1. *Oliver Twist* 1:3. All references to this novel are by chapter and page, inserted parenthetically in my text.
2. Partridge, entries "Twist" and "Oliver." For "Oliver" as a slang term in fiction by Dickens' contemporaries, see Bulwer-Lytton (I:197; II:37) and Ainsworth (19, 186, 273-4). Has King Charles's head also inserted itself into Oliver's story? Oliver suggests Cromwell, who dethroned and decapitated Charles I; Monks recalls George Monk, created Duke of Albemarle in 1660, who engineered the restoration of Charles II.
3. Wheeler. My discussion of the structure and development of *Oliver Twist* is generally indebted to this article. The "Mudfog Papers" were "Public Life of Mr. Tulrumble" (January 1837); "The Mudfog Association for the Advancement of Everything" (October); and "Full Report of the Second Meeting of the Mudfog Association for the Advancement of Everything" (September 1838). In *Bentley's, Oliver Twist* began, "Among other public buildings in the town of Mudfog" (1:1n).
4. In *Bentley's*, Fagin asks Bet to go to the police office to find out what has happened to Oliver after his arrest. When Bet refuses, Fagin "turned to the other young lady: who was gaily, not to say gorgeously attired, in a red gown, green boots, and yellow curl-papers. 'Nancy, my dear,' said the Jew . . . ." Revising for book publication, Dickens changed this to "he turned from this young lady: who was gaily . . . yellow curl-papers; to the other female. 'Nancy, my dear,' said the Jew . . . ."
5. Could the volume Mr. Brownlow reads at the bookstall "with the greatest interest and eagerness" (10: 58) in the July 1837 number possibly be *Sketches*, second series, published in December 1836? Reading about society's victims may have prepared Brownlow to intervene and help Oliver, and so shift from reading to social action, as Dickens hoped his readers would do.
6. *Pickwick Papers* appeared from April 1836 to November 1837; *Nicholas Nickleby*, April 1838–November 1839; *Memoirs of Joseph Grimaldi*, illustrated by Cruikshank, on February 26, 1838; *The Pic Nic Papers* not until 1841 (*Letters* I: 371n). *The Pic Nic Papers* were contributed by a number of writers to aid the widow of the publisher Macrone.
7. Dickens first met Cruikshank on November 17, 1835 (*Letters* I: 93n), after he had been proposed as illustrator of *Sketches* and eagerly accepted (I: 82; CD to Macrone, October ?27, 1835). Dickens had long admired his work (I: 89; CD to Macrone, November 7). Cruikshank portrayed Dickens in several plates for *Sketches*. He and Dickens appear together in the frontispiece as the two men ascending in a balloon, and are both shown ushering a band of orphans in the plate "Public Dinners."
8. George Cruikshank, "The Origin of *Oliver Twist*," letter to the *Times* (London), December 30, 1871, page 8, column 4. The letter is partly reprinted in Jerrold I: 208–211; and in full in Kitton 19–22. Since neither text is accurate, I have added the *Times* version to this paper as an appendix.

9. E. S. Morgan, untitled manuscript, University of Illinois collection of Richard Bentley's papers, page 14 (Wheeler 59, note 8).

10. Cruikshank, "Origin"; letter to R. Shelton Mackenzie, January 22, 1872 (Vogler, "Cruikshank and Dickens"). My discussion of Cruikshank's role in *Oliver Twist* draws on Vogler's well-argued essay, the first to examine Cruikshank's claims seriously. See also the appendix "Cruikshank and *Oliver Twist*" (Harvey 199–210) and, for evidence that Cruikshank played an important role in developing some of Ainsworth's novels, Harvey 34–42.

11. Cruikshank, "Origin." Cf. Dickens' description of Oliver when he attacks Noah Claypole: "A minute ago, the boy had looked the quiet, mild, dejected creature that harsh treatment had made him. But his spirit was roused at last; the cruel insult to his dead mother had set his blood on fire. His breast heaved; his attitude was erect; his eye bright and vivid; his whole person changed, as he stood glaring over the cowardly tormentor . . . and defied him with an energy he had never known before" (6: 37). Dickens never develops this "manly" Oliver.

12. Vogler, in "Cruikshank and Dickens" (74–77), describes Cruikshank sketches that may represent the earlier "London Thief" project. For published drawings, see Vogler, "*Oliver Twist*."

13. This was revised to "through all the struggles and sufferings, and troubles and changes, of his after life, he never once forgot it" (7: 43–44); Dickens dropped "all" in 1850.

14. Cohen reproduces Cruikshank's self-caricature, "George Cruikshank frightening Society" (1842), in which the resemblance to Fagin is strong. There is another curious linkage of Fagin and Cruikshank which may have associated them, perhaps unconsciously, in Dickens' mind. Dickens named Fagin after Bob Fagin, an older boy who worked with him during his employment at Warren's Blacking; in his autobiographical fragment describing this period of his life, he speaks of sinking "into this companionship" and remarks that neglect and low associates might have made him "a little robber or a little vagabond" (Forster I: 26, 30). Oliver's life with Fagin is clearly a disguised version of this episode, which Dickens was to use again, more circumstantially, in *David Copperfield*. But Cruikshank was also associated with Warren's Blacking, for whom he had drawn advertisements in the early 1830s (Cohen 15; Cohn, entries 591, 2092–2096). Thackeray remembered one of these advertisements, and assumed his readers would also remember it, in *Vanity Fair* (1847–48; 22: 207). Cohn attributes the doggerel verses accompanying these advertisements to Dickens, accepting as true a statement by John Henry Barrow, Dickens' uncle, who in July 1833 told Collier that Dickens had "assisted Warren, the blacking-man, in the conduct of his extensive business," and had implied that this assistance involved the writing of jingles. Though Collier's unreliability concerning Shakespearean texts is notorious, he may be telling the truth, misled by Barrow, who understandably avoided the true nature of his nephew's work at Warren's (Collier; Johnson I: 89–91).

15. Egan 378–379. See, for example, Egan's explanations of plates (219, 226–227, 315, 363). The plate depicting a masquerade supper at the Opera House includes a man disguised as a Jewish money-lender, Mordecai, who strongly resembles the Fagin who is to be.

16. Bulwer changed his name to Bulwer-Lytton in 1843.

17. *Pelham* opens his account by remarking that "There are few offenders whose name and whose character are more universally known than Ikey Solomon." *Pelham's Chronicles* appeared in book form in 1841, but had probably earlier

been issued in parts, as was common with "'Newgate series'' (Patten, *Charles Dickens* 53; Heppenstall viii). Solomon was well enough known for Thackeray to call himself "'Ikey Solomons, Esq., Junior'' when publishing *Catherine* in *Fraser's* (May 1839–February 1840). See also Hollingsworth 112–113; I am greatly indebted to Hollingsworth's study for my own account of the development of the Newgate novel. Dickens described boy pickpockets in "'A Visit to Newgate'' (*Sketches* 207). For Cruikshank's frontispiece to the Solomon chapbook, see Vogler, "'*Oliver Twist*''; Cohn, entry 387.

18. Dickens celebrates Catnach in "'Seven Dials'': "'Seven Dials! the region of song and poetry—first effusions, and last dying speeches: hallowed by the names of Catnach and of Pitts—names that will entwine themselves with costermongers and barrel-organs, when penny magazines shall have superseded penny yards of song and capital punishment be unknown'' (*Sketches* 69). Catnach was said to have made over £500 from the 1823 murder of William Weare and the trial and execution of Thurtell and Hunt, his murderers; and to have distributed 1.65 million copies of the "'Execution Papers'' of James Greenacre, the 1837 Edgeware Road murderer (Hindley, *History* 69, 92; *Life and Times* 143, 281). Catnach pirated Egan's *Tom and Jerry* soon after publication, in a two-penny sheet for street sale containing four-line verse summaries of each episode and crude woodcuts copied from the Cruikshanks' plates (Hindley, *History* 57–64; fuller text, with songs and the quatrains swollen to octets, *Life and Times* 121–135).

19. Edmund Kean, for example, played Shylock with red hair and beard, and is so portrayed in a colored mezzotint made from a picture painted on ivory by W. H. Watts in March 1814. The mezzotint is in the Theatre Museum of the Victoria and Albert Museum.

20. "' 'Don't be afraid,' '' Brownlow reassures him. "' 'We won't make an author of you, while there's an honest trade to be learnt, or brick-making to turn to' '' (14: 85). Michal Ginsburg, in "'Truth and Persuasion: the Language of Realism and of Ideology in *Oliver Twist*'' (unpublished lecture; 1985 Dickens Conference, University of California, Santa Cruz), points out that Oliver's chance to narrate his own story, "' 'a full, true, and particular account of the life and adventures of Oliver Twist' '' (14: 89), is thwarted by events—or, more precisely, by Fagin's plot to prevent that story from being told. Grimwig, who distrusts Oliver, deliberately gives this "' 'true account' '' a title reminiscent of eighteenth-century novels.

## WORKS CITED

Ainsworth, William Harrison. *Rookwood: a Romance*. London: George Routledge [1892].

Bulwer-Lytton, Edward George. *Paul Clifford*. Edinburgh and London: William Blackwood, 1862 (volumes 33 and 34 of Bulwer's novels).

Chesterton, G. K. *Charles Dickens*. 1906; repr. New York: Dodd Mead, 1910.

Cohen, Jane R. *Charles Dickens and His Original Illustrators*. Columbus: Ohio State University Press, 1980.

Cohn, Albert M. *George Cruikshank: A Catalogue Raisonné*. London: Bookman's Journal, 1924.

Collier, John Payne. *An Old Man's Diary, Forty Years Ago*. London: Richards, 1872.

Cruikshank, George. "The Origin of *Oliver Twist*." *Times*, December 30, 1871.

Dickens, Charles. *Letters*. Eds. Madeline House and Graham Storey. Oxford: Clarendon Press, 1965—.

——. *Oliver Twist*. Ed. Kathleen Tillotson. Oxford: Clarendon Press, 1966.

——. *Pickwick Papers*. Ed. Robert L. Patten. Penguin, 1972.

——. *Sketches by Boz*. London: Oxford University Press, 1957.

Egan, Pierce. *Tom and Jerry: Life in London*. London: John Camden Hotten, 1869.

Forster, John. *The Life of Charles Dickens*. 1871–74; repr. London: Chapman and Hall, 1899.

Harvey, J. R. *Victorian Novelists and Their Illustrators*. London: Sidgwick and Jackson, 1970.

Heppenstall, Rayner. *Reflections on the Newgate Calendar*. London: W. H. Allen, 1975.

Hindley, Charles. *The History of the Catnach Press*. London: Charles Hindley, 1886.

——. *The Life and Times of James Catnach*. London: Reeves and Turner, 1878.

Hollingsworth, Keith. *The Newgate Novel 1830–1847*. Detroit: Wayne State University Press, 1963.

House, Humphry. *The Dickens World*. Second edition, London: Oxford University Press, 1942.

Jerrold, Blanchard. *The Life of George Cruikshank in Two Epochs*. New York: Scribner and Welford, 1882.

Johnson, Edgar. *Charles Dickens: His Tragedy and Triumph*. New York: Simon and Schuster, 1952.

Kitton, Frederic G. *Dickens and His Illustrators*. London: George Redway, 1899.

Lane, Lauriat, Jr. "The Devil in *Oliver Twist*." *Dickensian* 52 (1956): 132–136.

*The Complete Newgate Calendar*. Ed. G. T. Crook. London: Navarre Society, 1926.

Partridge, Eric. *A Dictionary of Slang and Unconventional English*. Seventh edition; New York: Macmillan, 1970.

Patten, Robert L. *Charles Dickens and His Publishers*. Oxford: Clarendon Press, 1978.

——, ed. *George Cruikshank: A Revaluation*. Princeton: Princeton University Library, 1974. This volume reprints a double issue of *Princeton University Library Chronicle* 35 (1973–74).

Pelham, Camden (pseud.). *The Chronicles of Crime; or, The New Newgate Calendar*. London: Thomas Tegg, 1841.

Thackeray, W. M. *Vanity Fair*. Eds. Geoffrey and Kathleen Tillotson. Boston: Houghton Mifflin, 1963.

Vogler, Richard A. "Cruikshank and Dickens: A Reassessment of the Role of the Artist and the Author." *George Cruikshank*, ed. Robert L. Patten, 61–91.

———. "*Oliver Twist*: Cruikshank's Pictorial Prototypes." *Dickens Studies Annual* 2, ed. Robert B. Partlow, Jr. (Carbondale and Edwardsville: Southern Illinois University Press, 1971), 98–118.

Wheeler, Burton M. "The Text and Plan of *Oliver Twist*." *Dickens Studies Annual* 12, eds. Michael Timko, Fred Kaplan, and Edward Guiliano (New York: AMS Press, 1983), 41–61.

# Mr. Wopsle's Hamlet: "Something Too Much of This"

## George J. Worth

In the thirty-first chapter of *Great Expectations*, Pip and Herbert Pocket attend a performance of *Hamlet*, starring Pip's old nemesis Mr. Wopsle, at a seedy Thames-side theater in London. The acting is incompetent, the staging clumsy, the audience unruly: artistically, and for Wopsle personally (though he seems unaware of it), the evening is a disaster. Chapter 31 has been something of a crux for those critics of the novel who have given it more than passing attention;[1] or, to change the metaphor, it has served as a kind of litmus test, bringing out some of the characteristic preconceptions of these commentators. There have been those who have failed to see any structural justification for the inclusion of this episode and who have been honest enough to say so: Sylvère Monod, for example, who called "the *Hamlet* chapter" "as nearly gratuitous as anything can be in such a close-knit story," while conceding that it is "uproariously funny."[2] Others have cited the chapter as an indication of Dickens' affectionate recollection of the popular London theater of his youth, with special emphasis on its ridiculous features;[3] and at least two critics have used it as evidence to support their (contradictory) conclusions about the dating of the action of *Great Expectations*.[4] My concern in this paper will be with those critics of the last three decades or so who have found in chapter 31 revealing clues to what they take to be central issues in *Great Expectations*. I shall suggest that in the process they have failed to do justice to what is genuinely important both in that chapter and in *Great Expectations* as a whole.

Once regarded as nothing more than one of Dickens' eccentric and self-deluded buffoons,[5] Wopsle—the parish clerk in Pip's village who goes to London to seek theatrical fame and fortune under the stage name of Mr. Waldengarver[6]—began to receive serious critical attention in the 1950s, a time when, under the influence of the New Criticism, writers on *Great Expectations* strove to discover all kinds of unity in it and generally succeeded in finding what they were looking for.[7] Wopsle, displaying an "unquenchable expectation of reviving the drama, with himself as a famous actor, receiving the applause of multitudes," then came to stand as one of several "comic parodies" of Pip in the novel, setting off and accentuating the folly of his misguided aspirations.[8]

Four years before J. Hillis Miller made this point in his influential *Charles Dickens: The World of His Novels*, John Hagan said much the same thing in almost the same words in an article in *ELH*,[9] but zeroed in on chapter 31, "an episode that has absolutely nothing to do with the plot." Or does it? Hagan observes that, though initially "the incident seems to be no more than a humorous interlude, comic relief to offset the more serious action," the reader soon recalls that in the preceding chapter Pip has had a humiliating encounter with Trabb's boy on the High Street of the market town near his village, and this memory gives Wopsle's performance "an entirely new dimension":

> Wopsle and his fellow actors are trying, like Pip, to play roles for which they are not fitted; they are a parody of Pip himself whose pretensions far outreach his natural habits and instincts. And the jeers they receive from the gallery are delivered in the same spirit as those which Pip received from Trabb's boy. Pip himself has become a ham actor like the detestable Wopsle; unconsciously, in his egotism, he has become more and more like the very type of man he hated in his boyhood. His only saving grace is that, unlike Wopsle who remains stupidly indifferent to the audience's reception of him, he is not invulnerable: the mockery of Trabb's boy hits the mark.

By the mid-1960s, the thematic significance of Wopsle in general and chapter 31 in particular had become something of a critical commonplace, insofar as there can be such a thing in a pursuit—sometimes common but often private and highly individualistic—whose practitioners cannot always be relied on to know and use the work of their forerunners. But it remained for William Axton, a diligent student of the way Dickens organized his "serial novels" who laid great stress on the "unifying techniques" Dickens used,[10] to elevate the *Hamlet* chapter to the status of "the crucial symbolic episode in the novel," "a hugely comic paradigm of the whole," throwing into sharp relief "the dominant theme being worked out in more leisurely fashion throughout the novel—the folly of entertaining great expectations in excess of the limiting conditions of human nature, man's mortal situation, and one's own imperfect talents."[11]

Like Pip, Wopsle has come to London . . . with foolish expectations of reviving the English theatre by his histrionic genius. The result is depicted in this scene, where Wopsle is hooted off the stage, and even Pip is highly sensible of his friend's shortcomings as an actor. It is not only that Wopsle, like Pip, is ignorant of his true situation, but that, like Pip again, the would-be tragedian is as self-deluded as his friend the would-be gentleman; for he sees his failure behind the footlights as the result of a conspiracy by his enemies, rather than as a result of his entire lack of talent. Indeed, so far does Wopsle lose his hold on reality that he imagines his debut to have been a great artistic success and his future to be assured, just as Pip imagines himself to be Miss Havisham's protégé, sent up to London to acquire the polish to make him worthy to fall heir to Estella. Again like Pip, Wopsle is chiefly deluded by his personal vanity that makes him strut and preen in the costume of the tragic hero, just as Pip is enamored of the image he presents as a gentleman far removed from the frailties, vulgarities, and meannesses of other men.

The author of a pithy 1968 article, James Barry, effectively summarized the positions taken by his predecessors during the previous fifteen years regarding the functions in *Great Expectations* of Wopsle in general and Chapter 31 in particular, while adding some insights of his own.[11] Meticulously explicating "the significance of Wopsle to the themes of *Great Expectations* and Dickens's use of him in terms of plot and character" and proposing "artistic reasons . . . for the presence of the *Hamlet* chapter," Barry nevertheless left room in his interpretation for Dickens' characteristic use of what George Orwell had called "unnecessary detail."[12] In several respects, Barry's essay was the end of a distinct line of criticism of the 1950s and 1960s: like the earlier critics I have discussed, he based his findings squarely on a close study of the text of *Great Expectations* and what he saw as its major structural features; unlike some of his successors, who seem unaware of his brief but important article or choose to ignore it, he took careful account of the relevant criticism of this novel rather than using as his point of departure elements of critical theory far removed from most readers' experience of *Great Expectations*.

Also, like his forerunners Hagan, Miller, and Axton, Barry took no special notice of the fact that it was a performance of *Hamlet* in which Wopsle played: none of these critics, therefore, was in a position to draw any particular inferences from that fact. The process of looking to Shakespeare's play rather than Wopsle's performance as a key element in chapter 31 did not start until the 1970s. A. L. French began his 1974 essay on *Great Expectations* by remarking on the comic nature and the thematic significance of Wopsle's humiliation but very quickly (before the end of his opening paragraph) went on to consider "the possible connections between" the Shakespeare tragedy

and the Dickens novel—connections that he regarded as all the more telling
because Dickens was probably unaware of them.[13] These include the way
both *Hamlet* and *Great Expectations* address the question of how "the past
influences the present," the difficulty each protagonist has in discovering
how to "be himself," and the resemblances between the reappearance of
Hamlet's father's Ghost and the reappearance of Magwitch and between what
both revenants say and cause others to say and do (for example, swearing
oaths of secrecy). Finally abandoning these "*Hamlet* parallels," French con-
ceded that they "offer no more than a way into thinking about the recurrent
human situations that Dickens is interested in" in *Great Expectations* and got
on with the main body of his argument.

For Edward Said, writing in *Critical Inquiry* four years after the appearance
of French's article, chapter 31 was also full of significance derived from the
representation of *Hamlet* on which it centers; but by now, the critic—here
borrowing deliberately from the strategies of Jacques Derrida—could, and
indeed felt obliged to, refer to this episode as undermining rather than rein-
forcing the reader's sense of the coherence of *Great Expectations*—indeed,
of the concept of "textuality" itself.[14] Recognizing that "what [Pip] and
Herbert see on the stage is meant to be a mocking allusion to Pip's own
pretensions at being a gentleman," Said saw the unsettling comic effect of
the scene as growing out of the juxtapositions of several sets of mutually
clashing entities: "actor and role," "audience and performer," "speaker and
words," "supposed setting and actual scene"; "all of these are out of joint
with each other, and nothing during this hilariously inept performance perfectly represents what we expect to be represented." What goes wrong—what
is bound to go wrong with the representation of *any* text, presumably including
that of *Great Expectations*—is that the text of Shakespeare's play, which
"is there offstage," wields "imperfect or insufficient power to command this
particular performance." This "is in some measure due not only to the
company's and the audience's incompetence but also to the text's insufficient
authority to make a representation or performance of itself work 'properly'."
But Shakespeare's—or, one assumes, anybody's—text plays other tricks on
the performer, the interpreter, the reader: it "commands and indeed permits,
invents, all the misrepresentations and misreadings which are functions of
itself."

Unlike Derrida as mediated by Said, the last and most recent critic I want
to consider here, William A. Wilson, raises no fundamental questions about
the integrity of *Great Expectations*, even though he too sees instability and
vulnerability in Shakespeare's text.[15] But he goes further than anybody else

whose work I know in finding meaningful echoes of *Hamlet* in Dickens' novel: Wilson's "intertextuality" takes us well beyond French's "possible connections" between these two works of literature (some of Wilson's examples are, to be sure, the same as French's); and the crucial influence on Pip's development and on the course of the plot that he attributes to Wopsle's rendition of this particular tragedy cuts much deeper than Axton's thesis about the "symbolic" significance of that other self-deceiver's acting of a role that just happened to be Hamlet's. One of Wilson's major contentions is that in *Great Expectations* "Dickens violently and humorously wrenches the characteristic form of Elizabethan revenge tragedy—*Hamlet* is the major text—and attempts to reshape it into a Victorian comedy of forgiveness." In the process, chapter 31 serves as a spectacular "ironic deflation" of the concept of "revenge tragedy," with Pip "recoiling from those louts who treat *Hamlet* as if it were a slice of their own squalid lives."

What are we to make of all these interpretations of the significance of Wopsle's *Hamlet* that the last thirty-odd years have brought forth? All of them are based on perceptive close reading; none will leave unaffected one's own reading of *Great Expectations*. And yet there are some problems here.

Perhaps one way to begin dealing with these is to refer to the debate that has surrounded another feature of *Great Expectations*—a character and not an incident this time—that used to be widely regarded as extraneous to the overall design of the novel. Before the appearance of Julian Moynahan's pathbreaking article on the role of Dolge Orlick,[16] critics found it very difficult to account for the presence of this surly and violent journeyman blacksmith in *Great Expectations*. During the past quarter-century, however, all that has changed: no one seriously concerned with this character can afford to disregard Moynahan's closely reasoned and copiously documented argument. But this did not persuade everybody. Within a year of its publication, two critics took issue with Moynahan's thesis in the same journal that printed his essay, and their reservations may be instructive here. The first, Donald Crompton, though acknowledging that Moynahan's reading of *Great Expectations* was ingenious, objected to his rearrangement of materials in the novel to fit a preconceived thesis and to his basing his case on the premise "that the presence of an underlying unifying theme is by itself a sufficient guarantee of a book's quality."[17] Six months later, Barbara Hardy found fault with Moynahan for paying too little attention to "the literal level" of the novel, deeming it a breach of "critical decorum" to disregard "such matters as the literal reading, the novelist's tone, and the general habits of the individual and controlling artistic fashion."[18]

It is probably late in the day to invoke the "common sense" standards of critics like Crompton and Hardy, not by any stretch of the imagination *faux naïfs*; but it is certainly clear to anyone familiar with the history of *Great Expectations* criticism and the broader trends it reflects that something very foreign to the reasonably alert reader's reaction to the novel has been made not only of the character Dolge Orlick but also of the *Hamlet* chapter, which has been transformed from a diverting but largely irrelevant piece of comic relief into a crucial critical problem yielding very different solutions. As to poor Wopsle himself, he has undergone a transformation, too: from a stock Dickensian flat character he has been turned into a monitory example for Pip—one of several in the novel—and then the critical perspective on him has narrowed further so as to concentrate on his absurd portrayal of Hamlet, which is held to embody some sobering lessons for Dickens' protagonist, before he is made to disappear into and beyond the Shakespearian tragedy with all its alleged parallels to and anticipations of Dickens' novel.

What is the reaction of my "reasonably alert reader" on returning to chapter 31 of *Great Expectations* after trying to make sense of the divergent approaches that have been taken to it during the past thirty years? Even if one disagrees with some, much, or all of that criticism, it cannot simply be disregarded or wished away: one's own reading *has* been affected, whether one likes it or not. Though, or perhaps because, the chapter does interrupt the flow of the action in a way that Pip's second visit to the waterside theater where Wopsle performs (chapter 47) does not, it is impossible any longer to regard this chapter as purely a comic digression, just as it is impossible to assert that Orlick serves no function in *Great Expectations*.

Nor can the prominent position of the *Hamlet* chapter in the novel—almost exactly at the midpoint, concluding the nineteenth of thirty-six weekly installments—be ignored by anyone who has read Axton; indeed, it is possible to go even further than Axton, who had many other issues to deal with, in anchoring it in its context in *Great Expectations*. Chapter 31 shows us a Pip who is, in Hamlet's words, "passion's slave" (II, ii, 77): at the height of his infatuation with Estella, he has in the preceding chapter been warned off her by Herbert Pocket, who takes this opportunity to tell Pip of his own apparently hopeless engagement to Clara Barley, but cannot get her out of his mind. Pip has just returned to London from the country, where he has been berating himself, not unlike the Hamlet of some of the soliloquies, as the worst of "self-swindlers": making excuses for not staying at the forge with Joe, avoiding his old nemesis Pumblechook, and being humiliated for his pretensions to gentility by Trabb's boy. It is largely because Pip, like Herbert, finds himself at an emotional impasse that the two young men at the end of chapter 30 "resolve to go to the play"—impulsively, much as Pip had sent his troublesome servant "to the Play" earlier in the same chapter in a desperate attempt to get rid of him.

John Hagan was quite right to point out that the memory of "the mockery of Trabb's boy" in chapter 30 lingers in the reader's, if not in Pip's, mind in the following chapter. But another memory lingers as well: the memory of Pip's avoidance of Pumblechook, Wopsle's erstwhile ally, whom he continues to think of with dread and loathing as late as chapter 30. There was a time—for instance, during the ghastly Christmas dinner at the forge in chapter 3—when Pumblechook and Wopsle were joined in Pip's mind as his tormentors, exceeded in their cruelty toward the boy only by the rough-handed, rough-tongued Mrs. Joe; indeed, throughout his childhood, at least until he heard of his expectations in chapter 18, these two overbearing men together represented the brutal power that insensitive adult males can exert on a defenseless lad. Though Pumblechook has changed his tune since Pip came into his fortune, now fawning on Pip and posing as his "earliest patron, companion, and friend" (chapter 28), Pip still abhors him—so much so that in chapter 30 his "terrors of Pumblechook" (more specifically his fear that he will meet him in the market town near his village, where he has been staying at the Blue Boar) afflict him so keenly that his breakfast cup shakes in his trembling hand and he makes "a loop of about a couple of miles into the open country" in order to avoid having to pass by Pumblechook's shop on the High Street.

But in the *Hamlet* chapter that follows immediately, Pip behaves very differently toward his other arch-tormentor, Wopsle. He is of course amused by the acting of "Mr. Waldengarver" but also pities Wopsle because of the rude treatment he is accorded by the vocally disrespectful audience in the theater. He describes himself and Herbert as "feeling keenly for him, but laughing, nevertheless from ear to ear." After the performance, they try to avoid Wopsle—out of embarrassment and pity, not out of dread and aversion, as Pip tried to avoid Pumblechook in chapter 30—but are maneuvered into his tiny dressing room, where his self-satisfied remarks indicate that he has no idea what a fool he has made of himself. As they listen to Wopsle's fantasies, Pip says, he is "so sorry for him" that he suggests to Herbert that they invite him "home to supper"; back at Barnard's Inn, they patiently endure Wopsle's "reviewing his success and developing his plans" until two o'clock in the morning.

If, as William Wilson suggests, *Great Expectations* is to be read as "a comedy of forgiveness''—the label will do, as well as any other, and better than some[19]—it would seem that chapter 31 is indeed an important part of that pattern. But this is so because of the moral behavior Pip exhibits toward his old adversary rather than because he absorbs a moral lesson either from Wopsle's acting and the audience's response to it or from Shakespeare's tragedy itself. Why has he obviously forgiven Wopsle in chapter 31 whereas, equally obviously, he had not forgiven Pumblechook in chapter 30? Pip does not tell us: it may be because he recognizes the element of kinship between himself and the former parish clerk, but it is far more likely at this early stage of his moral education to be because Wopsle, quite unlike Pumblechook, here shows himself to be vulnerable, an object of pity. The reader can understand Pip's feelings about Pumblechook without either approving or disapproving of what may be described as his comic cowardice at the thought of encountering him in the market town; but Pip's indulgent and compassionate feelings toward Wopsle, though similarly rich in comic overtones, are clearly to be taken as praiseworthy.

Later in our reading of the novel, we may recall chapter 31 as an anticipation of Pip's change of heart toward Magwitch after the ex-convict returns from transportation in chapter 39: Pip's terror and revulsion, much stronger than anything he had felt for Pumblechook or Wopsle, are converted into compassion and finally love once Magwitch turns out to be, like Wopsle but much more so, a man in danger who elicits all that is best in his evolving moral nature. Magwitch's "crime" against Pip as initially perceived by the young man—his destroying of Pip's delusions and his bringing about Pip's remorse for the way he has acted, especially toward Joe, while under their spell—is much more shattering than any of the injuries that Wopsle had inflicted on him; and yet Pip forgives Magwitch, too. This transformation in Pip's character, whose first signs were observable in the *Hamlet* chapter, is complete by chapter 54, when Pip says, after Magwitch has been gravely injured in his aborted attempt to escape from England:

> For now my repugnance to him had all melted away, and in the hunted wounded shackled creature who held my hand in his, I only saw a man who had meant to be my benefactor, and who had felt affectionately, gratefully, and generously, towards me with great constancy through a series of years. I only saw in him a much better man than I had been to Joe.

But reading *Great Expectations* as a *Hamlet*-like revenge tragedy "translated" into a comedy of forgiveness, as Wilson does, also requires some bending of the evidence. At the end of chapter 31, weary and depressed after listening to Wopsle's foolish talk till the small hours of the morning, Pip retires:

> Miserably I went to bed after all, and miserably thought of Estella, and miserably dreamed that my expectations were all cancelled, and that I had to give my hand in marriage to Herbert's Clara, or play Hamlet to Miss Havisham's Ghost, before twenty thousand people, without knowing twenty words of it.

If I follow Wilson's reading here, he interprets the fact that "Pip dreams of being forced to play either Hamlet or a middle-class husband" as a warning to him. "By forgiving those who have offended him, Pip eventually avoids the fate of the one, but his act of forgiveness does not necessarily make him the other" (p. 171). Can this dream of Pip's really bear the weight of such an analysis? Pip has already, in this very chapter, demonstrated his capacity for forgiveness; and whether or not he ever becomes "a middle-class husband" is a question that Dickens carefully leaves unresolved at the end of the published versions of the novel. More to the point, unlike other dreams of Pip's—most notably the delirious one he has in chapter 57[20]—this one grows naturally out of his experiences and thoughts during the immediate past as well as his two greatest abiding fears at this stage of his story: that his life as a gentleman is itself a dream and that he will go on being humiliated despite his genteel pretensions.[21] Surely it is this latter fear and not anything in Hamlet's tragic story that accounts for Pip's dream, which no thesis should cause us to regard as anything but essentially comic, of his public failure as an actor in Shakespeare's play.

Why is it *Hamlet* that Dickens chooses to have Wopsle and his ragtag company perform in chapter 31? A. L. French may well have been right in his suggestion that the choice was made for reasons of which Dickens was unaware. What we do know is that, as far back as the "Private Theatres" sketch by Boz in Dickens' first book, his fiction often displayed what Angus Wilson called Dickens' "comic delight in the great gulf between the play and what the poor players make of it (particularly of Shakespeare)."[22] We also know that *Tom Jones* was one of Dickens' early and enduring favorites among English novels and that Fielding, too, depicts his young protagonist attending a performance of *Hamlet* (Book XVI, chapter 5) for reasons that are not immediately discernible but with purposes that are manifestly comic in nature. Finally, we know that, having grown up with productions of *Hamlet* that were not much superior to Wopsle's, Dickens took Shakespeare's tragedy much less solemnly than the more portentous critics of our own day are likely to do: indeed, as Michael Slater has shown,[23] in his frequent allusions to

*Hamlet* throughout his fiction Dickens tended to treat both the play and its hero in deflatingly comic rather than in exaltingly tragic terms.

In what sense, if any, is Pip a Hamlet-figure? As French pointed out, the "*Hamlet* parallels" are more suggestive than definitive, and certainly Shakespeare's Prince is not the only literary figure between whom and Pip instructive comparisons (and contrasts) can be made.[24] I myself have borrowed a term from *Hamlet* in referring to Pip as "passion's slave," but I might equally well have gone elsewhere for a characterizing expression—to *Othello*, for instance, if I were to confine my search for illustrative quotations to Shakespeare, where the Moor, just before his suicide, refers to himself as "one that loved not wisely but too well" (V, ii, 344). Similarities among literary characters, plots, and themes are to be found almost anywhere we look, if we look carefully and purposefully enough, and our awareness of them undeniably expands our sense of the significance of the particular text under consideration; but we should not let ourselves get carried away into claiming too much for such resemblances as a result of ignoring generic, historical, linguistic, and cultural considerations.

Pip does resemble Shakespeare's tragic hero in his self-lacerating emotional turmoil, and his attendance at a production of the barely recognizable *Hamlet* at a strategic point in his story may possibly serve to remind him—and, more importantly, the reader or *some* readers—of that element of kinship; but, as I have tried to show, there are more important matters in chapter 31 to claim our attention and our delight, and in any case it does justice neither to Dickens' novel nor to Shakespeare's play to elevate accidental similarities into essential parallels between two very different masterpieces.

## NOTES

1. As he often did in the critical chapters of his biography of Dickens, Edgar Johnson expressed a kind of consensus when he referred briefly to "Mr. Wopsle's famous performance of *Hamlet*" as one of the "many scenes of high-spirited enjoyment and . . . comic gusto in *Great Expectations*" (*Charles Dickens: His Tragedy and Triumph* [New York: Simon and Schuster, 1952], II, 993).
2. Sylvère Monod, "*Great Expectations* a Hundred Years After," *Dickensian* 56 (Autumn 1960), 134.
3. See T. Edgar Pemberton, *Charles Dickens and the Stage* (London: Redway, 1888), pp. 55–66; and J. B. Van Amerongen, *The Actor in Dickens* (New York: Appleton, 1927), pp. 161–163.
4. See Mary Edminson, "The Date of the Action of *Great Expectations*," *Nineteenth-Century Fiction* 13 (June 1958), 22–35; and V. C. Clinton-Baddeley, "Wopsle," *Dickensian* 57 (Autumn 1961), 150–159.

5. See, for example, Edwin Pugh, *Charles Dickens: The Apostle of the People* (London: New Age Press, 1908), p. 251.

6. The origin of Wopsle's stage name was the subject of some plausible speculation in a 1932 letter to the editor of the *Dickensian* (Gilbert Hudson, "Mr. Wopsle," *Dickensian* 28 [Summer 1932], 243). For a belated reply and some further speculation, see Edgar Rosenberg, "Wopsle's Consecration," *Dickens Studies Newsletter* 8 (March 1977), 6–11.

7. "Each element of the action is made to carry the weight of the implicit theme of the novel," according to one of the shrewdest of them (Thomas E. Connolly, "Technique in *Great Expectations*," *Philological Quarterly* 34 [January 1955], 49). But perhaps there is nothing really new under the critical sun. One of the earliest reviewers of *Great Expectations*, writing shortly after the publication of the first three-volume edition, praised the skill with which the novel is constructed, with a careful interrelation among the parts and a subordination of the parts to the whole, using Wopsle as an example of how Dickens integrated even minor characters into the structure of his plot (*Examiner*, 20 July 1861, p. 453). This reviewer may or may not have been John Forster; see my *"Great Expectations": An Annotated Bibliography* (New York: Garland, 1986), p. 52.

8. J. Hillis Miller, *Charles Dickens: The World of His Novels* (Cambridge, Mass.: Harvard University Press, 1958), p. 262.

9. John H. Hagan, Jr., "Structural Patterns in Dickens's *Great Expectations*," *ELH* 21 (March 1954), 61. The quotations that follow appear on p. 62.

10. William Axton, " 'Keystone' Structure in Dickens' Serial Novels," *University of Toronto Quarterly* 37 (October 1967), 32. The quotations that follow appear on pp. 48–49. Cf. Axton's *Circle of Fire: Dickens' Vision & Style & The Popular Victorian Theater* (Lexington: University of Kentucky Press), pp. 110–136.

11. James D. Barry, "Wopsle Once More," *Dickensian* 64 (January 1968), 43–47. Cf. Daniel Belden, "Dickens's GREAT EXPECTATIONS, XXXI," *Explicator* 35, iv (Summer 1977), 6–7.

12. George Orwell, *Inside the Whale and Other Essays* (London: Victor Gollancz, 1940), p. 69.

13. A. L. French, "Beating and Cringing: *Great Expectations*," *Essays in Criticism* 24 (April 1974), 147. The quotations that follow appear on pp. 147–148. Lionel Morton ascribes great significance to the fact that the actor who plays the Ghost in this production carries "a ghostly manuscript" wrapped around a truncheon: see " 'His Truncheon's Length': A Recurrent Allusion to *Hamlet* in Dickens's Novels," *Dickens Studies Newsletter* 11 (June 1980), 47–49.

14. Edward Said, "The Problem of Textuality: Two Exemplary Positions," *Critical Inquiry* 4 (Summer 1978), 673–714. Said concentrates on *Great Expectations* on pp. 685–689; this section of his essay appears, with minor changes, in his *The World, the Text, and the Critic* (Cambridge, Mass.: Harvard University Press, 1983), pp. 196–200.

15. William A. Wilson, "The Magic Circle of Genius: Dickens' Translations of Shakespearian Drama in *Great Expectations*," *Nineteenth-Century Fiction* 40 (September 1985), 154–174.

16. Julian Moynahan, "The Hero's Guilt: The Case of *Great Expectations*," *Essays in Criticism* 10 (January 1960), 60–79.

17. Donald W. Crompton, "The New Criticism: A Caveat," *Essays in Criticism* 10 (July 1960), 360.

18. Barbara Hardy, "Formal Analysis and Common Sense," *Essays in Criticism* 11

(January 1961), 112. I have resisted the temptation to work into my text another apposite observation by Hardy, reacting to three critics of another Dickens novel: the *Martin Chuzzlewit* of Jack Lindsay, Dorothy Van Ghent, and J. Hillis Miller, she says, "is a novel—or rather, three different novels—which I should like to read" (*The Moral Art of Dickens* [London: Athlone Press, 1970], p. 101).

19.  I find it difficult to regard *Great Expectations* as a potential "revenge tragedy" or Pip as the hero of a work of that kind. After all, the revenge Magwitch has in mind is very different from that which old Hamlet's Ghost urges on his son; and if, as Wilson says, "Magwitch's return to London effectively ends the [revenge plot] he himself authored" (p. 159), it is not easy to grasp what he means in the previous paragraph when he refers to the returned Magwitch as swearing Pip and Herbert "to secret complicity in a revenge plot."

20.  Of the published discussions of that later, much more complicated, dream, the most suggestive is Garrett Stewart's (*Dickens and the Trials of the Imagination* [Cambridge, Mass.: Harvard University Press, 1974), pp. 193–195.

21.  The point I make in the main clause of this sentence should not require either amplification or documentation; but perhaps it will be reassuring if I remark that Freud himself recognized the great importance of recent impressions, especially those from the immediate past, in the shaping of dreams; see, for example, *The Interpretation of Dreams*, third edition (London: Allen and Unwin, 1937), pp. 167–184. Joseph Butwin's interpretation of Pip's dream in chapter 31 differs both from Wilson's and mine; see "The Paradox of the Clown in Dickens," *Dickens Studies Annual*, 5, ed. Robert B. Partlow, Jr. (Carbondale and Edwardsville: Southern Illinois University Press, 1976), p. 122.

22.  Angus Wilson, *The World of Charles Dickens* (London: Martin Secker and Warburg, 1970), p. 38.

23.  Michael Slater, "Some Remarks on Dickens's Use of Shakespearian Allusions," *Studies in English and American Literature in Honour of Witold Ostrowski* (Warsaw: Polish Scientific Publishers, 1984), pp. 141–147. I am grateful to Paul Schlicke for calling Slater's essay to my attention as well as for making a number of helpful comments about the version of this paper that I delivered at the University of California, Santa Cruz, in August 1986.

24.  See, for example, John L. Warner, "Dickens Looks at Homer," *Dickensian* 60 (Winter 1964), 52–54; Bernard Schilling, "Balzac, Dickens, and 'This Harsh World'," *ADAM International Review* 34, Nos. 331–333 (1969), 109–122; J. M. Ridley, "Huck, Pip, and Plot," *Nineteenth-Century Fiction* 20 (December 1965), 286–290; and Philip Collins, "Pip the Obscure: *Great Expectations* and Hardy's *Jude*," *Critical Quarterly* 19, iv (Winter 1977), 23–35.

# Dickens' *Nickleby* and Cavalcanti's: Comedy and Fear

## Sylvia Manning

> Film takes our very distance and power-
> lessness over the world as the condition of
> the world's natural appearance.
> —Stanley Cavell[1]

In 1947 Ealing Studios of London released a film version of *Nicholas Nickleby*, directed by Alberto Cavalcanti. It is the only sound film version of this novel, if one excludes the videotape of the Royal Shakespeare Company's stage version, and it still shows up fairly often as late-night television fare. My interest in the firm began on one of those late-night occasions, when I watched it, for the first time, in the company of a sophisticated literary critic who had read a lot of Dickens, but not *Nickleby*. As we watched, my companion was gripped by the horror of the story, which even the commercial interruptions could not dissipate. I, on the other hand, kept assuring him that the whole thing was really very funny and would momentarily appear so. It never did, and after a while I realized that my relative comfort as audience was maintained by my ability to ignore the film and remember the novel.

This divergence in responses to the film raises the problem of the two audiences that any adaptation must anticipate: the audience that has read the novel, and the audience that has not. Though I will treat the problem briefly, I wish to concentrate this essay upon differences between the novel and the film, taking each experience, so far as possible, independently of the other—for the most part to assume, that is, a film audience that does not know the novel. The differences I seek will be those that appear to account, at least partially, for the degree to which the film is more frightening than the novel. At the end of the essay, I will discuss the contrasts offered by certain aspects of the Royal Shakespeare Company stage production.[2]

The film focuses upon a strand of terror that in the text is subdued, virtually hidden, by both the novel's humor and its melodrama. That strand is the myth of Kronos, the father destroying his sons, that the humor camouflages because it is a contrapuntal environment and the melodrama obscures because it distracts us with an intricate congeries of villains, plots, and counterplots. In the novel the main line of tension is between humor and melodrama. In the film, it is between comedy and terror, with terror ascendant until the very end, its climax marked by the storm that accompanies Ralph's death. This difference in the generative principle of the discourse of the film, as compared to the discourse of the novel, undergirds the several procedures and conditions that contribute to the film's effect of having extracted from the novel a vision of fear. The distinction I intend between ''procedures'' and ''conditions'' is that between features relatively independent of the particular medium of film—features that might equally have marked an adaptation for stage, comic book, or digest—and features that are particularly filmic. The elimination of minor characters, for example, might occur in any form of adaptation; close-ups, however, are confined to pictorial adaptations, unbroken superpositions to motion pictures. The Dickensian voice of the narrator is a mixed case: it might well disappear from an abridgment but seems almost necessarily absent, setting aside a persistent voice-over, from a film version.

My assumptions are, first, that a film adaptation constitutes an interpretation of a novel, a reading expressed not in critical discourse but through a rendition of the story in another medium. Second, the medium, film, has powers and constraints particular to it that have their effect upon the rendition. Third, the rendition in story creates an interpretation with a strong life of its own, tending to free and intentional re-vision of the tale. The audience may or may not have read the novel, but the screenwriter and director certainly have (there are exceptions with regard to the director, but they are not relevant in this instance), and therefore the film is defined against the novel. The film represents a pattern taken from an ensemble present in some degree, possibly submerged or only latent, in the novel and elaborated through changes, interpolations, and the inevitable differences of visual concretization. Extended comparison of the film to the novel can in consequence make evident procedures and conditions of both texts.

The discussion that follows, therefore, can be regarded as heuristic. It explores differences between the film and novel, in procedures and conditions, that not merely explain the film's foregrounding of elements in the novel that are occluded by the plenitude of early Dickensian style but that serve, hermeneutically, to guide us to this stratum of the novel that our defenses tend to gloss over. Because I imagine that most of my readers will be familiar with the novel but will not have seen the film or not seen it in some time, I will present much more detailed description of the latter; that imbalance should not obscure the direction of the argument, which is always to turn the film's variances back upon the novel. Returned thus to the novel, what we find clarified are its myth of Kronos, as suggested above, set within an oppositional structure of bad and good fathers. It is that structure that the film above all aborts: the Crummles troupe is relegated to a world of make-believe markedly apart from the "reality" the central characters inhabit and the Cheerybles' role is severely abridged. In Cavalcanti's story, therefore, the sons must go it alone against the bad father, with no support from the earlier generation. The film in this way exhumes both the myth of Kronos with the psychic tensions that it renders, and the countervailing ideology that offers us security against those fears. We may perceive more clearly that Crummles, like his successor Micawber, is the weak good father, and the Cherrybles are (conjointly) the strong good father. Their doubleness is emblematic of their double strength and double goodness and of the duplicative potential of good. That they are simultaneously signs for modern mercantile enterprise—in opposition or contrast to the ancient professions of usury (Ralph), schoolteaching (Squeers), and acting (Crummles)—will not surprise us: the novel sees the new bourgeois patriarchy as protecting where the feudal one has failed, become, indeed, the enemy itself (only Ralph consorts with titles).

Each instance of the film's adaptations discussed below may be understood to serve its interpretation of the novel, an interpretation that is realized largely by intense and near-exclusive focus upon one side only of the dialectic that shapes the novel and that in the novel is superficially resolved in the communal acts of adoption and marriage. Not that the film forgoes the superficial resolution: it simply tacks it on so inorganically that the resolution has little bearing on the total effect. It may even reveal its own factitiousness. Certainly it sharpens for us the dark side of the novel's oppositions and the novel's insistence on muting that darkness through humor and dispersion. As I hope to demonstrate, the film is claustrophobic; to be entombed for the duration in its dark interiority is to be trapped in a distillate of the novel's powerful underside, a side uncongenial to the view of Dickens that must share the triumph of light. In this essay, then, I am seeking to uncover strategies of the novel that the film reveals, often by omitting them, at other times by altering, replacing, or condensing them, and occasionally by adding to them.

For *Nicholas Nickleby*, the voice of the narrator is crucial. In the novel, it dominates: it comments, expands, indulges in word-play, and remains always in control. From the very start, it reminds the reader of this control:

> From what we have said of this young gentleman [Ralph Nickleby], and the natural admiration the reader will immediately conceive of his character, it may perhaps be inferred that he is to be the hero of the work which we shall presently begin. To set this point at rest for once and for ever, we hasten to undeceive them, and stride to its commencement.[3]

There are several layers of irony here, including the lack of control implied by the agreement error between ''reader'' in the first sentence and ''them'' in the second. To limit discussion to the more probably intentional, we may note that no reader is likely to have conceived a natural admiration for Ralph and that Dickens is not likely to have expected anyone to do so. Is the narrator being sarcastic at the reader's expense, or Dickens sarcastic at the narrator's? Are we to imagine any reader who would admire Ralph, or any narrator who would expect admiration? This sort of confused jocularity is not uncommon in early Dickens, and whatever the answers to the questions it raises if logically pursued, the direction of the paragraph remains the same: an assertion of narratorial control, both in determining our attitude toward a character and in deciding to ''stride'' to the story. As important as the control of the narrator is his benevolence. The narrator has a clear moral vision (and therefore does not participate in any mistaken admiration for Ralph) and is always on the side of the good. We feel the company of a presence, a persona, and because the narrator is good and is in control, we are in a world that is safe for morality and truth.

The narratorial voice offers reassurance, benevolence, humor, and the vitality of its language against the menacing features of the plot. It is resilient through twenty numbers. In the film, in contrast, the human sense of a narrator is minimized and no comforting presence is in control; the camera is as mute as possible. The camera is omniscient, but almost never does this omniscience offer a grand sweep of perspective or suggest a multiplicity of viewpoints. Rather, perspective is at once limited—narrow—and undefined. Character point-of-view shots are rare. In this context, a conventional technique loses some of its transparency: even the normal avoidance of frontal address to the camera contributes to the avoidance of any identified human point of view (that is, when in an interchange of dialogue the camera follows the interlocutors in alternating shot-reverse shot, we tend to see each face from an angle more or less but always distinctly different from the other character's). Thus the automatism[4] of photography is enhanced, and the automatism in turn enhances both the illusion of realism (as freedom from subjectivity) and the isolation of the audience from the world within the film. There are cuts that signify clearly and strongly, but the agent creating the significance is unknown, unheard, unnamed, and unseen, a condition that contributes to the persistently ominous quality of the significance. No narrator human enough to be capable of awkward joking mediates or accompanies our seeing.

For example, in the first scene Newman Noggs brings Ralph the letter announcing his brother's death and the family's arrival in London. Ralph looks at the superscript and mutters, "I know something of that hand" (exactly as in the novel). Then there is a cut to Noggs, who is standing beside the desk, first to a close-up of his face, then to his hands: he is cracking his knuckles, and the hands fill the screen. When Ralph says he knows hands, hands get nervous. We see Noggs's response and we also wonder uneasily about the extent of Ralph's knowledge. But who makes this pun, points these connections? We infer a director or photographer or screenwriter, perhaps, but only from our knowledge of how films are made, not from any presence in the film. The film gives us only, at most, an intuition of a disembodied intelligence. In contrast to the human narrator of the novel, whom we can vaguely characterize, the film creates a sense of pervasive, unknowable fatality.

Throughout the film, a recurrent object takes various forms: Squeers's switch, Ralph's baton (which has no purpose other than to be held by Ralph and struck against his own palm as he thinks about Verisopht and Nicholas), Hawk's whip. The recurrence is much emphasized by visual effect, as each time the object fills the screen and twice we see cuts across the face (Squeers hitting Nicholas and Nicholas hitting Hawk, both times with the face full screen). Again, the connections—the recurrence—are effectively agent-less and the meaning is threatening.

A third instance of connection depends upon frame composition. We see Kate introduced to the Mantalini establishment, then taken to her seat at the sewing table. It is a long table, with Miss Knag at the head and some ten girls down either side. It fills the screen, viewed at an angle that reaches from the lower left to almost the upper right. The girls ask Kate where she worked before and when she replies "Nowhere" they burst out in mockery: "Oh, nowhere!" "Oh, superior!" There is a fade-out: the screen lightens again on the Dotheboys dining room. The table is exactly symmetrical: a long table with some ten boys down either side, filling the screen and viewed at an angle that reaches from the lower right to almost the upper left. The head and foot of the table are obscured. There is a still moment, just enough for us to absorb the symmetry, and then we hear, more forcefully than see, Squeers burst into the room. As he says a quick grace the camera moves up, with the boys' eyes, to contemplate the framed motto on the wall: "Subdue your appetites and you have subdued human nature." The boys leave the table, carrying their bowls, and the camera lingers, allowing us to contemplate the bare board, sign of emptiness. Kate has been mocked by the other girls, the boys have been fed a mockery of a meal, and Squeers mocks God in his blessing. But these parallels are again without agent, arising only from an ominous tendency to signify.

If the film elides the comic energy of the narrator, it also is spared his sentimental and melodramatic tones, tones that led J. Hillis Miller to write about Dickens in this novel as "in a kind of frenzy of false feeling."[5] Such theatrical rhetoric survives in the dialogue, but the film has substituted images for language as the narrative medium: a hundred and fifty years later, the language does not work for us; forty years later, the manipulation of the images seems stylized, but their power remains strong. In fact, one technological happenstance may have enhanced that power with time. Our growing assumption of color as the norm in film tends to make black-and-white films seem, our better historical knowledge notwithstanding, comparatively austere, especially when lit mainly in high contrast, as *Nicholas Nickleby* is. Cavalcanti's softer lighting for scenes of pathos or sentiment provides only a plaintive counterpoint to the harsh contrasts in scenes of conflict and threat. We tend to color them cruel.

The omission of the narrator does not surprise us in a film of this period. Other omissions are dictated generally by the simple need to shorten the story, though any particular omission should still be regarded as a matter of choice by director or scriptwriter.[6] To take a fairly straightforward instance: the Kenwigs plot is cut entirely except for a brief, single scene in which Nicholas attempts to serve as tutor to the girls. Uncle Lillyvick is present to deliver his remarks on the cheerlessness of the French language, but none of the family relationships, as we know them in the novel, are explained. The scene ends with Nicholas in despair, and the Kenwigses disappear from the film. In the novel, the Kenwigs story is a comic version of two motifs: the major theme of the rich uncle, and the secondary theme of the January-and-May marriage. Furthermore, we understand that these themes are motifs because we see two instances of them. Thus the doubling both offers a comic *reductio*, lightening the theme, and by providing a second instance turns the theme to *topos*, makes it a bit trite and so a bit less powerful. In the film, the horror of the story is unique and therefore all the worse; the story has no benign or comic version of itself to distance our perception of it.

This vignette also points out some of the problems in considering the differences in the film when an audience knows the novel and when it does not, because for an audience that knows the novel the scene functions as an allusion. For an audience that does not know the novel, it is merely a brief bit of business on Nicholas's difficult road to the Cheeryble brothers. But how the allusion functions is less clear. The allusion imports the text alluded to and in so doing also announces the pre-existence of the tale being told, reminding us that there is another, prior version with other details than those shown here. Does this establishment of a fuller story outside the film increase our sense of artifice or our sense of realism? Do we assimilate into a seamless experience what we see and what the allusion causes us to remember? That may be what happened when I watched the film for the first time and what produced the stubbornly different response from my companion's. It seems equally possible, however, that the effect might be to detach viewers from the experience of the film by reminding them of aesthetic experience as experience, bounded in time, as, for example, was their experience of reading the novel. Because such an effect would defeat pleasurable absorption in the story, perhaps it is what underlies the familiar obsession of litterateurs with the infidelities of film adaptation. Either way, even when the scene functions as an allusion, something of the role of the subplot is not available to the film.

As Uncle Lillyvick in the novel achieves his January-and-May marriage (and is appropriately punished), so Mr. Mantalini offers a comic version of profligacy, John Browdie of youthful courtship and rivalry, and the mad gentleman who courts Mrs. Nickleby of adult sexuality in general. In the film, none of these appear except Mr. Mantalini, and he is confined to a couple of mildly lascivious glances at Kate and one typical interchange with Mrs. Mantalini. The domestic billing is mocked by a parrot reminiscent of Mrs. Merdle's but it is neither extensive nor light enough to function in relation to the story's sexual threats as the Mantalini relationship functions in the novel, where it presents a comic side to sexual manipulation (as Lillyvick does to the theme of the rich uncle and to the pursuit of young women by aged bachelors).

At other points the film seeks economy through condensation. The most important of these is the substitution of Ralph for Gride as the courtier of Madeline. One effect is to make Gride oddly irrelevant; Cavalcanti and his screenwriter John Dighton may not have noticed as much and kept him in the film in a sort of oversight. By making Ralph the one to attempt the marriage, the film concentrates the evil of its world in him. Ralph is not merely the devourer of children, he is also the sexual marauder. This role is intensified when he also threatens Kate, as he does in the novel, by setting her as bait for Verisopht. In consequence we have in the film a more thorough inversion of Oedipal struggle. In both novel and film, Ralph is openly out to get his nephew, and covertly out to get his son. (Covert in two senses: that he and we do not know that Smike is his son, and that Nicholas stands as his son in the psychodrama of the plot.) But in the film the father (uncle) not only kills the alter-ego of the son (Smike), as he does in the novel, he also threatens to take the son's rightful bride.

Although film adaptation must usually cut from the original text to save time, it can also add to the original text without adding time when what it adds are images. Two additions in this film deserve attention: faces and doors. Over and over, the camera comes close in to a face, until the frame is a portrait. The single portraits are complemented by a large number of paired faces. The face of Ralph (Cedric Hardwicke) is immobile, except for certain dilations of the eyes and the abrupt movements of the jaw when he talks. The immobility is an index of hauteur, sangfroid, and inhumanity. When they first meet, Ralph takes Kate by the chin and stares at her face. Mrs. Squeers shines her lantern in Nicholas's face and stares. But mostly, the camera stares and the faces, filling the screen, look back at us: Ralph, Squeers, Fanny, Mrs. Squeers, Wackford with something in his mouth, Snawley, Noggs, Kate and Madeline in fear or terror, Nicholas (Derek Bond), whose face is beautiful and clear, Smike in pain, even an anonymous man at the employment office. Close-ups of Smike establish his beauty, both a spiritual emblem and the basis for Noggs's recognition of him as the image of his mother. Close-ups of Nicholas and Ralph (there are many more of these two and about the same number for each) serve as notation for the struggle between purity and power. Close-ups of Kate and Madeline (second in frequency to Nicholas and Ralph, about the same number for each and half as many as Nicholas or Ralph) establish their beauty and their fear or pain. With the evil characters the effect is to magnify the threat they present. The camera makes it easy for Cavalcanti to force us into confrontation with these figures and so into a share of the fear they inspire or the pain they suffer. The effect is a staple of film, without correspondence in the novel. Here it works in the same direction as the excision of the narrator: the novel's narrator distances us from the tale; the film's close-ups increase our emotional involvement.

As striking as the close-up faces in this film are the doors. Ninety-five times in the course of the film a door is opened or closed or knocked at or peered through (one of those times it is a gate, and once it is a window, through which the police climb in pursuit of Ralph at the end). The film begins with a door: Noggs opens it, receives and pays for a letter—while we see the letter-carrier and a barely defined open space behind him—closes the door, and turns. On more than one occasion we see three doors in the course of moving from one scene to the next (as I count these, I count each appearance as a door, without regard to whether the particular door has appeared before). The doors may have special effects. Because Derek Bond is tall, Nicholas must stoop every time he passes through a door, even the relatively high ones. Smike, in contrast, comes through stooping though he does not have to, and so that stoop of deprivation is accentuated. The boys are always hustled through the doors.

Perhaps the most striking door is the yard-gate at Dotheboys hall. The gate is composed of vertical metal bars. When the coach with Nicholas, Squeers, and the new boys arrives at the gate, Smike comes to open it. The camera looks at him through the gate—so that our first sight of Smike is behind bars, and it takes a minute to realize that what we are looking at is a gate. The motif is picked up with a real jail-gate, of the same vertical bars, that guards the entry to the Brays' lodging in the Rules. The bars of this gate are repeated immediately in the shadow thrown on the wall by the bannister of the stairway Nicholas mounts to the Brays' flat. The shadow covers the full wall, and screen, as Nicholas approaches and knocks at the door. Later, when Ralph comes to call at the same landing, the shadow is not shown, until Madeline flees down the staircase. Finally, when Nicholas comes back to plead with Madeline not to marry Ralph, as he stands beside her we see her in her bridal gown and behind her a deep pattern of bars on the wall, thrown from the windowpane. At its third appearance the lock-gate is an ordinary but locked house door that the police pry open in order to reach Ralph in the garret where he has hanged himself.

Most of the doors, however, are plain interior or exterior household doors, and almost once a minute a character goes in or out of one. Perhaps the most noticeable is the door that does not quite appear, but is called for: when Gregsbury dismisses Nicholas for having queried his proposed salary, he does so simply by shouting, "Door, Matthews!" He does this in the novel too, but only after some further altercation, and the note is not emphasized, as it is in the film, by the excessive presence of doors around it. As Noggs shouts the full revelation of what he has pieced together, Ralph hastens to leave, but he is delayed by a fumble at the door. And the last we see of Ralph is a door closing.

These doors create a persistent sense of enclosed spaces, as movement in and out is carefully defined, noted, by the door. We are reminded continually of the possibilities of closed doors, slammed doors, or undesirably opened doors. We seem to jump from door to door rather than scene to scene; the doors increase rather than diminish our awareness of the cuts from one short indoor scene to the next. And the doors emblematize the themes: imprisonment (all the boys at Dotheboys, with Smike at the head; Bray in the Rules); false entry (as assault and battery; in Squeers' kidnapping of Smike; in the sexual advances upon Kate and Madeline); locked-in secrecy (Ralph's secret, which is also Smike's); denial of rightful admission (to the family circle; to honest work; and for Nicholas, to Madeline).

The doors and the enclosures they create should be contrasted to the sense of traversing distances that we find in the novel. Not only are major distances covered—from Devonshire to London to Yorkshire to London, back to Yorkshire and back to London—but within London we are conscious of a great deal of movement between locations, along its streets and across its districts, by Nicholas especially and by others, such as Kate, as well. Although these distances often represent obstacles or difficulties, they also create a sense of space, and the frequent references to specific places tie the novel to a world we know. There are such references in the film too—East as opposed to West End London, London, Yorkshire, the village of Bow where the Cheerybles give the Nicklebys a cottage—but what we see of the places is almost exclusively interior, interiors that could be anywhere. We move from one interior to the next, with exteriors that are used mainly to locate interiors (the Saracen's Head or Miss La Creevy's house) or are themselves enclosed, like the courtyard of the Saracen's Head. This film in doors is emphatically indoors.

There are some exceptions, including the cottage garden at Bow, which is a paradisal island, and the first meeting of Nicholas and Madeline outside the employment agency. But the first time we see the garden it is also observed by the snake, Wackford, Jr., spying out Smike. And when Nicholas and Madeline meet, the scene is filmed so that no sky is visible and their being outdoors signifies mainly their being excluded from the interior, where employment is held and withheld. This exclusion is made clear in the last frame of the scene, when a hostile and disdainful man glares out at Nicholas through a pane of the large window to the interior. Elsewhere when the film is out of doors the elements are threatening, as in the snow outside Dotheboys when Nicholas arrives, when Squeers hunts Smike and when Nicholas escapes, and the thunderstorm that pursues Ralph home the last time. Ralph and Mrs. Nickleby meet Kate outside the Mantalinis' when Ralph invites her to his dinner, but it is a dark and enclosed outside, with no sky.

The few real exceptions—when the outdoors is open—mark the moments of relief or the anticipations of ultimate comic resolution: the shot of Nicholas and Smike approaching the inn where they will meet Mr. Crummles; their arrival with the Crummles troupe in Portsmouth; Nicholas's second meeting with Madeline on his way out of London. Even the latter is qualified, for though the scene begins with a view of trees lining the street accompanied by a young-love motif in the music it rapidly devolves to Bray shut up in the box of the hackney and taken under arrest, leaving Nicholas, in a rare instance of the camera taking his point of view, to watch the departing coach. The trees become visible again and the music returns; the sky is still beyond the frame. Only at the very end of the film does the sky arch overhead. Anyone who may have doubted the emblematic function of sky (or its absence) and weather will be assured by the segue to the final scene: the camera looks out the window of the room in which Ralph is hanging, as the thunderstorm diminishes; the camera moves through the frame into the rapidly lightening outdoors where the smoking chimneys of the stormy scene are virtually transformed into a church spire (by a superposition of images that looks like a zoom forward). We go into the church for the triple wedding, which concludes with the camera sweeping up the wall, as it did in the Dotheboys dining hall, but to find, instead of a motto on repression, "Gloria in Excelsis" and the organist and the pipes of the church organ, reaching ever upwards. (Cavell describes this "old ending" *topos* as the "outside pull-away, up from the house or neighborhood in which the drama has ended, letting the world return" [p. 135].)

Differences between film and novel in the ordering of events also heighten discomfort. In the novel, when Nicholas leaves Dotheboys after flogging Squeers, he first encounters John Browdie. We and he anticipate a conflict, and in consequence Browdie's friendship and laughter seem all the warmer. After this meeting, we are told that it is snowing—but Nicholas is already warm, and so are we, from the comedy of Browdie's delight. In the film, Cavalcanti could not very well withhold the information that it is snowing, though he could have had the snow begin after the encounter. But there is no encounter, because Browdie has been cut entirely. Nicholas and Smike leave Dotheboys together (in the novel, Smike follows Nicholas and catches up with him in a barn, after the meeting with Browdie) and they go out the gate into a dark snowstorm. The exterior is merely bleak and hostile.

In the novel, Smike dies in Devonshire, on a trip taken in the hope of easing his illness. Only two chapters later do we learn that Ralph is his father. In the film, first we learn of Ralph's paternity, and then Smike dies (in London). Thus whereas the novel splits off the knowledge of the father's responsibility for the boy's death from the scene of the death, the film brings them together. It goes even further. As Nicholas rises from the side of Smike's deathbed, he moves to the bureau and puts away the miniature of Kate that Smike had been cherishing. He looks up into the mirror to see Ralph enter. A mirror shows us ourselves, and Nicholas is Ralph in the sense that the film also imputes to Nicholas a degree of guilt for Smike's death, an imputation never developed in the novel: Smike dies for Nicholas, in his place, the victim of Ralph's hatred for Nicholas. At the level of plot, Ralph pursues Smike only to hurt Nicholas. And so it is Nicholas who should have died and who caused the death of Smike by being invulnerable to Ralph's machinations. The novel never makes this connection clear and certainly does not suggest a taint of survivor's guilt in Nicholas.

In this scene in the film, both Ralph and Nicholas are wordless. Ralph looks, we see a last close-up of his face, he turns, and goes out the door. So we see Smike's death with the knowledge that he is Ralph's son and Nicholas's cousin, and we see Ralph confronting the dead boy. While Ralph looks on, Nicholas covers Smike's face with the bedsheet, so stating in gesture what Noggs stated in words and will repeat as the voice-over of Ralph's conscience: Too Late. By covering Smike's face, Nicholas for the last time shields Smike from Ralph. And in so far as Nicholas and Smike vis-a-vis Ralph are one, this covering is also a turning away. This face is turned, or turns, away from Ralph, who is now the one rejected. The film moves to highly melodramatic (and Dickensian) tropes for the psychic condition of Ralph—the storm and its trappings—but although they build a certain momentum of chase, they do not create fear. Because Ralph has lost power we are no longer afraid of him, and because, unlike Dickens, Cavalcanti allows him no remorse, we do not fear for him. Cavalcanti's Ralph first tries to get away, but when we see the money fall from his hands—a tidy contrast to Noggs's nervous hands at the opening—we know that he is trapped. In the film Ralph hangs himself only in desperation, not at all in despair.

The reorderings may include additions as well as deletions. In the film, Mrs. Nickleby arrives with Kate at Ralph's house while Sir Mulberry Hawk and Lord Frederick Verisopht are there. The men invite her and Kate to the opera, and she consents. As she babbles in characteristic fashion, we see her face and Kate's close together, Kate a little to the rear. We are conscious of the large brim of Mrs. Nickleby's hat, compared to Kate's trimmer but otherwise similar bonnet style. That brim brims over, as she does, and her babble is more annoying than it is in the novel, less amusing, because beside it we see Kate's pained face. In the novel, Mrs. Nickleby comes to Ralph's alone, and in the following chapter we see her alone with Pyke and Pluck. In the latter scene the arrangement for theater is made. She goes to the theater with Sir Mulberry, Lord Frederick, Pyke, and Pluck—where they meet Kate, to Mrs. Nickleby's genuine surprise but not Hawk's, because she has been brought thither by the Wititterlys (who do not appear in the film). The film version, in which Kate is brought to the opera by her mother, both in the planning of the evening and then as we see them in the box, leaves a suggestion that Mrs. Nickleby's negligence borders upon selling her daughter. While Mrs. Nickleby chatters, we watch Kate silent. It is altogether more sinister. In the film, the emphasis of the scene at the opera is on *Norma* on the stage (with its concern for virginity under siege) and on Kate's face; in the novel, it is on the exuberantly comic social pretensions of Mrs. Nickleby and Mrs. Wititterly and on Kate only when, leaving, she breaks away from Hawk. The film has intensified the threat and deleted the comedy.

In the film, as in the novel, Nicholas on his first day at Dotheboys takes over the class to teach them some reading. The first class has spelled WINDER and BOTTINNEY and has been sent on its way. And now Cavalcanti interpolates. Nicholas begins to read from *Pilgrim's Progress*. The camera watches him, from the boys' point of view, as he reads. Over his shoulder we see BOTTIN. As he comes to "I dreamed a dream" there is a dissolve to Kate in Mrs. Mantalini's salon. The scene has an operatic, Hollywood lushness that one associates with the film settings of stars' boudoirs. It is a secular, material dream of the Cinderella variety, but the irony of its secularity and materialism is quickly undercut as we realize that the dream even for what it is is factitious: it is all millinery, it is a miserable life for Kate, and it is decorated with Mr. Mantalini and the contemptuous parrot.

Finally, there are differences in valence between the novel and the film. These are most apparent in the effect of the Crummles company. In the novel, Nicholas's stint with this troupe is a sort of holiday and the segment a hiatus in the march of the plot. For the Crummles family, all the world's a stage and all of life is a drama. The narrator remains aloof from them, and so does Nicholas; we are aware that the serious business of life is taking place elsewhere. The episode reminds us of the artifice of art, including the art of the novel, and of its generic warranties of happy endings. We return to the most melodramatic portion of the novel refreshed and bemused by comic melodrama. In the film, the Crummles sequence provides comic counterpoint to the main plot, but little relief. The badness of the troupe's acting—its keynote struck in the appearance of Mrs. Crummles *en scene*—suggests that this is "acting" and that what surrounds it, in the main plot, is real. Because the film does not develop any of the little tales of company life that spark the novel, the Ralph/Squeers plot hangs ominously over this sequence. Like other forms of delay, the sequence heightens suspense, and the break that it offers is not refreshing as it is in the novel.

Cavalcanti's streamlining of the Crummles episode and the much shorter duration of the film as a whole combine to accentuate a subplot function that is also present in the novel but comparatively submerged by the dominant sense of hiatus. The parallel emerges visually. This film shoots scenes of two, three, sometimes four or five people. Larger groups are rare and briefly shown: the miscellaneous street crowds seen when Ralph walks to Miss La Creevy's and in the courtyard of the Saracen's Head, the company in the coffee-room where Nicholas meets Hawk, the group of employment-seekers at the agency when Mr. Cheeryble arrives there, the Kenwigs family circle, the roomful of seamstresses whom Kate joins at Mrs. Mantalini's, and the stageful of singers (but no audience) at the opera. But there are really only two parts of the film in which the subject of a sequence of shots is a large group: at Dotheboys, and in the Crummles company. From the visual parallel other likenesses become apparent. Both groups are social microcosms. Both are controlled by a male figure assisted by a wife whom he eulogizes and supported in his work by a child (Wackford, Jr. and the Infant Phenomenon) around whose accomplishments there hangs a certain deception. Both employ Nicholas for a short time. These likenesses are in the novel as in the film, but because in the film they constitute almost the total of what we see of the Crummleses, they are much more readily noticeable.[7] In addition, in the film the two sequences present two of the three meals: the empty tea at Dotheboys discussed above, the dinner at Ralph's where Kate is set upon, and the dinner at the inn that brings Nicholas and Smike into the Crummles troupe. These meals are meals for males only: at the first the boys are starved, at the second Kate is set as bait and baited, but at the last Smike is secure enough to fall asleep. Thus the film points a schematic contrast between tyranny and benevolent patriarchy.

The patriarchy, however, is a world of make-believe, a wonderland with no possibility for reality, an interlude. In the novel, its structure is realized in the real world by the ascendancy of the Cheerybles and their beneficent control of the resolution. In the film, the role of the Cheerybles is truncated:

except for a silent glimpse of their presence at the wedding they disappear from the screen after the scene in which they assign Nicholas the job of collecting Madeline's artwork. Thus the film enhances the contrast between tyranny and patriarchy and diminishes the presence of patriarchy outside the world of fantasy. It is possible that at the close of World War II patriarchy seemed safe nowhere else.

Cavalcanti uses comedy as comic relief and to anticipate the happy ending, which is assured mainly through Nicholas's good looks and height. The overriding difference in tonality between the novel and the film takes us to an essential feature of early Dickens: that Dickens keeps us laughing at things that are not really funny at all. Cavalcanti, like many American Dickensians, has looked more at the frightening things than at the humor and by excising or altering several bases of the novel's comedy has shown us their importance. The film's abridgment of the Kenwigses, Mantalini, the Crummles troupe, and the Cheerybles and its elimination of John Browdie show us how these figures are integral to the novel if not to its plot. The plot alteration whereby Ralph is made Madeline's suitor shows us how by splitting this role onto Gride the novel moderates, or hides, the intensity of the threat Ralph represents.

That Cavalcanti's emphasis is not inevitable to adaptation of this novel can be seen in part from comparison to a stage production. The Royal Shakespeare Company's 1980 *Nickleby*, like the film, is twentieth-century, though one should not suggest that the thirty-three years between the film and the stage version are negligible. The major differences between the film and this version arise from RSC's very modern allegiance to the original text. Others may be attributed to characteristics of the stage exploited by this production, as the film exploited certain characteristics of cinema.

The RSC Nickleby was performed on a slightly thrust stage with a gangway down the center aisle of the theater. Although this structure brings the play somewhat closer to some members of the audience, its primary effect is to create, in contrast to the proscenium stage, a greater sense of staginess. It helps keep the entire play very much a play. So too did the actors' hanging about the stage and talking with the audience during the intermissions, the stunning ticket prices (in the U.S.), and the arrangement whereby one saw the eight-and-one-half-hour play in two sessions, which tended to foster a heightened self-consciousness in the audience of itself as audience. In comparison, the film is very much a proscenium film, in keeping with the dominant style of the medium at the time and reinforced by the general absence of human point of view for the camera.

The RSC production also went to great length to retain the narratorial voice, by distributing narrative portions to various characters. It thus retained a certain amount of verbal connection between scenes—in contrast to the jumps through doors and from scene to scene in the film—introduced another irrealistic element, and broke with the convention of the audience's invisibility. With the Crummles troupe it heightened our awareness of the entire experience as theater, an effect enhanced in the American tour when the audience roared in response to an interpolated line announcing that in America audiences will pay any price.

Only at one point in the RSC production did real fear strike. Direct personal violence is more frightening on stage than on film because in the theater the audience can be much less sure that the scene has somehow been faked. The RSC built up very high tension as the flogging of Smike approached, topped only by the event itself. Whereas the film spared us any actual blows, the stage made us watch two: the difference is in keeping with the difference between the film's high-heroic Nicholas, who intervened immediately and strongly, and the hesitant, more slowly sparked and less self-confident Nicholas of the stage. The stage production also milked a great deal of sentiment for the death of Smike. All told, however, it sustained a level of comic buoyancy as merry-Dickensian as one could wish, and quite foreign to the film.[8] Just the wide focus of the stage—kept wide by frequent full movement, the second storey created by bridges, the presence on stage of the choral characters, even when they were not speaking, and a great deal of activity along the backdrop—brought the production closer to the novel's sense of possibility and space for movement and freedom, a sense reversed by the film's close-ups, doors, and interiors.

The redundant life of Dickens' novel, which the Royal Shakespeare Company recreated in the high energy of its production, is absent from the film. It is a film that, despite its commitment to a happy ending, is dominated by Ralph. Of the three versions, it is also the closest to the layer of filicide and incest in the story. The film is more "closed" than "open"—in Leo Braudy's description, more schematic in form, more self-enclosed and self-contained, more confined to detail that signifies, more architectural than pictorial.[9] For example, Braudy points out that characters who wander in and out of the frame and irrelevant, "detail" characters who appear at odd moments in the background are more typical of open films. In *Nicholas Nickleby*, while the main characters usually either are found by the camera when it opens a new scene or enter the scene through a door, in a few scenes some unnamed irrelevant characters—extras—walk by through the frame: when Ralph reaches Miss La Creevy's house, he passes a virtual crowd pushing in the opposite direction (it is never explained); there is the expected bustle of porters, travellers, and loungers in the courtyard of the Saracen's Head as Nicholas and the boys depart for Yorkshire; when Madeline and Nicholas meet outside the employment agency a few passers-by cross the screen, one right in front of the two principals. In all these scenes, empty streets would have been simply unrealistic and would have suggested significance: the detail is here not so much to signify or not signify as to prevent its absence from signifying in some undesired way.

The novel establishes itself as a reader's book and indulges in such extreme irrelevance as the interpolated tales in chapter 6. Critical ingenuity can of course always find relationships between the tales and the main story, but they remain an indulgence, smacking of the need to round out a number (they come in the middle of number 2). It is not merely that the film, with its limited length, has no time for such fillips, but that the intensity of the film and the effects of paranoid claustrophobia and looming threat that it achieves depend upon a relatively rigorous exclusion of non-signifying details. The rigor is only "relative" because a total exclusion would reduce the realism and so lessen the effect.

David Paroissien notes that the obvious result of the several cuts required to bring the film within a two hours' compass (108 minutes, in fact) is to make its narrative line much tauter than the novel's, more orderly and less digressive. Some of the contemporary reviews saw this compression as important to the film's relative failure, complaining of a lack of room to develop character or pace incident.[10] What the film lost—or renounced—is perhaps best put in Margaret Ganz's description of where the novel most gains. Following G. K. Chesterton, she argues that the characters irrelevant to the plot "have the power to affect us most, if in a very subtle, unconventional way. What is best in the novel is truly independent of story or main characters, as a seemingly gratuitous but hardly meaningless impulse of imaginative energy projects a humorous vision of the world."[11]

This humor is the comedic essence of the novel and this is what is excised in a film that chooses the plot first. For example, as the crisis of the theater visit approaches, Mrs. Nickleby is described by the narrator:

> There was one great source of uneasiness in the midst of this good fortune, and that was the having nobody by, to whom she could confide it. Once or twice she almost resolved to walk straight to Miss La Creevy's and tell it all to her. "But I don't know," thought Mrs. Nickleby; "she is a very worthy person, but I am afraid too much beneath Sir Mulberry's station for us to make

a companion of. Poor thing!'' Acting upon this grave consideration she rejected
the idea of taking the little portrait-painter into her confidence, and contented
herself with holding out sundry vague and mysterious hopes of preferment to
the servant-girl, who received these obscure hints of dawning greatness with
much veneration and respect.                                (chapter 27)

The veneration and respect of the servant-girl are a triumph of excess; the
film does not attempt to create anything equivalent. Similarly, when in the
film Fanny composes her letter to Ralph reporting on Nicholas's attack,
Cavalcanti employs the conventional film technique of having us watch her
write as her voice-over reads. It is well done, but what comes through is only
Fanny's spite and meanness. In the novel, a significant element of comedy
comes from her spelling. In both these instances, what the film omits are
linguistic features probably impossible to translate directly to film. But a third
instance suggests that such humor is also willingly forgone. After the death
of Ralph, the film moves directly to the triple wedding, a scene that offers
relief limited by its brevity and its confinement of language to two marginal
voices, the minister and Mrs. Nickleby, the former reassuring and the latter
rattling on. That last scene reproduces the solemn and sentimental note of the
novel's final chapter. What the film omits is the chapter in the novel (64)
between the death of Ralph and the "Conclusion," which is made up of Mr.
Mantalini's reprise ("I am always turning. I am perpetually turning, like a
demd old horse in a demnition mill. My life is one demd horrid grind!") and
the glorious breakup of Dotheboys, led by John Browdie ("Tak' a good breath
noo—Squeers be in jail—the school's brokken oop—it's a' ower—past and
gone—think o' thot, and let it be a hearty 'un! Hurrah!"). Language and
accent have here, as ever, a good deal to do with the comedy, but the scenes
remain obviously dramatizable.

    The film gained a tighter structure—though in noticeable degree the story
remained ineluctably episodic—by its strict focus on the main lines of the
plot. The RSC production attempted, with admirable success, to avoid such
condensation: "here was an essentially Dickensian looseness of structure,
with the main line of the plot clear but constantly varied or subsumed in local
issues."[12] In the space free of the plot that the RSC retained, it was possible
to develop a large part of the high-flying humor of Dickens' novel. It was
possible, as in the novel, to keep us laughing at things that are not really very
funny by turning us away from them and into the counter-life of the humor,
irrelevant to the main action.

    Having drastically cut the irrelevancies, in all their glory, did Dighton and
Cavalcanti create a mere rigid melodrama, marked by machinations of evil

figures, plots, concealments, and discoveries that one can barely follow as the novel unfolds, let alone remember? Or, as Paroissien argues, an allegory for which underdeveloped characters and a simpler plot were appropriate? Neither, I think. Cavalcanti curtails the comic life of the novel, to lift out its tragic substratum. He brings to the foreground what was always present in the novel, what in fact required the enormous comic creation and made the triumph over reality so gratifying. His means include a variety of elements, some intrinsic to film, some chosen by decisions in the making of this particular film: large and several cuts; condensations and reorderings of events; changes in tonality; the sense of confinement arising from repeated focus on doors and faces; the depopulation of *Nickleby*'s world; and above all the excision of the narrative voice, without compensation. Thus the film version cut to the bedrock of the plot and found there a fundamental story that speaks to primal fears: a story of filicide and incest in a world where age and cruelty war upon youth and the human spirit, and sometimes win. And in the film, the terror of this myth of Kronos is amplified by the effects of camera and set: in a world presented by no narrator and comprised of small groups in confining spaces, we are all the more vulnerable.

My language has suggested that the story of filicide and incest is primal—bedrock—to the plot of the novel, and the humor a sort of overlay or defense. Ganz would probably reverse the relationship. I would like to leave it rather less defined. It seems plausible to argue that the two major strands in the novel, humor and terror, are co-equal, each perhaps dependent on the other for its energy. Cavalcanti's different emphasis, in this light, offers us not a revelation of a deeper layer of meaning but a perspective upon that half of a dialectic that we tend to underacknowledge—as he, Cavalcanti, seems to have underacknowledged the humor. We go back from the film to the novel less with an alternative version of the story than with an interpretation that enhances our understanding of its dynamics. In this view, terror and humor in the novel are not kernel and husk but two interwoven patterns on a single verbal plane. Most literary criticism, and perhaps most readers, have responded, at least consciously, to one; the Cavalcanti film emphasizes the other. Virtually all the film's "deviations" or "infidelities" serve that emphasis, and so even do several apparently invariant conditions of the medium, such as the absence of color or the use of close-ups. The example of *Nickleby* suggests the value of seeing the film adaptation not as translation, to be measured by likeness to the original, but as hermeneutic and interpretation, in which the differences from the original are most telling.

## NOTES

1. *The World Viewed*, enl. ed. (Cambridge, Mass. and London: Harvard University Press, 1979), p. 119.
2. My premises, it should be apparent, are different from David Paroissien's in "The Life and Adventures of Nicholas Nickleby: Alberto Cavalcanti Interprets Dickens" (*HSL* 9 [1977], 17–28) and my conclusions correspondingly different. To a large extent, our two essays take up essentially different problems. Paroissien does anticipate my interest (below) in the film sequence from Nicholas reading *Pilgrim's Progress* through the boys' tea at Dotheboys, though he makes more of the presence of Bunyan than I do.
3. Quotations are from the facsimile of the first edition in parts introduced by Michael Slater (Philadelphia: University of Pennsylania Press, 1982).
4. I am using the term as Cavell does, pp. 20 and 25.
5. *Charles Dickens: The World of His Novels* (Cambridge, Mass.: Harvard University Press, 1959), p. 93.
6. In an interview with John Harrington and David Paroissien ("Alberto Cavalcanti on *Nicholas Nickleby*," *Literature/Film Quarterly* 6 [1978], 48–56), Cavalcanti took credit for a good part of the writing: "Harrington: What part did you play in the writing of the script of *Nicholas Nickleby*? Cavalcanti: Quite a lot. I had a very intelligent script writer, John Dighton, whom I knew while working at Ealing. Dighton and I worked together very well. He had all the dialogue from Dickens; there is very little of the scriptwriter in it. But he was very good in the literary work of adaptations. Harrington: Did he make the decisions on how the novel was going to be shaped for the film? Cavalcanti: We did it together."
7. The relationship in the novel between Squeers and Crummles is noted by John Archer Carter, "The World of Squeers and the World of Crummles," *Dickensian* 58 (1962), 50–53. Carter's focus is on the issue of teaching; he emphasizes the contrast between Squeers as pedagogue and Crummles's first appearance in his role of teacher to the two boys learning to stage-duel. This is play-violence, Carter notes, in the same way that on stage "Smike's starvation will be a fabrication." Jerome Meckier, in "Faint Image of Eden: The Many Worlds of *Nicholas Nickleby*," *Dickens Studies Annual*, 1, ed. Robert B. Partlow, Jr. (Carbondale and Edwardsville: Southern Illinois University Press, 1970), 129–146, includes the Squeers and Crummles domains among the several circles through which Kate and Nicholas must pass in their search for a better world.
8. An odd piece of evidence for this spirit is the tendency for people occasionally to remember the play as a musical—not just a play with some music, which it was, but a musical in the way that *Oliver!* is. More direct is the kind of comment made by Andrew Sanders: "The joy, the exuberance, the eccentricity, the villainy, the confusion, the twists and turns, the pathos were all there" ("Nicholas Nickleby at the Aldwych," *Dickensian* 76 [1980], 174–175).
9. *The World in a Frame: What We See in Films* (Chicago and London: University of Chicago Press, 1976), pp. 44ff. This paper is also indebted to Braudy directly, for his comments on a draft, and to Ronald Gottesman.
10. See *The New York Times*, Dec. 1, 1947, p. 27, and *Variety*, March 26, 1947, p. 12. Leslie Staples was more generous in the *Dickensian* 43 (1947), 131–132.
11. "*Nicholas Nickleby*: The Victories of Humor," *Mosaic* 9, iv (1976), 131–148.
12. Sanders, *op. cit.*

# The Shaping of *The Battle of Life*: Dickens' Manuscript Revisions

### *Ruth Glancy*

"I wouldn't have it limp, if it can fly."[1] So wrote Dickens to Forster in November 1846, when he was busy altering the proofs of *The Battle of Life*, and as usual called on his friend for advice. Few if any readers since then have credited the book with flight; most would hardly even allow that it limps, since it is now universally regarded as Dickens' greatest failure, a moribund creation with no possibility of movement at all. For Dickens, though, the possibility of the book's flight was urgent and exciting because he saw in its theme of heroic sacrifice the potentialities which were later to be properly realized in *A Tale of Two Cities*. He blamed the failure of the Christmas book on its shortness: "What an affecting story I could have made of it in one octavo volume,"[2] he complained, while busy with last-minute revisions of the proofs. And undoubtedly the working out of the plot without the super-natural machinery used in his previous Christmas books to telescope time was a difficulty that he tried unsuccessfully to overcome. As well as an implausible plot, though, the book lacks a convincing theme because Marion's sacrifice is essentially faulty. In Dickens' letters and in the manuscript we have in-teresting evidence of his attempts to rectify both problems, as well as insights into his working methods: his meticulousness in finding the right word or phrase; his concern with keeping the threads of the story in the reader's mind while maintaining necessary suspense and secrecy; and his desire to make the final version as plausible and affecting as possible. A study of the manuscript reveals that Dickens had great difficulty in composing the story, and made some major alterations at proof stage in the hope that his little love story would indeed fly.

*The Battle of Life* was conceived and written at Rosemont, Dickens' home in Switzerland from June to December 1846, a location that influenced both the setting and the theme of the book. His letters speak repeatedly of the effect of the Swiss countryside upon him. In July he wrote to Lord Robertson that London did not exist: "Mountains, valleys, lakes, vines, and green lanes, are all I believe in, in the way of locality."[3] His house overlooked an apple orchard, surely the source of the opening scene of the book, which he wrote at harvesting time in September. He was particularly struck by the marked contrast in Swiss scenery between such awesome and heroic sights as the mountains, summer thunderstorms, and monuments like the Castle of Chillon, and the quiet orderliness of everyday life in the fields, orchards, and small towns. This blending of heroic and simple, of history on a grand scale and rural day-to-day life on a small, formed his theme, as explained by Alfred Heathfield to the cynics, Dr. Jeddler and Snitchey: "I believe . . . there are quiet victories and struggles, great sacrifices of self, and noble acts of heroism . . . done every day in nooks and corners, and in little households, and in men's and women's hearts."[4] As *Dombey and Son*, written concurrently, is almost wholly rooted in London and the mercantile world, it is hardly surprising that Dickens transferred some of his response to the Swiss scenery to the Christmas book.

When on 28 June Dickens began *Dombey and Son*, he was in two minds about the Christmas book, feeling both "the suddenest and wildest enthusiasm" and "solitary and anxious consideration."[5] He hoped to "clear it off"[6] between the first two numbers of the novel in July, but the first number took longer to write than he had foreseen, and when he began the second number on 5 August he still had not started on the Christmas book. It was a continual worry to him that he was "wasting the marrow of the larger book"[7] by working on both at once, but in fact he was able to complete the Christmas book between numbers two and three of *Dombey and Son*, beginning it on September 9. For a week he had thought of abandoning it, having had difficulty with the opening lines and with a passage on p. 3 of the manuscript, which he deleted with a wafer, introducing Doctor Jeddler instead. In the omitted portion Dickens had intended to reinforce the battlefield motif by having the Jeddlers' land a tourist attraction:

> This gave three men without an opportunity of coming in, for they had been waiting all this time by the gate, or peeping over the low wall, as I should certainly have mentioned but for having waited for an opportunity myself.
>
> "Don't hang back gentlemen," said the small man, in advance of the other two, holding the gate open with an air of patronage. "Pray don't hang back. I have leave to show strangers this point. It's perhaps the most interesting point of the battlefield. Don't deprive yourselves gentlemen."

The other two, being thus strongly pressed to come in, came in, but only a few steps, and there stood: looking about them.

"The last charge, gentlemen," said their attendant, flourishing his right arm, with an air of great importance, "is supposed to have been made from the rising ground there, slap into this very nook. The troops were tumbled down here gentlemen, o' both sides, dead and wounded, like flies. More bones have been dug up at one time and another from round that little bank."[8]

Dickens perhaps felt that the passage was becoming too morbid, the attendant's lecture too stark a contrast to the orchard scene. At proof stage he added references to the battlefield at different places in the text to reinforce the theme, but they did not recall the physical siting of Jeddler's house on the gory remains, which this deleted passage would have emphasized.[9]

The manuscript shows that Dickens further toned down the battlefield description in the first scene by deleting with a wafer a passage that followed on in paragraph two from his exhortations to Heaven to keep us from a knowledge of the wind's secrets "that blew across the scene of that day's work and that night's death and suffering!":

War, long remembered: Glory, soon forgotten; War, comprehending in its miseries and outrages whole nations; Glory shining on the hearts of half a dozen out of half a dozen hundred thousand fighting men: both fade away before the truth of time.

Dickens perhaps felt that this passage was wandering from the motif of the field, and was introducing the new subject of glory for a few, which was out of keeping with the emphasis on the great numbers who fell needlessly and absurdly. Its moralizing broke into the descriptive tenor of the passage.

Dickens' letter to Forster on September 20 emphasizes the ease with which he wrote Part One of the story, once he overcame the opening difficulties. The manuscript contains many emendations and additions, but few corrections were needed at proof stage, unlike Part Three, which required considerable rewriting. At this point he considered it "a pretty story, with some delicate notions in it agreeably presented, and with a good human Christmas groundwork."[10] Most problematical was the character of Doctor Jeddler, whose transformation from a cynical, rather flippant "philosopher" to a sympathetic and sensitive man is the chief link between this unusual Christmas book and Dickens' four others: in each of the books a central character is forced to realize the wrongness of his previous attitudes. But whereas many commentators have argued that the unreformed Scrooge is more interesting and believable than the one who emerges at the end of *A Christmas Carol*, Doctor Jeddler's cynicism is unconvincing. The passage which tries to account for his crustiness was an addition on the back of p. 5, and its lack of credibility is one of the many faults of the book. It blames Jeddler's state of mind on his stumbling "by chance" over the stone which turns "every precious thing to poor account," hardly a plausible or even understandable explanation. To provide a more convincing argument and to connect Jeddler's transformation to the central motif of the book Dickens then introduces the siting of Jeddler's house on the old battlefield as the reason for his belief in the absurdity of human endeavor. In answer to Alfred's statement that "great sacrifices of self, and noble acts of heroism" occur every day in humble homes, Jeddler replies that he is too old to be converted because in sixty years he has "never seen the Christian world, including Heaven knows how many loving mothers and good enough girls like mine here, anything but mad for a battle-field" (252). Originally Dickens had placed a version of this passage at the conclusion of Snitchey's speech on the seriousness of law, which Snitchey sees as counter-balancing the stupidity of war (251). On Snitchey's pausing for tea, Jeddler then asks Alfred if he has been listening, and gives an abbreviated version of the speech that in the final version occurs a page later. Dickens cancelled this, wanting to bring in Alfred's statement of the theme at this point. On a wafer over Jeddler's passage Snitchey returns to the seriousness of the game of life, and in reply Dickens again intended to bring in Jeddler's battlefield passage. The second version of the passage is longer than the first, but not identical to the final version, as can be seen by comparing the three:

| Covered by a wafer in manuscript | Deleted in manuscript | Manuscript |
|---|---|---|
| "You have been listening, Alfred?" said the Doctor, with a merry eye. "And yet you see, I haven't been convinced in nearly sixty years. No no!" he added more [illegible]. Even here on an old battlefield—my attention was directed young to battlefields—I have seen [illegible] people [illegible] the whole world, mad for battle-fields. I have known the young and gentle | "Tut, tut," said the doctor, "let it pass. I am too old to be converted—even by friend Snitchey. I was born upon this battlefield. I began, as a boy, to have my thoughts directed to the real history of a battlefield. Sixty years have gone over my head, and I have never seen the Christian world —including Heaven knows how many loving mothers and good girls | "Well, well!" said the Doctor, "I am too old to be converted, even by my friend Snitchey here, or my good spinster sister, Sally Jeddler; who had what she calls her domestic trials ages ago, and has led a sympathizing life with all sorts of people ever since; and who is so much of your opinion (only she's more obstinate, being a woman), that we can't agree, and seldom meet. I was born upon this battlefield. I began, as a boy, to have my thoughts directed to the real history of a battle-field. Sixty years have gone over my head, and I have never |

exult in dreadful battle-
fields

like mine here—any-
thing but mad for a bat-
tlefield. One must either
laugh or cry at such stu-
pendous inconsisten-
cies. And I prefer to
laugh."

seen the Christian world, including Heaven knows how many
loving mothers and good girls,
like mine here, anything but mad
for a battle-field. The same contradictions prevail in everything.
One must either laugh or cry at
such stupendous inconsistencies;
and I prefer to laugh."

The rewritings increase Jeddler's connection with the battlefield, expand the
inconsistency of gentle people revelling in battlefields (although Dickens
replaced "exult" with the more colloquial "mad for"), and introduce Martha
(altered from Sally at proof stage) as a sympathetic person who knows what
it is to suffer. The important passage in which Alfred and Snitchey disagree
about the battle of life, and Alfred argues for the heroism of humble people,
occurs in the manuscript on the back of p. 10, replacing the deleted second
version of Jeddler's passage. That Dickens experimented with the passage
twice before arriving at the final version, and twice decided to add more
dialogue between Snitchey and Alfred, indicates that he realized the importance of establishing the thematic function of the battlefield setting and its
relationship to Dr. Jeddler, and of defining the roles of Alfred and Martha,
who do not return to the stage until Part Three.

Manuscript emendations show the care with which Dickens worked to
foreshadow the plot and establish character and motivation, even at this early
stage when the story was still not fully conceived. Additions show that Dickens
wanted to establish Dr. Jeddler's essential kindliness and affection, qualities
that will overcome his veneer of cynicism after he sees his daughters' heroism.
The doctor's soliloquy about the girls' dancing on the day they dreaded was
added in very small writing to the manuscript, to foreshadow Alfred's departure, and reveal the doctor's private sensitivity to the girls' feelings. It also
introduces the doctor's stock phrase:

"Music and dancing *to-day!*" said the Doctor, stopping short, and speaking
to himself. "I thought they dreaded to-day. But it's a world of
contradictions.                                                          (242)[11]

Minor additions such as "Puss" and "going close to him" in the next passage
emphasize the affection between father and daughters. Dickens also added
to the conversation between Jeddler and Britain to show that Britain had been
instructed about the breakfast the night before, and had not brought it outside
as directed (245). This minor change adds to the sense that Dr. Jeddler is as

conscious of Alfred's departure and its effect on the girls as they are, despite his attempts to remain merely amused.

Alfred's character is established more clearly in the passage mentioned above, which Dickens worked in on the back of a manuscript page. Later, the passage in which Jeddler discusses Alfred's upbringing is rewritten on a wafer to add two details:

"But this is not our business, Alfred," said the doctor. "Ceasing to be my ward (as you have said) today, and leaving us full to the brim of such learning as the grammar-school down here has been able to give you, and such practical knowledge as a dull old country doctor like me could graft upon it, you are away now into the world. The term of probation, fixed by your poor father, is over, and away you go. You'll forget us, in six months."

"If I do! But you know better. Why should I talk to you!" said Alfred, laughing.

"But this is not our business, Alfred," said the Doctor. "Ceasing to be my ward (as you have said) to-day; and leaving us full to the brim of such learning as the Grammar School down here was able to give you, and your studies in London could add to that, and such practical knowledge as a dull old country Doctor like myself could graft upon both; you are away, now, into the world. The first term of probation appointed by your poor father, being over, away you go now, your own master, to fulfil his second desire: and long before your three years' tour among the foreign schools of medicine is finished, you'll have forgotten us. Lord, you'll forget us easily in six months!"

"If I do—But you know better; why should I speak to you!" said Alfred, laughing. (253–254)[12]

While composing the first draft Dickens clearly saw here an opportunity to explain Alfred's absence and give it a time limit, thus preparing for Alfred's return, which forms the climax of Part Two. Earlier, Dickens had cancelled a passage about Alfred when the girls are talking about him. When Marion accuses Grace of teasing her about him, Grace had originally replied, "Such a true lover," and laughed. Dickens cancelled this in favor of " 'Teaze you by mentioning your lover!' said her sister," which allows him to expand on Alfred's fidelity in Grace's next response:

"Hush! Don't speak lightly of a true heart, which is all your own, Marion," cried her sister, "even in jest. There is not a truer heart than Alfred's in the world!" (244)

At proof stage Dickens made another important deletion to a later passage, removing "or can ever be" from Alfred's parting words to Grace about Marion: "dear to my heart as nothing else in life is—or can ever be" (257). As Alfred has to transfer his affections from Marion to Grace in Part Three, this declaration is out of keeping with the story line.

Marion's character also underwent subtle changes during the writing. Her name was originally Mary; on p. 8 of the manuscript (250) Dickens writes

Marion, and apparently at that stage went back and altered all previous references. She remains Marion from then on. Much has been written on the identification of Marion with Mary Hogarth, Grace with Georgina, and Alfred with Dickens.[13] Perhaps Dickens wished to make the identification less obvious. It does suggest that the identification was conscious, however. The most important emendations occur in the scene in which the girls have been discussing Alfred's love for Marion. A minor alteration to Marion's stripping petals from the flowers changes "throwing them away" to the more suggestive "scattering them on the ground," emphasizing Marion's emotional turmoil rather than her willfulness, which at this point is shown to be a cover for her feelings. In the speech Dickens has to portray the younger sister as in love with Alfred, but also as hiding some other feeling, the reason for which will be revealed at the end of the story. At this point Dickens wants to prepare for the later revelation of Marion's sacrifice without showing his hand. The manuscript shows that this dilemma, on which the plausibility of the plot rests, was difficult to overcome. To show Marion's resolve in seeming to be indifferent to Alfred (because she wants him to turn to Grace instead) Dickens altered the description of her as "casting down her eyes" to "raising her eyebrows," which he reinforced by the words "with a pleasant air of careless consideration" (244). A passage on the back of manuscript p. 4, intended to come in at this point but deleted, would have given the narrator's voice too flippant a tone, and would have pointed out Marion's deception too obviously:

> You are not curious, I dare engage, and yet you might have wondered what the doctor's younger daughter meant by this. Not that we wonder very much in life, when anybody's daughter is capricious or unintelligible, but because there was something in the manner at variance with the matter.

Another addition on the back of p. 4 was retained in the final version, which made clear the deception but in a more sympathetic way:

> And it was very curious indeed to see the younger sister's eyes suffused with tears, and something fervently and deeply felt, breaking through the wilfulness of what she said, and striving with it painfully.                    (244)[14]

A small change in the last line of Part One shows Dickens' awareness of the subtlety with which he had to both suggest and disguise Marion's sacrifice. When Alfred leaves in Part One, the reader has to see that Marion is upset by more than just her lover's departure. Dickens has to suggest here that she is already contemplating stepping aside to let Grace become Alfred's wife, and is torn by the sacrifice. The last line was to have been "But I cannot bear to see it, Grace! My heart is breaking," but Dickens altered the last phrase to "It breaks my heart." The ambiguity of the second phrase (what is the "it" which distresses Marion so much?—her lover's departure? her intended sacrifice? her knowledge that Grace also mourns Alfred's departure?) subtly lays the foundation for the events to come, and reveals without giving anything away the complexity of Marion's feelings.

The only alteration to Grace's portrayal in the first part comes at proof stage, when Dickens added "before sunrise" to Clemency's reference to the fact that Grace was walking outside early (248). The addition suggests Grace's emotional involvement in Alfred's departure, an involvement which can only be hinted at, as it is central to the plot that Marion realizes her sister's love for Alfred only because of her own love for Grace, and sensitivity to her. Grace is shown to be hiding her feelings totally from her family; she does not suspect that Marion has guessed the truth. This addition provides a very minor foreshadowing for the reader of what is to be revealed later.

On September 26 Dickens wrote to Forster at length, explaining that he had finished Part One on Wednesday the 23rd, and had felt "full of eagerness and pleasure." But the opening of Part Two was proving so difficult that he contemplated abandoning the book altogether, rather than risk damaging *Dombey and Son*, whose third part he hoped to complete before leaving for Paris in the middle of November. He felt ill, and missed the streets of a city, but was reluctant to abandon a story in which he was "deeply interested." He knew "the end and upshot of the second [part]; and the whole of the third," continuing:

> I know the purport of each character, and the plain idea that each is to work out; and I have the principal effects sketched on paper. It cannot end *quite* happily, but will end cheerfully and pleasantly. But my soul sinks before the commencement of the second part—the longest—and the introduction of the under-idea. (The main one already developed, with interest).

He planned to go to Geneva the next day and work on it there, hoping that the change of scene would help. He also recognized the problems inherent in the short Christmas book form when the plot is a straight narrative with no supernatural overcoming of time, as was used in the previous three books:

> It promises to be pretty; quite a new idea in the story, I hope; but to manage it without the supernatural agency now impossible of introduction, and yet to move it naturally within the required space, or with any shorter limit than a *Vicar of Wakefield*, I find to be a difficulty so perplexing . . . that I am fearful of wearing myself out if I go on.[15]

time on p. 26 of the manuscript, when Marion first speaks to him in private
(276). Dickens went back then and altered the previous references. He changed
"young man" to the more specific "man of thirty" (261), having decided
to make Warden's early misspent career a lengthy one, and altered "stranger"
to "client" (262). The passage in which Warden and Snitchey are described
as knowing each other, and speaking accordingly (263), is heavily deleted
and amended in small writing, suggesting with the deletion of "stranger" that
Dickens changed his mind about Warden's role, and decided while actually
in the process of writing to introduce Warden's romantic fall from his horse
at the Jeddlers' door, which forced him to stay with the family and allowed
him to observe Marion and fall in love with her. That Dickens had Warden
in mind as the red herring with whom Marion is to appear to elope is clear
from the reference in the manuscript to the nursing of his estate. Snitchey
says that Warden will have to leave his estate for ten years in order for it to
recover; this was altered at proof stage to six or seven, to accord with Forster's
good advice that Marion's absence from home should not be as long as ten
years. (Dickens forgot to alter one of these references when he went over the
proofs. Warden says "ten years hence as my wife" [267].) Thus although
at this stage Dickens wanted Warden's absence to coincide with Marion's,
the alterations suggest that the idea of the fall from the horse and Warden's
sojourn at the Jeddlers, which is revealed through the dialogue of the lawyers
and Warden, was conceived while Dickens was actually writing. Contrived
as it is, it allowed him to get the subplot moving without having to establish
Warden's relationship with Marion in the action of the story itself. We know
that Dickens wrote for only a morning on September 30, and felt unable to
fit the story into the necessary space. It is likely that in Geneva while continuing with the writing he thought of making the Warden-Marion plot predate the action by using flashback dialogue, thereby saving time and making
the supposed elopement more probable. Warden's reference to living in the
Jeddlers' house "some few months ago" was added to the manuscript, and
several short deletions introduced a little later indicate that Dickens wanted
to expand this scene while he was writing it. Warden's reiteration that he is
"deep in love" was such an addition, and Snitchey's query that the woman
in question is neither rich nor married was added on the back of p. 18 of the
manuscript. Originally Craggs asked the question, but Dickens changed it to
the more likely Snitchey. An important addition was Warden's declaration
that he was "not going to carry the young lady off, without her own consent.
There's nothing illegal in it" (265). Dickens wanted to make it quite clear

that Marion appeared to agree to an elopement, that she was not coerced by fear or force.

Warden's long speech (266–267) setting himself up as rival to Heathfield is heavily amended in the manuscript, and Dickens also altered the time within which Warden had to leave, changing Snitchey's proposed "tomorrow" to "in a week," and Craggs's "in a fortnight at full" to "in something less, I should say." "Today is Thursday" is added to Warden's speech to make his departure coincide exactly with Heathfield's return. Warden's reference to Marion as "the star of my destiny" and Snitchey's pun on it, that Warden had better take care on the stairs because "she don't shine there," was a happy lightening of Warden's earnestness added on the back of manuscript p. 20. Dickens also added the qualification that Snitchey was a good-natured man (268), having found that his lawyer was becoming much more human than his first appearance would have permitted. Other manuscript emendations show that Dickens softened the portraits of other characters to give them all the potential for warmth, sincerity, and genuine sympathy with human endeavor, in keeping with Jeddler's transformation. In Britain's recital of his history, his reference to carrying "nothing but deceptions" about in "oilskin baskets" when employed by a stay and mantua maker, which "soured [his] spirits and disturbed [his] confidence in human nature" (274), is added on the back of the manuscript page. Other changes soften Dickens' portrayal of Britain and Clemency. When Britain says to her, "What have you taken into your head? Not an idea, eh?" (277) the manuscript continues: " 'By George,' said Mr. Britain, meditating, 'perhaps she's got one at last and it's upset the nervous system'." A proof stage Dickens removed this more cynical retort. The narrator was also made less cynical, when Dickens altered "Clemency Newcome was rendered quite ecstatic by this avowal" to the milder "observed Clemency, folding her arms comfortably in her delight at this avowal" (275).

Dickens had trouble with the opening of each part of the book, and he had to rewrite the opening of the last scene in Part Two, when Alfred returns home to find the party in progress and Marion gone. The opening passage originally began in the same way as in the printed version, but Dickens altered "a bleak, cold, raging winter day" to just "a raging winter day," and "the fireside and the chimney-corner" to just "the chimney-corner" (279). Originally the passage continued, "to shed a ruddier glow upon the faces gathered round the hearth, and knit such domestic groups" and stopped there, replaced by a wafer that took up the fireplace image and contrasted the group clustered around it with "the roaring elements without." Such was the care with which Dickens wrote, that he rewrote a whole paragraph in order to expand this simple image. Dickens deleted a passage at the bottom of the wafer, which originally came in after the description of the English Christmas scene which would welcome Alfred back: "And the red berries gleamed an English welcome to him, peeping from among the leaves." The deleted passage read:

> There was a company of bell-ringers in the little town—young fellows of that country who delighted in the art—who, knowing Alfred, they resolved to set the bells a-going with a joyous peal when he arrived, in honour of an old acquaintance, and the Doctor's lovely daughter. All these preparations gave the Doctor infinite delight—for though this is a [world?] of trifles only worth a wise man's laughter, he was in a trifling humour for the time, or thought himself some [illegible] engaged with serious things.

Dickens may have rejected the bell-ringers because they would be unlikely to wish to disturb the whole town near midnight.

Dickens posted Parts One and Two, comprising 35 manuscript pages, to Forster in twelve separate parcels beginning on October 10. He asks Forster to read the two parts together, and says he finds "interest in it, and a pretty idea; and it is unlike the others [Christmas books]." He also suggests "The Battle of Life. A Love Story" as the complete title for the book, "to express both a love story in the common acceptation of the phrase, and also a story of love," and sees the need for "some slight alterations in one or two of the Doctor's speeches in the first part."[17] These alterations were the changing of "returned the Doctor" to "replied the Doctor" in his answer to Britain (245); the addition of "less reasonable and" to his parenthetical comment on Martha that "she's less reasonable and more obstinate, being a woman" (252); the addition of "enough" to his reference to his daughters as "good enough girls" (252); and the addition of "any serious correspondence or" to the phrase "To talk about any serious correspondence or serious affections, and engagements and so forth" (259), when he is saying goodbye to Alfred. None of these is important, although the last one does prepare for Alfred's continued communication with the family.

Dickens wrote Part Three between October 12 and 18, and as usual he had difficulty with the opening, the following cancelled passage appearing on the back of what became manuscript p. 36:

> One pleasant evening, when the world had grown ten years older since that night of the return: when the snow of ten winter seasons had melted from the earth, and had accumulated on the heads of ancient men: when flowers and fruits had sprung up from the ashes of those withered leaves in the old orchard, and had

The new opening altered "ten years" to "nearly ten" (which at proof was altered to six), changed the time of day from evening to afternoon, brought in the battlefield, and changed the original suggestion of spring to the more suitable one of autumn, with its implications of maturity and ripeness in the sisters. A wafer on manuscript p. 37 rewrites the passage about Clemency's arrival in the chaise cart. Although the alterations are very minor, Dickens clearly felt that they were important enough to warrant rewriting the passage:

| | |
|---|---|
| A chaise came clattering along the road, driven by a boy: and seated in it in a chair with a large saturated umbrella spread out to dry behind her, was the plump figure of a matronly woman with her arms folded across a basket which she carried on her knee, and a large loose umbrella by her side, several other baskets and parcels crowded about her, and a certain bright good nature in her face, and contented awkwardness in her bearing, which smacked at a little distance, of old times. Nor | A chaise-cart, driven by a boy, came clattering along the road: and seated in it, in a chair, with a large well-saturated umbrella spread out to dry behind her, was the plump figure of a matronly woman, with her bare arms folded across a basket which she carried on her knee, several other baskets and parcels lying crowded around her, and a certain bright good nature in her face and contented awkwardness in her manner, as she jogged to and fro with the motion of her carriage, which smacked of old times, even in the distance (291). |

The rewritten passage removes the repeated reference to the umbrella, qualifies the umbrella as "well" saturated and Clemency's arms as "bare," and changes the emphasis of the first and last sentences by re-ordering the phrases "driven by a boy" and "at a little distance."

In the passage introducing the day of Marion's return, Dickens altered the reference to the passing seasons from "since Alfred Heathfield had come back to find her lost to him" to "since she had fled" (301). Dickens correctly saw that at this point he does not want to remind the reader of Alfred's disappointment, as it is crucial to the story that Alfred has found his truer lover in Grace. The autumnal mood is emphasized in the correction of the landscape here from "bright" to "tranquil and serene." A final wafer on manuscript p. 45 (305) extends the meeting of the two sisters from a simple scene to a more staged and sentimental final version:

| | |
|---|---|
| As she clung to her sister, smiling through her tears, and looked into her face so tenderly, she whispered, "Let me tell you all, dear Grace." | Clinging to her sister, who had dropped upon a seat and bent down over her: and smiling through her tears, and kneeling close before her, with both arms twining round her, and never turning for an instant from her face: and with the glory of the setting sun upon her brow, and with the soft tranquillity of evening gathering around |

> them: Marion at length broke silence; her voice, so calm,
> low, clear, and pleasant, well-tuned to the time.[18]

Dickens wrote Part Three quickly, knowing it would need emendation, but anxious to send it to Forster and have his comments on the whole book. Differences between the manuscript and the printed text show that Part Three required the most correction. In his letter to Forster which accompanied the manuscript Dickens wrote:

> I really do not know what this story is worth. I am so floored: wanting sleep, and never having had my head free from it for this month past. I think there are some places in this last part which I may bring better together in the proof, and where a touch or two may be of service; particularly in the scene between Craggs and Michael Warden, where, as it stands, the interest seems anticipated. But I shall have the benefit of your suggestions, and my own then cooler head, I hope; and I will be very careful with the proofs, and keep them by me as long as I can.[19]

Dickens goes on to acknowledge Forster's criticism of Britain's Christian name. In Parts One and Two Britain has no Christian name; it is only in Part Three that his Christian name appears sometimes as John deleted to Tim, sometimes just as Tim, and sometimes just as John. Dickens altered them all to Britain, Mr. Britain or Benjamin on the proof copy, although three references to Tim slipped into the first and 1852 editions. Dickens also refers to his alteration of "Sally" to "Martha" in Part Three, and asks Forster if he would leave the concluding paragraph as it is "for happiness' sake? It is merely experimental." It was left, with "four or five-and-thirty," a clear reference to Dickens' own age, altered to the easier but less accurate "five-and-thirty," and the rather awkward "Time confuses facts most dreadfully sometimes" altered to "Time confuses facts occasionally." On the 28th, still waiting for Forster's comments and wondering "whether [Forster] foresaw the end of the Christmas book!"[20] Dickens either has the proofs, or has heard from Forster that the printers have turned Dr. Jeddler, "my kindly cynical old father," into Doctor Taddler, an understandable mistake considering Dickens' writing. The following day he suggests to Forster that the illustrators use eighteenth-century costumes, and the proof copy was emended accordingly, adding the phrase "about a hundred years ago" to the description of the orchard (241).

Back at work on the third number of *Dombey and Son*, Dickens writes to Forster on October 31 that he has received the proofs of Part Three, and notes that the printers have made mistakes in the section dealing with Grace and Alfred's marriage. Forster has complained that this topic is "unsatisfactory," but Dickens counters that the mistakes have misrepresented the scene, and that "whatever is done about that must be done with the lightest hand, for the reader MUST take something for granted." Dickens finds it "next to impossible, without dreadful injury to the effect, to introduce a scene between Marion and Michael. The introduction must be in the scene between the sisters, and must be put, mainly, into the mouth of Grace."[21] Dickens is correct in this; at this point he wishes to emphasize that there was no liaison at all between Marion and Michael, and that the whole story rests upon the love between the sisters. He has to reveal in the homecoming Marion's constancy to Grace alone, and avoid any reference to the red herring of Warden's scene with Marion at the end of Book Two. With such an addition, and a few other minor touches, Dickens hoped to make the book "pretty and affecting, and comfortable too." Dickens did, however, slip in an important scene between Marion and Michael at the end of the book, which will be discussed later.

Dickens decided that rather than have Grace discuss her marriage with Marion, he would put the addition into the scene between Grace and Alfred, before Marion appears. This large addition to the proof begins after the reference to Alfred's and Marion's birthday (301–302), and constitutes the alteration referred to in Dickens' letter to Forster of November 4. Dickens was waiting for Forster's advice before altering the proofs, but saw this scene as "a good place for introducing a few lines of dialogue."[22] He actually introduced several pages of new material. The addition ends with the words "how red the sun was" (303). Dickens added "raising her head quickly at these words" at proof stage to Grace's reply, to link the new passage to the text. The new passage describes Alfred's quiet, unambitious but wholly worthwhile vocation as a country doctor, bringing in a reference to the battlefield, and the "better purpose" won in this small sphere than if he had attempted a greater glory. The couple then discuss Marion, and Grace produces a letter which Marion had left behind for her when she disappeared. Dickens tells Forster of his plans for including the letter in a long letter on November 7:

> BUT (keep your eye on me) when Marion went away, she left a letter for Grace in which she charged her to encourage the love that Alfred would conceive for her, and FOREWARNED her that years would pass before they met again, etc. etc. This coming out in the scene between the sisters, and something like it being expressed in the opening of the little scene between Grace and her husband before the messenger at the gate, will make (I hope) a prodigious difference.[23]

Dickens decided to put the whole reference to the letter in the scene between

Grace and Alfred, a wise decision as the book already shows the two sisters manipulating the affections of the man, and a further scene between them would only emphasize Alfred's passive role. The new addition stresses that Grace resisted Alfred's love, that Alfred had to win Grace on his own merit, and that Grace did not take for granted Marion's avowal in the letter that he would transfer his affection to Grace. The new passage fills in the gap in the story concerning the courtship and marriage of Alfred and Grace, but does not do so very satisfactorily, for the reader is still left with the impression that Marion's sacrifice took little account of Alfred's feelings. This problem, inherent to the plot, could not be corrected by last-minute alterations.

Dickens made a few minor alterations to enhance Marion's homecoming. In the manuscript Grace has two daughters; this became one daughter at proof stage, perhaps to avoid too obvious a repetition of the sisters, and to give greater importance to the one little girl, whose name is Marion. When Marion appears, Dickens added to the overwrought description of her ghost-like apparition the words "with a cry," to humanize the "figure, with its white garments rustling in the evening air" (304), which waves its hands and sinks down in Grace's embrace. The addition of speech does alleviate the suggestion, which Dickens actually spells out, that the figure is a vision. Dickens added a wafer to expand the description of the sisters' meeting, and inserted another passage at proof stage:

> "When this was my dear home, Grace, as it will be now again—"
> "Stay, my sweet love! A moment! Oh Marion, to hear you speak again!"
> She could not bear the voice she loved so well, at first.          (305)

This rather unnecessary addition provides an element of suspense, and reiterates the importance of the vision's voice in proving her reality.

In his letter of November 7 Dickens answered several of Forster's objections. Forster had suggested the addition of a little scene with Marion following Warden's final speech at the end of the book, but Dickens refused this, saying that only a printer's line could go between the speech and the concluding paragraph. As Kathleen Tillotson points out,[24] in the first edition the final illustration provided a large break, the final paragraph appearing alone on the facing page. Dickens added a line to Warden's speech at proof stage, the manuscript giving only "Forget and Forgive" and omitting Clemency's other injunction, "Do as you would be done by!" Forster evidently thought that the conclusion of Part Three was hurried, but Dickens answered this objection also:

I wish to remark generally of the third part that all the passion that can be got into it, through my interpretation at all events, is there. I know that, by what it cost me; and I take it to be, as a question of art and interest, in the very nature of the story that it *should* move at a swift pace after the sisters are in each other's arms again. Anything after that would drag like lead, and must.

Dickens made very few alterations at proof stage to the story after Marion's return. To Grace's exclamation that Marion married Warden out of self-sacrifice he added, "You never loved him" (306), to emphasize the enormity of what Grace believes was the sacrifice. In Marion's reply Dickens added the words "told me what his condition and prospects really were" to make Warden's proposal more realistic. A few lines later he altered Marion's reference to "crowded streets and poor men's houses" to "crowded places, and among its busy life, and trying to assist and cheer it and to do some good" (307). This alteration to the sphere of action of other self-sacrificing sisters is more in keeping with the setting and moral of the book, which unlike the other Christmas books has nothing to do with the nobility of the poor. In the description of Grace's reaction to Marion's story Dickens removed the words "she tried to smile" after "her face relaxed" (307), and at the conclusion of that passage asked the printer for a very small space, which is not generally adhered to in modern printings. After the space Dickens added a long passage between Dr. Jeddler and Aunt Martha which foreshadows Marion's marriage to Warden and thus helps to answer Forster's objections. In his letter of November 7 Dickens tells Forster that he will try to put in a passage between Aunt Martha and the doctor "which shall carry the tale back more distinctly and unmistakeably to the battle-ground." In the added passage Martha refers to "such a farce as—," but her brother, "a converted brother," no longer retains his cynical views. There is no reference in the added passage to the battlefield, but in the doctor's later speech Dickens added the words "a world on which the sun never rises, but it looks upon a thousand bloodless battles that are some set-off against the miseries and wickedness of Battle-Fields" (308). In the same speech a reference to the Creator's "roughest image" is altered to the more poetic "lightest image."

Following the break after this speech, Dickens added the words "long ago," to explain that Jeddler had known the truth of Marion's sacrifice for a long time, and the words "and to that daughter's side" to show that Jeddler had actually visited Marion not long after her exile. To the next paragraph Dickens added that Marion had not just promised Alfred, but had seen him, and that Grace should know the whole story "at last." These small details were intended to make the plot more plausible, as one of the difficulties was that Aunt Martha was not estranged from her brother, and would have been unlikely to be out of touch for six years. It is still unlikely, however, that Jeddler and Alfred could know of Marion's whereabouts without Grace discovering it.

An important addition foreshadowed Michael's marriage to Marion. The new passage shows Michael slipping in unnoticed, and standing alone dejectedly. Aunt Martha goes over to him, then whispers something to Marion, who, flustered, joins her aunt in conversation with him. This is one of the most useful of Dickens' proof additions, as without it Warden appears only at the very end, and his marriage to Marion seems even more contrived than in the printed version. As Dickens said to Forster on October 31, he could not introduce the Michael/Marion theme earlier, as their blossoming love had to develop *after* the sacrifice had been revealed to Grace. Marion's sacrifice had to be completely unspoiled by any thought of a liaison with Warden.

Forster had requested at this time the lessening of the exile from ten years to six, to which Dickens agreed, and also "a word from Alfred in his misery," to which Dickens replied:

> Impossible: You might as well try to speak to somebody in an express train. The preparation for his change is in the first part, and he kneels down beside her in that return scene. He is left alone with her, as it were, in the world. I am quite confident it is wholly impossible for me to alter that.

The only alteration that Dickens made to Alfred's return and Marion's flight in Part Two was the important addition of the words "clasping one of Grace's cold hands in his own" to the sentence describing Alfred's reaction to the news:

> He started up, as if to follow in pursuit; but, when they gave way to let him pass, looking wildly round upon them, staggered back, and sunk down in his former attitude, clasping one of Grace's cold hands in his own.    (287)

The scene ends with Alfred silently preventing the others from removing Grace into the house, and the snow quickly obliterating Marion's footsteps and memory. The addition of "whitening" to "ground" at proof stage added to the sense of Marion's obliteration, and Grace and Alfred's isolation. The "preparation for his change" is not very convincingly shown in the first part. In Alfred's farewell speech he talks exclusively to Grace, because Marion refuses to talk at all, but his continual references to Grace as their sister, and her sisterly role in their threesome, is hardly indicative of the later transfer of affection. Alfred stresses Grace's role as their anchor, the firm base on which the flightier lovers can rely, and Dickens may have had this in mind. Alfred's words about Grace show her in a role similar to that of Agnes Wickfield, the sister/guardian who wins out over the flighty Dora a few years later in *David Copperfield*:

> "Ah, Grace! If I had your well-governed heart, and tranquil mind, how bravely I would leave this place to-day!"
>                                                                       (257)[25]

Grace, in other words, is portrayed throughout as "true and steadfast," a much more suitable wife for the young country doctor than the impulsive, emotional Marion whose rightful husband is the impulsive, emotional Michael.

Proof corrections to Part One are chiefly small ones which indicate the care with which Dickens went over his work. He changed Clemency's apron from "grey woollen" to "white," and deleted after "printed gown" (246) the words "available anywhere above the waist as a pincushion." The pincushion bodice is reserved for Dickens' anti-mothers such as Pip's sister Mrs. Joe, whose armor against breast-feeding even extends to the pins, which become detached and stick in the bread she is cutting for Pip and Joe. Clearly this armor is inappropriate for the maternal Clemency. Dickens also altered the tone of Clemency's answer to Mr. Snitchey from "vacantly" to "vaguely" (256), perhaps to make her sound confused rather than stupid.

Added to the proofs of Part Two was Marion's reply when Grace tells her to stop reading because she is weeping.

> "I cannot," she replied, and closed the book. "The words seem all on fire!"
>                                                                       (269)

This addition makes clearer the correspondence between what Marion has just been reading and her own situation, and also makes more acceptable the next line, "the Doctor was amused at this," as now he is amused not by his daughter's tears but by her voiced response to the book. When the Doctor refers to Grace's childhood play-acting as Alfred's wife, Dickens altered the proof from the rather harsh "ridiculous as it seems now" to "odd as it seems now" (272). As this early play is to come true, "ridiculous" has clearly the wrong tone.

Dickens returned the corrected proofs to Forster on November 13, hoping that Forster would find the third part "very much improved" with the corrections. Dickens thought it was, but added that if Forster had more recommendations to tell Dickens about them in Paris. "I am bent on having it right, if I can. . . . If in going over the proofs you find the tendency to blank verse (I *cannot* help it, when I am very much in earnest) too strong, knock out a word's brains here and there."[26] No such alterations were necessary. Writing to Forster on November 21, Dickens sent him the dedication, "This Christmas Book is cordially inscribed To my English Friends in Switzerland," and said that when he had the proofs back he "may manage another word or two about the battle-field, with advantage."[27] Clearly the lack of a sustained metaphor in the book was still worrying him. Forster had approved of the alterations, however, and Dickens replied that "they make it complete. . . . it would have been incomplete without your suggestions." Dickens is referring here, I think, to the passages which fill in the courtship of Grace and Alfred, and prepare for Marion's marriage to Michael, a concession to the Christmas book happy ending, which as we have seen was probably not a part of the original design.

When Bulwer Lytton suggested that Dickens rework *The Battle of Life* in a longer form, Dickens replied that he was tempted to try the theme again, but for "an insuperable aversion"[28] he had to reworking old material. It could be argued that in *A Tale of Two Cities* he did in fact "forge that bit of metal again," and coincidentally, his concluding phrase to Bulwer Lytton, "One of these days, perhaps," was one of his suggested titles for the novel.[29] *A Tale of Two Cities* was conceived while Dickens was acting in *The Frozen Deep*, but the germ of the book had actually occurred to him eleven years earlier, while he was composing *The Battle of Life*. Writing to Forster in July 1846 about *Dombey and Son*, Dickens says:

> I have been thinking this last day or two that good Christmas characters might be grown out of the idea of a man imprisoned for ten or fifteen years: his imprisonment being the gap between the people and cicumstances of the first part and the altered people and circumstances of the second, and his own changed mind. Though I shall probably proceed with the Battle idea, I should like to know what you think of this one?[30]

Dickens referred to the idea of a gap in time in his memoranda book also, in which he planned the novel: "How as to a story in two periods—with a lapse of time between, like a French Drama?"[31] Such a lapse had first been tried in *The Battle of Life*, but while the lapse provided by Marion's absence is a serious flaw, in the novel Dr. Manette's imprisonment is central to the working out of the historical events of the revolution and to the eventual conviction of Charles Darnay. The "gap" also becomes one of the most powerful aspects of the novel, when Dr. Manette repeatedly relapses into his former state of mind, forgetting his new life while he works obsessively at the shoe-making which had occupied him totally during his imprisonment. The novel also reworks and improves the book's theme of heroic sacrifice. Marion's manipulation of Alfred to transfer his love from herself to her sister is similar to the self-sacrifice of the hero of Dickens' 1868 story "George Silverman's Explanation," in which Silverman turns a young admirer's love away from himself to someone he considers more suitable for her. In both Christmas book and story the sacrifice is of doubtful value. Marion and George both appear to be sacrificing themselves for the good of others, but at the same time they have to be seen as manipulative, and calculatedly blind to the wishes of those around them. Dickens does not convincingly show that Alfred's marriage to Grace, and Adelina's to Silverman's young student, are anything other than contrivances brought about to satisfy the self-denying compulsion of Marion and Silverman. In contrast, Sydney Carton's sacrifice of himself for Charles Darnay is clearly shown to be a noble act that will benefit the other characters. The important difference between Carton and Marion or Silverman is that Carton's love for Lucy Manette is not returned; while Marion manipulates her lover Alfred, and Silverman Adelina, Carton manipulates nobody, and his final sacrifice is truly heroic, the ultimate act that he can perform for the woman he loves. Dickens thus had to alter the whole conception of the sacrifice in order to make it acceptable. The emendations which he made to *The Battle of Life* before publication improved it as much as was possible, given the problems inherent to the story-line and the theme themselves.

## NOTES

1. *The Letters of Charles Dickens*, vol. IV, 1844–46, ed. Kathleen Tillotson (Oxford: The Clarendon Press, 1977), 654.
2. *Ibid.*, 648.
3. *Ibid.*, 579.
4. *Christmas Books*, ed. Eleanor Farjeon (London: Oxford University Press, 1966), p. 252. All quotations from *The Battle of Life* are taken from this edition (commonly known as the *New Oxford Illustrated Dickens*) and are cited by page number in the text.
5. *The Letters of Charles Dickens*, IV, 573.
6. *Ibid.*, 586.
7. *Ibid.*, 626.
8. The fifty-page manuscript is now in the Pierpont Morgan Library, New York, item MA 98. All references to and quotations from this manuscript are made with the permission of the Pierpont Morgan Library. Proof copies are not extant. I disagree with Tillotson (*The Letters of Charles Dickens*, IV, 623n) that the

attendant is Britain. The attendant has been waiting outside and has obviously been showing the two men remains from the battlefield outside Jeddler's land. He has special permission to take them into Jeddler's, so there is no reason to suppose that Britain would be such a guide.

9. Dickens complained to Forster that he had been troubled by having to cancel "the beginning of a first scene" (*The Letters of Charles Dickens*, IV, 623), something he claims never to have done before. Kathleen Tillotson suggests that Dickens was here referring to the deleted passage about the visitors to the battle site, but it is likely that he meant the opening of the book, which he also cancelled. It is possible that Forster made a mistake in transcribing the letter, as "the beginning of a first scene" does not make grammatical sense; Ley's edition of Forster's *Life of Charles Dickens* actually gives the passage as the more understandable "beginning of the first scene" (John Forster, *The Life of Charles Dickens*, ed. J. W. T. Ley. New York: Doubleday, Doran, 1928, p. 425). On the back of p. 3 of the manuscript Dickens had begun, "Once upon a time, it is no matter when—and in stalwart Old England—it is no matter where—there stood by itself," presumably intending to introduce Dr. Jeddler's house immediately. It is likely that Dickens was referring to this cancellation, and that the "notion" which he had trouble pinning down was the battlefield motif, which he then introduced by showing the difference between the same piece of land then and now. It is unlikely that Dickens would never before have cancelled a passage which occurred several pages into a new work; he would be more concerned by having difficulty with the opening paragraph.

10. *The Letters of Charles Dickens*, IV, 623.

11. The Oxford edition is in error in placing a period after "speaking to himself." All other editions have a comma.

12. Dickens altered the punctuation in this passage from "desire: and long" to "desire. And long" for the Cheap Edition (London: Chapman and Hall, 1852), p. 169.

13. See, for example, Albert J. Guerard, *The Triumph of the Novel: Dickens, Dostoevsky, Faulkner* (New York: Oxford University Press, 1976), pp. 73–74; Christopher Hibbert, *The Making of Charles Dickens* (London: Longmans, Green, 1967), pp. 195–197; Steven Marcus, *Dickens from Pickwick to Dombey* (New York: Simon and Schuster, 1968), pp. 269–292; Michael Slater, *Dickens and Women* (London: J. M. Dent, 1983), pp. 96–99, 368.

14. Dickens changed a semicolon after "tears" to a comma for the 1852 Cheap Edition, p. 163.

15. *The Letters of Charles Dickens*, IV, 625–626.

16. *Ibid.*, 626.

17. *Ibid.*, 630–631.

18. Dickens made several minor alterations in punctuation in this passage for the 1852 Cheap Edition.

19. *The Letters of Charles Dickens*, IV, 637. Dickens made no significant changes to the scene with Warden, and as Craggs became Snitchey in the manuscript after the first two references to him it appears that Dickens' reference to Craggs in the letter was accidental.

20. *Ibid.*, 648.

21. *Ibid.*, 650.

22. *Ibid.*, 652.

23. *Ibid.*, 654.

24. *Ibid.*

25. ''Ah, good Grace!'' was altered to ''Ah, Grace!'' for the 1852 Cheap Edition, p. 172.

26. *The Letters of Charles Dickens*, IV, 656.

27. *Ibid.*, 657–658.

28. *The Letters of Charles Dickens*, vol. V, 1847–49, eds. Graham Storey and K. J. Fielding (Oxford: The Clarendon Press, 1981), p. 383.

29. John Forster, *The Life of Charles Dickens*, ed. A. J. Hoppé (London: J. M. Dent, 1966), II, 280.

30. *The Letters of Charles Dickens*, IV, 590. Tillotson points out that Dickens used this idea also in *Little Dorrit*.

31. *The Life of Charles Dickens*, II, 300.

# *Hard Times* and Dickens'
# Concept of Imagination

## *Robert Higbie*

More directly than any other Dickens novel, *Hard Times* is concerned with what the imagination is and what its role should be. Dickens makes imagination one of the novel's central subjects: the main plot shows the way utilitarian, rationalist materialism (as represented by Gradgrind) fails to satisfy a child's imaginative (and emotional) needs. Dickens makes numerous statements about imagination in the novel, and in addition he uses the symbol of the circus to express his sense of what imagination is like. If we examine this evidence, it can help us more fully compehend his concept of imagination. Although Garrett Stewart has given us an interesting discussion of imagination in Dickens' work in general, I do not think critics have yet completely understood what Dickens is saying about it in *Hard Times*.[1] On the one hand, some critics (such as F. R. Leavis) overrate the impulse which the circus symbolizes, seeing it as a strong positive force.[2] Most critics, however, find Dickens' treatment of the imagination and the circus inadequate.[3] These latter are right, I think, in seeing the circus as weak, but they seem mistaken when they treat this as unintentional, a failure on Dickens' part. I think we should assume that (as the internal evidence indicates) Dickens is quite aware of what he is doing. He is not trying to make the imagination strong and accidentally failing; instead he is deliberately examining its weakness. What I want to discuss here, then, is what *Hard Times*—especially the circus—reveals about Dickens' view of the imagination. The evidence indicates he was coming to feel that imagination alone was unable to counteract the bleakness of reality and needed to be supplemented by a more serious belief like that offered by religion. In *Hard Times* he therefore attempts to find a way of joining imagination with faith, giving imagination a serious purpose it could not have alone.

91

Dickens uses imagination (or fancy, a term which he sometimes uses interchangeably with imagination) in two main ways, roughly corresponding to the meanings imagination and fancy have for Coleridge. On the one hand, imagination sometimes, as with the Romantics, means a force able to transform or transcend reality and create a vision of an ideal, as in the case of Paul Dombey's and Jenny Wren's visions of paradise.[4] On the other hand, Dickens often refers to what Coleridge would consider a lower kind of ability, a fanciful playing with reality as comic characters like Dick Swiveller and Sairey Gamp do. What he says in *Hard Times* is mainly concerned with the former of these, but since he partly merges the two, some of what I shall be saying will apply to both.

The clearest indication that Dickens was beginning to have doubts about the imagination's ability to create some transcendent ideal is the fact that here for the first time he writes a novel without a happy ending. Garrett Stewart has discussed the decline of imagination in Dickens[5] (though he is concerned mostly with what I would call fancy); but although Dickens' novels become increasingly dark throughout his career, it is only with *Hard Times* that he gives us not a wish-fulfilling ending but rather what we may call a "realistic" ending—one which largely denies wish-fulfillment. As W. H. Auden pointed out (408–409), in *Pickwick* Dickens creates a world that resembles Eden. This vision of paradise is repeated, though with decreasing confidence, in the more or less idealized worlds at the end of all the novels through *Bleak House*. But with *Hard Times* such an ideal is no longer possible; and in Dickens' later novels (though I do not have the space to discuss them here in any detail) the endings, if not always unhappy, are at least somber and chastened, not offering a retreat to a paradise. If there is a happy ending, it must take place within the limits of a realistic world. For various reasons (unhappiness with his marriage, perhaps, and disillusionment with society) Dickens' sense of the unidealness of reality has become too strong for imagination to overcome; he can no longer transcend or transform the fictional reality and create a final wish-fulfilling world. Certainly he has not entirely lost faith in imagination; but he is questioning it—indeed, making it the central concern of a novel, as if trying to find some part it can still play if it can no longer create a fictional ideal.

His sense of the limits of imagination is clearly shown in his treatment of the circus. There is considerable evidence that he did intend the circus to represent imagination. He associates it with Pegasus (21; pt. 1, ch. 6), as if Pegasus is the horse the performers really ride; Jupe's performance is "Shaksperean" (9; pt. 1, ch. 3); and Gradgrind associates going to the circus with "reading poetry" (13; pt. 1, ch. 4). In addition, Dickens connects the circus with fairy tales (27; pt. 1, ch. 7; and 213; pt. 3, ch. 7), which he often relates to fancy, as in "Frauds on the Fairies."

However, when we look closely at the details of his presentation of the circus, it also seems clear that he wants to emphasize its imperfection. Here is our first glimpse of it:

> He had reached the neutral ground upon the outskirts of the town, which was neither town nor country, and yet was either spoiled, when his ears were invaded by the sound of music. The clashing and banging band attached to the horse-riding establishment . . . was in full bray. . . .
> A space of stunted grass and dry rubbish . . .          (8–9; pt. 1, ch. 3)

He probably makes this scene ugly partly because that is how the circus appears to Gradgrind, the observer here. It is he, presumably, who feels the music is an invasion of his world and therefore ugly. His attitude represents society's attitude toward the circus, reflecting society's attitude toward the imagination. The place is "spoiled" and "stunted" as society tries to stunt the imagination. Instead of valuing the circus, Gradgrind's world sees it as little better than "rubbish," just as society tries to stifle imagination (e.g., 10, pt. 1, ch. 3; and 19; pt. 1, ch. 5).

But the ugliness here tells us about the nature of the circus as well as about society's attitude. Dickens is very conscious of first impressions on the reader; especially in this novel, he is concerned with striking the right "keynote" (16; pt. 1, ch. 5). And he has deliberately chosen to give us a negative impression of the circus, an impression which is not much contradicted by what we see of it later. Because society rejects it, the circus (like the imagination) is partly disabled, "spoiled" like the place. The braying of the music suggests that no matter how praiseworthy their intentions, the circus people are not able to give very adequate expression to imagination in this unsympathetic world. And what we see of them later reinforces this sense of their weakness. Sleary seems "broken" (27; pt. 1, ch. 6) by this world, as the imagination is weakened by reality; and his lisp suggests that (like imagination) he can't find a full, serious, natural outlet. His very name makes us feel he has been somehow diminished, bleared and smeared with the world's toil. Jupe is also a weak man, a drunken clown, suggesting that imagination can't become fully serious. Later on, the circus appears to be a "skeleton" (211; pt. 3, ch. 7), as if society can destroy it (and imagination) entirely, though of course it does survive.

If we compare the circus with similar institutions in earlier Dickens, there are two main differences. First of all, the circus has a consistent, serious, intentional symbolic and thematic function of a sort which there is no evidence to make us believe Dickens intended in such earlier counterparts as Crummles's theatre and Mrs. Jarley's waxworks. Those earlier refuges of fancy are quite marginal to the plot, unlike the circus at the climax of *Hard Times*. Nor does Dickens try to invest them with significance. They are expressions of fancy, but not symbols of it. Crummles and his troupe exist not to serve some external purpose but for their own sake, as a comic outlet for Dickens' energy, independent of any moral concern. Where Sleary preaches (though with a lisp), Crummles plays parts. Thus although Crummles and his players certainly have as many imperfections as the circus performers, we need not take those imperfections as a statement about the imperfections of fancy. On the contrary, we can simply enjoy them as sources of comedy, whereas the imperfections of the circus performers are thematic rather than comic. In his early novels, Dickens values the play of fancy as an end in itself; but in *Hard Times* he is self-conscious about it and must give it a thematic significance in the story in an attempt to understand and justify it.

The other way the circus differs from these precursors is that it fails to function as a refuge. In earlier novels, Dickens often uses imagination to create some sort of idyllic retreat within which his more childlike characters can remain at least largely innocent, at least temporarily untouched by the outer world—imperfect versions of the paradise they reach at the novel's end. Even Crummles and Mrs. Jarley are able to offer havens of this sort, imperfect and temporary though these are. In addition, the earlier novels offer other, more fulfilling refuges such as the Wooden Midshipman in *Dombey* and Aunt Betsey's in *Copperfield*. Such sanctuaries reproduce the way imagination offers some escape from reality, even if an imperfect, temporary one. The circus does retain a vestige of this function; it provides a momentary haven for Tom. But he cannot stay there, and it provides no refuge for other characters. Earlier novels also create relatively idealized parent-figures like Pickwick and Jarndyce who can offer this kind of protection. Sleary is the nearest thing *Hard Times* offers to a father-substitute; but he cannot replace Gradgrind, as the circus cannot provide an alternative home. Sleary is not only a fairly weak character but he also remains largely cut off from the novel's plot, able to function only within the circus. It is as if he cannot enter the novel's "reality."

The shortcomings of the circus suggest that imagination has similar weaknesses. Because the circus remains marginal, unable to enter Coketown and barely able to act in the plot (with one notable exception, to which I shall return later), it cannot offer the characters fulfillment. Sissy cannot return to it or regain her father through it, and Louisa is even more cut off from its help. If it cannot bring about a happy ending, this suggests that Dickens feels imagination cannot do so. The fact that (unlike Sissy) Louisa is relatively realistic and enclosed within the novel's reality seems to place her beyond the help of Dickens' imagination. She is forced to seek fulfillment within a social world where the circus cannot help her. Similarly, imagination cannot help her; it cannot make her world wish-fulfilling. This failure is reflected in the failure of her own imagination: she marries Bounderby because the Gradgrindian world has denied her the imagination to conceive of any fulfillment that is not simply social.

Dickens apparently feels that imagination, like the circus, is unable to deal directly with social reality, to transform it as the Romantics hoped was possible (Coketown remains unchanged)—perhaps even unable to face reality fully. Imagination evidently cannot overcome Dickens' sense of the unidealness of reality. In a society whose values were based on a Gradgrindian belief that all that matters is material reality (especially profit and loss), Dickens must have felt the imagination was doomed, like the circus, to a marginal, ineffectual existence. Perhaps he felt rather like a circus performer himself, unable to affect society as he wished and instead relegated to the role of a mere entertainer, not taken seriously.

Since Dickens tends to merge imagination and fancy, the decline of one is accompanied by a decrease in the other. There is less of the play of fancy, the exuberant elaboration of detail, in *Hard Times* than in any previous novel. Of course *Hard Times* is Dickens' shortest novel; but that can be seen as an effect of the decrease in fancy as much as a cause. The fact that he was willing to write a shorter novel indicates that he was not as concerned with using fancy. What playfulness there is in *Hard Times* almost never exists as an end in itself as in the case of earlier characters like Mrs. Gamp; imaginative play is strictly subordinated to what the novel is saying about the world, as if fancy is no longer as important as dealing with reality is. As some critics have noticed, Dickens is showing that the world of *Hard Times* suppresses playfulness in characters or perverts it into narrowly selfish and mechanical forms (Bracher 306–312; Stewart 148, 151–154). Dickens is clearly trying here to make us resent the way society denies fancy. But he may also be implying that, if reality is so grim, to become playful and fanciful is not an adequate response. Similarly, to retreat to a wish-fulfilling happy ending would mean failing to face up to the way society makes such fulfillment impossible.

We can also see Dickens' growing doubts about how effective imagination could be in a letter Forster quotes from 1854, the year *Hard Times* was written, in which Dickens describes himself as seeking his "realities in unrealities" and says such an "escape from the disappointment of heart" around him was a "dangerous comfort" (2: 196). If imagination is merely an escape into unrealities, that means he cannot fully believe in it any more, cannot accept it as a valid substitute for reality. And if escape is dangerous, one should face reality, even if it disappoints the heart. This disillusionment is not unlike that we find in Dickens' Romantic predecessors. Perhaps the Romantic search for an ideal inevitably leads to disillusion. We could say, then, that like Keats Dickens feels that "the fancy cannot cheat so well" as he had believed. His sense of the loss of a "guileless belief" in imagination which he had as a child (Forster 1: 7) resembles the sense of loss one encounters in Wordsworth. And he evidently feels something like what Byron feels in *Don Juan* when he says "Imagination droops her pinion" and one is left facing "the sad truth" (4: 3).

If imagination is no longer fulfilling, what then does Dickens turn to in its place? Instead of relying on the circus as his main agent of salvation, he uses Sissy instead. And Sissy I would say represents not imagination (which she does not display) but rather faith. What exactly Dickens means by faith remains somewhat unclear, probably because his own beliefs were never completely certain, but it is close to Christian belief, even if not wholly conventional. For our purposes here, the details of what Dickens believes are not crucial, since what Sissy evidently represents is not any particular object of belief but rather the act of belief itself—the mental state in which one accepts the existence of some ideal. The value Dickens offers us is no explicit set of beliefs but the condition of the mind (or heart) in which one can transcend one's doubts. Such a state is opposed to Gradgrindian realism, and so it is closely related to imagination. But there is a difference; imagination lacks the seriousness of faith. In both cases the mind envisions an ideal, but faith is able to accept that ideal as if it were real, whereas when we merely imagine an ideal we know it is not real. That is, our reason remains at least partly detached from what is imagined and does not take it too seriously. We can see, then, why Dickens would like to replace imagination with faith; he wants to find an ideal he can believe in seriously, not just imagine as if in play. His sense of the way reality prevents fulfillment has evidently become too strong to overcome without something more serious than imagination. Such a retreat from the Romantic reliance on imagination, trying to replace that with some more serious, more explicitly religious belief is typical, I think, of Victorian writers; Tennyson's "Palace of Art," for example, criticizes imagination for failing to provide a moral control like that which religion might offer.

The connection between Sissy and spiritual belief is clearly shown in her faith that her father will come back (42; pt. 1, ch. 9) and that he loves her, a belief she holds onto as religiously as she holds onto his medicine bottle. There seems to be a deliberate religious suggestion here: she believes in a father who (like God) is absent from this world. (Indeed, God seems especially missing from Coketown.) Despite a lack of rational evidence, Sissy believes that this father loves her and is sacrificing himself for her sake, just as the Christian believes in God's love and sacrifice. She does this, like the Christian, "in defiance" of Reason (42; pt. 1, ch. 9). Perhaps her medicine implies that this belief has healing power. Of course this is not to say that we should take Jupe as equivalent to God, although he does resemble God in remaining unknowable. Rather it is to say that Sissy's belief in him is like a religious belief. Because she has been left without anything in this world to believe in, she believes in a father beyond her world. Perhaps Dickens is suggesting that belief in God can grow out of a child's belief in his parent. And because of her faith, Sissy can become Christlike: she has been sent into this world to redeem people. She represents faith, for example, in the way she gives Louisa something to live for. And she acts for faith when she defeats Harthouse. Her "simple confidence" in a higher love is able to overcome his lack of "belief" (177; pt. 3, ch. 2) in a scene which seems meant to act out the way faith vanquishes doubt.

For Dickens, the purpose of faith is to create belief in a merciful power able to replace the repressive, punitive control society tries to impose on people. This social control is analogous to the control of an unloving parent, as the novel makes evident by paralleling Gradgrind's treatment of his children with Bounderby's treatment of his workers. This kind of repressive control can cause a loss of belief in any loving power like God's, as happens in Bitzer's case and nearly happens in Stephen Blackpool's and Louisa's; and it can lead to resentment and rebellion like Tom Gradgrind's. Dickens himself, perhaps remembering the inadequacy of his own parents, evidently felt the need to defend against this kind of resentment. He speaks of the conflict in Louisa between "doubts and resentments" and a natural "disposition to believe" (127; pt. 2, ch. 7), and I think this is the basic conflict not only within Louisa but in the whole novel: Dickens is seeking a way to overcome unbelief. To oppose doubt and resentment he turns to faith, embodied in Sissy. She has even more reason to resent an inadequate father than Tom has, but she can overcome resentment by believing in an ideal father. And the faith she represents can save others as well. Louisa could resent her father and become like Tom, who corresponds to the resentful side of her character; but Sissy helps Louisa learn to forgive her father as Sissy has forgiven her own. Similarly, Stephen could be driven into rebellion by Bounderby and join the strikers (who are resentful like Tom), but instead he learns to become like Rachel (who corresponds to Sissy in his plot) and believe in forgiveness. Thus the function of faith and the characters who embody it (Sissy and Rachel) is to save these two protagonists from resentment and hatred.

However, if Dickens believes that imagination alone is inadequate, he evidently feels that faith is not enough either. Like the circus, Sissy seems deliberately limited. Dickens does not make her the protagonist as he does comparable earlier characters like Little Nell and Florence Dombey; he does not let her enter into the novel's plot and act in it much more than the circus can. Her role remains largely a defensive one, as in defying Harthouse, which implies that Dickens believes that the best faith can do is ward off doubt. Sissy does of course obtain some fulfillment, but she never fulfills the main desire associated with her: she cannot regain her father. Nor can she even find an idealized character to replace him, in contrast to earlier Dickens novels where there is at least some sort of parent-substitute available for analogous characters. This suggests that although Dickens values faith, he no longer believes it can attain its object in this world; it cannot overcome reality. His reservations about faith are also implied by the fact that Sissy's belief in her father, though presented sympathetically, is shown as a delusion, something "fantastic" (48; pt. 1, ch. 9), childish, and irrational.

In addition, Dickens' sense of the limitations of faith is shown by the way he shifts emphasis from Sissy to Louisa. The latter embodies neither faith nor fancy but rather the awareness of reality which Dickens seeks to reconcile with faith. What he makes central in the novel, then, is the doubting mind which seeks belief, the heart struggling to find a way out of rationalism. By the end of the novel he can partly reconcile this consciousness with faith: Louisa can value what Sissy stands for. But Louisa still cannot fully share Sissy's faith nor participate in the fulfillment that faith earns for Sissy. Sissy's faith is no more able than imagination is to transform the reality Louisa perceives. In earlier Dickens doubts like Louisa's can be transcended, enabling him to create his final visions of an ideal world. These happy endings are not, of course, explicitly religious, but they are like paradise, and the attitude he asks us to take towards them is analogous to belief in a religious ideal. In *Hard Times*, however, though we may possibly share Sissy's faith, we can't help also seeing that the world Louisa lives in remains unideal. Instead of escaping to a pastoral paradise, Louisa must come to terms with an un-fulfilling world.

The fact that Louisa is denied fulfillment implies that reason (represented by Louisa) is cut off from belief in fulfillment. Reason, that aspect of the self which is aware of the unidealness of reality, remains separate from faith, as Louisa remains separate from Sissy, unable to become like her. That is, there seems to be an unresolved division in Dickens' mind between reason and faith. He is unable entirely to overcome his rational sense that the ideal cannot exist in reality. Sissy's happy ending does not belong within the novel's reality where Louisa lives; we do not even know Sissy's mate. She seems to exist on a level above reality, a level where one can believe in the ideal. Thus we are left at the end with a sense that the ideal in which faith believes is separate from the reality that reason must accept. Similarly, Stephen's star remains distant and the faith it represents only seems attainable beyond this life. It is as if only part of Dickens, not his reason, can believe in an ideal.

This division in Dickens' mind first finds open expression in the preceding novel, *Bleak House*, in which it seems as if there are two Dickenses speaking. The side of him that seeks to believe in an ideal speaks through Esther's narrative, which is concerned with the search for an ideal (in the form of parent-like love and a paradise-like home). But the other half of the novel gives expression to the side of Dickens that remains aware of how unideal reality is. Dennis Walder has pointed out how this division in *Bleak House* implies a conflict between belief and unbelief (145). And Edwin M. Eigner discusses the split between idealism and realism not only here but elsewhere in Dickens (172–173, 178). But although there has always been this tension in Dickens, at this point in his career it becomes increasingly difficult for him to believe that the ideal he seeks can exist in the reality he perceives. *Bleak House* brings this division out into the open, and *Hard Times* pursues the problem further, trying to find a more complete solution to it.

Part of Dickens' solution is an attempt to let faith and doubt coexist. If Sissy cannot get fulfillment for Louisa, at least Louisa doesn't prevent Sissy from getting her happy ending. Similarly, if faith cannot wholly overcome doubt, doubt doesn't destroy faith. Although Dickens cannot locate an ideal fulfillment in the fictional world, he still believes in one, even if it must exist somewhere beyond this world, on the level where Sissy and the faith she represents are possible. Even though Louisa is unfulfilled, she can value Sissy's fulfillment, which is like believing in an ideal even though one does not believe one can attain it—at least not in this life. If faith cannot overcome reality, it can present a vision of the ideal (like Stephen's vision of the star) which can enable us (like Louisa) to bear the reality we are caught in. Thus Sissy teaches Louisa not to resent reality by keeping a belief in something beyond it.

Dickens also turns to the imagination in his attempt to resolve the conflict between realism and faith. Since faith alone is unable to overcome his sense of reality, he cannot simply abandon imagination for faith but rather must try to combine the two in some way. He is trying to redeem imagination by finding a new way of using it, by giving it a serious purpose so that it will no longer be separate from faith (as Swiveller and Nell, for example, remain separate) but rather allied with it. Just as the circus seems reduced to a skeleton but then is revived, he hopes to keep the "heart of infancy," with its capacity for imagining, from dying (226; pt. 3, ch. 9). And this redemption involves finding a way for imagination to work along with faith.

Here again we can use the circus to understand what he believes the role of imagination is. First of all, Sissy comes from the circus. If she represents faith, this should mean that faith comes from imagination. Some critics have mentioned Dickens' belief that faith can grow out of imagination (Stewart xxi; Walder 124, 137, 149), but I don't think they fully explain the process. In *Hard Times* Dickens tells us how it can take place. He is talking about what should have been but was not done for Louisa:

> The dreams of childhood—its airy fables; its graceful, beautiful, humane, impossible adornments of the world beyond: so good to be believed in once, so good to be remembered when outgrown, for then the least among them rises to the stature of a great Charity in the heart, suffering little children to come into the midst of it, and to keep with their pure hands a garden in the stony ways of this world, wherein it were better for all the children of Adam that they should oftener sun themselves, simple and trustful, and not worldly-wise—what had she to do with these? Remembrances of how she had journeyed to the little that she knew, by the enchanted roads of what she and millions of innocent creatures had hoped and imagined; of how, first coming upon Reason through the tender light of Fancy, she had seen it a beneficent god, deferring to gods as great as itself; not a grim Idol, cruel and cold, . . . never to be moved by anything but so many calculated tons of leverage—what had she to do with these? (150–151; pt. 2, ch. 9)

"The dreams of childhood," then, enable us to create something "to be believed in." But those dreams are "impossible"; we cannot keep that childhood belief in an imaginary ideal. Yet we do not lose it entirely. As we grow up, we convert it through memory (as in Wordsworth) into belief in something higher, a Christlike love, "suffering little children to come into the midst of it.'' This conversion from fancy to faith involves partly giving up imagination: the child's dreams are "outgrown" and we develop "Reason," which evidently involves becoming aware of how "stony" reality is. Yet despite this awareness, faith enables us to "keep" a "pure" belief in "a garden," a paradise like that of which imagination first enabled us to conceive, if imperfectly, when we were innocent.

Although this passage, like most of Dickens' statements about religion (and I suspect like his beliefs themselves) remains somewhat vague, it describes the kind of change his fiction is undergoing. He has outgrown the heavy reliance on imagination he had in his earlier work. He is journeying to "Reason" through "Fancy," becoming more aware of the stony nature of reality and thus trying to replace imagination with a serious belief that can deal more successfully with his sense of how unideal reality is. He may also be saying that some disillusionment with imagination is necessary in order to develop faith. That is, one must learn that imagination's childlike belief in wish-fulfillment is not enough; one must face the unidealness of reality in order to learn the need for serious belief, chastening oneself into looking for something higher than one's own fancy, giving up the illusion that one can create an ideal oneself as the endings to the earlier novels do. This acceptance can transform imagination into an unselfish form, a "Charity in the heart."

This movement beyond imagination is reproduced by the way Sissy must leave the circus and go out to face reality. The fact that she cannot return to the circus may reflect Dickens' sense that he is unable to return to a child's belief in the imagination. But he uses Sissy to seek a substitute for that belief. Perhaps it is facing reality that enables Sissy to go beyond the childishness of the circus people and learn serious faith. Gradgrind's taking Sissy from the circus is like rationalism trying to overcome faith, destroying her childlike belief in an ideal, trying to make her become like Louisa. However, the opposite happens. By accepting Gradgrind, Sissy faces up to that rationalist awareness of reality that cannot believe in more fancy; but this discovery teaches her the pity through which she is able to overcome his rationalism. By facing Gradgrind's reality she learns to move beyond imagination to belief in the heart's charity. This process resembles the one David Copperfield undergoes. At his climactic conversion he is at first still like a "dreamer" in a place where "Fancy" abides, but then he looks up from his "dream" to a "dawn" for which he thanks "Heaven." Thus he moves from his childish "wild fancies" to the "higher tendency" associated with the "sacred" Agnes (ch. 58).

Dickens also implies a connection between imagination and faith in some of his descriptions of the circus, as Thomas M. Linehan has pointed out (31–32). The circus box-office is "ecclesiastical"; the circus contains "hidden glories" (9; pt. 1, ch. 3); the circus people are found in the "upper regions" (27; pt. 1, ch. 6); and the circus is associated with the "idealities" of an "ethereal" Pegasus covered with "stars" (21; pt. 1, ch. 6). We can connect these stars with the star that leads Stephen to his final trust in the existence of a Christlike forgiveness, as the magi were led by a star. And if Pegasus is ethereal, this may suggest that imagination can rise up to faith. Furthermore, the circus presents "strictly moral wonders" (9; pt. 1, ch. 3). The word *wonder* also has spiritual connotations, and I think Dickens has these in mind in the chapter entitled "Never Wonder": Louisa wonders as she gazes into the fire, watching the sparks "dying." It is as if she is facing mortality and seeking a belief (in something that can make her feel wonder) that can enable her to deal with the idea of death. Yet at the same time, as Garrett Stewart points out (160–170), Dickens relates fire-gazing to imagination, a relationship implied by saying she might see a "circus" in the fire (41; pt. 1, ch. 8), presumably if she had learned how to imagine wonders instead of only seeing reality. Thus the circus is associated with the capacity for wonder on which religion is based. The association of imagination with faith is also implied by the seemingly random quotation (as an example of what appeals to a child's fancy) of "Twinkle, twinkle, little star; how I wonder what you are" (7; pt. 1, ch. 3), which brings together the ideas of wonder and the star, both having spiritual connotations. Dickens is suggesting that the Gradgrind children have been prevented from feeling religious wonder because they have not been taught to use their imagination, not even through nursery rhymes.

But although the circus and imagination are thus connected to belief, they still seem inferior. Dickens points out that Sleary is no "angel" (29; pt. 1, ch. 6), and clearly the circus is not very spiritual. Perhaps its imperfections imply that idealistic impulses cannot find any purer, more convincing expression than this in a society whose churches remain empty. The circus also suggests that imagination, though related to belief, cannot provide a complete, serious belief by itself. It needs to be combined with faith, as both the circus and Sissy are needed to resolve the novel's conflict.

How can imagination supplement faith? Once more we can look to the circus for an answer. To bring about the final plot resolution Louisa needs the help of the circus. Though she cannot have fulfillment herself, she is allowed a diminished substitute for it: the rescue of Tom. If Tom embodies resentment against their father (and on a more general, symbolic level, resentment against the failure of society to provide the individual with something to love and believe in), then Louisa's rescuing him is like overcoming her own resentment and lack of belief. And this substitute fulfillment is only possible with the help of the circus. Its aid implies that although imagination cannot create belief in an ideal, it can enable us to overcome the resentment that an unideal reality can cause. We can understand how imagination does this by looking at what the circus does. The circus performers keep Bitzer at bay so that Tom can escape (220; pt. 3, ch. 8). Bitzer represents rationalism pushed to its logical extreme, an inability to believe in anything beyond reality, leaving the individual with no value but self-interest. This is the moral condition produced by a society whose only real belief is in profit. Such a belief is the opposite of spiritual faith, as Bitzer is the opposite of Sissy, an opposition implied by the contrast between them at the start. If the circus can thwart Bitzer, that implies that imagination can similarly keep at bay the loss of faith that rationalism can cause. The circus people cannot actually punish or reform Bitzer, just as imagination cannot overcome rationalism. But imagination can prevent rationalist doubts from gaining complete control and leaving us like Bitzer with nothing but materialism, as the circus prevents Bitzer from triumphing. Imagination resists unbelief by enabling us to envision some ideal beyond reality. This process of fending off doubt is repeated in Sissy's victory over Harthouse. Imagination and faith are both necessary, acting together to defeat unbelief. Thus imagination can help lead to something like spiritual salvation; Tom is "saved" (210; pt. 3, ch. 7) by the circus. And when his blackness is washed off, it is as if he is being cleansed of guilt.

Imagination, then, offers Dickens a way of coming to terms with realism. Imagination's role seems by this point in his career to be primarily negative. If it cannot provide a positive belief, it can at least disarm doubt, protecting faith from realism, inducing rationalism to give up its rejection of belief as the circus helps soften Gradgrind. In seeking an accommodation of this sort, Dickens is trying to heal the dissociation of sensibility, the split between realism and idealism that I have already mentioned. To reconcile them, he wants to overcome what he sees as the intransigence not so much of reality as of the realistic view of it. What he dislikes about rational materialism of the kind embodied in Gradgrind is its intolerance of imagination, an intolerance that cuts it off not just from art but more importantly from faith. Like Louisa, the mind can become "chained . . . down to material realities" which can cause it to lose "faith in anything else" (127; pt. 3, ch. 7). In other words, Dickens feels rationalism is threatening because it demands belief in nothing beyond reality. It leaves no room for faith or fancy. Forster quotes Dickens as saying that literature was entering a "dark age," becoming too realistic—"frightfully literal and catalogue-like" (2: 279); in other words, people no longer valued imagination. As he says in his "Preliminary Word" to *Household Words*, such a "utilitarian" attitude results in an "iron binding of the mind to grim realities" (*Collected Papers* 223). Realism imprisons imagination, preventing it from escaping a sense of reality's unidealness. Thus, as he says in *Hard Times*, reality itself comes to seem "uncompromising" (8; pt. 1, ch. 3). If one is prevented from conceiving of anything beyond reality, one is liable to lose faith as Harthouse does and become resentful as Tom does. Realism destroys belief in any religious ideal, creating an infidel creed (125; pt. 2, ch. 6) that replaces God with Fact, an attitude summed up by the Gradgrindian statement "Fact forbid!" (7; pt. 1, ch. 3). Whereas God's control is forgiving, this rationalist creed is forbidding, refusing to compromise, as exemplified by Gradgrind's opposition to the circus.

If realism is too uncompromising, faith may be also; they may be too opposed to each other to allow for any reconciliation. Each demands serious belief. It is here, I think, that Dickens finds a role for imagination. It may seem weak because it cannot command serious belief, but this very lack of seriousness can be to its advantage. By not insisting on total belief it can disarm reason, making it temporarily suspend its doubts. If reason could accept faith, imagination might not be necessary; but since reason remains unconvinced, imagination is necessary to create a substitute for serious faith. It creates playful belief instead, something reason can accept because imagination does not demand serious acquiescence. We needn't worry about whether a vision of the ideal is real if we know it is only imaginary. Similarly the circus can deal with Gradgrind and Tom because no one takes it too seriously. It remains rather childlike and so doesn't try to control Tom repressively the way Gradgrind does, and thus it doesn't arouse Tom's resentment as Gradgrind does. Like the imagination, the circus succeeds because it is not too demanding. And like the circus, imagination can act as a go-between, standing in for faith as the circus does for Sissy.

This process resembles the way the circus keeps Bitzer at bay: imagination fends off rationalist doubt. And it is also what Dickens is evidently describing, in a passage I have already quoted, when he hopes that fancy can soften reason, making it "a beneficent god, deferring" to other beliefs (151; pt. 2, ch. 9). Instead of seeking to replace religion, demanding total belief in the god of fact, reason should be made to defer, to allow the mind to conceive of things beyond its comprehension. Like Gradgrind, rationalism should accept the need for belief. And this passage suggests that such an acceptance will enable the mind to reach belief in a god—that is, imagination will enable us to move from reason to (or at least toward) faith.

Such a process involves not a victory over realism but a compromise with it. Dickens' statements about imagination indicate that by this point in his career he accepts the need for such a compromise. He does not advocate an escape from realism, much as he might like to. On the contrary, he concedes the need to accept reality. Evidently he feels imagination is unconvincing if it is unrealistic, just as realism is unsatisfactory if it does not allow for imagination. He is trying to rescue imagination, to find a way for it to accommodate realism and yet continue to exist. We can see this sense of a compromise when he says imagination is "Another Thing Needful" (167; pt. 3, ch. 1), not the only thing; it is a "holiday" (19, pt. 1, ch. 5), to be balanced with acceptance of the workaday world. In a speech (to workers like those in *Hard Times*) he spells out the nature of this balance in more detail: in a world so concerned with the kind of "knowledge which can be proved upon a slate," he says, "do not let us . . . neglect the fancy and the imagination. . . . Let the child have its fables; let the man or woman into which it changes, always remember these fables tenderly. . . . The hardest head may coexist with the softest heart." And the example he offers of this "blending" of "the understanding and the imagination" is Christ (*Speeches* 284), again implying that the imagination can lead us beyond realism to some higher belief.

This idea of a compromise between imagination and realism is implied by the way the circus lies between the town and the country, as Bornstein (159) and Smith (117, 193) have suggested. Though the circus cannot enter Coketown, it cannot escape to the country either. This may indicate that Dickens believes imagination cannot wholly escape reality and regain the natural child-like state in which one could believe in an ideal. As the circus lies between social reality and idealized nature, so the imagination is caught between realism and escapism, or between disillusion and belief in an ideal. In other words, Dickens is both unwilling to accept reality completely, to believe in nothing more, and unable to believe he can escape it completely. This double attitude is like Sleary's eyes, one "fixed" and one "loose" (27; pt. 1, ch. 6). Like Sleary, imagination keeps one eye fixed on reality but at the same time remains partly free of it, able to conceive of something beyond reality's limits. This double attitude enables it to act as a mediator, leading from realism toward a sense of the ideal, neither wholly giving in to realism nor seeking simply to escape to an ideal as in earlier Dickens. As the circus retreats to neutral ground between town and country, Dickens retreats to the neutral ground of imagination, where he can partly accept reality because he distances it, does not take it entirely seriously, and so can balance realism with belief in something beyond reality.

This compromise is embodied in *Hard Times*. Though the novel seems relatively realistic in its denial of wish-fulfillment, it is of course far from being a mere reproduction of reality. The "realistic" representation of a grim social world is constantly affected by the narrator's imagination. Imagination and "realism" coexist and interact throughout the novel, each modifying the other. Dickens presents a picture of what he considers to be reality, but a picture that is imaginatively transformed. As he says in the Preface to *Bleak House*, he dwells on the "romantic side of familiar things," showing (as he says in the "Preliminary Word") "that in all familiar things, even in those which are repellent on their surface, there is Romance enough" (*Collected Papers* 223). In a letter he adds that this modification of merely "literal" realism can be brought about through "fanciful treatment": "The exact truth must be there," but art lies not simply in reproducing it but in "the manner of stating the truth" (Forster 2: 279). Since imagination cannot overcome realism, it must color it, altering the way we perceive reality. Like Wordsworth, Dickens wants to half create what he sees.

One way he enables the "real" and the fanciful to coexist is through the use of metaphor. In Coleridge's terms, Dickens' metaphors involve fancy more than imagination, not seeking to create a vision of the ideal as the Romantic imagination does but rather manipulating reality playfully. As Dickens says, this use of fancy can "ornament" reality (125; pt. 2, ch. 6), as his metaphors ornament his comparatively realistic text—as, for example, in his comparison of the Coketown factories to fairy palaces (49; pt. 1, ch. 10). A metaphor like this accepts the realistic object, but it simultaneously induces us to supplement realism with an imaginative way of seeing, as in fairy tales. Thus we feel that even though fancy cannot make reality go away, it can deal with it. Since the rational side of our minds still sees reality, we do not wholly accept fancy's vision; rather we partly set aside rational seriousness and entertain the fanciful idea as if in play. We partly admit reality and partly escape it, seeing the factories as if they are real but not entirely so. This makes reality more bearable; we no longer feel it is all that matters and take it as seriously as Gradgrind does.

But in *Hard Times* and his other late novels Dickens relies less on simple metaphors and instead extends the metaphorical way of seeing into a fundamental organizing principle. In other words, he replaces metaphors with symbols. Instead of being merely local, making an object represent something just for the moment as metaphors do, his symbols are more fully related to the work as a whole and thus able to take on more complex meaning and more thematic significance. In this way Dickens tends to transform fancy into imagination. The thematic significance that symbols acquire enables them more adequately to serve the function that the Romantics especially assign to imagination, namely creating a vision of the ideal. The Romantics see symbol-making as one of the imagination's main functions (Engell 349, 363; Warnock 99), since symbols enable them to reach beyond the image to a transcendental meaning. Dickens moves towards a similar use of symbols. While keeping the metaphor's ability to let us distance reality, his symbols try to add a positive function onto this, making us see a serious value beyond reality, offering a vision of the ideal that is not merely playful. Of course not all of them represent an ideal as Stephen's star does, but I think they generally are related to the search for an ideal; many of them are negative, ironic symbols (like the fog in *Bleak House*) and what they signify is the absence of an ideal. And others represent a state of mind related to the ideal, such as the presence or absence of belief or imagination.

This attempt to raise fancy to imagination resembles the way Dickens transforms the circus, which at first seems only playful and childish but comes to have a serious purpose and meaning. And the shift from fancy to imagination seems related to his increased concern with faith. We could describe the Romantic idealistic imagination as an attempt to merge fancy with faith, trying to make fancy serve faith's search for an ideal and thus giving it a new, serious function. In contrast, in Dickens' early novels fancy and serious purpose tend to remain separate, as Dick Swiveller and Little Nell remain in separate areas of *The Old Curiosity Shop*. There is little play of fancy in serious scenes like Nell's death, and there is little serious searching for an ideal in scenes involving comic characters like Dick or Sairey Gamp. Dickens does not seem bothered by this tension between faith and fancy in his earlier fiction, but now he no longer seems content to let the two remain unreconciled. He wants imagination to serve a higher purpose.

Dickens uses symbols, then, more consciously and pervasively in *Hard Times* than in his earlier fiction. As a result, the novel's technique becomes his answer to the problem the novel raises: the novel both asks and demonstrates how imagination can survive realism. It is both a statement of the problems facing imagination in dealing with reality and also Dickens' way of working out an answer to these problems, offering an explanation and justification of his fiction. And he does this primarily through symbols. Almost every character and even object in *Hard Times* has an important symbolic function; there are almost no characters who exist simply for their own sakes as Dick Swiveller and Sairey Gamp do. Bounderby stands for repressive, unforgiving social control, Stephen for the virtue that society victimizes, and so on; I have already mentioned what qualities I think Louisa, Sissy and other characters symbolize. As the circus does for the children, these symbols offer us a kind of "loophole" (7; pt. 1, ch. 3) through which we can catch a glimpse of something beyond the novel's reality, of a spiritual meaning that cannot be perceived by mere rationalism like Gradgrind's. Stephen finds a similar kind of loophole, offering him a view beyond reality, when he looks up out of the pit into which this world has caused him to fall (as society causes the individual to fall into a hell-like despair) and sees something beyond this world, a symbolic meaning represented by the star. He (and we) see this spiritual ideal through the medium of reality, since that ideal is symbolized by an image in the novel's reality. But it is imagination that makes such a revelation possible, for it is imagination which reads the object as a symbol. Thus imagination acts as a kind of loophole in reason, an area where rational materialism is no longer fully in control, so that we can glimpse something beyond what we know.

In this way imagination is trying to restore to reality the meaning that religion once gave it and that rationalism has tried to strip away from it. And if imagination cannot fully replace religion, it can at least offer us something to believe in instead—itself. Just as the circus is the best help Louisa can find in this world, since she cannot move beyond the world as Sissy (like faith) seems to, so imagination is the best substitute for faith like Sissy's that we can hope for in this world. Even if we cannot fully believe in Sissy and the faith she represents, even if we cannot fully believe that the ideal can exist in the reality Louisa inhabits, we can still believe in the circus. That is, we can believe in the imagination, the act of seeking to envision some ideal, as an end in itself. If serious belief is no longer possible, this make-believe may be the best one can hope for.

## NOTES

1. Sonstroem (especially 521, 525–526, 528–529) provides a good discussion of Dickens' use of fancy in *Hard Times*. Stewart offers the best discussion of Dickens' use of imagination in general, though I disagree with his opinion that there is little use of imagination in *Hard Times* (151–154). Imagination is less obvious in that novel because it is integrated into the presentation of "reality" in the way I shall describe.
2. Among the critics who I think overrate the circus and what it represents are Leavis 278–279 and Miller 226–227, 332.

3. Among the critics who find Dickens' treatment of the circus and imagination inadequate are Dyson 198–199; Engel 175; Hirsch 4–7, 10; Holloway 168–169, 172; Sonstroem 527; Hornback 115; and Stewart 148, 151–154.
4. Engell presents much evidence on the Romantic concept of the imagination as idealistic; see especially 7–8, 244–275, 363–365. Abrams discusses the Romantic use of imagination to replace religion; see especially 65–67, 118–119, 121, 212, 258–262, 296, 334–340, 347, 458, 466–467. Stewart (105 and 197) compares Dickens' attitude to the Romantic faith in imagination.
5. Stewart *passim*; see especially 103–104, 116–117, 144–152, 178–185, and 223–226.

## WORKS CITED

Abrams, M. H. *Natural Supernaturalism: Tradition and Revolution in Romantic Literature*. New York: W. W. Norton, 1971.

Auden, W. H. *The Dyer's Hand and other Essays*. New York: Vintage, 1968.

Bornstein, George. "Miscultivated Field and Corrupted Garden: Imagery in *Hard Times*." *Nineteenth-Century Fiction* 26 (1971): 158–170.

Bracher, Peter. "Muddle and Wonderful No-Meaning: Verbal Irresponsibility and Verbal Failures in *Hard Times*." *Studies in the Novel* 10 (1978): 305–319.

Dickens, Charles. *Collected Papers*, Vol. I. *The Nonesuch Dickens*. Bloomsbury: Nonesuch Press, 1937.

———. *Hard Times*. New York: Norton, 1966.

———. *The Speeches of Charles Dickens*. Ed. K. J. Fielding. Oxford: Oxford University Press, 1960.

Dyson, A. E. *The Inimitable Dickens: A Reading of the Novels*. London: Macmillan, 1970.

Eigner, Edwin M. *The Metaphysical Novel in England and America: Dickens, Bulwer, Melville, and Hawthorne*. Berkeley: University of California Press, 1978.

Engel, Monroe. *The Maturity of Dickens*. Cambridge, Mass.: Harvard University Press, 1959.

Engell, James. *The Creative Imagination: Enlightenment to Romanticism*. Cambridge, Mass.: Harvard University Press, 1981.

Forster, John. *The Life of Charles Dickens*. New York: Everyman, 1966.

Hirsch, David M. "*Hard Times* and Dr. Leavis." *Criticism* 6 (Winter 1964): 1–16.

Holloway, John. "*Hard Times*: A History and a Criticism." *Dickens and the Twentieth Century*. Eds. John Gross and Gabriel Pearson. London: Routledge and Kegan Paul, 1962.

Hornback, Bert G. *"Noah's Arkitecture": A Study of Dickens's Mythology*. Athens: Ohio University Press, 1972.

Leavis, F. R. *The Great Tradition*. Garden City: Doubleday, 1954.

Linehan, Thomas M. "Rhetorical Technique and Moral Purpose in Dickens's *Hard Times.*" *University of Toronto Quarterly* 4 (1977–78).

Miller, J. Hillis. *Charles Dickens: The World of his Novels*. Cambridge, Mass.: Harvard University Press, 1959.

Smith, Frank Edmund. "Perverted Balance: Expressive Form in *Hard Times.*" *Dickens Studies Annual*, 6, ed. Robert B. Partlow, Jr. (Carbondale and Edwardsville: Southern Illinois University Press, 1977), 102–118.

Sonstroem, David. "Fettered Fancy in *Hard Times.*" *PMLA* 84 (1969): 520–529.

Stewart, Garrett. *Dickens and the Trials of Imagination*. Cambridge, Mass.: Harvard University Press, 1974.

Walder, Dennis. *Dickens and Religion*. London: George Allen and Unwin, 1981.

Warnock, Mary. *Imagination*. Berkeley: University of California Press, 1976.

# A Considerate Ghost:
# George Rouncewell in *Bleak House*

## Stanley Friedman

As various readers have observed, a major motif in *Bleak House* is that of actual or figurative ghosts. Esther herself is triply a "revenant": (1) after birth she "had been laid aside as dead" and only later was discovered to be alive (ch. 36, 452); (2) next, Miss Barbary falsely told Esther's mother that the infant had perished, a lie accepted by Lady Dedlock for more than two decades (ch. 29, 364); (3) later, after recovering from a disfiguring disease, Esther must adjust to a "strange" face in the mirror (ch. 36, 444–445), and she subsequently states that she feels for her "old self as the dead may feel if they ever revisit these scenes" (ch. 45, 551).[1] In addition, her anonymous co-narrator seems a strange, mysterious presence, characters like Hawdon, Lady Dedlock, Bucket, Tulkinghorn, Smallweed, and Vholes are at times referred to as though they were phantoms or other kinds of supernatural creatures, and spectral attributes have also been noticed in such figures as Woodcourt, Mrs. Snagsby, Richard Carstone, Gridley, and the inhabitants of the slum called Tom-all-Alone's.[2] Even with all these names, the list of ghosts is incomplete, for the anonymous narrator appears obsessed with this theme. For instance, he compares the Snagsbys' servant Guster to "a popular ghost" (ch. 19, 235), regards Krook as a "Hobgoblin" (ch. 20, 254), sees Phil Squod as George's "Familiar" (ch. 26, 324), likens Smallweed's grand-daughter Judy to "some shrill spectre" (ch. 34, 426), and has previously suggested that Chesney Wold, the Dedlocks' Lincolnshire estate, is haunted not only by the ghost of Sir Morbury Dedlock's lady, but also by all the other "dead and buried Dedlocks" (ch. 29, 357).

All of the overt or indirect references to phantoms keep this idea prominent, but no previous commentator, I believe, has examined the status of one other person in the novel as a ghost, even though this figure's role as a revenant is especially significant. George Rouncewell, like Esther, is a child lost for many years, and he, too, is eventually found. While remaining only a minor character, he serves in a remarkable way to link many diverse figures in *Bleak House*, and he is also employed to emphasize another motif besides that of ghosts—the theme of *interest*. Together with these functions, the timing of his appearances in the narrative and the ways in which his responses and actions influence our perception of major events give him both an importance and an attractiveness that seem greatly to exceed the relatively small number of pages that directly deal with him.

## I

Most important is George's role as a parallel and contrast to Esther. Since George, when a soldier, evidently acted as Hawdon's attendant or orderly, he may be seen in a sense as his former captain's "child," like Esther. Both Esther and George provide shelter for Jo, although neither benefactor is aware of the boy's having previously been befriended by Hawdon. Like Esther, George also instinctively shows friendly interest in Charley Neckett, whom he encounters at the Smallweed establishment (ch. 21, 266), shortly before she is retained by John Jarndyce as Esther's maid. And just as Esther comes to fear harming Lady Dedlock by word or deed, so George is apprehensive that showing Tulkinghorn a sample of Hawdon's handwriting would be a betrayal of the dead captain. Although George is a "prodigal son" (so labeled in one of Dickens' running headlines),[3] a figure who ran away from his mother after an idyllic early life, while Esther was unwittingly abandoned by her mother and then suffered a miserable childhood, various parallels besides those already noted are discernible.

In the church at Chesney Wold, Esther perceives the resemblance between her late godmother and Lady Dedlock, whom she sees again in the keeper's lodge and on other occasions in church. These meetings, of course, eventually lead to Esther's learning that she is Lady Dedlock's child, although the mother's own prior realization comes only after Guppy has provided important information. In the installment preceding the one in which Lady Dedlock discloses herself to Esther, Mrs. Rouncewell, even though she sees only George's back in Tulkinghorn's outer office, instinctively recalls her long-lost son, but the anonymous narrator does not here mention George's true identity and records merely that the former trooper "is so occupied with the almanack over the fire-place . . . that he does not look round until she has gone away'' (ch. 34, 427). Subsequent details make us think that George has been aware of Mrs. Rouncewell and sought to evade her attention, for Bagnet soon notices his friend's dejection, and we learn much later that George has indeed recognized his mother during this scene (ch. 55, 655–656).

Interestingly, the actual reunion scenes involving, first, Esther and Lady Dedlock and, later, George and Mrs. Rouncewell occur during a period of crisis for each child: Esther, convalescing after her illness, must adjust to her changed appearance; George is in prison, wrongly suspected of Tulkinghorn's murder. The connection between these scenes seems to be further emphasized by Hablot Browne's illustrations (see pp. 112–114). In each the child being recognized is seated, while the mother stands, and in each a third figure (in one case, Charley Neckett, Esther's maid, and in the other, Mrs. Bagnet, George's friend) is nearby. Moreover, George is shown writing at a desk, his pose (eyes looking down) suggestive of Esther's in a much earlier illustration depicting her response to Guppy's marriage proposal.[4] Returning to Dickens' text, we find still further associations between these parent-child recognition scenes: at Chesney Wold and in the prison, one character kneels to beseech forgiveness of the other and readily receives it—Lady Dedlock from her daughter, George from his mother.

Other similarities are also evident in these melodramatic encounters. In each case both of the participants are deeply emotional, and in each meeting a handkerchief is a ''prop,'' held for at least a time by the penitent person: Lady Dedlock carries Esther's handkerchief, which she had taken from Jenny's cottage as a memento, Esther having used the cloth to cover Jenny's dead infant, and George takes out a handkerchief to dry his tear-filled eyes. In both scenes, too, the guilt-ridden person explains the reasons for past behavior, indicates that there was no intention to cause sorrow, and expresses a wish to remain unknown to others: George requests that his older brother not be told; Lady Dedlock stipulates that, although Jarndyce may be informed of the discovery, Esther and she ''shall meet no more'' (ch. 36, 451–452)—a resolution that she does not really try to break, for at the end of the novel her futile attempt to see her daughter one additional time would not have involved the latter's seeing her (ch. 59, 709–710). We may be reminded here of George's revelation that he has at times secretly visited Chesney Wold to observe his mother from a distance (ch. 55, 659). The child-parent relationship in each recognition scene is the reverse of that in the other.

In addition, when we again look beyond these two scenes, we find other resemblances, as well as further differences that nevertheless suggest links.

*Lady Dedlock in the Wood*

*Mrs. Bagnet Returns from her Expedition*

*In re Guppy. Extraordinary Proceedings*

George and his mother remain together, while Esther and Lady Dedlock separate.[5] George also states that when he ran away he was "making believe to think that I cared for nobody . . . and that nobody cared for me" (ch. 55, 658); but, of course, he is clearly a caring person, "open-hearted and compassionate," to use Jarndyce's words (ch. 52, 617).[6] Lady Dedlock, the erring person in the other relationship, while lacking the kind of warmth that George possesses, is still more emotional than she seems. Despite her aloofness and apparent coldness, she shows maternal affection toward Rosa, who replaces the maid Hortense, as well as toward Esther. George retains a letter from Hawdon as a souvenir of his former captain, a "parent" figure, while Lady Dedlock acquires a handkerchief as a memento of her child, Esther. Prodigal son and errant mother, George Rouncewell and Honoria Dedlock are associated in still other ways. Both are harried by Tulkinghorn and wrongly suspected of his murder, actually perpetrated by Hortense, Lady Dedlock's former maid and apparently a former customer of George's shooting gallery (ch. 24, 305). For both Lady Dedlock and George, Mrs. Rouncewell is a maternal figure. And, at the novel's close, both return to Chesney Wold, Lady Dedlock to be buried in the family mausoleum, George to serve as a retainer to the bereaved Sir Leicester, who calls him "another self" (ch. 58, 697) and also tells the former trooper, "You are familiar to me, . . . very familiar" (ch. 58, 697), Dickens perhaps here intending a pun, since Phil Squod was previously called George's "Familiar" or attending spirit (ch. 26, 324). As Sir Leicester's companion, George, in a sense, seems to replace Lady Dedlock.

Earlier in *Bleak House*, George, on first meeting Esther, remarks, "I thought I had seen you somewhere" (ch. 24, 305). Although Robert Newsom suggests that George had known Lady Dedlock long ago at Chesney Wold and is being influenced by Esther's resemblance to her,[7] various details indicate that George's departure preceded Sir Leicester's marriage. George, who is fifty (ch. 21, 264), left home some thirty-five years before (ch. 26, 325), when fifteen; since Esther was about twenty-one when Jarndyce employed her as Ada's companion (ch. 17, 213), and since Lady Dedlock did not marry until after Esther's birth, George was not living at Chesney Wold when she became its lady. Of course, he later discloses that he has made furtive visits to the estate to observe his mother, and he may then also have noticed Lady Dedlock. Moreover, he apparently did see Lady Dedlock once *before* her marriage, when Hawdon asked him to deliver a letter to her (ch. 63, 747). Another possibility is that George is unconsciously responding to a resemblance between Esther and her father. In any case, the former trooper becomes devoted to Esther and later states that he would "esteem it a privilege to do that young lady any service, however small" (ch. 47, 563), when Woodcourt asks, partly in her name, that shelter be given to the ailing Jo.

By assisting Jo, George unknowingly associates himself more strongly with Hawdon, who also once befriended the boy. Indeed, at times George almost seems a surrogate for Hawdon, who, in a way, unwittingly led him to Small-weed (ch. 26, 334). As Gordon D. Hirsch notices, George, Hawdon, and Richard Carstone (to whom George gives fencing lessons) are all linked by their indebtedness to the old usurer (ch. 26, 332).[8] Moreover, Tulkinghorn, at different times, seeks out and disparages both Hawdon and George, each of whom has been unsuccessful in worldly matters. At one point, when the lawyer contemptuously dismisses George, the former soldier is associated with Gridley, for Tulkinghorn's label for that character, "dangerous fellow," is taken by a passing clerk to be a reference to George (ch. 27, 346). The latter is also connected to Boythorn here, for we may recall that Sir Leicester was previously quoted as considering Boythorn an "extremely dangerous person" (ch. 12, 147); and, still earlier, we heard Boythorn, the generous friend whom Jarndyce likens to "an old soldier" (ch. 9, 105), mention his very brief military career (ch. 9, 110).[9]

Besides being connected with Esther and each of her parents, as well as with Sir Leicester, Richard, Gridley, and Boythorn, George is linked with Allan Woodcourt; for just as George looks like a former soldier (ch. 21, 264; ch. 34, 427), so Allan, on first presenting himself to George, is mistaken for a sailor (ch. 47, 562). And, of course, Woodcourt and George are together at Jo's deathbed.

George is also associated, by verbal echoes, with Bucket, who claims to envy the former trooper's physique (ch. 24, 312). When confronting Tulk-inghorn, George "sits . . . very forward in his chair, as if the full complement of regulation appendages for a field-day hung about him" (ch. 27, 337); the term "field-day" reappears later, for when Bucket gets ready to apprehend Hortense we are told twice that the detective prepares for a "field-day" (ch. 54, 636; ch. 55, 654).[10] Afterwards, while searching for Lady Dedlock, Bucket calls Esther, who is accompanying him, "a pattern" (ch. 59, 704); in a subsequent chapter, George shows his elder brother a letter of explanation addressed to Esther and asks whether the message is suitable for "a pattern young lady" (ch. 63, 747). Police officer and former trooper both reveal appreciation of Esther, a somewhat paternal affection that reflects favorably on both men, even though George is a much less ambiguous figure than Bucket.[11]

George, by serving as an antithesis and yet a parallel to Esther, and by linking many other characters,[12] helps develop the theme of connections, stressed by the often-quoted passage in chapter 16:

> What connexion can there be, between the place in Lincolnshire, the house in town, the Mercury in powder, and the whereabout of Jo the outlaw with the broom, who had that distant ray of light upon him when he swept the churchyard step? What connexion can there have been between many people in the innumerable histories of this world, who, from opposite sides of great gulfs, have, nevertheless, been very curiously brought together!          (ch. 16, 197)

The former orderly of Esther's father is revealed to be the long-lost younger son of her mother's housekeeper. Like the novel's heroine, George is a revenant who is self-disparaging and remarkably caring, his kindness to others being revealed by his adoption of Phil Squod, as well as by his assistance to other victims, ranging from Gridley and Jo to Sir Leicester.


## II


Like Esther, the former trooper is closely connected to the theme of *interest*. Very early in the narrative, Esther emphasizes this motif when she writes of the way in which emotion affects perception: "I have not by any means a quick understanding. When I love a person very tenderly indeed, it seems to brighten" (ch. 3, 17). Later, she repeats, "I have mentioned that, unless my vanity should deceive me, . . . my comprehension is quickened when my affection is" (ch. 3, 18). Of course, the manner in which perception is influenced depends on the kind of interest and its degree. In *Bleak House* Dickens clearly stresses the distinction between a person like Allan Woodcourt, who characteristically displays "compassionate interest" (ch. 46, 553), and someone like Smallweed, whose father was an "old pagan" devoted to the worship of "Compound Interest" (ch. 21, 257). Among the numerous figures in the novel, many can readily be judged in terms of sensitivity or callousness, with some persons always showing appropriate feeling for other human beings, others remaining constant in cold detachment or else displaying the wrong kinds of involvement, and a few—like Lady Dedlock, Sir Leicester, and Bucket—evidently moving from the negative to the positive side of the moral scale. Indeed, forms of the word *interest* recur with noteworthy frequency.

Speaking to Woodcourt about Jo, the compassionate George Rouncewell remarks, "It seemed to me probable that you might take more than a common interest in this poor creature, because Miss Summerson had taken that unfortunate interest in him. 'Tis *my* case, sir, I assure you'' (ch. 47, 565–566)—a comment that Dickens wishes us to consider in its relation to the anonymous narrator's preceding ironic apostrophe telling Jo, who is neither a Tockahoopo Indian nor a resident of Borrioboola-Gha, "From the sole of thy foot to the crown of thy head, there is nothing interesting about thee'' (ch. 47, 564). George, a sensitive person, later admits to being "rather knocked . . . over'' by Jo's death (ch. 49, 591). At the end of the novel, the former trooper's great "sympathy'' enables him to comfort the stricken Sir Leicester (ch. 58, 697).

Contrasted with George and his capacity for generous human involvement is Tulkinghorn. At the deathbed of Nemo (Hawdon), he remains "inexpressive'' (ch. 11, 127). Arriving at Chesney Wold, "he wears his usual expressionless mask—if it be a mask'' (ch. 12, 147). In his talks with George, he shows "self-possession'' (ch. 27, 340) and, later, a "perfect assumption of indifference,'' a "dry, passionless manner'' (ch. 34, 428). Lady Dedlock, speaking to Esther, describes him as a person "too passionless'' to be friend or enemy, "mechanically faithful without attachment,'' without pity or anger, "indifferent to everything but his calling,'' which is "the acquisition of secrets, and the holding possession of such power as they give him'' (ch. 36, 451). Later, after threatening Lady Dedlock by presenting a veiled version of her story, the lawyer is called "severely and strictly self-repressed'' by the anonymous narrator (ch. 41, 507). Subsequently, the deaths of both Jo, who was questioned by Bucket at the request of Tulkinghorn (ch. 22, 281–283), and Gridley, against whom Tulkinghorn asked for a warrant (ch. 25, 314), are "mixed up'' in George's mind "with a flinty old rascal who had to do with both. And to think of that rusty carbine, stock and barrel, standing up on end in his corner, hard, indifferent, taking everything so evenly—it made flesh and blood tingle'' (ch. 49, 592).[13] The open, excitable George is repelled by the furtive, unfeeling lawyer, a character in some ways like Vholes, who, according to Esther, speaks "as though there were not a human passion or emotion in his nature'' (ch. 60, 720).

Dickens, however, does not suggest approval of emotion for its own sake, since he wishes to discriminate among different kinds of involvement and interest. For example, the anonymous narrator, in describing how Nemo's corpse is found, notices that Tulkinghorn appears "equally removed . . . from all three kinds of interest exhibited'' by the others present: Woodcourt's "professional interest in death, noticeable as being quite apart from his remarks on the deceased as an individual''; Krook's "unction,'' previously called "the unction of a horrible interest"; and Miss Flite's "awe" (ch. 11, 126–127). In addition to these different kinds of interest, as well as Tulkinghorn's evident detachment, we may observe the anonymous narrator's own attitude, suggested by his chapter's title, "Our Dear Brother," a reference to the Anglican burial service and an anticipation of the bitter satire used in describing the cemetery where Nemo is put to rest.

In diverse contexts the word *interest* can range in meaning from selfishness to dispassionate curiosity to affectionate concern. Tulkinghorn mentions Jobling's "strong interest in the fashionable great" (ch. 39, 494); Esther assures Woodcourt that she and Miss Flite read of the shipwreck with "the truest interest" (ch. 45, 549); George notices Phil Squod's "natural interest" in Jo (ch. 47, 565); Smallweed, storming into the Dedlocks' town house, demands that the police look "where the interest and the motive was" in Tulkinghorn's murder (ch. 54, 642); and Vholes, slowly guiding Richard to self-destruction, tells the young man, "It is my duty to attend to your interests with a cool head" (ch. 39, 485). The list of examples could be greatly extended, yet throughout *Bleak House* Dickens' moral stance is clear: the interest that deserves approbation is that which is linked to love and compassion.

As we have already noticed, George Rouncewell, who gave refuge to Gridley, reveals "more than a common interest" in Jo and also later shows sympathetic concern for an unfortunate at the other end of the social scale, Sir Leicester. George, however, besides serving as a character who connects many other persons, and as one of the book's exemplary figures who display "compassionate interest," is important in still other ways, especially in the novel's final six numbers, the last two appearing together, of course, as a double-installment. In presenting George, Dickens displays great narrative artistry.

### III

Although George does not actually appear in *Bleak House* until after almost the first third of the novel, he is developed quickly, and the considerable amount of detail provided suggests that he will be of significance in the resolution of major questions. He is, however, after being very visible in four of five successive monthly numbers, suddenly removed from view and ignored in three consecutive installments, only to re-emerge as a figure involved in a number of events crucial to the book's conclusion. Just as Dickens has gradually prepared us for the revelation that Lady Dedlock is Esther's mother, so we have been made increasingly confident of George's identity as Mrs. Rouncewell's runaway son. At the end of *Bleak House*, he is ideally suited to provide consolation and assistance to Sir Leicester.

In the second number of *Bleak House*, the anonymous narrator reports that the younger of the two sons of Mrs. Rouncewell, the Dedlock's housekeeper, "ran wild, and went for a soldier, and never came back" (ch. 7, 78). After being informed that the elderly woman remembers this boy as "a gay, good-humoured, clever lad" (ch. 7, 79), we hear her tell Watt, the son of her older child, that he looks like his "poor uncle George" (ch. 7, 79).

Not until the seventh number of the novel, an installment originally appearing five months later, does the reader meet a character named "Mr. George," "a swarthy browned man of fifty; well-made, and good-looking," who inspires the anonymous narrator to remark, "one might guess Mr. George to have been a trooper once upon a time" (ch. 21, 264), a guess confirmed later in the chapter when this figure tells of his service with Captain Hawdon. Four clues suggest that Mr. George is Mrs. Rouncewell's second-born son: his surname, which is the same as the runaway's given name; his age; his former military status; and his claim that he "was a thundering bad son" (ch. 21, 265). After five months, however, not all of the novel's original readers would even have remembered that Mrs. Rouncewell had a younger child.

Mr. George is quickly established as a likable man, for he provides a "special contrast" to the Smallweed family in "figure," "manner," and "voice" (ch. 21, 264). Visiting the old usurer to make a payment on an outstanding debt, George sees through Smallweed's claim to be merely the agent of a "friend in the city" and suggests that the latter is diabolical, not human: "The name of your friend in the city begins with a D, comrade" (ch. 21, 267).[14] After leaving the Smallweed home, George attends a performance at Astley's Theatre and "is touched home by the sentiments": "In the last scene, when the Emperor of Tartary gets up into a cart and condescends to bless the united lovers by hovering over them with the Union-Jack, his eye-lashes are moistened with emotion" (ch. 21, 271). George's susceptibility to feelings aroused by a fictitious spectacle again emphasizes his difference from "the house of Smallweed," which, we have been told, "has discarded all amusements, discountenanced all story-books, fairy tales, fictions, and fables, and banished all levities whatsoever" (ch. 21, 258). Our interest in George has been stimulated by the attention paid him throughout the chapter and also by the threat uttered by Smallweed after the former trooper has left him: "I'll lime you, you dog, I'll lime you" (ch. 21, 270).

In the following installment of *Bleak House*, one of the two chapters narrated by Esther includes her account of meeting Mr. George, who has been hired "to fence with Richard" (ch. 24, 304), as part of the young man's preparation for a military career. Esther, who shares her co-narrator's evident approval of the former soldier, later tells of her visit to his shooting gallery, where she witnesses the moving death of Gridley, who has been given refuge by the benevolent George.

The latter receives even more notice in the next number, presented entirely by the anonymous narrator. Speaking to Phil Squod, George refers to his own country upbringing: "My good mother lived in the country" (ch. 26, 326). After a few more words, however, he exclaims, "What set me on about country boys, and runaways, and good-for-nothings?" (ch. 26, 326). Following this further clue about George's identity, we are informed of his generous sheltering of Phil and then see Smallweed begin the eventually successful attempt to get the trooper to allow Tulkinghorn to see "some fragment in Captain Hawdon's writing" (ch. 26, 333). Subsequently, Tulkinghorn employs the threat of proceedings against Bagnet, who has provided security for a loan to George, to get the former soldier to show the lawyer a sample of Hawdon's handwriting. This specimen enables Tulkinghorn to identify Nemo as Hawdon and to continue to acquire information that can be used against Lady Dedlock. By using completely unethical tactics to coerce George into compliance, the lawyer confirms our earlier sense of his villainous nature.

In chapter 34, when George visits Tulkinghorn's office and notices but avoids directly meeting Mrs. Rouncewell, we receive the strongest hint yet about the trooper's identity. Earlier, in chapter 28, devoted to George's older brother's first interview with the Dedlocks concerning Rosa, Sir Leicester has reminded us that Mrs. Rouncewell is the mother of two sons (ch. 28, 350). In both the ninth and eleventh installments, George and his problems are given a great deal of attention, since three of the seven chapters in these numbers, enclosing the central installment of the novel, focus directly on him.

In the four months between Nos. 11 and 15, readers of the original serial installments found no further news of this character, but in all of the novel's last six numbers, Nos. 15–20, George plays a part. Just as he had rendered assistance to Gridley, so he also gives aid to Jo, another ailing fugitive from Bucket. In each case, too, George observes the victim's death. Shortly before the account of Jo's demise, we learn, moreover, that Tulkinghorn has continued to harass the former soldier by causing him anxiety about the renewal of the outstanding debt (ch. 47, 566). In the very next chapter, appearing in the same installment (No. 15), we see Tulkinghorn tormenting Lady Dedlock. This juxtaposition emphasizes the link between the two victims, both of whom, as well as Hortense, visit the lawyer's chambers on the night of the murder, one of the circumstances that lead to George's arrest by Bucket.

In the sixteenth installment, Esther, for the second and final time in the novel, includes George in one of her chapters. After noting that confidence in his innocence of the murder has been expressed by both Woodcourt and Jarndyce, she quotes her guardian's words, "We will stand by him, as he himself stood by the two poor creatures who are gone," a reference, she explains, to Gridley and Jo (ch. 52, 617). George's refusal to accept legal representation, however, creates a difficulty leading to Mrs. Bagnet's announcement that she knows the identity of his mother and will bring her to him.

In chapter 55 of No. 17, Esther's co-narrator describes the emotional reunion between Mrs. Rouncewell and her younger son. As we previously noticed, this meeting, in a prison cell, includes many features that recall the preceding reunion, in a beautiful outdoor setting, between Esther and her mother.

The circumstances of George's incarceration, when considered with his first name and the second syllable of his surname, suggest that this "prodigal son" is in some ways an inversion of George Lillo's protagonist in the famous play *The London Merchant: with the Tragical History of George Barnwell* (1731), a character developed from an old ballad and later depicted in various narratives and other dramas. Unlike Barnwell, George is not guilty of theft, but he is in debt. Both men are accused of murder, even though Rouncewell is innocent, and both feel shame when visited in prison by their friends. In contrast to the erring apprentice, George Rouncewell has been a "prodigal" only in deserting his mother, and he, unlike the biblical prototype, expressly states his wish not to reduce a worthier brother's inheritance (ch. 63, 744–745).[15]

In No. 18 George is seen ministering to Sir Leicester. The reappearance of Mrs. Rouncewell's lost son has stirred the baronet to speech for the first time since his stroke, and his thoughts are suggested by the anonymous narrator's question, "Does this discovery of some one lost, this return of some one so long gone, come upon him as a strong confirmation of his hopes?" (ch. 58, 695). These hopes for Lady Dedlock's safe return remain, of course, sadly thwarted. George has been restored at just the time that the legend of the Ghost's Walk is evidently being fulfilled by her disgrace and death. Early in the novel, George has been associated with this legend, for the first reference to the runaway son of Mrs. Rouncewell comes just before she relates this old tale, in chapter 7, "The Ghost's Walk." In addition, after she has found her long-lost child, he reacts to her references to the legend. At first, George tries to allay his mother's "old-story fears," but, after seeing Lady Dedlock's empty rooms, he concedes, "I begin to understand how you come to think as you do think, mother" (ch. 58, 693).

In the novel's final double-number, George is reunited with his successful older brother and indicates his desire to relinquish any inheritance from their mother, an ironically unusual attitude in a book in which so much suffering is attributed to disputes arising from the wish to procure rather than surrender legacies. Then, in the penultimate chapter, the last one presented by Esther's co-narrator, we find an approving notice of George's devotion to his mother, and to Phil Squod, the Bagnets, and the infirm Sir Leicester, whom he accompanies on daily rides to the mausoleum in which Lady Dedlock rests.

## IV

Even though George Rouncewell appears in only thirteen of the sixty-seven chapters in *Bleak House* and is referred to in just three other chapters, he proves highly significant to the book's overall effects. One more example of a revenant, he helps to connect many characters, repeatedly displays "compassionate interest," and is involved in actions leading to the novel's conclusion. As I observed earlier, however, his most noteworthy function is in relation to the heroine, Esther.

Whatever limitations Esther may have, she must, as Robert Donovan maintains, be accepted as a moral guide.[16] In the fourteenth and fifteenth installments of *Bleak House*, we find praise of Esther when she is not present to record it, her unnamed collaborator telling us of the loving admiration of her expressed by Jenny, Woodcourt, Jo, and George Rouncewell. And, later in the novel, George, when visiting his elder brother, again indicates great esteem for Esther. In this same chapter, part of the novel's final, double installment, we are once more shown George's unusual sensitivity when he does not wish to send Esther, whose mother has very recently died, a letter from Chesney Wold, since for her that "might be a painful name just now" (ch. 63, 746). Such sensitivity is in keeping with his character. Much earlier, Allan Woodcourt, responding to George's suggestion that Phil Squod take the ailing Jo to a bath and purchase some clothing for the boy, has called the former trooper "my considerate friend" (ch. 47, 565). The emphasis on George's considerateness may remind us that this quality is one of Esther's greatest virtues.

Nearly two years before the serialization of *Bleak House* began, Dickens published "A Preliminary Word" in the first issue of *Household Words* (March 30, 1850) and announced his wish to provide in that periodical "moving lessons of compassion and consideration." Despite all its darkness, *Bleak House* fulfills the same goal, for it includes an optimistic note in that a number of its figurative spectres display "compassionate interest," for Dickens a supremely important quality. Indeed, in *Nicholas Nickleby* the narrator describes compassion as "the one great cardinal virtue, which, properly nourished and exercised, leads to, if it does not necessarily include, all the others" (ch. 18). Like Esther Summerson, George Rouncewell is a long-lost child who becomes a source of great comfort to others. In the regretful cry, "Mankind was my business," uttered by Dickens' most famous ghost, the spirit of Jacob Marley, we find an implicit urging toward the values that motivate both the heroine of *Bleak House* and her dead father's former orderly—warmth, generosity, and consideration.[17]

## NOTES

1. When citing *Bleak House*, I use George Ford and Sylvère Monod's edition (New York: Norton, 1977) and provide chapter and page references in parentheses. For other Dickens works, I employ the Oxford Illustrated Dickens (1947–58) and indicate parenthetically chapter or book and chapter numbers.

2. Ghostly elements in *Bleak House* are considered by Robert Newsom, in *Dickens on the Romantic Side of Familiar Things: "Bleak House" and the Novel Tradition* (New York: Columbia University Press, 1977), pp. 8, 55, 57–58, 65–67, 155 (n. 4), and 156 (n. 10); Jonathan Arac, in *Commissioned Spirits: The Shaping of Social Motion in Dickens, Carlyle, Melville, and Hawthorne* (New Brunswick, N.J.: Rutgers University Press, 1979), pp. 126–128; Michael Ragussis, in "The Ghostly Signs of *Bleak House*," *Nineteenth-Century Fiction* 34 (Dec. 1979), 253–280; and Christopher Herbert, in "The Occult in *Bleak House*," *Novel* 17 (Winter 1984), 101–115. For commentary on a related topic, demonic characters, see Marilyn Georgas, "Dickens, Defoe, the Devil and the Dedlocks: The 'Faust Motif' in *Bleak House*," in *Dickens Studies Annual*, 10, eds. Michael Timko, Fred Kaplan, and Edward Guiliano (New York: AMS Press, 1982), 23–44.

3. These headlines, composed by Dickens for the Charles Dickens Edition (1868), are reprinted by Ford and Monod—see p. 802, which indicates that "The Prodigal Son" was one of the headlines for the chapter (55) presenting George's reunion with his mother. Stephen C. Gill, in "Allusion in *Bleak House*: A Narrative Device," *Nineteenth-Century Fiction* 22 (Sept. 1967), 150–151, observes that when the anonymous narrator, speaking of Mrs. Rouncewell's grandson Watt, uses the words "a journey in far countries" (ch. 7, 79), there is an echo of an

expression in Luke 15:13 concerning the prodigal son, a figure who eventually returns from spiritual death; this allusion, as Gill explains, refers not to Watt, but to his uncle, George, whom he physically resembles, according to Mrs. Rouncewell.

4. For these three illustrations, see, in the Oxford Illustrated Dickens, *Bleak House* (New York: Oxford University Press, 1948), intro. Sir Osbert Sitwell, the plates "Lady Dedlock in the Wood" (facing p. 512), "Mrs. Bagnet Returns from her Expedition" (facing p. 745), and "In re Guppy. Extraordinary Proceedings" (facing p. 120).

5. Louis Crompton, in "Satire and Symbolism in *Bleak House*," *Nineteenth-Century Fiction* 12 (March 1958), 286, observes that the novel contrasts these two parent-child relationships.

6. Trevor Blount, in "The Importance of Place in 'Bleak House'," *Dickensian* 61 (Sept. 1965), 147, states that George's "moral worth" is "comparable to Esther's." T. W. Hill, in "Notes on *Bleak House*," *Dickensian* 40 (June 1944), 139, points out that George, in his remark about not caring or being cared for, is using a line from the song "The Miller of the Dee," found in Isaac Bickerstaffe's comedy *Love in a Village* (1762). In *A Tale of Two Cities* Sydney Carton tells Darnay, "I care for no man on earth, and no man on earth cares for me" (II, ch. 4).

7. P. 53.

8. "The Mysteries in *Bleak House*: A Psychoanalytic Study," in *Dickens Studies Annual*, 4, ed. Robert B. Partlow, Jr. (Carbondale and Edwardsville: Southern Illinois University Press, 1975), p. 132. Steven Cohan, in " 'They Are All Secret': The Fantasy Content of *Bleak House*," *Literature and Psychology* 26 (1976), 86, suggests that George "acts as a double for the dead lover in the latter part of the novel."

9. Crompton, p. 289, remarks that Boythorn's "large size links him with trooper George as one of the book's good giants."

10. This expression in *Bleak House* may be a previously unnoted example of Dickens' interest in private jokes, since Bucket was modeled on Inspector Charles Frederick Field. See, in John Forster's *The Life of Charles Dickens*, ed. J. W. T. Ley (London: Cecil Palmer, 1928), Bk. XI, ch. 3, p. 843, Ley's n. 501. My later references to Forster indicate book, chapter, and page numbers in this volume. In *Dickens: Interviews and Recollections*, 2 vols. (Totowa, N.J.: Barnes & Noble, 1981), II, 329, n. 1, Philip Collins, the editor, observes that Dickens, in an 1867 conversation, used "field-days" as an undetected pun in referring to trips to thieves' dens with Field.

11. Edwin M. Eigner, in *The Metaphysical Novel in England and America: Dickens, Bulwer, Melville, and Hawthorne* (Berkeley: University of California Press, 1978), p. 201, notices that Esther is praised in similar ways by both Bucket and George.

12. W. J. Harvey, in "Chance and Design in *Bleak House*," in *Dickens and the Twentieth Century*, eds. John Gross and Gabriel Pearson (Toronto: University of Toronto Press, 1962), pp. 153–154, observes "various narrative strands converging on George." Robert Alan Donovan, in *The Shaping Vision: Imagination in the English Novel from Defoe to Dickens* (Ithaca, N.Y.: Cornell University Press, 1966), p. 226, refers to Dickens' "careful husbandry of characters" in *Bleak House* and comments on the relationships George has with Richard, Smallweed, and Hawdon.

13. Forster, XI, ch. 3, 838, remarks of the novelist, "The one thing entirely hateful to him, was indifference."

14. Luther S. Luedtke, in "System and Sympathy: The Structural Dialectic of Dickens' *Bleak House*," in *Literatur in Wissenschaft und Unterricht* (Kiel) 3 (1970), 6, sees the "friend" as real, as does Georgas, p. 39, who identifies this figure as "none other than Tulkinghorn himself"; but Smallweed is clearly creating a fiction to evade responsibility, for the anonymous narrator describes the "friend in the city" as "the one solitary flight" of the old usurer's imagination (ch. 21, 266).

15. The Barnwell story is used by Dickens in *Great Expectations* (ch. 15–16), and the character is mentioned briefly in *Pickwick Papers* (ch. 10) and *Martin Chuzzlewit* (ch. 9). Rouncewell's name may also ironically reflect that of the scapegrace Tom *Rakewell*, the protagonist in Hogarth's *The Rake's Progress*. A connection with the theme of the prodigal is found, too, in still another possible inspiration for the former trooper's name: *George* Herbert Buonaparte *Rodwell* was the author of the play *Azael; or, The Prodigal in London* (apparently based on the opera *L'enfant prodigue* or *Azaël the Prodigal*, by Augustin Eugène Scribe and the composer Daniel-François-Esprit Auber). Rodwell's play, listed by Allardyce Nicoll, in *Late Nineteenth Century Drama, 1850–1900*, 2nd ed., vol. 5 of *A History of English Drama, 1660–1900* (Cambridge: Cambridge University Press, 1959), p. 548, was performed in London on Oct. 13, 1851, about a month before Dickens, according to Forster, VII, ch. 1, 559, began writing *Bleak House*. Moreover, Dickens knew Rodwell, who had prepared the songs for Edward Stirling's 1844 dramatization of *A Christmas Carol*—see the Pilgrim Edition of *The Letters of Charles Dickens*, 4: *1844–1846*, ed. Kathleen Tillotson (Oxford: Clarendon Press, 1977), p. 40 (to Rodwell, Feb. 6, 1844), and also pp. 107–108 (to Thomas Mitton, Apr. 17, 1844).

16. P. 236.

17. I wish to thank Professor Robert Newsom for helpful advice concerning the presentation of this material.

# Designs in Disorder:
# The Language of Death
# in *Our Mutual Friend*

## Patrick McCarthy

I have been reading the novels and stories of Dickens as embodiments of his primordial myth of the nature of existence, taking special note of the linguistic means he uses, and finally observing how death enters his world and is dealt with in terms of the myth. My paper will review these aspects of his work in a broad, generalizing fashion and then go on to rather more detailed consideration of their presence in *Our Mutual Friend*. The juxtaposition of myth, language, and death emerged for me over time as the relationship of Dickens' primary vision to its constitutive parts and its threatened dissolution. Much in that novel as well as its connection with other Dickens work becomes clearer when the myth and these relations are kept in mind.[1]

Briefly, Dickens' world is one of radical disorder in which energetic self-will induces each entity to affirm itself at the expense of everything else. All creatures great and small, be they animal, vegetable, or mineral, are engaged in continuous struggle. Energies embroil themselves everywhere; the plenum is packed; there is no safe enclave. Everything is at risk: amid universal expressiveness parts revolt against the whole, servants against masters, things against owners. Whatever stands in the way is liable to attack: one's possessions, one's liberty, one's name, oneself. Humans appear to be special targets but in fact are targets only as they get in the way of others, humans and non-humans. Things, for example, often find themselves contending with multitudinous other things so that jumbles are common, but there are no dividing lines, and humans may find themselves almost overwhelmed by massive disorders in things. We remember—and how typical they are—the helter-skelter miscellaneousness of Fagin's London, Skaggs's Gardens in *Dombey and Son*, and the ink-stained correspondence and nightmarish closets of Mrs. Jellyby in *Bleak House*. We remember, too, the darker legacies of wild, self-asserting energies: fragmentation, dissolution, decay, violence, and sudden death.

When the center cannot hold, indeed when there seems to be no center, heroes and heroines find their places to stand only with great difficulty. That they are people of moral probity and worthy of sympathy and understanding is assumed, but they find themselves victims from the beginning, born in a kind of bondage. They have entered life encumbered, for the will of the past weighs them down and to a degree imprisons them. Oliver Twist's mother leaves him a heritage of possible disgrace; David Copperfield's kindly father leaves him a weak, unproviding mother; Arthur Clennam and Esther Summerson live under the shadow of their own bastardy and the assumption that they share in its stigma and blame.

While casting off the bonds of the past, they must constantly resist the destroying wills of insistent antipathetic energies. Certain attractions and expectations add to the peril: fool's gold and romantic, self-flattering love may try them and in a measure corrupt them, as with young Martin Chuzzlewit and Pip and David Copperfield. They may grow weary amid the hostile pressures and disappointing illusions. They may drift into despair and self-neglect as with Arthur Clennam, self-questioning and uncertainty as again with Pip and David. In time the experience of failure serves to chasten them and widen their intellectual and imaginative visions. But they will require help—Oliver Twist and David most acutely—and usually it comes as some version of benevolent spirit in human form, the Maylies, the Garlands, the Cheerybles, or Betsy Trotwood, for example.[2] They may also need the strengthening and healing effects of altruistic love, and not just romantic love, for we think of Mr. Paul Dombey saved by his daughter Florence.

For Dickens' heroes, as for Keats, life is a vale of soul-making, and in a world of competing wills they must seek, not to make their own prevail, but modestly to secure independent survival. However misguided or self-deluded they may be for a time, they may not sink into passivity. Not to have plans or take action is to be swept up in the plans and actions of others. Heroes need designs of their own and a certain tenacity of self-reliance in executing them. In the arc of rising self-esteem and understanding they must act with purpose and direction and meet contrary energies with energies that, if they may not command, comprehend prudence and wise limitation. They become devotees of order, public and private, for they know the power of chaos.[3] In enforcing their own order, they are not required to be fastidious; they may be secret or devious, or candid or direct, as need serves. They may, when necessary, administer physical punishment and can take satisfying pleasure in settling their own desserts and those of their enemies.

The language in which Dickens bodies forth his energetic, dangerous world gathers together every rhetorical, imagistic, enlivening, heightening, revitalizing, and energy-bearing device he can think of as well as a variety of modes and tones. I have earlier designated these devices as animism, animal imagery, superlative expressions, odd collocations, lists, and reworked clichés, and sought to assess their effects on meaning.[4] Already at work in his *Sketches by Boz* and reaching a point of development in *Martin Chuzzlewit*, they become Dickens' standard procedures to suggest the vivid turbulence in which his opposing forces dispose themselves. Some deplore the results as false intensity, as Dickens' particular way—as he said himself—of "[getting his] steam up,"[5] and we understand the charge.[6] But what others see as an expense of spirit in a waste of style is also and primarily Dickens in action. "There is," as Conrad suggests, "a sort of lucidity proper to extravagant language,"[7] a lucidity he found useful in his own "Heart of Darkness" and *The Secret Agent* and just as useful to the dynamic, pressure-filled, unstable atmosphere in which Dickens' characters work out their destinies.

In time, one way and another, they escape into a private domain of order and satisfactions, but it is no fairy-tale world, and accommodation must be made, especially to the challenging presence of death. It is not that Mary Hogarth brought death into Dickens' world, but she brought its woe. The strolling player, the widow's son, and others had died in his early pages, but Mary through her fictional self, Little Nell, faced him with the problem of evil in its most radical form, the death of a child. As a Christian sharing many traditional views, Dickens tended toward a belief in immortality, but he made no parade of his views. In the event, he worked out a rhetoric of consolation for the novel that echoes what he expressed about actual deaths he knew of. His primary concern at such times was for the living, for the ways death bore back upon those who survived. With the deaths of Fagin, Bill Sikes, and Ralph Nickleby, Dickens undertook explorations of several kinds of fatality—explorations that continue through the novels and stories and that, as with the deaths of the children, concern themselves with death as a comment on the life that precedes and on its effects for survivors. The subject is for him inextricable from any serious consideration of life, and *Our Mutual Friend* marks his furthest excursus into its place in his mythical schemes.

The novel takes up at the point in the myth reached by *Great Expectations* and at once pushes back and widens the meaning of death and opens to a chosen band the possibilities of satisfying fulfillment. We had seen Pip, like other Dickens protagonists before him, faced with the need to free himself from several kinds of imprisonment, including his own mind-chains, and in the battle for freedom and self-assertion being almost murdered, almost incinerated, and almost destroyed by fever. What he finally achieves is, we remember, a clear sense of the modest, severely limited successes open to him. His fate reminds us that, years before, Dombey is rescued at the verge of committing suicide and is last seen weeping tears of joy and regret, and that Arthur Clennam, from a point of hopelessness in debtors' prison, "went down [with little Dorrit] into a modest life of usefulness and happiness." In the present novel, John Harmon will make his way in the same Dickens universe, the world of mythical vision and the world of contemporary social and mercantile practice, and the circle he describes will also move from darkness into light. For much of the book, as Dickens' memorandum states, he will be "dead to all intents and purposes external to himself,"[8] but he will rise, higher than Pip, into a life of assured happiness. He will go beyond his predecessors toward death, and he will move more fully into a life of happiness through love. Even further, his experience will be mirrored and reasserted in that of a fellow victim, Eugene Wrayburn.

Astonishingly, in what appears so highly ramified a work, the principal forces of the novel are juxtaposed in the first three chapters. A central concern of the myth, how beleaguered life may make its way in the face of and by the use of death, is figured by Gaffer Hexam's search into the depths of the river for what may be taken from death.[9] Gaffer's dirty boat, stained as though with the blood of corpses, then gives way to the spick-and-span newness of the Veneerings, all surface and no depths, all assurance, power, and smooth exclusiveness. Two guests of the Veneerings betake themselves with Hexam to the place of order, the police station, and are joined unexplainedly by our mutual friend, whose first words are, "I am lost!" Though calmly competent, the representative of order can do nothing but record the disruptive facts, and we wander off with Gaffer's son to be introduced to other central elements of the myth, love and imagination. We see Lizzie at home, skilled at reading reality in the embers of a fire and (as she says) for the happiness of her father and brother "a'most content to die."[10]

Already at work in the beginning chapters are Dickens' standard verbal procedures to suggest the vivid turbulence in which his opposing forces dispose themselves.[11] Four of the procedures are worth pointing out at this point: animal imagery, animism, odd collocations, and superlative expressions. The book begins predictably enough with birds of prey swooping down and angling up the living and the dead, and we recognize the terrain as Dickens' when serpents, dragons, wolves, and monsters freely roam about. Fledgby as fox, Wegg as serpent, and Riah (misunderstood) as wolf make the obvious point that men are brutes, but we are both comically and unpredictably taken aback by Wegg as extinct bird, ostrich, and mud-worm, Boffin as rhinoceros, and Wrayburn's father as eel. Animal energies turn the world into mad unpredictables when the wounded Fledgby "plung[es] and gambol[s] all over his bed, like a porpose" (793), while "contending with every mortal disease incidental to poultry" (790), though perhaps we are not quite out of complete rationality until Mrs. Wilfer kisses her daughter Lavinia "once on the brow (as if accepting an oyster)" (742).

Further down the chain of being, the device we blandly call personification or animation makes lifeless objects bristle with secret life as they plot hazards for beasts and men. The forehead of a building swells with a rotten wart of wood; vessels get ashore and stare into windows; a mangle lunges at two infants "like a catapult designed for their destruction" (245). At yet another level at which orderly intentions seem completely to have abandoned themselves, a dreadful loose miscellaneousness thrusts everything into meaningless collocation with everything else. For *Our Mutual Friend* the dust heaps are the resident symbol of the blind indiscriminateness deep down in things, but we also recall the rich multitudinousness of Venus's shop with its "Tools. Bones, warious. Skulls, warious. Preserved Indian baby. African ditto. Bottled preparations, warious," and so on at length. We recognize that it is to Charlie's credit that he "had risen in the jumble, taught in the jumble, and been received from the jumble" (265), but neither he nor anyone is quite free. The new district in which he teaches looks like a box of blocks on a table to which a child "of particularly incoherent mind" had given a kick (268), and the London he walks through with Bradley Headstone is another chaos of "melancholy waifs and strays" of people, porters, papers and pins (450).

Disruption under irrational pressures, fragmentation or deep hardening after long stress: these are the exerting forces and their results in Dickens' world. In *Our Mutual Friend* language forces the issue at every turn, exerting pressures locally and generally. Even the least important of the ones I shall mention here, superlative expressions, easily dismissed as mere Cockney bad taste, join in at the level of pulse and punctuation. Thus adjectives and adverbs continually swell their expressiveness to the highest degree. Every word suggestive of unusualness, uniqueness, or ultimateness crowds the lines.

Unqualified "no's" and "never's" and "every's" confederate with the bristling exclusiveness of words like "perfect" and "only" and "nothing." Vulgarian Dickens is indiscriminate and incorrigible, of couse: everything serves his turn, the forcible feebleness of "very's," "so's," and "such's," along with everything else. Even quiet corners of the text are inflected constantly with small but multiple expressive charges. Here at her birthday party is mild Georgiana Podsnap on the subject of dancing: "it *always* has been . . . *such* a trial to me! I *so* dread being awful. And it is *so* awful. *No one* knows what I suffered at Madame Sauteuse's, where I learnt to dance" (184, emphases mine).

Reading on in the passage, we see how language devices gather together to produce an intimidating, dehumanizing, pressure-filled world. Directly after these words of Georgiana, her mother, cantering like a rocking horse, approaches with the ogreish Mr. Grompus, doing so, Georgiana thinks, to "torment" her and making her, in turn, wish to "kill" him (308, 183). It goes on:

> And now, the grand chain [of the dancers] riveted to the *last* link, the discreet automaton [of a pianist] ceased, and the sixteen [dancers], two and two, took a walk among the furniture. And herein, the unconsciousness of the Ogre Grompus was pleasantly conspicuous; for, that complacent monster, believing that he was giving Miss Podsnap a treat, prolonged to the *utmost stretch of possibility* a peripatetic account of an archery meeting; while his victim, heading the procession of sixteen as it slowly circled about, like a revolving funeral, *never* raised her eyes except *once* to steal a glance at Mrs. Lammle, expressive of *intense* despair.
> At length the procession was dissolved by the violent arrival of a nutmeg, before which the drawing-room door bounced open as if it were a cannonball."
>                                                                 (184–185, italics mine)

The drawing-room setting and humor are deceptive. The scene is of a piece with the darker passages of the novel. The tone allows the narrator to connect Georgiana's plight with the novel's most serious implications. Her complacent partner is a monster quite real enough, her mother a wooden horse of insensitivity, the dance a chain that binds her physically, the pianist a machine, and the arriving refreshments terrifying intruders. In its adverbs and adverbial phrases the language at once attenuates and condenses her genuine anguish so that her suffering is both instantaneous and prolonged. She *is* a victim, and her dance of life threatens to become a funeral procession. That without her knowledge she is also being victimized by Sophronia and Alfred Lammle makes her position all the more dangerous and pathetic while adding an almost Jamesian note of sophisticated evil.[12]

Their approach in this world of words is principally verbal, and it is with names, the private possession most open to public appropriation, that they begin. The Lammles call their victim Georgiana and insist that she also call them by their first names. In doing so, they reinforce the novel's special sense of names as both one's own and open to appropriation or alteration by others. The Lammles belong with the aggressors who seek to take over; Georgiana on the other hand belongs with those—Riah and Twemlow, for example—who lack sufficient force of will to resist such intrusions.

Characteristically all aggressive characters refashion the names of others as a mode of exerting control.[13] Beginning with Riderhood with his repeated use of "pardner" to assert his right to share Gaffer Hexam's grisly find, the practice continues throughout the novel. Riderhood's low cunning, partly defensive and always assertive, initially keeps separate Lightwood as "Governor," Wrayburn as "T'other Governor" and Headstone as "T'otherest Governor" but moves powerfully to rename Headstone as "Schoolmaster" (as Wrayburn had done earlier) and finally to induce Headstone to erase his own name from the blackboard. Wrayburn, in his unredeemed state, says of Riah, "*I* gave him the name of Aaron" (598), and he contemptuously names Jenny Wren's father Mr. Dolls as a preliminary to bribing him for information. Mrs. Wilfer and Lady Tippins, as we might expect, twist the names of others to their own purposes, and it is the almost faceless Veneering who dubs John Harmon "the man from Somewhere" (55). But it is Wegg, the verbal creator, who is the aesthete of appellations, rebaptizing the inhabitants of "Our House," pronouncing downright, immutable judgement on the names of Nicholas Boffin, boasting of his taste and power of language, and finally reducing Boffin to "the minion and worm" (91, 554, 560).

With access to one's name open to all, one may in response call oneself what one chooses and with others' permission develop pet names to express affection. Jenny Wren, who most famously has denominated herself anew, is quick to change Riah's name from "godmother" to "wolf" when she suspects him of treachery, and lovingly transforms Lizzie into "Lizzie-Mizzie-Wizzie." Harmon, of course, also redesignates himself, into Handford and Rokesmith, and even into an animate-inanimate "secretary." Almost no one in the novel escapes nominal alteration or transformation with, of course, the narrator (himself a self-named "Inimitable") taking an active hand as he dubs Bella's baby "the Inexhaustible" and Twemlow the "Knight of the Simple Heart" (841, 632).

The issue here is one of control where intrusions and apprehensions and fracturings continuously threaten. Owners of names are at risk in another way. As so often in other Dickens novels, parts of people's bodies revolt against their possessors' wills and act quite on their own. Pleasant Riderhood, like her father, is swivel-eyed, and Georgiana Podsnap's dancing partner has "one eye screwed up into extinction and the other framed and glazed" (186). Silas Wegg not only worries about the disposition of his amputated leg but also has to contend with a wooden substitute that has a will of its own (551), not to mention a mind unable to bear insults (645). The arm of Mary Anne, Miss Peecher's pupil, is afflicted with the Dr. Strangelove syndrome: her arm stretches out when she speaks and requires hooking under by her left hand; Gaffer Hexam's dead hand holds the silver he has robbed in a tight grip and the left hand of a pew holder "voluntarily double[s] up to act as a money-box" (163). But it is Headstone, as we guess, for whom the problem of control is most acute: his right hand digs painfully into his left with a screwing motion, clenches itself spasmodically, and during his interview with Lizzie breaks from him and lays its "knuckles raw and bleeding" on the coping of the cemetery wall (456).

Too long over-controlled and repressed in the struggle to rise from poverty to respectable employment (345), insulted and taunted by Wrayburn, Headstone fights (and loses) his own *psychomachia* before revenging himself against Wrayburn and clasping Riderhood to himself in an iron ring of death.[14] And yet the spectacular violence of his attempted act of murder and death proceeds from the same intense, violence-prone world the other characters also inhabit. All of us, the inspector wisely says, are up to murder, whenever pressures mount unbearably (69). This is a world, the language tells us insistently, where violent actions or the threat of such action toward others and toward oneself is a constant. The words *terrific, terrible, horrible, fearful, shocking, stunning, frightening* and others of like import stud the text like cloves a baked ham. Ordinary domestic life bristles with it: old John Harmon has "anathematised" and turned out his two children, Gaffer Hexam has often struck his son, Rogue Riderhood has beaten and strapped his daughter so that she has learned to look on marriage as a license to quarrel and fight. The mother of the potboy at the Six Jolly Fellowship Porters "systematically accelerated his retirement to rest with a poker" (114).

My last example suggests that it is not just the reckless angry people, like the drunken woman in the cell banging herself about, who live in an atmosphere of casual violence but others, like gentle Miss Peecher, who while sewing quietly thrusts a needle through her dress in the place where her heart would have been (283). It is shy Miss Podsnap who wants would-be suitors who "torment" her (308) "trampled upon" (309), and Jenny Wren who considers the danger of a suitor blowing up and taking her with him (402) and plans to pour boiling liquor down his throat (294). With her experience of children, her "queer" legs and crooked back, Jenny can convene terrors and the feisty will to combat them. She says she would refuse to give Wrayburn the information he requires if he had "brought pincers with [him] to tear it out" (596).

Yet perhaps even more symptomatic than these examples is the offhanded way the narrator hits upon illustrations flecked with violence. We expect the "savage" Alfred Lammle to decant a bottle of soda-water "as though he were wringing the neck of some unlucky creature and pouring its blood down his throat" (319), but do we expect the narrator to remark that an old school-master, looking at boyish Rumty Wilfer, "might have been unable to with-stand the temptation of caning him on the spot" (75)?

Again, as Gaffer Hexam in the scene following Charlie's departure punc-tuates each sentence by striking downward with his knife, we see as Lizzie does the murderous implications of his action (120). When Wrayburn at the Veneerings' table "trifles quite ferociously with his dessert-knife" (57), we laugh, and laugh again during the long night-wait for Gaffer Hexam when he whispers, "Three burglaries, two forgeries, and a midnight assassination" (216). But what save a disposition to casual violence sets Lightwood's idle office boy to "chopping at the flies on the windowsill with his penknife" (136)? Benevolent Nicodemus Boffin tells us that he had to be restrained from giving old John Harmon "a rattler for himself" (134) and later listens to John Rokesmith's proposals that Boffin employ him with his stick ready to "knock him down" (140).

Resistance to compulsion of any kind may spill over into violence of its own especially of a punishing sort. In earlier novels, most notably *Nicholas Nickleby*, Dickens made punishers of his protagonists. Here much-put-upon Jenny who had long contemplated blowing pepper on her youthful torturers gleefully sprinkles pepper on wounds Alfred Lammle and the author have already inflicted. The same zest for physical chastisement makes inoffensive Soapy catapult Silas Wegg onto the scavenger's cart, and for readers carried along by the novel's verbal and thematic insistence on intense physicality across its moral spectrum, the moment is a delight.

In such a context, murder is the logical endpoint, and so it is, although of itself it is not an important conceptual category. As subject of mystery, it is none of Dickens' concern: he never tells us who murdered Radfoot.[15] As a defining action, it serves principally as the necessary *terminus ad quem* of Bradley Headstone's self-destroying life. As a kind of death, it serves as the ultimate contrary example of what the novel demonstrates. Headstone is the dark fulfillment of the dark side of the myth.

Headstone of course is a special and interesting case. He does not belong with the hopelessly corrupt world of the Veneerings and Podsnaps. He has not been self-indulgent; he has been "obliged habitually to keep [his strong feelings] down" (400), and though the word *victim* is not used of him as it is used of Harmon, Wrayburn and others, he is something of a victim, too.[16] But he is wedded to the stone of his own inexorable nature, and the language devices suggest he has been rendered by a hard, mechanical system into an automaton, and he retains the physical aggressiveness of a wild animal or nightbird (266, 609, 618). His hand flies out of control, as we have seen, and his body racks itself with epileptic tortures. The clear implications are of irrepressible, physical desire that would in Empson's phrase "rip to blood" but cannot heed Empson's injunction: "Leave what you die for and be safe to die."

Ultimately, of course, the novel does not affirm the dark side of its myth but, because it must, it accepts its conditions: the feral, aggressive, omnipresent energies; the tendencies to fragmentation, miscellaneousness, dissolution, and decay; the hardening, dehumanizing effects, and above all the fact of death. Facing these and facing them down, it discovers paradoxically that death grants freedom from the imprisoning contexts of life. Death, the endpoint of the myth of life, the final dissolver of the individual life, opens or re-opens the myth to new constructions, to new life.[17]

Dealing with death, as I said earlier, is not new to Dickens. The lessons offered by the death of Nell in *The Old Curiosity Shop* are a legacy to all the other novels, a legacy most obviously present in *Our Mutual Friend* as the death of little Johnny. His death I take to be a kind of ground note: the central fact of death is not blurred. The clergyman presiding at the burial puts aside misgivings of his brethren that "they were required to bury the dead too hopefully" (386). But there is a certain softening: the blue-eyed and dimpled toddler can ask whether God will cure children of their pain, gives away all his toys to a suffering child, and as a last wish sends "A kiss for the boofer lady," Bella Wilfer. We are meant to be distressed and moved but not to puzzle the question any more than the clergyman does. The Boffins learn that they cannot re-create the child they once knew as John Harmon; the fact that the child must be given up is to be accepted and indeed had already been accepted by Betty Higden, the remarkable woman who had given him up for adoption.

For those who live on to the normal term of existence, Betty's death sets a standard for dying, her death being a constant affirmation of her life. The conditions of the myth are fully present; the hostile energies, the forces that would dissolve and destroy her essential self press upon her. Her response is to be more than equal to their power to destroy her before the fact of death destroys all together. She asserts her independence, makes gestures of love and acceptance, and finally gains for herself a gesture of love. As she has agreed to give up Johnny for adoption, she leaves Sloppy, her only help, that he may advance himself. Despite her years she refuses all help as she trudges her way to death across the English countryside. She dies as a burden neither to the parish nor to her friends and achieves a sense of what her death, and deaths like hers, may be.[18]

That sense is multifold, and the language of the novel stretches to suggest a breadth that is social, pagan, Romantic, and Christian. She has visions: the Thames, in which other characters die so violently, is "the tender river" (567), calling sweetly, and on its waves she sees her dead children coming for her on a funeral barge. The tree under which she chooses to die reminds her of "the foot of the Cross, and she [commits] herself to Him who died upon it" (575). She has chosen the particular tree because from it the lighted windows of a factory are visible. Fleeing from the Parish workhouse, envisioning "many furious horsemen" (574) who hunt her down as a criminal, Betty had wanted to be found by one of her class and kind who would understand her. She dies, as she wishes, in the arms of a factory hand, Lizzie Hexam, who does understand and who, at the last moment, lifts "her as high as Heaven" (577). We think of the purposive ambiguity of similar phrases when Little Nell and Johnny die. Betty's death has become the crown and ultimate reality of her life.

Betty has considered what her coming death would mean, has taken the knowledge seriously, and used it to protect her essential self. Two other deaths and one near-death in the novel point the moral by contrary example. Gaffer is the first of the selfish, guilt-tainted characters to die. Caught in his own lines, he drowns, and, as his body is being recovered, the taunting, vatic wind asks whether he has been "baptized unto Death." Has he never seen himself, it asks, as he is lying now, as a "shape soaking into [his own] boat"? The wind means to shame the corpse, and it forces "his face towards the rising sun, that he may be shamed the more" (222). His last act, as death steals him from life, has been to steal from the dead. Mr. Dolls is a later minor example. Dolls has so immersed himself in rum that no saving baptismal waters can awaken him to self-consciousness, and long before dying he has devolved into the child of his own daughter, Jenny Wren. She, his lone mourner, has a brief cry and then cheers up again.

The near-death of Riderhood has similar thematic resonances. "Riderhood suspended between life and death is a mystery to be looked on with awe," says A. E. Dyson, but the mystery and its possible meanings work no change on him when he is revived.[19] Given a second chance at life, he can only return to his foul and truculent ways and takes from the experience one lesson, an incorrect one that he need not fear death by water. In the manner of all the myth's blind, self-interested energies, he meets Headstone's attempt to take over his life by forcefully taking over Headstone's. He claims oneness with the master by giving the latter's class a lesson in marine geography and fishing. He thus helps Headstone forge the tight, unbreakable union in which they fall to violent, meaningless death.

The near-death Harmon suffers just before the novel opens was for Dickens the key action of *Our Mutual Friend*, and its doubling later to include Wrayburn joins the double plot in shared significance. Both men are victims, imprisoned by the wills of their fathers and able to free themselves only by consenting to their own deaths.

In terms of the myth Harmon's choice to remain dead is only apparently negative, for in effect he is taking positive action to validate goodness. It is true that for a time the attack and the drugged coffee drive him out of a sense of who he is, and the first words he speaks in the novel are "I am lost!"[20] But "the living-dead man" (430) gradually understands that his "death" has rewarded the faithful, deserving Boffins and that, had he not "died," his marriage with the beautiful Bella Wilfer would have been a purely mercenary affair. Alive, he would only have conformed to the corrupted will of his father. When previously alive, so to speak, he has influenced others only to the extent that his lonely, unhappy childhood has been "an incentive to good actions done [by the Boffins] in [his] name" (429), and he had better remain dead.

Since his "death" has "pronounced lastly on each deed" of his first life, he may say with a smile, "I have now to begin life" (142). He takes it up once more but this time under no compulsion. Since he knows what the malevolent energies can do, he is prudent and wily. Since he knows the standards by which death will judge him, he will not put on his old self until he has fair certainty that he will do no harm.

The near-death of Eugene Wrayburn, which also baptizes him into new life, inscribes the same relation we have seen earlier between life and aftermath, self-making and fulfillment, altruism and selfishness. In Wrayburn's case, however, the scales of judgement tip precariously one way and another. Likeable, witty, and sympathetic, he is also feckless, self-indulgent, and undirected. The language of myth characterizes him as both victim and brute beast, but such is his self-knowledge that he uses these terms of himself. He can see the surpassing value of Lizzie but has neither the character nor will to act definitively. The crisis is social and sexual; class differences make them unsuitable partners, and he should give her up, but he cannot do so.

As they meet by the river, the terms of their discourse are proleptic of fatality. She has "struck dead" "the cursed carelessness" of his old life, and he almost wishes she "had struck [him] dead along with it" (760). She tells him of Betty Higden, who made her "promise that her purpose should be kept to, after she was dead, so settled was her determination." Like her, Lizzie says, she will not yield up her determination even though Wrayburn "should drive [her] to death" (762). He has already forced her to take flight once; now he "force[s] her to disclose her heart, . . . and he made her do it" (763). The words show him still partially on the side of the aggressors and enforcers, and we recall his taking over other people's names, the rough way he seizes Charlie's face when they first meet, and his calculated cruelties to Headstone.

Yet now, in response to her love and her resolution, he holds her "almost as if she were sanctified to him by death" and kisses her "almost as he might have kissed the dead" (640). This is startling since the one word "almost" keeps the action from symbolically yielding Lizzie up to death while affirming that such a death (like Nell's and Betty's) would bless her for him. But he is irresolute, and though his thoughts cannot conceal "their wickedness," he is still pondering "The crisis!" as Headstone strikes him from behind.

In the stages of Wrayburn's slow recovery, it is not enough that he indicates he wishes to marry Lizzie that the "reparation may be complete" (811). More is required for him to meet the criteria by which John Harmon and Betty Higden have been measured: he must be willing to die for another. And he is. That he may not betray Lizzie's deep, forgiving love of him, he says to her, "I ought to die, my dear!" (825). The acceptance frees him, and thereafter there is no question that he will survive. Like Harmon, he has "now to begin life."

For the most part, the regenerative terms with which we have been dealing do not apply to the other characters. But Bella Wilfer, as often has been noticed, describes a pattern less violent yet almost as radical as Wrayburn's. And Mr. Venus, who makes his living from death,[21] nevertheless articulates his own unpromising parts into a fair replica of a lover. But as for Jenny

Wren, we see in retrospect that her breath-taking invitation, "Come up and be dead! Come up and be dead!" (291), brilliantly and proleptically sets the terms for salvation in the novel's mythic world. She does more of course, for hers is an imaginative creativeness that transforms the tattered materials of her life so that soul can clap its hands and sing. She is angry and bright, and defiant of circumstance and cruelty, as she needs to be. But it is her art, the mimic life of her dolls and her visions of angel children, that moves to escape artistry of another order, escape from self into self-transcendence, from hopeless pity into "sorrowful happiness" (334).[22]

An argument might be made that Dickens' mind, over-burdened with thoughts of his own death, is in *Our Mutual Friend* turning his back on normal expectations for happiness and wishing only for easeful acceptance. Edgar Johnson notes the incidence of death among Dickens' friends in the 1860s and entitles his chapter for the period "Intimations of Mortality." But Dickens' correspondence in the years when *Our Mutual Friend* was forming in his mind betrays no morbidity.[23] The word *death*, its cognates, and words suggestive of death appear in their hundreds in the novel, and dozens of references to death are simply gratuitous. Dickens' mind was on death, no doubt, but positively in the manner of an explorer of meaning. Unlike earlier, when he looked at death in life and cried, "Oh, the pity of it!", now he looks at life through death and finds it sad but not an enemy of happiness.

As a sign, his comic inventiveness, as Chesterton joyfully noted, bursts into a glorious Indian summer,[24] and he spends it freely on Wegg and the whole of Veneering society. His final scene leaves their world behind, politely dismissed by the polite and finally forceful Twemlow. The final passage reminds us of Yeats and the old seers of "Lapis Lazuli" with whom his sense of life and death has much in common. Their eyes are gay, and Mortimer Lockwood, accompanying Twemlow as they leave the society of the dead and faring toward the Temple, does so "gaily."

### NOTES

1. Geoffrey Thurley uses "myth" in a yet broader sense than mine to include Dickens' attitudes toward society and money. He sees *Our Mutual Friend* interestingly as a "last period" work, comparable to *The Tempest, John Gabriel Borkman*, and *The Magic Flute*. See *The Dickens Myth: Its Genesis and Structure* (London: Routledge and Kegan Paul, 1976).
2. As Edwin Eigner has pointed out, *Great Expectations* is the exception to Dickens' usual practice in this regard. See his "The Absent Clown in *Great Expectations*," *Dickens Studies Annual: Essays on Victorian Fiction*, 11, eds. Michael Timko,

Fred Kaplan, and Edward Guiliano (New York: AMS Press, 1983), pp. 115–133, and in vol. 14 of the same publication (1985) his "David Copperfield and the Benevolent Spirit," pp. 1–15.

3. The conservative side of Dickens' political and social ideas is explored for the early novels in Myron Magnet's *Dickens and the Social Order* (Philadelphia: University of Pennsylvania Press, 1985).

4. "The Language of *Martin Chuzzlewit*," *Studies in English Literature, 1500–1900*, 20 (1980), 637–649.

5. The Pilgrim Edition of *The Letters of Charles Dickens*, eds. Madeline House and Graham Storey (Oxford: Clarendon Press, 1965—), I, 97 (referred to hereinafter as *Letters*).

6. Ruskin's remark is the most famous: Dickens, he said, "chooses to speak in a circle of stage fire." But he also said, "The things he tells us are always true." See *The Works of John Ruskin*, eds. E. T. Cook and A. Wedderburn, Library Edition, London: George Allen, 1903–12, XVII, 31.

7. Joseph Conrad, *The Secret Agent: A Simple Tale* (London: J. M. Dent and Sons, 1947), p. 220.

8. Fred Kaplan, ed., *Charles Dickens' Book of Memoranda* (New York: The New York Public Library, 1981), p. 19.

9. Hexam is seen as a debased version of the Christian fisher of men in Barry V. Qualls's *The Secular Pilgrims of Victorian Fiction* (Cambridge: Cambridge University Press, 1982), p. 123.

10. *Our Mutual Friend*, ed. Stephen Gill (Harmondsworth: Penguin Books, 1971), p. 70. All subsequent citations from the novel will be from this edition.

11. John Kucich considers the extent to which the excessive language of Dickens is "non-signifying" and the help to reading given by the stylistic modes in which it is presented. My reading, by contrast, is what he would call "context-oriented." See his "Dickens' Fantastic Rhetoric: The Semantics of Reality and Unreality in *Our Mutual Friend*," *Dickens Studies Annual*, 14, eds. Michael Timko, Fred Kaplan, and Edward Guiliano (New York: AMS Press, 1985), pp. 167–189.

12. The suggestion is Angus Wilson's in his *World of Charles Dickens* (New York: Viking Press, 1970), p. 280.

13. G. W. Kennedy's "Naming and Language in *Our Mutual Friend*," *Nineteenth-Century Fiction* 28 (1973), 165–178, first alerted me to the kinds of uses names served in the novel.

14. In *Between Men: English Literature and Male Homosexual Desire* (New York: Columbia University Press, 1985), p. 169, Eve K. Sedgwick says that their deaths are described in the language of male rape. In general, labeling male relationships in the novel as homophobia or homophylia distorts by oversimplification.

15. See Stanley Friedman, "A Loose Thread in *Our Mutual Friend*," *Dickens Studies Newsletter* 1, no. 2 (1970), 18–20.

16. For an informed and sympathetic account of the difficulties of teachers like Headstone see Philip Collins's *Dickens and Education* (London: Macmillan, 1963), pp. 159–171. Using the insights of modern psychology and sociology, John Kucich argues that repression and violence in characters like Headstone are part of the same "general economy." See his "Repression and Representation: Dickens's General Economy," *Nineteenth-Century Fiction* 38, (1983), 62–77.

17. For an excellent general treatment of death in Dickens, see Alexander Welsh, *The City of Dickens* (Oxford: Clarendon Press, 1971), pp. 180–212. Death in *Our Mutual Friend* has attracted much attention but not as the test and final

resolution of Dickens' central myth. The subject is part of J. Hillis Miller's excellent structuralist analysis in *Charles Dickens: The World of His Novels* (Cambridge, Mass.: Harvard University Press, 1965), pp. 314–327. In addition to method and emphasis, the present discussion differs from Miller's in stressing the judgmental importance of death throughout the novel. Andrew Sanders's *Charles Dickens: Resurrectionist* (New York: St. Martin's Press, 1982) follows a discussion of Dickens' views on resurrection by reading *Our Mutual Friend* as expressing "the reality of the hope that the resurrected few may show the way to the many" (197). In *Dickens Quarterly* 1 (1984), 97–105, Garrett Stewart objects to Sanders's reading as "biography passing over . . . toward Christian apologetics," and his own essay, "The Secret Life of Death in Dickens," *Dickens Studies Annual*, 11, eds. Michael Timko, Fred Kaplan, and Edward Guiliano (New York: AMS Press, 1983), pp. 177–207, brilliantly illustrates the kind of reading he prefers though he does not there consider *Our Mutual Friend*. His *Death Sentences* (Cambridge, Mass.: Harvard University Press, 1984) devotes three analytical pages to the death of Betty Higden.

18. In *Laughter and Despair: Readings in Ten Novels of the Victorian Era* (Berkeley: University of California Press, 1971), pp. 156–160, U. C. Knoepflmacher stresses notions of resurrection, regeneration, and salvation in *Our Mutual Friend* as aspects of the characters' imaginative beliefs.

19. A. E. Dyson, *The Inimitable Dickens: A Reading of the Novels* (London: St. Martin's Press, 1970), p. 266.

20. In his deconstructive reading Steven Connor suggests that Harmon's account is "not necessarily a privileged version" because Harmon says, "There was no such thing as I, within my knowledge" (*OMF*, 426). The blurring is caused by his having just drunk drugged coffee. But only when drugged is Harmon absent from himself; before the blurred period and to the end of the section he refers to himself unqualifiedly as "I." See Connor's *Charles Dickens* (Oxford: Basil Blackwell, 1985), p. 157.

21. The point is noticed by James R. Kincaid in *Dickens and the Rhetoric of Laughter* (Oxford: Clarendon Press, 1971), p. 251.

22. The phrase "escape artistry" is Garrett Stewart's from his brilliant analysis of Jenny in *Dickens and the Trials of Imagination* (Cambridge, Mass.: Harvard University Press, 1974), p. 214.

23. An interesting exception might be noted. On the night of December 31, 1863, Dickens had made a device representing the Goddess of Discord to be used in charades with his children. It came into his head that it was like the dismal things used in funerals. He cut away at its black calico, but the image of death so much persisted that he slashed it to pieces before he went to sleep. "All this would have been exactly the same," he wrote, "if poor Walter had *not* died that night. And examining my mind closely since I received the news [of his death in India], I recall that at Thackeray's funeral I had sat looking at the very object of which I was reminded." *The Nonesuch Letters*, eds. Arthur Waugh, Hugh Walpole, Walter Dexter, and Thomas Hatton (Bloomsbury: The Nonesuch Press, 1937–38), III, 379–380.

24. G. K. Chesterton, *Appreciations and Criticisms of the Works of Charles Dickens* (London: J. M. Dent & Sons, 1933), p. 207.

# Social Harmony
# and Dickens' Revolutionary Cookery

## James E. Marlow

In 1850, when Charles Dickens launched *Household Words*, the condition
of England was still grim. If physical hunger was less widespread than it had
been in the 1830s and 1840s, a spiritual hunger seemed nevertheless to cling
to the nation. Dickens announced that the purpose of *Household Words* was
no less than "to bring the greater and lesser in degree, together . . . and
mutually dispose them to a better acquaintance and a kinder understanding."[1]
In a word, he was promising to root out social disharmony. This intention
was carried on from 1859 by the new periodical *All the Year Round*, whose
projected but discarded name made his intention evident.[2] For harmony to
come about he would first have to expose and remove the causes of alienation,
illness, and hunger. Both periodicals were conducted on the premise that the
education of the "People governed" would do more to ameliorate the spiritual
hunger of England and to move towards social harmony than all the legislation,
industrialization, unionization, patronage, policing, and sermonizing could
ever do.

The disharmony had many causes, some of which could be remedied by
material changes. Dickens' journals were from the very first fervent in their
concern for improvements in the realms of political economy and public
policy. Certainly, Dickens' efforts on behalf of improvements in sanitation,
housing, education, and the factory laws are well known. Not so well known
are his efforts as the editor of two popular journals to alter the national disgrace
in private realms of animal economy and domestic economy known as English
cookery. It is arguable that no subject receives more continuous attention over
the course of his editorship than cookery. Articles about food, nutrition,
cooks, cooking, and dining customs pepper his journals. To trace the decided

emphasis on concerns of domestic economy that is evident in the journals—even leaving aside the ample but well-known evidence of this concern in the novels, such as *David Copperfield*—is to discover a coherent and determined editorial policy.

Dickens' journals were not the only nor even the first journals in the early Victorian period to feature articles on food, restaurants, the physiology of digestion, and the customs of dining. The *London Quarterly Review*, *Chamber's Journal* and *Blackwood's*, for example, frequently had articles on cookery before *Household Words* even came into being. By the same token, other journals such as *Good Words* and Thackeray's *Cornhill* included such topics as soon as they began, ten years later. Obviously, food is an attractive subject for magazines because it is a topic largely immune to political, religious, or social biases, and articles about it would offend few readers. The growing popularity of the subject notwithstanding, there is in Dickens' journals a consistent, didactic, even proselytizing strain that is missing elsewhere. Although the majority of the articles were not by Dickens, many were written by such tried and trusted hands as Morley, Wills, Sala, and others; all told, I believe the articles, as they analyze, debunk, inform, and reform English attitudes toward food and its consumption, reveal Dickens' editorial concerns and personal values.

Englishmen in general had begun to pay more attention to what went into their stomachs. Part of this was due to the new realization that the health of the individual could be directly affected by the food he ate. As Bruce Haley states in *The Healthy Body*, "No topic more occupied the Victorian mind than Health—not religion, or politics, or Improvement, or Darwinism."[3]

Science had made great advances in the understanding of digestion and of food value. Indeed, it can be argued that the naive etiological thrust and materialist bias of nineteenth-century science attributed too much to the direct effects of diet, from personal health to national characteristics. For some scientists, the edict *"Mann ist was er iszt"* was scarcely an exaggeration. A typical example is that of the famous chemist Justus von Liebig:

> It is certain that three men, one of whom has had a full meal of beef and bread, the second cheese or salt fish, and the third potatoes, regard a difficulty which presents itself from entirely different points of view. The effect of the different articles of food on the brain and nervous system is different, according to certain constituents peculiar to each of these forms of food.[4]

The reactions to such reductive hypotheses were frequent and predictably humorous.[5] But for the most part—the utter disregard for the economic and social status of those who eat the beef, cheese, or potatoes notwithstand-ing—invaluable information on the nutritional values of various foods and the processes of assimilation was being discovered. News of these discoveries was eagerly awaited by the reading public.

Another reason for the increase in interest in food was reflected in and perhaps stimulated by the popular work of Brillat-Savarin *Physiologie du Gout*, which had been translated early in the century. Despite the surface bias of a materialist and physiologist, and occasional references to issues of health, this writer portrayed dining as an art. Company and conversation were scarcely less important than the food itself. Brillat-Savarin writes that the science of gastronomy not only watches over the preservation of mankind by "laying down certain principles to direct the search, supply, or preparation of ali-mentary substances" but it "also considers how food may influence the moral nature of man, his imagination, his mind, his reason, his courage and his perceptions, whether awake or asleep, whether in action or repose."[6] The title of an English variation on Brillat-Savarin's theme is instructive. Thomas Walker called his book *The Art of Dining and of Attaining High Health*, by a Bon Vivant.[7] Walker concludes, "I consider what I have said on the 'Art of Dining' to be part of my observations on the 'Art of Health.' One reviewer risked the obvious to quote, "Health obviously depends in a great measure on the number, quality, and quantity of our meals."[8] But, in fact, concern for health gets very little more attention than that in either of the books. For Dickens, as for Brillat-Savarin and for Walker, the company with whom we take our meals was quite as important and quite as subject to improvement as the content of our meals.

Between chemists and bon vivants, the interest in cookery was accelerating in England. But, also, science was clarifying the methods of improving the health of both rich and poor, and Dickens dedicated a significant portion of his journals to the propagation of these methods. Public harmony, Dickens evidently assumed, would naturally follow.

I

To judge by the majority of the articles published on the subject, the fact was that the English suffered dreadfully from food. For the poor in England, both the quantity and quality of the food they consumed left much to be desired. In the first place the poor sometimes suffered from a total want of food because during the Victorian period there were erratic rises and falls in

manufacturing activity. A working-class family might find itself with plenty
to eat for one half of the year and with next to nothing in the succeeding half.
What was worse, among the many orphaned and neglected children of slum
London come to be fed on charity, one could see

> the keen look of conscious hunger—God help them!—and the deadened look
> of creatures who, by the brutalization of poverty, have never attained the full
> use of their faculties. Some come half famished, and are scarcely to be satisfied;
> but, after a short course of sufficing "dinings-out," the wolfish hunger is
> appeased, and the appetite becomes more natural and healthy. Others cannot
> eat much at first . . . [which] is a sadder thing to see than wolfish hunger;
> telling as it does, of depressed vital functions and organs absolutely undeveloped
> through privation.                                      (*AYR*, XV, 132)

The "wolfish hunger" no doubt reminded many readers of the bestial qualities
of the revolutionaries in Carlyle's *The French Revolution*.

In "Houseless and Hungry," written by Augustus Sala,[9] there is a bitter
outburst which is reminiscent of some of those by Dickens in *Our Mutual
Friend*:

> I abide by the assertion, that men and women die nightly in our golden streets,
> because they have no bread to put into their mouths, no roofs to shelter their
> wretched heads. It is no less a god-known, man-neglected fact, that in any state
> of society in which such things can be, there must be something essentially
> bad, rotten.                                      (*HW*, XIII, 125–126)

But even those who are not destitute do not eat well in England:

> The school of adversity teaches the poor to hunger patiently when the cupboard
> is empty, but to reward themselves, by hasty cooking and large meals, when
> they have a chance of filling it. The food they throw away from ignorance of
> correct culinary principles, when food is to be had, would, properly husbanded
> and prepared, satisfy the cravings of hunger when money is scarce.
>                                                  (*HW*, XVI, 162)

If the facts about the working-class meal at home are dismal, the working
man who attempted to eat out was no better off. Addressing the "gentlemen
of the Imperial Commission for Ameliorating the Condition of Mankind,"
another of Dickens' writers points out that one need not, like Mrs. Jellyby,
"go all the way to Central Africa, or the wilds of South America, to study
the condition and habits of savages, when the New Cut, Lambeth, is within
ten minutes' walk of the House of Parliament" (*AYR*, XV, 589). Savages
abound in London, the journal suggests, not because of poverty only but

because of official indifference to the facilities available to the poor. The (generic) Mr. Whelks mentioned by the article

> is spending money freely in meat and drink, paying more for a coarse meal, served in a beastly eating-house than you, honorable sir, are charged for your elegantly served lunch in the splendid salon of the Reform club.

Each Mr. Whelks spends his "evenings in sloppy beer-shops, or in some wretched dusthole of a 'gaff.' And yet that man earns money enough to live cleanly and wholesomely" (590). We note in passing that Mr. Whelks has a hunger for solid entertainment as well as good food—these hungers are given equivalency here, as they often are in Dickens' work, for both are necessary to the human spirit. But his environment offers the typical English working man little to satisfy either hunger.

The facts in the case of the middle class are no more promising. "Innutricious, wasteful, and unsavory cooking is our national characteristic. . . . Prosperity is also a bad school for the middle classes, whose gastronomic ambition is literally bounded by roast and boiled" (*HW*, XVI, 162). Among the well-to-do the national cookery also has a severe effect. "It may seem a dreadful doctrine to poetical people, but two-thirds of a man's woes begin in his stomach" (*AYR*, XV, 295). Illness, one source claimed, is often the result of "eating raw mutton chops, and from indigestion caused by potato-bullets."

> Medical statistics tell us that of all diseases with which the English are afflicted, those arising directly or indirectly from impaired digestive organs are the most prevalent. . . . A Frenchman or a German devours much more at one of his own inexhaustible *tables d'hote* than an Englishman consumes at his dining-table—and with impunity; for the foreigner's food being properly prepared is easily digested.
> (*HW*, I, 139)

To eat less, and to suffer more: surely this is to add injury to national insult. The fact is that in England even those who can afford to eat very well generally eat very badly, for the preparation of food in England leads all too often to dyspepsia. It is no laughing matter: "People die of indigestion as well as of starvation; the sufferings of the one case are equal to those in the other" (*HW*, XII, 70). And suffering is but a poor basis for establishing equality and harmony. For the middle class also, the national cookery was a dismal art.

Insufficient food or indigestible food—the results of both spell misery for the mass of Englishmen. The *sine qua non* of both good nutrition and pleasant dining was the art of cookery. As Brillat-Savarin's Fundamental Truth III says, "The fate of nations depends upon how they are fed." Therefore, to a large degree, it is upon a revolution in the kitchen that Dickens will make his bid to establish a new harmony in England.

II

The results of the dismal art of English cookery go far beyond the matter of wasted or inedible food and dyspepsia. A deep demoralization of society has set in. As one result, the waste of provisions that is concomitant with the English style of cooking reduces the amount of money available for other purposes. This point is reiterated several times: the "foreign tribes who live on the other side of the channel, get very much more out of their money than we do" (*AYR*, VIII, 477). Even granting a preference for English taste, "Our system of plain cookery is very nice, but very extravagant" (*AYR*, XIX, 58). Unable to make the most of their food, the poor are unable to make the most of their wages; unable to make the most of their wages, they are unable to make the most of their lives. "Enjoyments of life are few to the poor; eating was meant to be a common pleasure, and is unwholesome when it is unpleasant" (*AYR*, IX, 353). The results of English cooking are manifold—wasted food, wasted money, wasted health, wasted opportunities, and wasted spirit.

It is difficult to exaggerate the consequences which Dickens' periodicals saw issuing from bad cooking. The majority of working men found their home dinners inedible. The results? "The man quarrels with his wife because there is nothing he can eat, and he generally makes up in drink for the deficiencies in the article of food. Gin is the consolation to the spirits and the resource to the balked appetite" (*HW*, I, 140). Of course drinking both taxes the resources with which to purchase food and impairs the capacity to work and provide a sufficiency. Thus, an entire segment of the population was in danger of losing social purpose and personal dignity—and English cookery had to bear a real proportion of the blame. Obviously, large-scale economic, political, and ideological factors were also at work; but from Dickens' point of view these larger factors not only found representation in but also exercised, as we shall see, a direct effect on British cookery. In several ways, then, British cookery added a real increment to the dissatisfaction of the poor, and spawned another barrier to national harmony.

Among the well-to-do, home dinners were, like those of Dora in *David Copperfield* and those of Mrs. Pocket in *Great Expectations*, all too often marred by culinary incompetence, both on the part of the cook and on the part of the mistress of the house.

> At any rate, many poor husbands, tired of their Barmecide feasts—which disappoint the taste the more because they have often a promising look to the eye—prefer better fare at their clubs; and escape the Scylla of bad digestion to be wrecked on the Charybdis of domestic discord. All this is owing to the wife's culinary ignorance, and to your 'Good Plain Cooks.' (*HW*, I, 140)

A "good plain cook" implies a cook not boasting French "tricks," such as pot-au-feus, but who cooks only simple roasts and chops. Although the subject of "good plain" cookery is often treated humorously, the recurrence of the phrase in the jourals brings home what appears to have been a general problem: "I advertised for a plain cook, but I never expected such a very plain cook; such a Salisbury-plain cook as this" (*AYR*, II, 7). Even when there is "a fine, portly lioness at home, to keep house for me, and rule the roast, as it is pleasantly termed" (*HW*, XVII, 453), she apparently managed so badly that she often failed to please the British lion at home (apparently driving him to pun).

Other consequences besides indigestion and domestic disharmony attend this failure of English cookery. The system has a decided tendency to ruin the morality of servants. Mrs. Pocket's servant, lying drunk with butter tied up to sell, is a fictional example. In his journalism Dickens cites a letter from a butcher who had admitted continual cheating of a household through collusion with the cook (*AYR*, VIII, 474–478). Such cheating was made too easy by the culinary ignorance and the managerial incompetence of the housewife. But, alas,

> What is she to do? If she discharge her cook, she tumbles back straight into a morass of cold soup, ice-bound gravy, and public humiliation. If she retain that wicked, wicked woman, she is in a manner conniving and pandering to crime (475).

The great reluctance on the part of the English mistress of the house to inspect the books frequently, and to familiarize herself with markets and prices, causes much of the cheating. And again:

> Our ladies of London cannot now go to the market, and those who have a personal interview with the butcher are the exception. The rule is a red book, in which the weights sent by the butcher are accepted by the cook or housekeeper, or by any other grander person who rules the roast and boiled, the stewed and fried. . . . The system destroys the butcher's conscience, if he had any to start with. (*AYR*, XIX, 57)

Thus English cookery affects not only personal health and domestic harmony, it has a discernible and deleterious effect on the moral condition of the society as a whole.

Another result of the current state of English cookery, and a symptom of the general demoralization of England, was the wholesale adulteration of foodstuffs. The frequent rumors and incidental reports were scientifically verified by Arthur Hill Hallam, MD, in *The Lancet* in 1854 and 1855. He showed the adulteration of foodstuffs was of such a scale as to create a real concern for health of the nation, casting grave doubts about the ethics of the majority of wholesalers. Of 56 samples of cocoa bought in stores in London, for instance, only 8 proved to be genuine. *The Parliamentary Debates* (Hansard, Vol. 156, 1860) reports that "The Committee, however, has established the fact that adulteration was practised wherever it was possible" (p. 2025). For example, the gunpowder tea they examined turned out to be a lovely mixture of "large quantities of tea and silkworm's dung" (p. 2027). Such revelations eventually prompted the passage of legislation outlawing the adulteration of foods. The legislation received Royal Assent on August 6, 1860, but the culinary condition of England was not to be improved by fiat, nor quickly.

In any case the laws would not have been in time to save the narrator of a humorous article printed in 1855 in *Household Words*, called "The Starvation of an Alderman." Shocked by news of the widespread adulteration of food, the narrator writes,

> We decided that it was impossible to go on taking our meals, and that our dinner-party must be put off until I had time to reconstitute society and make the dealers in food honest, as I hope they will be come when they have heard how dreadfully we suffer.     (*HW*, XI, 216)

Despite the humorous tone, Dickens did intend to reconstitute society, and in a manner more likely to succeed, he believed, than legislation. The problems that beset the nation's cookery had the same cause as the adulteration of foodstuffs, and this cause could best be eliminated through publicity and education.

The Victorian custom of dragging dinner parties into the late hour is another result of English dining customs which militates against healthy sociability. In fact, these late soirees after large dinner parties have a deleterious effect on true civilization:

> No doubt the theatres suffer by this to a considerable extent, and it is even possible that the general decline in dramatic matters may have been brought

James Gillray's satiric view of the contrast between French and English economics and nutrition.

about by this among other causes; it being well-nigh impossible to get together
an audience of enlightened people, ready to devote a whole evening to the
consideration of a carefully elaborated work of art. After a modern dinner it
is too late to think of going to a play.                              (*AYR*, XV, 82)

If we remember that for Dickens the hunger for entertainment that sustains
the spirit is nearly as important as hunger for physical sustenance, we realize
what a menace the Victorian system of dinings-out was. "Guests upon the
continent always take leave of their host about seven, so that he is not bored
to death with them all the evening. A dinner means a dinner, and nothing
more, and a dinner party is not, as with us, the miserable waste of hours."
And the cause of this unhappy and, indeed, "miserable waste of hours" was
conspicuous consumption, a potlatch of display, like that of the Veneerings
(*OMF*, I, 2), which lacked even the desire to make people happy.

Victorians were not slow to express their consciousness that attending such
social gatherings was little more than an onerous duty. They knew that their
customs had turned what ought to be an occasion of the most humane pleasure
into what was only pretense, discomfort, and dissatisfaction. As one writer
was dressing to attend such an evening dinner party, he paradoxically felt
that "my heart was fainting within me at the prospect of going out to dinner"
(*AYR*, I, 396). The prospect grows no fairer as it nears:

How should I feel in three hours' time, when the evening party, which was to
follow the dinner, began, and when I and a hundred other polite propagators
of animal heat were all smothering each other within the space of two drawing-
rooms . . . ?

After smothering a while, the victim slips outside, and, in looking back inside,
he is aware of his narrow escape. "It is the Black Hole of Calcutta, ornamented
and lit up. It is a refinement of slow torture unknown to the Inquisition and
the North American savages. And the name of it in England is pleasure."
It is called pleasure but it has been subverted by the style of conspicuous
consumption. To be truly free the individual must escape from the confines
of such misplaced priorities. In this case, the writer escapes outside. Standing
out on the street beside some poor people looking into the ornamented rooms
he has just left, he can remain superior to their illusions: " 'And sich lots to
drink!' Artless street innocent! unsophisticated costermonger! he actually en-
vies his suffering superiors inside" (398). The extravagance might look attractive to the poor, but the experience is quite otherwise.[10] What caused the
English to rise above comfort and to change pleasure into duty?

## III

The causes of the demoralization of the English table were not far to seek. From Dickens' journals it would seem that there were two prevailing attitudes in England about dining. It was either a necessary but onerous task of re-fueling, or an occasion of conspicuous consumption. Speaking of Dr. Johnson and his times, one writer remarks, "It is plain there were schismatics in his day who did *not* dine—who, at least, found no relish in that enjoyment—and who preached it down as a nuisance, necessary perhaps, and almost una-voidable but still to be pruned and curtailed, and in practice nullified" (*AYR*, IV, 465). The ornate Black Hole of Calcutta, of course, represented the other wrongful attitude. In neither case was the taking of food considered pleasure.

*Household Words* points out that displeasure is not the universal attitude towards the taking of dinner. "People don't ask you to take a bit of dinner with them in Paris. With the French, dinner is an institution" (*HW*, VI, 231). It is a pleasant occasion, to be looked forward to, but not because of its pomp and ceremony. "There is something very sociable and pleasant about the way in which a French bourgeois family prepares a meal" (*AYR*, XX, 228). To dine together is the primary motive, to enjoy company as well as food. "Do not dine alone if you can help it" (*HW*, VI, 231), admonishes the "Roving Englishman" in one of his long series of articles, which, interestingly enough, was entitled "Philosophy of Dining." Dinner in France is neither mere re-fueling nor conspicuous consumption. The question remains then, what has caused the difference in England?

A point reiterated with some frequency in the journals is that it is not often sheer want that dooms the working class to meager portions. It is, rather, ignorance. The wife of an English working man, "on a moderate calculation, throws away one-third of her family's food. She has no culinary resources" (*HW*, IX, 44). After a description of how a poor Frenchman's wife gets the maximum benefit from a piece of beef, the writer makes a comparison to the English mode:

> Had that same joint of ros bif fallen into the hands of an English cook, half of it would have been wasted; two-thirds of the fat would have found their way to the grease-pot, and the bones would have been caste into the dusthole.
> (*HW*, IX, 44)

Besides her outright waste, the working-class wife was unlikely to have the education or imagination to make a meal either nutritious or attractive.

It was expedient to blame the demoralizing cookery of the poor upon their willful ignorance. It had become a commonplace that the "prejudices of the poor are so extraordinary that it has always been a matter of great difficulty to coax them into the use of any new article of food" (*HW*, XIII, 42). Yet, no one prefers indigestion and waste to pleasure and satisfaction. Therefore, there must be causes beyond ignorance since human beings will naturally accept suggestions that lead to real improvements in their comfort. Dickens would be the last person to believe that the culinary habits of the poor were incapable of improvement. The prejudices of the poor imply more than custom; an ideal is also implied. Dickens saw that ignorance was often enough an act of will, the flying of a banner that proclaimed a vice as a virtue; one example is the factitious naturalness implied by the phrase "a good plain cook."

As for the middle class, ignorance was clearly the result of false ideals. One such false ideal was the notion that superior status for a woman required culinary ignorance. Dickens himself argued that no longer can the "daughters of Albion" be "too busy with less useful—though to them scarcely less essential accomplishments"; they must learn to recognize the vast importance of the principles of cookery, "a subject they have never been taught to regard as worthy of their attention" (*HW*, I, 139).[11] Both classes, then, appear to maintain practices created by a false consciousness. If this were the case, then social harmony is by no means beyond the scope of Dickens' journals, for what better weapon could there be against a false consciousness than an impassioned and informed journalism?

One rampant form of false consciousness afflicting both classes is chauvinism. For the majority of Englishmen, all things French were suspicious, and cookery was no exception. The traditional disdain for French cooking can be reduced to what might be called a judgment by cannon:

> Insular vanity has willingly connected our military supremacy with the supposed superiority of our national diet; and, when Hogarth exhibited the stalwart grenadier making a hearty meal off a baron of beef done to a turn, in the presence of several half-starved cuirassiers, who looked pitifully at their bouilli, this was accepted as a witty and pleasing illustration of one of the circumstances which mainly contributed to turn the scale to our favour at Waterloo.
>
> (*HW*, XIX, 522)

The effect being desirable, it seemed that all possible causes must also be desirable. And if the doctrine of materialism turned roast beef into courage, and Englishmen were courageous, who is to contemn the English mode of cooking roast beef? In this way, ignorance could be given the mask of superiority.

The arrogant ignorance, the chauvinism, and the other forms of false consciousness have a cause which Dickens has identified over and over again in his novels[12]—that there was at the heart of the English culture a carelessness, a caringlessness, which has been institutionalized and almost deified as the dominant ideology. Unnatural, unsatisfying, the doctrine nevertheless seems to be the matrix out of which so many approved values derive. Dickens identified an official manifestation of it in *Little Dorrit* as the Circumlocution Office, whose maxim of "How Not To Do It" seems to have permeated society as a whole. Certainly Mrs. Merdle speaks for the official value system when she tells her husband, "I simply request you to care about nothing—or seem to care about nothing—as everyone else does" (*LD*, I, 33). It is this decorous stunting of the capacity to feel that Dickens sees as the primary cause of so many of the ills of English society. For this carelessness (by which Dickens means a lack of *caritas*)—which characterizes the philosophy of government in England—has percolated to all levels of English life. It is the economic doctrine of laissez-faire generalized into the fundamental maxim of English society.

The official side of the doctrine is readily visible in the failure of the government to take responsibility for the enlightenment and improvement of the working classes. When the government is not indifferent to a fault, it seems to be only perverse. As one article argues in its very title, if you enter a pub in England, "You Must Drink!" (*AYR*, XI, 437–440). It says: "The whole system of licensed victualling has been carefully designed and elaborately built up, to compel people to drink and to prevent them from doing anything else" (437). With the complicity of the government, then, public houses do not provide the traveller with what his spirit most requires. The large class of working men are "utterly neglected and left to their own helplessness" (*AYR*, XV, 590).

The problems mentioned by the Uncommercial Traveller may be taken as typical of the problems of English cookery. If the Uncommercial could find nothing worth eating and only disdainful service during his travels to and from London, there were specific causes. In England, railway refreshment bars were supposedly a matter of free enterprise, and competition was supposed to eliminate, according to the venerable doctrine of laissez-faire, the bad and inefficient. But the fact was in England that free enterprise was a sham. Too often an individual was given the monopoly of operating the railroad refreshment stand as a charitable sinecure. In the following example, "old Robert" has obtained such a sinecure and the consequences are grave for both free enterprise and good digestion:

> let us recal [sic] the last time it was our fortune to be allowed behind the scenes
> of a railway refreshment bar. . . . The little bar and the comfortless closet
> attached to it were, after all, neither better nor worse than scores of others on
> the Great Mudland line. . . . Robert's pastry was supplied from the little shop
> around the corner (kept by the head porter's wife), and his beer by the local
> brewer (a director), and his wines and spirits by the leading wine-merchant
> (a large share holder).                                    (*AYR*, XIX, 61)

Under these conditions, "charity to Robert meant cruelty to the public." Not
only was free enterprise a hoax, but the term "refreshment bar" was a wild
misnomer.

Savages abound in London, by 1866 not so much because of economic
factors as because of official indifference to the housing, dining, and recre-
ational facilities of the working classes. If the more generous emotions are
not aroused in the hearts of the ruling classes to know of this wasteland, this
mass of neglected and lowering men, then perhaps they will be stricken by
fear to realize that this savage place is only ten minutes from the seat of
government. Thus the English ideology, which after all does not tolerate
teaching the working class to husband the resources they do have, may be
subverted by a fear of an entire class that has no resources to live a civilized
life. The same doctrine of carelessness that created that apotheosis of carelessness, the New Poor Law, in the first place, has for too long been able to
rationalize neglecting an entire needy class and has even been able to justify
starvation in the streets under the spurious banner of freedom, economic as
well as political.

As the *Uncommercial Traveller*, Dickens indicts some of the public masks
under which the unofficial side of the doctrine of carelessness is concealed.
"I very seldom have been blown to any English place in my life where I
could get anything good to eat and drink in five minutes, or where, if I sought
it, I was received with a welcome" (*AYR*, II, 512). Dickens is referring
specifically to the refreshment stands in railroad stations, where, he writes,
the young ladies who are supposed to restore him have "been from their
infancy directed to the assumption of a defiant dramatic show that I am *not*
expected." Custom seems to have established that it is bad form to suppose
that food and drink were meant to restore body and soul, and that to serve
such restoratives could be considered a high calling. Dickens goes on to mock
the national habit of falling back upon Thomson's lyrics to hide flaws in the
system:

> I am a Briton, and, as such, I am aware that I never will be a slave—and yet
> I have a latent suspicion that there must be some slavery of wrong custom in
> this matter (513).

Dickens frequently seizes upon this vocal and trivialized idea of freedom, suggesting that the insistence on being undominated has made inroads upon true freedom, including freedom to cook well, and freedom to accept human responsibility. Under the banner of political freedom, to exercise care about anything or anybody becomes tantamount to slavishness.

Given the definition of man as the cooking animal,[13] such freedom means the freedom not to be human. The slavery of false custom in this matter is the apparent pretense that food—well-cooked and pleasantly served and shared—could never occupy a respectable person's attention or serve any important function in the march of civilization.

Out of the cherished national principle of laissez faire comes all of the specific and interrelated ailments of the animal and kitchen economies in England: indigestion, unpleasant dinner parties, and, for the poor, ignorance of simple management practices and resulting hunger and excessive reliance on drink. For these specific ailments and the social disharmony that they generate, Dickens' journals recommend remedies to make England whole again.

## IV

The journals engage the causes of disharmony on two different fronts. On the one, they present the specific and positive recommendations for improvements in the content and methods of cookery, in the training of those to be entrusted with the crucial responsibility of cooking, and in the management of the household, that is, the kitchen economy. Simultaneously, the journals hammer away with varied rhetorical attacks on the false ideals that split the nation from other nations, split one class from another class, split man from wife, and split a person from his own "better self." The varied rhetoric used to expose the false ideals that support bad cookery range from muck-raking exposé, to humor, to satire, to comparisons to superior methods, and rational adjuration to do all that is possible to promote health and happiness.

Humor was one of the favored rhetorical devices. A humorous letter, published as a "Chip. English Cookery," called for foreign aid to England:

> The culinary condition of the English is so bad, that nothing but a root and branch reform will ever do them good. With respect to pastry and sweetmeats, there is but one way, and one way only to stem the tide. Let Parliament decree that a Vienna mehlspeis Kochin, or female cook of puddings, be forthwith engaged, brought over to England, and endowed with a salary.
>
> (*HW*, XIII, 116)

But of course Dickens, like Carlyle, was dubious that Parliament was capable of a "root and branch reform" in any field. Fortunately, the reformation of rudimentary attitudes can be achieved in other ways, such as popular journalism. By disseminating information, one might realize genuine improvements. The first step is to expose the causes of the dyspeptic and social disasters that characterized English cooking and dining.

A black humor permeates some of Dickens' perspectives on English society when he writes as the Uncommercial Traveller, especially when he continues to report on the trials of eating out in England. For, contrary to their *raison d'etre*, public houses and restaurants in England seemed to set up barriers to the restoration of the public's spirit. Waiting to be served at one seaside restaurant, the Uncommercial had, with foreboding,

> been taking note of the crumbs on all the tables, the dirty table-clothes, the stuffy, soupy, airless atmosphere, the stale leavings everywhere about, the deep gloom of the waiter who ought to wait upon us, and the stomach-ache with which a lonely traveller at a distant table in a corner was too evidently afflicted.                                    (*AYR*, n.s. I, 109)

Even in 1868, when Dickens puts in his hand to create humor from the dismal condition of English dining-places, the argument nevertheless implies that an evil custom has the nation in thrall. Dickens' humor points up the well-established custom of carelessness that starves the English in both body and soul.

By making direct comparisons to superior culinary ways, the journals keep undermining the false customs obtaining in England. For example, in railway stations throughout England travellers expected only "pork and veal pies, with their bumps of delusive promise, and their little cubes of gristle and bad fat, the scalding infusion satirically called tea, the stale bad buns with their veneering of furniture polish"; even worse is the "icy stare from the counter, the insolent ignoring of every customer's existence, which drives the hungry frantic" (*AYR*, XIX, 60). The only delicious element found in the English system is the irony: "We boast in England of free trade: but, in this particular respect we are far behind France." There "a public house is a place combining elegance with comfort and convenience" (*AYR*, 11, 439). The worst rub is that early in the century, French writers looked to England as the land of superior inns and public taverns.

In France the customer is actually refreshed when he seeks refreshment. "What agreeable memories the travelled English brings with him too from the Continent, of his dinners at French railway stations. Such kindly promptitude, such bland alacrity to oblige'' (*AYR*, XX, 228). Somehow, the French public eating places combined cleanliness, promptness, good service, and delicious food with frugality: "I thought of the many thousands in London who starve more expensively than they could dine at the *Petit Romponneau*" (*HW*, V, 493), a modest restaurant in Paris. Bit by bit, French customs and French cookery are taken as the standard in the pages of the two journals. The evident goal of Dickens' editorial policy is manifested when he speaks of "the peculiar abuses against which we have so long inveighed in vain." Particular abuses may be remedied, in part, by a study of the French diet, policy, and cookery. "Many scientific brains, and many artful heads, have for centuries experimented on French cooking, which, if less solid than the English, is more appetising, more alluring" (*AYR*, XX, 229). It took a generation after Napoleon's death to lay the fears of things French sufficiently to rest to take advantage of the experiments by the French, but the English were finally being induced to consider the French methods.

Dickens has a quintessential English character called Monied Interest offer his "objections" to the French mode of quick refreshment:

> "Says the manner of refreshing is 'not bad,' but considers it French. Admits great dexterity and politeness in the attendants. Thinks a decimal currency may have something to do with their despatch in settling accounts, and don't know but what it's sensible and convenient. Adds, however, as a general protest, that they're a revolutionary people—and always at it" (*Reprinted Pieces*, Oxford University Press, p. 481).

A revolutionary people is precisely what Dickens wishes to raise in England. His journals find in France an acceptable model for the reformation of English cookery. France shows that it is possible to waste less, eat better, and care more. There will be no slavish imitation of the French, but revolutionary cookery in England will restore England to her better self.

In a word, the whole system of French kitchen economy is to be emulated. The French variety of dishes is superior; their preparation excels in flavor and nutrition; the waste is less in both rich and poor households; the dinners are more attractive and satisfying social occasions (which promotes better digestion); the service in restaurants is better; and the domestic servants are more trustworthy. If the task of a critic, of whatever art, is to know the best that is known and thought in the world, as Matthew Arnold wrote, then the pages of Dickens' journals qualify as genuine criticism. For they continuously

inform, and judge, the art of cooking. In the end they leave no doubt for the
necessity of revolution, for "England, alas, must hang her head for shame,
having no children who have fought in this good fight" (*HW*, XIX, 380).
Consequently,

> Britons, in a curious spirit of self-assertion, may protest that they never, never
> shall be slaves; but, for all that, shall suffer frightful slaveship horror for ever
> and aye, through indigestion and unskilfully treated viands.
>
> (*HW*, XIX, 380–381)

Freedom from indigestion, from ill service, ignorance propagated or condoned
by the government, from insular peculiarities, and from the familial and
national disharmony which results from the former is the object of Dickens'
revolution in the kitchen.

It was against a pervasive English contempt for foreign practices, this fear
of physical, moral, and social infection, that *Household Words* and *All the
Year Round* had to wage their struggle to radically alter British culinary
attitudes and practices.

> We have even embodied our contempt in certain popular sneers at the kitchen
> world of some of our neighbors; whose economy seems to us mean rather than
> ingenious, and whose culinary contrivances we suspect to be unwholesome,
> instead of admiring as infinitely better than our own.          (*HW*, XIII, 42)

But there are some sops thrown to patriots: There was not to be a total
abandonment of the British style, for plain dishes could be "admirable of
their kind" (42).

By and large, nineteenth-century materialism implied that among necessary
effects of positive causes, such as race, climate, and era, were "local peculiarities," like cooking.

> It has its own physiognomy, which the wise may decipher. Every local pecu-
> liarity is translated by a corresponding culinary variation.     (*HW*, XIX, 522)

Against the prejudices that prevent improvement Dickens wages war. Materialism therefore seemed to be an ally in the struggle for the revolution, for
its impetus across the entire breadth of culture was to subject customs and
"local peculiarities" to analysis. This kind of tone removed cookery from
the reach of unexamined value judgements, so that suggestions could be
advanced without jingoistic or lapsarian objections being leveled against them.
One article notes that "Monsieur the Cook," M. Victor, can produce "a
most satisfactory and wholesome little dinner" from the scantiest provisions.

The materials, which, in England, would produce only the most unpalatable food, become, in his dexterous hands, the foundations of little dishes of the most various descriptions. Yet M. Victor is not expensive. He laughs at all he hears of English cookery, and wonders how masters can support its extravagance.

(HW, IX, 44)

With a strange assortment of allies, from gourmets to positivists, Dickens' journals argued for a new attitude towards cookery. A new society would be built on what is called "Aristology, or the Science of Dinner-Fellowship" in the article entitled "Home Dinners," (*AYR*, XI, 64). In 1852, citing Thomas Walker, Abraham Hayward had found the etymology of the word "aristology" in "the Greek for *dinner* . . . Ariston," and goes on, "I call the art of dining aristology."[14] Dickens' writer works the root the other way, saying that the Greeks gave the evening meal "the most dignified of names, as 'to Ariston,' the Best" (p. 63).[15] In any case, the task of the man who chooses not to be a slave to archaic dining customs is first to "scout and despise the miserable notion of one fixed form of a conventional dinner-party"; he will instead "delight to give a dinner *like himself*." Such gatherings are "Home Dinners," an occasion which provides,

> whatever its degree of costliness, a sincere welcome, hearty intercourse, and meats and drinks, however modest in their character and small their variety, pleasantly set forth, each the best after its kind.

The conspicuous consumption that so often produces nothing but indigestion will be banished. Pretense of all sorts is banned. Thus Carlyle's concern that friendship in England had degenerated into a state of official dinner-hostings and -guestings is indirectly answered. The precepts of aristology goes beyond the food; the term means "everybody at the great round table making the best—for a wonder—of himself and his neighbor" (67).

> Away, then, we say again, with the whole, greasy indigestible sham of conventional dinner-parties, aping a style inconsistent with the natural means of the giver. Let us substitute for it the Home Dinner everywhere, honest and characteristic.

The Home Dinner, hence, makes of such "local peculiarities" as class and taste a basis on which to build fellowship.

On the basis of this "dinner-fellowship," difference in rank no longer precludes social intercourse. The well-to-do and those of modest income may come together at any dining-board where cleanliness, intelligent choice of viands, educated cookery, and unpretentious good fellowship obtain. In overturning the slavery of wrong custom, aristology is nothing less than revolution by cooking.

The revolution requires that Englishmen revolt against the illusions of privilege. "Paint and varnish, too, overlie the whole system of hospitality . . . where there is no enjoyment, no sociability, no real hospitality, and no real pleasure, but only paint and varnish" (*AYR*, X, 355). Again comparing the usual overcrowded, ostentatious dinner-parties to the "Black Hole of Calcutta," this article goes on:

> But what is *not* paint and varnish, is the pleasant supper. If any one wants to know the meaning of good company, let him inaugurate a series of small suppers, where the men have brains and can talk, and the women are amiable and pretty, perhaps some of them too with brains and the power of being vocal—let him compare his creed with that other code of gilded magnificence, and say which is best.

The condescension here toward women shouldn't blind us to the revolution[16] that *is* nevertheless in progress. For one stage of the Victorian dining ritual was to draw the cloth when the women departed so that the men can get down to serious talk. As the revolution in cookery progresses, the presence of women is no longer restricted to the time for frivolous conversations. For women's presence at the table was coming to be seen by more people than George Meredith as essential: "Now that women had come back to the dining-table to humanize society by their presence there were hopes for good and refined cooking once more" (*AYR*, XX, 225). Under aristology, each man and woman will be at his and her best, and the presence of women will not only humanize the occasions but improve the food.

As the thesis develops in Dickens' periodicals, aristology ultimately becomes a matter of morality. A review of Soyer's *Modern Housewife, or Menagere*, repeated the same concern, voiced earlier by Dr. Kitchener in his *Cook's Oracle*, that poorer men were expected to reciprocate by giving equally grand repasts to richer men. "Few had the moral courage to refrain from this ridiculous assumption of pocket equality" (*Fraser's* 44 [1851], 200). Dickens is obviously intent upon wiping out inequality of income as a barrier to the harmony of the classes. Therefore he insists that men of lower income can entertain men of wealth not by pretense but by honestly providing the best they can afford, not by pocket equality but by equality in cookery.

> Also it is a minor morality to entertain your friends in the best way possible to your means, if so be you are minded to entertain them at all. No mock Gunterisms! no bad Cape wine labelled with high-class names, no pretenses

of French cookery, which are simply English meat made uneatable. Every attempt at things beyond your means is an immorality just as the best you can do is your bounded duty.

(*AYR*, XX, 373)

It is clear that the revolution in cookery means for Dickens the dissolution of the false and pernicious class system; it means healing up the social wound between the two nations of England that Disraeli characterized: it means England can be united at last.

Science will doubtless continue to be devoted to this great art [cookery], which has done much to extend peace, binding families and nations by a common tie.

(*AYR*, XX, 229)

A revolutionary change is coming, and this moral and social change is necessary for the advancement of civilization. After peace and plenty reign at home, they will come to reign in the nation. (*HW*, VI, 232).

## V

Beyond these general attacks on the attitudes and ideas that supported, at once, conspicuous consumption and starvation, Dickens' journals provide numerous specific recommendations of means of achieving changes, as well as words of praise when improvements manifest themselves. From its very first issue, *Household Words* was engaged upon a program of culinary education and indoctrination, both practical and theoretical, aimed at both the individual and society at large. About more formal culinary education, however, it is at first somewhat diffident:

Let us hope that these hints will fructify and be improved upon, and that the first principles of cooking will become, in some way, a part of female education. In schools, however, this will be difficult. It can only be a branch of household education: and until it does so become, we shall continue to be afflicted with "Good Plain Cooks."

(*HW*, I, 141)

Attention was at first directed instead to informal forms of education, such as the book written by the famous chef Alexis Soyer,[17] of whom Dickens thought highly. Later, even a review of a 1660 cookery book brings out this familiar idea:

Passing by the bad taste which took delight in such vandalisms, we might perhaps find some useful hints in our old cookery-book. Certainly we might learn one good lesson—how to make use of every available article of food; how to multiply our present resources, and turn into nourishment and use, material now left wasting by the side of men dying of hunger.

(*HW*, XI, 21–24)

From any and every source the message is transmuted into that consistent with aristology.

Meanwhile, a change in English attitudes toward cookery was gradually taking more specific shape.

And thus the teaching of common things which has been lately talked of, should include, as a most important branch of popular education, the economy of the kitchen. To teach the young idea how to cook is to do a great social good, undoubtedly.          (*HW*, IX, 44)

But as a later article ruefully points out, "what is called common knowledge, is in reality common ignorance," and, what is worse is that what "ought to be the commonest of things found among our educated classes"—the power of independent thought—"is so rare" (*HW*, XIV, 39).

*Household Words* reports that Dickens' long-time friend, Miss Burdett-Coutts, the richest heiress in England, had offered to distribute among the Training Institutions in England "certain prizes varying in value, for the best answers to a set of questions upon which (reserving our own notion of the subject), we follow the rest of society in calling Common Things" (40). But for this writer, as for Dickens, precisely the source of the problem in England was that Common Things like cookery and the economic management of the kitchen are matters of "common ignorance." Too few cooks think and too few wives manage. Therefore, not a code of invariable rules is needed but merely a little thought about the "How and Why" of the kitchen economy. Immeasurable good would evolve from an intelligent woman having been "trained to live by How and Why—always pouring down through these conductors the whole energy of mind upon the matter actually in hand—she will surely make a wise wife or servant." Miss Coutts's prizes point the country in the right direction.

In 1857 *Household Words* asks a question that reveals a certain amount of progress: "Why, it is then asked, are not our national school girls taught to cook?" (*HW*, XVI, 162). The question at least reveals acceptance of the idea that cookery might be beneficially taught in England's training schools. The idea has not only been broached in the private sphere but it has been implemented. The journal reports: "Near to the Christ Church schools, in Albany Street, Regent's Park, this inscription appears on an otherwise blank shop window: SCHOOL OF COOKERY AND RESTAURANT.'' It is a sign to conjure a more harmonious future by.

The problem of ignorance is not, of course, instantly remedied. Two years later *All the Year Round* is complaining that in England the plain cook "never thinks: she does not take my wages to think; she is only a walking plate-warmer, a portable ladle, a human cruet-stand" (*AYR*, II, 7). And the practical, national solution is stated more firmly than ever:

> Why should not all our workhouses have steam-kitchens, where one experienced cook presided, and taught a certain number of the younger girls destined for service, to whom she could give certificates when they have attained sufficient skill to work alone.

To turn workhouse inmates into qualified cooks not only would improve their lot but would benefit society generally. "These schools would discover much latent cooking genius, and soon drive all uncertificated and worthless destroyers of digestion out of the service market." When the indigent are taught to cook, and the well-to-do realize the importance of managing their kitchens efficiently, not only will nutrition be improved but so will the economic condition of England. Beyond these improvements lay the improvement in personal good will and, hence, in public spirit. For, it is a commonplace to say, "how much hope, and love, and truth, and kindness, have been born of a good dinner!" (*HW*, VI, 232).

Although the rich will be served well by improved knowledge in their cooks, it is the poor who will perhaps benefit most, for proper education will show the working classes how to curb wasteful practices. For indeed,

> few blessings are of greater importance than that of well feeding a dense population; and if, by any application of unused material, or by new combinations of those already in use, the sum of the nations food can be increased, a larger national benefit will be wrought than many would like to acknowledge.
>
> (*HW*, XIII, 42)

Malthus had argued near the turn of the century that a man who contributes a few new acres to the production of foodstuffs provides more benefits to the poor than one who distributes great sums of money, which only serves to raise the prices of the available food. Dickens' journals thus propose to augment the culinary resources of the poor an immense one-third, the proportion which it was estimated that they waste in their present cookery. If proper education can achieve this, what a boon for the working man. Brillat-Savarin had asserted long before that the "discovery of a new dish does more for the happiness of the human race than the discovery of a planet.''[18] Given the condition of England, Dickens is likely to have agreed. Practical benefits, therefore, are seen as nearly unlimited: what was needed was practical instruction, and Dickens' journals were not loathe to supply these.

One of the first results of superior training will be a change of diet in England. In the first place, reputation must be replaced by reality. For example, the reputation of England for its roast beef is, ironically, quite undeserved, especially in the Army, whose success had long been popularly attributed to roast beef.

> Roast beef is to be had anywhere except among the Household Brigade. . . . It might be had by any one else, but not by our soldiers. These unfortunate victims of routine have been condemned to a penal diet of everlasting boiled beef. . . . Even if boiling were the best manner of cooking meat, it is indefensible to make it the sole method of dressing it; but, for ordinary purposes, it is the worst.                                               (*HW*, 17, 523)

What is true of the Army has been true of society at large, except when an even more indigestible method is used. When she does not boil meat, the good plain cook "fries everything, and prefers the greasy, unwholesome, soaking mode of cooking to the racy, chastened gridiron, that gives to a chop such a healthy flavour" (*AYR*, II, 7). Grilling, roasting, and stewing meats must come to replace the traditional methods of cooking meat. Moreover, chops and roasts will be supplemented as never before in the diet of Englishmen.

Fish is frequently extolled by both journals as an all-but-unknown entree in the English household. The ordinary Englishman apparently did not like it. In "A Popular Delusion," the question is asked: "Is this aversion to fish unconquerable? If it be not, what an enormous augmentation of wholesome food might be procured to relieve the increasing wants of the humble and needy" (*HW*, I, 220). However unlikely it may now seem that the land of fish and chips ever disdained seafood, such was largely the case.

Years later it is acknowledged that, in England, "We make little use of fish—partly because we don't know how to prepare it" (*HW*, XIII, 45).

> Justice for fish! for the increased use of fish as a cheap article of diet we have pleaded before, and we intend now to gossip further on the subject.

Once educated cookery is introduced, a change will be possible. For example, another article, years later, greeted with delight a "Cookery Manual for Days of Fasting and Abstinence,'' which made fish "exceedingly palatable and delicious" (*AYR*, n.s. I, 353).

The reason that the consumption of fish should be increased is obvious: ". . . the fecundity of the Ocean knows no limits. We may take and eat all we *can* take, without fear or scruple" (*AYR*, XVI, 493). Therefore,

> we say to the landsman, we cannot count the hungry mouths agape for food in this grand country. Let fish descend from the mahogany board of the epicure to the labourer's board.
> (*HW*, III, 421)

In an article entitled "Dear Meat and Cheap Fish," the inducement to alter the English diet toward fish continues: "The present scarcity and consequent high price of animal food is most alarming" (*AYR*, XIV, 537). The particular fish recommended here was the enormously fecund salmon. Scarcity is not yet a consideration.

Another kind of food that is strongly applauded is soup. "In this prejudiced country, the idea connected with soup is, that it is a poor, washy, meagre sort of food, not at all worthy of the true-born Briton" (*HW*, XIII, 44). But soup, declared *All the Year Round*, was the "cheapest, most savoury, and most nourishing food that could be procured" (*AYR*, IX, 353). The title of the article brings the issue to the fore: "The Soup Question." Count Rumford, the article recounts, tells us "that the cheapest, most savoury, and most nourishing food that could be procured, was a soup" (*AYR*, IX, 352). Rumford's notion was that with barley, potatoes, and bread, it required only a "thoughtful soup-maker in the poorest or richest household" to get from discretion, time, patience, and "only pepper, salt, and a few herbs or scraps of vegetable . . . good soup out of anything in which the elements of food exist" (p. 356). Soup would contribute a great deal to the good home dinners that will keep a well-to-do man from fleeing to his club and "a poor man from a bad dear drink abroad" (p. 355).

In a long article in praise of and entitled "French Domesticity," the French housewife is shown haggling with the *marchands*, telling them that they must "ask such prices of the English, who know no better." Having procured the articles at fair prices, because she is knowledgeable, she goes home to her kitchen, where

> she flits around like a fairy, creating magical messes out of raw material of the most ordinary description. She mixes up the milk and eggs that make the foundation of the soupe a l'oseille, if it be a meagre day. This sorrel soup is a great favourite in economical households, and is vaunted as being highly refraichissant for the blood.
> (*HW*, IX, 436)

New items for the menu and better forms of cooking are the major resources in the renovation of English cookery for both rich and poor. But many working men have need of other resources as well. Besides recruiting wives who have learned the lessons of kitchen economy, they can also club together when they are single or away from home. Working men can, "by merely clubbing the price of their separate meals, though but a few halfpence, and dining together, conduce considerable to their own comfort and the advance of the noble art of cookery" (*HW*, VI, 36).

The first volume of *All the Year Round* introduces the well-forgotten character "Philosewers" (whose laudable, eponymous concern for the public welfare can scarcely excuse his cognomen). In search of a temperate temperance, Philosewers and a friend discover a working man's club which is self-controlled and self-controlling. Operating on the principle, which Dickens propagated so often in both his journalism and his fiction, that the working man must be trusted to direct his own destiny, the club sets no limit to the amount of beer each member may buy. But the "club gets its beer direct from the brewer, by the barrel. So they get it good; at once much cheaper, and much better, than at the public house" (*AYR*, I, 14). (It should be noted that beer was one of the most frequently adulterated foods.) The gentleman (a clergyman) who sponsored the club provided primarily advice, using his greater experience in the world for the benefit of the working men, but without coercing or patronizing them. He explains as follows:

> The people are very ignorant, and have been much neglected, and I want to make *that* better, if I could. My utmost object was, to help them to a little self-government and a little homely pleasure. I only show the way to better things, and advise them. I never act for them; I never interfere; above all, I never patronize.

These practical steps toward helping the working man acquire "homely" pleasures at the same time as he achieves a measure of autonomy was high on Dickens' list of social priorities. We are reminded of Mr. Whelks, ten minutes from Parliament, who had sufficient income for a decent life if he and his "were not utterly neglected and left to their own helplessness." Clearly, part of the revolution requires the governing classes to find and adhere to that thin line between patronage and negligence.

The Working Men's Club and Institute Union, established in the autumn of 1862, and spreading rapidly, was an outgrowth of the temperance movement. In 1864 *All the Year Round* again sounds Dickens' persistent theme: the avoidance of patronage in the assistance of the poor.

Unless these clubs are made self-supporting, they can never be in a position of independence from external influences—from the caprices of well-intentioned tyranny, or the blight of patronage. *(AYR*, XI, 154)

To excise a working man's sense of autonomy is to excise his capacity to care. To its credit, the Working Men's Club did not deprive its members of their sense of self-regulation. Although they often did not serve food and drink, they nevertheless succeeded in providing for appetites almost as strong, appetites for "social rest and social recreation." Hence, they served to develop the capacity of the laborer to care (in both senses of the word) for themselves.

As the years passed, other signs appeared in England of a "newbirth" of the capacity to care. One such phenomenon, called the "Self-Supporting Cooking Depot" *(AYR*, IV, 588–591), is reported by Dickens as the Uncommercial Traveller. The journals cited such positive signs to rally others. Dickens visited one such institution in London and spoke well of the viands and the cookery. But he finds one thing objectionable in the depot he visits: no beer is served. Again, this "expresses distrust of the working man. It is a fragment of the old mantle of patronage in which so many estimable Thugs . . . are sworn to throttle him." Every effort must be made to foster the autonomy of the poor. Hence, it is well that even at the charitable "Sick Children's Dinner-Table," where "puny children should be made, if possible, into hale and wholesome men and women, and that the hungry should be fed when they are unable to feed themselves,"—which is, after all, a canon of law "as eternal as humanity itself" *(AYR*, XV, 134)—a penny is paid for the food. For, "this little, trifling as compared to the amount [of food] given . . . yet lifts the charity to the rank of a self-helping institution in the minds of the poor, and prevents that lazy dependence on others which is just the curse clinging to benevolence" (p. 132). Without so entrusting the poor, Dickens is arguing, the body politic cannot be made wholesome. Dickens feels strongly that any form of patronage that would starve the human spirit even while it feeds the body must be avoided.

A few years later Dickens is able to give the highest praise to a self-supporting cooking depot: "I dined at my club in Pall-Mall aforesaid, a few days afterwards, for exactly twelve times the money, and not half as well" *(AYR*, IX, 591). If this is the case, then the common opinion, that there "are very few things, indeed, in which wealth has any real advantage over poverty" *(HW*, VI, 232), which appeared merely to whitewash class inequities, may contain at least some substance. Once the lessons of revolutionary cookery are thoroughly learned, and genuine care has replaced the ideology of carelessness heretofore dominant, then true equality and therefore true social harmony will be possible. This will occur when the poor man has more than the notorious sauce of hunger for his "piece of boiled rusty bacon," and has not spent his dignity to gain a full stomach. On that great day, the poor man as well as the rich man may be able to claim, in the words of Dickens' dear friend, Rev. Sidney Smith, "Fate cannot harm me, I have dined today." Only when such assertions are universal can true social harmony be built.

By clubbing together, by broadening their diets, by cooking more economically, the poor may help themselves. A whole dimension of human enjoyment, a grand resource of physical, spiritual, and social benefit can be added to the lives of the working poor. But the revolution in cookery will benefit the bourgeoisie as well.

Involving the middle class in the revolution in cookery was, perhaps, an even more difficult task. Practical changes could not be introduced until a primary alteration in social values had occurred. The ancient linkage between social status and social uselessness had first to be severed. For despite the sway of Utilitarian/Carlylean ethics, the highest social esteem was still given to those who did and had to do least in the world. For confirmation of this, we need only look to Pip's great expectations, or to the definition of gentleman's behavior by Mr. Spenlow (*DC*, ch. 33) and by Blandois (*LD*, I, 1). In all these cases social rank was normally considered the inverse of one's social usefulness. It is no wonder that middle-class women also considered that the less they were called on to do the greater their position in society. The gentle classes must learn that to pay attention to domestic economy is no longer "common."

As such ideas of gentility were deleterious to the common health as well as to the commonwealth, the journals adjured the women readers to assume active management of their domestic destinies.

> It would be a great improvement in our social system if there were more markets—good markets—in different parts of London and if it might become the fashion for ladies to visit them every day, accompanied by a servant, and that great and glorious institution—a basket.                    (*AYR*, VIII, 477)

If "the grievance of dear meat falls chiefly on those who keep two or more servants, and is due mainly to their mismanagement" (*AYR*, XIX, 58), the middle-class housewives can go a long way to improve prices and therefore to equalize distribution of food supplies. Besides getting better articles to eat, they could in concert greatly reduce cheating, adulteration, and the ruination of servants.

Quoting M. Gogue's *Mysteries of the French Cuisine*, one writer suggests that by making every kitchen a "model of engaging purity" one might "win the mistress to enter with as much delight as into her own drawing-room" (*HW*, XIX, 381). Physical renovation must, of course, be accompanied by the psychological. Urging both specific dinners and personal management of them, the "Roving Englishman" declares

> A roast saddle of Welsh mutton, two sorts of vegetables, and a tart is dinner for a prince; but then there should not be more than four princes and princesses to eat it. It is the best dinner a young housewife, whose husband has five hundred pounds a year can, or ought, to put upon the table, and much better than any possible abominations contrived by the pastry-cook around the corner.
>                                                                    (*HW*, VI, 232)

The housewife is given to know that food is cheaper and better at home than food procured elsewhere. Both physical health and personal satisfactions would be vastly improved. Once she is able to accept this care for cookery, the middle-class wife would also be ready to dispense with what the "British Lion" called "the whole dining-out nuisance, the saddle of mutton nuisance, the choking cravat nuisance" (*HW*, XIII, 453). For the sake of health and contentment, then, the middle-class wife will throw over the old regime—those pretentious orgies of conspicuous consumption—and the old regimen—the deadly "vapour-bath of haunch of mutton" (*DC* and *OMF*).

As in Samuel Butler's *Erewhon*, the idea of health was already becoming associated with morality. The middle-class housewife has the duty to effect an improvement in the digestion of her family and thereby improve its health.

> All cooking is a preparatory digestion. The ancients consider digestion itself as only a process of cooking, and in some respects they were right. In proportion as the food has been well cooked there is less labour thrown upon the stomach.
>                                                                    (*AYR*, V, 8)

By combining scientific and classical rhetoric, this writer gives double authority to the idea that good cooking results in good health. In a review of the *Manual Annuaire de la Sante* by V. F. Raspail, it is noted that "Health, Raspail maintains, is the normal or regular state of life, fitting man for the performance of his natural and social duties" (*HW*, XII, 69). For the Victorian, perhaps, health is essential not only for purposes of pleasure but for purposes of work.

Creating health and contentment, simplicity and aristologic pleasure in family and friends, the modern British housewife performs her duty.

There are more showy accomplishments: fair fingers may be seen to better advantage than when partially buried in a light crust—but the light crust has something to do with the light heart, and the kitchen strongly influences the happiness of the parlor.                                                    (*HW*, IX, 44)

And the parlor, it follows, strongly influences the happiness of the family and, through the family, the entire nation. For upon good food depends good cheer, and "Good cheer . . . is one of the chief preservatives of health!" Dickens evidently felt that once the English middle class was apprised of the relationship between cookery and spirit, and between personal care and national welfare, they would join the forces of aristology to create harmony in England.

In the 1860s there were, for the middle-class railroad traveller, signs of a change, a change so miraculous that its perpetrators were called in the title of the article "Genii of the Cave." "The cave is a railway arch, and the genii are mighty modern magicians who have converted that arch into a gorgeous temple of luxury" (*AYR*, XIX, 60). The entrepreneurs, or genii, have created a system of refreshment stands which are competitive, comfortable, quick, and wholesome.

> Borrowing the bill of fare of the first-class dining-room, which is changed every day, we compare it half an hour later with that of one of the principal clubs in Pall-Mall, and find it superior in some particulars, and equal in all. Under the genii, the hungry Briton may count upon nourishing food and wholesome drinks, and recalling the miseries of the past, the insolence of Mugby, and the barrenness which has prevailed from Dan in England to Beersheba in North Britain, we mentally kiss the magician's hand, and pray that the outlying railway world may be shamed or coerced into imitation. (64)

Once the new view of cookery is in place, even commerce may make such improvements as will help eliminate "the vast amount of evil temper, and irritability, [which] arises from indigestion, [for] . . . indigestion is greatly helped, if not caused by bad cooking" (*HW*, XIII, 42). It is no exaggeration to suggest that partly upon the elimination of these evils—generated by the carelessness which is at the heart of the dominant English ideology and so of English cookery—the true harmony of England will depend.

## VI

In the middle of the nineteenth century, there was "evidence that death by starvation is no unknown horror amidst the wealth of London" (*AYR*, IX, 354) and there was gross over-indulgence. Dyspepsia from a surfeit of food was as common as malnutrition. There was a waste of spirit in the dinner-party custom, and there was demoralized and careless service. There was too frequent a recourse to drink and there was adulteration of foodstuffs. Dickens' critique was aimed at the carelessness of heart that generated both the slavery to custom by the well-to-do and the self-damaging prejudices and inattention of the poor. Dickens' basic maxim, which runs through all of his later work, is that there is an inextricable relationship between animal economy and political economy, a relationship in which domestic, or kitchen, economy was an ignored but essential mediator. It is a commonplace to speak of Dickens' sentimental politics and economics. To seek to foster harmony in Victorian England hardly seemed to be a practicable project. But from the point of view of either materialistic science or idealistic humanism, to speak of meddling with the political economy without first attending to animal economy and therefore to cookery is patently nonsense.

> All that is needed is for intelligence to be given to the art of cookery, which binds families and nations together by a common tie of social interest which no inroad of barbarians can snap. (*AYR*, XX, 229)

Even the most philosophical of radicals would be likely to admit the materialistic truism that the surest way to reform a nation was to reform its diet.

From Dickens' point of view, the barbarians, or Philistines, were dominant in society, and inroads had to be made by civilizing forces.

> This I take to be the true exposition of that complex notion, dining, as distinguished from eating; in this lies the chief triumph of civilization. (*AYR*, IV, 466)

Indeed, if less attention were paid to the problems of political economy and more to the problems of domestic economy, many of the problems of the former would disappear. "No man ever knew how to dine properly who could shut his heart afterwards to the distresses of one human being" (*HW*, VI, 232). The inequities, the conflicts, the soul-destroying voracity of the current system of political economy would be at least partially remedied by attending adequately to domestic economy. In practical application, therefore, a change of heart upon dining customs was likely to have a far greater effect on the nation than a change in the cabinet or a switch in the political majority. Since all reform takes compromise, and compromise is impossible without good intentions, how can one even consider reform without a requisite attention to personal temper? How can the proper temper be achieved without the good health and good cheer so largely provided by a good dinner? Hence, harmony had to be built meal by meal.

At the end of a long series of articles entitled "Leaves of a Mahogany Tree," late in Dickens' editorship of *All the Year Round*, it is pretended that "a cookery book, the property of the last chef of the King of the Sandwich Islands, has lately fallen into our hands" (*AYR*, XX, 586). The book supposedly contained such recipes as "English sailor a la Maitre d'Hotel." The style at the end of this article resembles that of Dickens, but whether his actual hand is present is not as important as the fact that the message here in 1868 is consistent with the entire trend of revolutionary cookery that we have been tracing. The acts of cannibalism supposed to have occurred on the Sandwich Islands are largely excused in the article as being the acts of hot blood. But the implication clearly is that the current system of English political economy constitutes cannibalism in cold blood, for it eats up the poor. Present English society, in both the economic and social sense, was barbarous.[19] This "English cannibalism" aristology, or revolutionary cookery, was intended to halt. Hence, it is not as surprising as it may on the surface seem that Dickens, the most popular novelist of his time, and nearing the end of his highly creative life, should have—as Philip Collins relates—as one of his last literary plans, a "great scheme for writing a cookery book."[20] Perhaps he would have called the book *Revolutionary Cookery*. Like Bella in *Our Mutual Friend*, a spoiled girl who learns to cook and thus brings her loved ones out of "Harmony Jail," Dickens saw the direct connection between home dinners and social harmony. But perhaps he did not have to write the cookbook, for he had already provided the rationale for the book in the pages of *Household Words* and *All the Year Round*.

## NOTES

1. Charles Dickens, "Preliminary Word," *Household Words* I (1850), 1. Hereafter the editorial direction of Dickens will be assumed, and all quotations from *HW* and *All the Year Round* (*AYR*) as well as any references to the novels will be cited in parentheses in the text.
2. An earlier name that Dickens thought of for *AYR* was *Household Harmony*.
3. Bruce Haley, *The Healthy Body and Victorian Culture* (Cambridge, Mass.: Harvard University Press, 1978), p. 3.
4. Justus von Liebig, *Familiar Letters on Chemistry* (London: Taylor Walton and Maberly, 1851), p. 452.
5. "I do not like to see them [Milton and Shakespeare] analysed by the irreverant hand of chemical science and I do not like to hear that beef and mutton made them what they were. I cannot submit, without a scruple, to alter the philosophical dogma and say, I eat—therefore I am" (*HW*, XIX, 467).

6. Jean Brillat-Savarin, *Gastronomy as a Fine Art*, tr. R. E. Anderson (London: Chatto & Windus, 1877), p. 32. The earlier English translation was called *The Handbook of Dining*, the emphasis on health signaled by its subtitle, *or Corpulency and Leanness Scientifically Considered*, tr. L. E. Simpson (London: Longman, Green, & Roberts, 1864). The even earlier American version also carried a significant title, *The Physiology of Taste; or Transcendental Gastronomy*, tr. Fayette Robinson (Philadelphia: Lindsay and Blakiston, 1854). All of these and many recent translations were inspired by the 1825 publication in Paris of *Physiologie du Gout*.

7. [Thomas Walker], *Aristology, or the Art of Dining* (London: Geo. Bell & Son, 1881), p. 85. The somewhat earlier American edition is the one that emphasizes health: *The Art of Dining and of Attaining High Health* (New York: DeWitt, 1874).

8. Article VII: "The Original. By Thomas Walker," *London Quarterly Review* 60 (February 1836), American Edition, 259.

9. According to Anne Lohrli (comp.), *Household Words . . . List of Contributors* (Toronto: University of Toronto, 1973).

10. Thackeray's *Cornhill* echoes the paradoxes of English dinners out: "And to think that there were some people who 'moved heaven and earth' to get invited to this party, while those who were there, the greater part seemed to think only of how they could get away soonest"—"At Home," III (1861), 499.

11. Almost ten years later Harriet Martineau re-enunciates the problem in English kitchen economy: "Middle-class housewives in England cannot cook, generally speaking: and, moreover, they do not know what to require, what to order, and how far to superintend. Their mother did not teach them; we have no schools for the homely domestic arts"—"Follies in Food," *Once A Week* I (1859), 301.

12. The carelessness assumes a different guise with each novel, from Podsnappery in *Our Mutual Friend* to the "Pickwickian point of view."

13. The definition of man as the "cooking animal" (*HW*, XIX, 380) becomes a commonplace in the Victorian period.

14. "Home Dinners," *AYR*, XI (1864), 63.

15. Mortimer Collins uses "Aristology" for the title of an article in *Belgravia* XV (1871), 342–346. He defined it as follows: "as the science which provides for man his best meal in the best way." In any case the word is an improvement over some of the efforts earlier in the century to create a jargon for the discussion of the science, such as the word "palatician," which is coined in "Cookery and Confectionary," *Monthly Review* 96 (1821), 395.

16. Given the frequently reiterated definition of man as the "cooking animal," it comes as no surprise that even the term "revolution" had been associated with cookery long before Dickens took up the battle. "The revolution as to dinner was the greatest in virtue and value ever accomplished. In fact, those are always the most operative revolutions which are brought about through social or domestic changes"—in "Dinner Real and Reputed," *Blackwood's* 46 (1839), 828. Dickens could not have agreed more.

17. Alexis Soyer, *The Modern Housewife, or Menagere* (London: Simpkin, Marshall, Co., 1851). A typical book reflecting the widening physiological interests is Andrew Coombe, *The Physiology of Digestion* (Edinburgh: Maclachlan & Stewart, 1836).

18. *Gastronomy as a Fine Art, or the Science of Good Living*, n.p., but listed as IX under the "Fundamental Truths of Science" section.

# "Where There's a Will . . ."

## *Sylvère Monod*

What author was defined as "that bard . . . who drew / The celebrated Jew," and by whom?[1] The answers are, of course, William Shakespeare, and that he is thus called by a Dickens character, one Miss Twinkleton. Her own name seems to invite us to emulate the more familiar style of our mutual friend Mr. Silas Wegg and drop thus early into poetry, by addressing Miss Twinkleton like this: "Twinkle, twinkle, little ton . . . of pedantry." Even so, the importance assumed by Shakespeare in a girls' school in Cloisterham is confirmation strong of his unique power over English education.

To anyone even moderately well acquainted with Dickens, it seems obvious that the theatre played an enormous part in his life, and that this major fact is to a certain extent reflected in his work. Of his life one may recall a few notable aspects: much has been said about his initial ambition to be an actor; about the innumerable private theatricals in which he took immense delight and to which he devoted extraordinary energy; about his public readings. Let us not forget in addition that he was a constant and avid playgoer wherever he went, or that he made close friendships with several actors, like Macready and Fechter. In his own work, there is not much that can count as dramatic literature, and not much good in what little there is. His collaborations with Wilkie Collins yielded mostly appalling melodramas, which can be fun to perform or to watch, but which are dreary and seem intellectually poor when read in the cold light of print. A word might perhaps be said in favor of Dickens as a writer of theatrical prologues.

But of course the bulk of the theatrical element in his writings is made up of episodes, phrases, and allusions, in the novels and stories, having to do with the life of the stage or with theatrical performances and theatrical literature. All the elements which have just been listed are important, interesting, relevant to our theme, and in part controversial. I shall content myself, though, with examples from the early and late periods of Dickens' career; but I shall also introduce an element of comparison, taking the case of another English novelist, whose Shakespeare came to him in a different way (with our Will there's more than one way), a way that was less immediate and intimate, and the inferences to be made on the basis of such a comparison will be pointed out. That other novelist is the foreign-born Joseph Conrad, whose very foreignness seems to be a significant element of his attitude to Will and his works.

A word or two is in order at this point about the difficulty of spotting Shakespearian allusions and quotations. We may not contrive a method enabling us to spot all the quotations and allusions there are in a work we are reading. There are things that are easy enough. "To be or not to be, that is the question," is quite plain sailing. But it is not certain that there is an infallible method in more difficult cases. The only infallible quotation-spotter would be someone having all Shakespeare's works at his or her fingertips, surely a rare case; perhaps actors who have played many parts come near enough to that ideal situation after many years. On the other hand, people who do a good deal of annotation acquire a specific training which the actor may lack. In any case, things usually happen in one of the following ways (again, there are several ways, and no doubt several of them may be in operation simultaneously). The most obvious references are easily spotted, though by no means always easily identified: they are the bracketed phrases, signalled by the writer as quotations. If some phrases placed between inverted commas may defeat the annotator all the same, it is because the signal may be ambiguous: Dickens' inverted commas may point to substandard speech, popular idioms, internal references; but even so, inverted commas invite investigation. Then, there are phrases that are easily identified, simply because they are well known to everybody—not only the Shakespeare saws, like that is the question, or the pound of flesh, or if we should fail, or band of brothers, etc., but also phrases coined by other writers: if one reads the announcement that the curfew tolls the knell, one should react with a normally cultured person's familiarity with such items in our common stock-in-trade. Then, unfortunately, there are numbers of phrases that ring a fainter bell, that sound like quotations, either because they give us the impression that we have heard or read them already, and so ought to recognize them, or simply because their style or tone or wording is foreign to the paragraph in which they occur.

In that last respect the protracted practice of annotating Victorian and Edwardian fiction for scholarly editions is good training for this quotation-spotting process. One's sense of the quotationese becomes sharper with practice; it is a slow but not hopeless evolution. Perhaps the difficulties of the task must not be exaggerated, for there are—from the point of view of their presentation—two main kinds of quotes: (a) those that are both signalled and signed, of the "as So-and-So wrote" type. Incidentally some writers are more perverse than others. Joseph Conrad, for instance, is addicted to the signalled but unsigned quote, his procedure in such cases consisting in no more than "as the poet says" or "as a French writer puts it." The signed quote occasionally makes use of rarefied knowledge, but even so it provides built-in data for the annotator's research. Apart from the curious case of Mr. Septimus Hicks in *Sketches by Boz*, who keeps quoting snatches from Byron's *Don Juan*,[2] Dickens does not use that kind of quotation very much. (b) The second kind is the unsigned, and as often as not unsignalled, quote or reference, which makes greater demands on the annotator, who must first detect, then identify it.

If I may, or must, now refer to the specific case on which the bulk of this essay will have to rest, such Shakespeare-spotting abilities as I may possess have been acquired in several ways (again, where there's the Great Will, there are several ways)—first of all, and quite naturally, through studying English literature. In French secondary schools, before the War, one was supposed to acquire the ability to speak English from reading *Julius Caesar, The Tempest*, and *Hamlet*. As a student of English at the Sorbonne, I took courses in *The Merchant of Venice* and *Macbeth*. The second way was more unexpected; it was through amateur acting of scenes from Shakespeare. I was a tormented young Hamlet in one memorable public performance (I mean, of course, memorable to me); I recited the great soliloquy, and the scene that follows. In that scene I mouthed the injunction "To a nunnery, go" with great fervor, but little persuasive power, for the advice was not taken. The student who acted Ophelia to my Hamlet duly deplored that after having seen what she had seen, she had to see what she now saw, and lamented the decline of one who had been the observed of all observers. But she did not commit suicide, nor did she go to a nunnery, in either the respectable or the immoral sense of the word; instead of which she married me eighteen months later.

The third way was less sensational. As a member of the teaching profession, in the course of thirty-three years of University teaching I discussed many of the plays. The fourth was through translating Shakespeare. I translated only one play, for a bilingual edition published in 1955 and which is still in print. My choice had been *Henry V*, in part because I had fallen in love with the Choruses, and forgotten about the bawdy Anglo-French jokes; that experience, alternately, or sometimes simultaneously, excruciating and exhilarating, may have influenced my approach to Shakespeare-spotting. And there is a fifth way, which is from reading, translating, and especially annotating authors like Dickens and Conrad, who are inveterate Shakespeare-quoters; and perhaps a sixth way, if we take into account the give-and-take of friendship, conversation and correspondence with people who cherish other gems than my own favorites and have impressed things like prophetic souls and towers of strength on my mind. Yet, one way, the most natural and obvious to most people, is conspicuously absent from my list, and that is theatergoing. I have of course attended Shakespearian performances in France, in Britain, and elsewhere, but not systematically, and not on a large scale. Television has helped slightly, with some good BBC productions being relayed by a French channel. But most of the Shakespeare that is performed in France is acted in French, and thus unlikely to impress the Great Will's very words on our memories.

Dickens' acquisition of his familiarity with Shakespeare was largely through reading, acting, on an immensely larger scale than mine, and through playgoing. Of course he did not have to translate, teach, or even study Shakespeare in an academic or scholarly way; his single reported emendation of a Shakespeare text was not a brilliant success. Conrad, however, seems to offer more similarities to the case of a Frenchman in that he was, or at least described himself once as "an amazing bloody foreigner writing in English."[3] He knew Shakespeare from reading him. A complete Shakespeare was among the very first books he bought when he became an English sailor. If not a translator himself, he was at least the son of a man who translated Shakespeare into Polish; and he came across Shakespeare quotations in the works of other authors.

After these preliminaries, laying down the principles of the quest, I may proceed to the inventory, or inventories, since the comparative element that appears desirable involves exploration of at least fragments of two writers' works. To begin at the beginning with Dickens means beginning with the *Sketches*. As everyone knows, in *Sketches by Boz* there are several pieces devoted entirely to the theater, the theater being more than once Shakespeare; that is the case in "Private Theaters" (Scenes, XIII), which describes a performance of *Richard III*; and it is the case again with "Mrs. Joseph Porter" (Tales, IX), which describes a performance of *Othello*. In both cases, the performance is amateurish and of very poor quality, a tradition that will be adhered to in the most famous example of Dickens' Shakespearian episodes, the performance of Hamlet by Mr. Wopsle as Waldengarver in *Great Expectations*.

The situation of Shakespearian and other quotations in *Sketches by Boz* is roughly as follows. Apart from Shakespeare, there are at least nine references to the Bible, and echoes of writers like Spenser, Sidney, Pope, Richardson, Sterne, Chesterfield, Hobbes, Bunyan, Blake, Goldsmith, Scott, and also Molière and Bernardin de Saint-Pierre (which proves that Dickens was not hostile to amazing foreigners). But his real favorites are present also: Thomas Moore, Burns, Byron's *Don Juan*. In addition to such literary quotations and allusions, there are innumerable references to theatrical places and persons of all sizes and periods: Drury Lane, Covent Garden, the Victoria Theatre, Astley's, Richardson's, Milton Street, private theaters in general, Sadler's Wells, White Conduit House, Vauxhall, and figures like Mrs. Siddons, Master Betty, Sheridan, Congreve. Minor writers for the stage are also mentioned: Moncrieff, Bayly, Poole, Holcroft, O'Keefe, Arne, Barnet, and a few others. As to Shakespeare himself, we have just seen that he is central to two sketches; one also finds from reading the *Sketches* that Boz was familiar with "the Cumberland edition" of the plays.[4] But the allusions and quotations are not very numerous. Twelve of the plays, or one third of the Shakespearian corpus, are pressed into Boz's service: *Hamlet* is particularly in evidence, but that is mostly in the prefaces, which are on the whole unremarkable and uncharacteristic.

The most curious case, among the Shakespeare quotations used in *Sketches by Boz*, occurs in the chapter devoted to "Private Theatres." It is from *Richard III*. In the brief passage in which it is encountered, Boz is explaining that the two pounds paid by the amateur who will act the part of Gloucester are really dirt cheap, and he goes into all the details, until he comes to "the bustle of the fourth act," which "can't be dear at ten shillings more—that's one pound ten, including the 'off with his head!'—which is sure to bring down the applause, and it is very easy to do—'Orf with his ed' (very quick and loud;—then slow and sneeringly)—'So much for Bu-u-u-uckingham!' Lay the emphasis on the 'uck'; get yourself gradually into a corner, and work with your right hand, while you're saying it, as if you were feeling your way, and it's sure to do." Excellent advice, no doubt, though none of us may have a chance of following it, either because we shall never act the part or because we shall—without speaking those very words. Indeed, the interest of the passage from "Private Theatres" is that it so beautifully illustrates the fate of the annotator. Working on Dickens involves a good deal of leafing through Shakespeare's plays. Nearly every time one has spotted a Shakespeare quotation, one manages to identify it precisely and to include chapter and verse, or act, scene and line, in the note. Not so, however, in the present case. The conscientious annotator happened to be fairly familiar with *Richard III*, and he reread the relevant passages, these having to do with Buckingham's rebellion against the arch-rebel, and his liquidation at the usurper's hands. In vain, through several of the current editions available on the annotator's shelves. The text, as given by Boz, "Off with his head! So much for Buckingham!" is simply not there at all. It is *not* a Shakespeare quotation! Admittedly Richard was ready enough to have people's heads cut off, and he did not shed too many tears over his victims' fate. But where Buckingham is concerned, all that Shakespeare's Richard does, once he has been informed that Buckingham is under arrest, is to make sure that he will be taken to Salisbury under suitable escort. So where do Boz's lines come from? Are we going to be cheated of them, if we pay two pounds for the privilege of playing the part, having been attracted by that sensational little piece? Actually, the passage in question, though not by Shakespeare, belongs to a stage-version of *Richard III* that was frequently acted in the eighteenth and early nineteenth centuries, the version adapted and improved by Colley Cibber. It is amusing to think that Dickens, an enthusiastic Shakespeare-lover, and a reasonably knowledgeable one, may have believed the "off with his head" piece was actually by Shakespeare. Apart from Richard's apocryphal cynicism about Buckingham's fate, the most interesting Shakespearian presence in the *Sketches* is provided by *Othello* and Mrs. Joseph Porter. In that sketch, as with the Byron-quoter of the Boarding-House, there are many quotations neatly interwoven with the comic narrative. Here Boz displays genuine familiarity with one Shakespeare play. The sketch is in addition valuable as being, characteristically, a satire of bad theater, which was a theme dear to Dickens' heart throughout life, and one close to the essence of his humour.

In *Martin Chuzzlewit*, we find a much more simple case. The two theatrical artists mentioned in that novel are Mrs. Siddons and Grimaldi. Mrs. Siddons had already put in an appearance in *Sketches by Boz*. And Grimaldi was the clown whose *Memoirs* Dickens had edited with his father's help, in the merry days when it seemed that life held infinite potentialities for work, energy, literature, and earnings. In *Chuzzlewit*, there are no theatrical performances as such, though there are theatrical figures galore, particularly though not exclusively among Americans. You will remember that General Fladdock, for instance, when he fell to the floor at the Norrises', was raised as stiff as a dead clown (XVII). And nothing could express the theatricality of Mrs. Hominy more eloquently than Dickens' description of her going through a room "in a procession of one" (XXXIV). She must have had something in common with Mrs. Crummles, after all, though her pretensions were far less good-natured than those of the aged ham-actress.

In *Martin Chuzzlewit* the non-Shakespearian allusions and references include Byron again, Milton and Pope, Defoe, Goldsmith, Bacon, Scott, Congreve, Gay, Percy, Wordsworth, Bunyan, Lesage, and Boccaccio, *The Arabian Nights* and *Tales of the Genii*, as well as minor authors like the usual Lillo, Bickerstaffe, Watts, and one Dorrington. And there are, by my count, twenty-seven biblical phrases (admittedly Mrs. Gamp is given to floating them in pairs) and one reference to the Book of Common Prayer. I find thirteen Shakespeare quotations and allusions in *Chuzzlewit*, including one from the Sonnets, while the plays represented are *As You Like It, Coriolanus, Hamlet* (with three appearances), *Julius Caesar, The Merchant of Venice, Richard III* and *Romeo and Juliet*. At the other end of Dickens' career, let us have a look at his last two novels, the finished *Our Mutual Friend* and the unfinished *Edwin Drood*. Here are my findings on *Our Mutual Friend*: twenty-eight biblical allusions and quotations (versus the twenty-seven of *Chuzzlewit*—no significant difference in that respect) and twelve from the Book of Common Prayer, which is a little surprising in that it seems to point to a more religious Dickens than in his earlier days. Admittedly, *Our Mutual Friend* has in its cast one of the few likable and respectable clergymen in Dickens' work, the Rev. Frank Milvey, which may account for this total of 40 religious, or religiose, allusions.

Authors other than Shakespeare are not very numerous; the most glamorous are in part our familiar friends Pope, Byron (mentioned twice), Boccaccio, and also Gay and Farquhar. There is a recrudescence of interest in the *Arabian Nights*, mentioned five times; Thomas Moore puts in three appearances; O'Keefe and Bickerstaffe one each. And there are fifteen Shakespearian quotations and allusions, with *Macbeth* at the head of the list (four times), followed by *Hamlet* (three) and *A Midsummer Night's Dream* (two); works mentioned or referred to only once are *Julius Caesar, Lear, The Merchant of Venice, Much Ado* and *Twelfth Night* and the Sonnets again.

*Edwin Drood* is an interesting case and might have been even more so if it had been completed. That half-novel shares with *Our Mutual Friend* the privilege of a congenial clergyman in the person of Crisparkle (Septimus), and it has many other ecclesiastics in its pages and a cathedral town for its *décor*; that is why the five biblical and the four Book of Common Prayer allusions seem meager. The number of literary authors other than Will seems also to have dwindled, peaked and pined. In *Edwin Drood*, Chaucer, Addison, and Spenser come in for one mention each; Milton appears twice. And that is all.

Among the nine (nine only!) Shakespeare quotations and allusions there are three from *Macbeth*, two from *Henry V* (or so it seems to me), and one each from *Henry IV*, Part II, *The Merchant of Venice*, *The Merry Wives*, *A Midsummer Night's Dream* (which is definitely an Old Faithful for Dickens). These findings call for three additional remarks: (a) *Hamlet* is spectacularly absent; (b) the total number ought to have been greater since *Edwin Drood* has in its cast a professional pedant in the person of Miss Twinkleton, whose allusions come thick and fast, and are ridiculous; (c) how does one treat, statistically speaking, a half-novel? Should I multiply all my figures by two? Obviously not. But it is only fair to stress that what we possess is half of the text Dickens intended to write, and also that what he had planned was a twelve-installment story, not the usual twenty numbers; what we have is thus in length, though not in interest or quality (in my opinion) barely one third of what is found in *Chuzzlewit* or *Our Mutual Friend*.

A more or less similar exploration of some of Conrad's works has been carried out on the basis of substantial and representative samples (though they were arbitrarily chosen). Conrad's works are in the process of being published in France—and in French—as a five-volume edition; volume I was issued in 1982, volume II in 1985. Volume I includes works from *Almayer's Folly* to *Lord Jim*, and volume IV, which has been selected as representative of the later period (because it is nearing completion now) covers the period from *Chance* to *The Shadow Line*.

Volume I yields one very interesting fact. *Almayer's Folly* and *An Outcast of the Islands*, i.e., Conrad's first and second novels, contain to the best of my knowledge and investigations *no* Shakespeare quotations or allusions; *Almayer's Folly* is even in one sense unliterary since it does not refer to any other author either; *An Outcast* has references to Calderon and Pope. Conrad's third fictional work to be published in book form, *The Nigger of the "Narcissus"*, opens out to Shakespeare with two unsensational allusions, and to the rest of literature with references to Pepys, Bulwer and, if that counts as literature, the Book of Common Prayer. *Tales of Unrest* has just one unusual, but eminently apposite line from *Henry IV*, Part II. And suddenly *Lord Jim*, admittedly a much longer piece of work, blossoms out in every direction. In *Lord Jim* one can spot thirteen biblical items, plus allusions to Goethe, Plato, Novalis, and Aquinas, and also seven full-fledged Shakespeare quotations, including three each from *Hamlet* and *Macbeth*. I call this finding interesting because to me the conclusion is irresistible that by the time he wrote *Lord*

*Jim*, and no earlier, Conrad had become a true English writer, who had the Bible at the fingertips of one hand, and some Shakespeare at the fingertips of the other. This gave him a more genuine British nationality than the deed by which he had become a British citizen in 1886.

Among the later works, to be included in our fourth volume, *Chance* has four Biblical items; a few . . . how shall I call them? A few "literary warious," if you see what I mean, in the light of your probable immersion in Mr. Venus's appetizing trade; *Chance*'s literary warious are Sterne, Rabelais, Bergson, Lombroso, Daudet, and Dickens—so you see that, like Mr. Venus again, Conrad runs very much into foreign! But he also has five Shakespeare items, from *Hamlet*, *Macbeth*, *2 Henry IV*, *Richard II*, and *Romeo and Juliet* (one each). *Victory*, which comes next, sports five biblical references and one to the Book of Common Prayer, several "warious," including two Dickens items, Milton, Twain, Marlowe, Blake, and the usual assortment of foreigners old and new in the persons or the words of Lamartine, Plato, and Seneca, and only two Shakespeare items, an astonishingly low number for such a long book. One is from *Macbeth*, an obvious and almost universal favorite; the other is naturally enough (*Victory* being eminently an island novel) from *The Tempest*, but the reference is not very original, I'm afraid. *Within the Tides*, a collection of four stories, is not much richer: it has three biblical references and four Shakespearian items, from *Hamlet* and *As You Like It* (one each) and two from *The Tempest*. *The Shadow Line*, admittedly one of the shortest of Conrad's book-length narratives, refers to the Bible three times, to four "human warious" (namely Baudelaire, Bulwer, Blake and Tennyson), and to Shakespeare four times (two of the references being to *Hamlet*, one to *Richard III*, and one to *The Tempest*).

Provisional conclusions, on the basis of such comparative inventories, might be that Conrad, not surprisingly, quotes more French authors than does Dickens, and that Conrad's non-Shakespearian literary sources are more in the fields of poetry and fiction than in that of the drama. It remains to be seen, and if possible demonstrated, that the major difference after all lies in the fact that, unlike Dickens', Conrad's Shakespeare is more verbal (or poetical) than theatrical. The demonstration requires a rapid sequence of phrases from the two novelists' works in which Shakespeare texts are made use of.

Beginning with Dickens once again, when we find a phrase like "a state of single blessedness," which is a trite joke in *Sketches by Boz* (Tales, X, i), we realize that many people, including perhaps the author himself, need not have known that this was coined by Shakespeare in *A Midsummer Night's Dream*. In two other cases, the ignorance is still more probable because of the misleading signal embodied in the text; Dickens writes (in *Chuzzlewit*, XI): "Does anyone doubt the old saw, that the Devil (being a layman) quotes Scripture for his own ends?" It seems slightly disrespectful to refer to Shakespeare as a mere author of old saws. And in the *Sketches* (Characters, X), there is this: "A very poor man, 'who has seen better days', as the phrase goes"; here "who has seen better days" is signalled as a quotation by being placed between inverted commas, but "as the phrase goes" hardly points to the fact that it goes in, or flows from, Shakespeare's *Timon*.

One or two quotations are more accurately signposted, though this is not Dickens' most familiar procedure. One example is from *Edwin Drood* (IX), *re* Crisparkle, who was "as confident in the sweetening power of Cloisterham Weir and a wholesome mind, as Lady Macbeth was hopeless of those of all the seas that roll." That is probably one of the most refined and genuine of Dickens' Shakespeare quotations; by genuine I mean serious, not jocular, and fully integrated into the narrative sentence.

Refinement of some kind is not absent from the following batch including several snippets from *Our Mutual Friend*: "while memory holds her seat" (II, xvi), is less trite than most of the words quoted from *Hamlet*; the dolls "with no speculation in their eyes" (IV, ix) rather elegantly recall *Macbeth* ("Thou hast no speculation in those eyes"). Jenny Wren is an unexpected Shakespeare-quoter, yet it is Jenny who says of her father: "He'd be sharper than a serpent's tooth, if he wasn't as dull as ditch water" (III, x), which is refinedly allusive, for it is the other half of the Shakespeare text that gives it its bearing on the situation in the Cleaver home. Jenny may not have been familiar with *King Lear*, but if she had read *Sketches by Boz*, she would have come across the complete text in Mr. Dumps's speech at "The Bloomsbury Christening" (Tales, XI): "How sharper than a serpent's tooth, it is to have a thankless child." And perhaps the most refined of all Dickens' Shakespearian references occurs in *Our Mutual Friend* also, when the narrator asserts that "Evil often stops short at itself and dies with the doer of it; but Good, never" (I, ix), in which the writer manages to coin an adage that gives the lie to the text it so clearly evokes (what Shakespeare had written in *Julius Caesar* was: "The evil, that men do, lives after them; / The good is oft interred with their bones".)

A special class may be reserved for Shakespeare quotations palmed off upon characters in the novels, not used by the narrator or author in his own name. In Dickens, such quotations are more often than not jocular, inaccurate and disrespectful. Dr. Jobling, in *Chuzzlewit* (XLI), thus says this: "Your bosom's lord sits lightly on its throne, Mr. Chuzzlewit, as what's-his-name says in the play." Dickens seems to have thought that quoting Shakespeare seriously was a fit occupation for gentlemanly persons, especially if they have been through university; that is the case of Eugene Wrayburn and his friend Mortimer in *Our Mutual Friend*. To the latter we owe an elegant reference to "local habitation" (I, ii); and the former once signals and adapts a Shakespearian text in "I can say to you of the healthful music of my pulse what Hamlet said of his" (IV, xvi). On another occasion he says—significantly, I think—"and being gone you are a man again" (III, ix); significantly because this happens to repeat a quotation made in *David Copperfield* (XXII) by James Steerforth, also a university student, and presumably a gentleman.

The really trite Shakespeare quotations in Dickens are not very many, and they fall into several sub-categories. There is the prefatory style (one of the most common ways with Will in other authors); of course the Prefaces to *Sketches by Boz* are all early, and that may account for their containing two allusions, one to "Brevity is the soul of wit" (not of breathtaking originality, surely), and the other speaking of the *Sketches* as published "with all their imperfections (a good many) on their heads" (a phrase to which I may refer in a moment, and in a different context). The trite quotations about which there is nothing to be said can be simply listed pell-mell: "chartered libertine" (in *Drood*, IV; about Durdles, of course, and perhaps enhanced by the reference nineteen chapters later to a "chartered bore"); my favorite "note of preparation" (favorite because it is from a *Henry V* chorus) occurs both in *Sketches* (Scenes, XIX) and in *Drood* (V), and elsewhere in Dickens (in *Bleak House*, for instance); "sinning more against himself than others"[5] (topsy-turvy, but unmistakable); "There was the rub!,"[6] "Take it for all in all,"[7] "When shall these three meet again?"[8]

But the really typical quotations found in Dickens are of a simpler and more characteristic kind, or rather two kinds (two more ways with Will). There is the crudely jocular or punning: "the spirits were speedily called—not from the vasty deep, but the adjacent wine-vaults"[9] (Dickens seems to have derived, if not produced, inexhaustible fun from the double meaning of *spirits*). The other characteristic kind is the reference to a visual or gestural aspect of a passage in Shakespeare rather than to the words spoken or printed in the text. In *Sketches by Boz* there is this: " 'With a marriage!' gasped Hicks, compared with whose expression of countenance Hamlet's, when he sees his father's ghost, is pleasing and composed" (Tales, I, i). In *Chuzzlewit* (XVII) there is this: "Mr Norris the son . . . dusted his fingers as Hamlet might after getting rid of Yorick's skull." In *Our Mutual Friend* now: "Mrs Wilfer, washing her hands of the Boffins, went to bed after the manner of

Lady Macbeth'' (III, xvi). And from *Edwin Drood* I would like to quote what
has become my favorite illustration of Dickens' way with Shakespeare, the
occasion being the leg of a waiter: "always lingering after he and the tray
had disappeared, like Macbeth's leg when accompanying him off the stage
with reluctance to the assassination of Duncan'' (XI). This is a really beautiful
evocation of ham-acting.

A brief survey of Conrad's way with Shakespeare quotations will bring out
the characteristics of both methods. To begin with, there are at least two
quotations used by the two writers. In *Lord Jim*, and of Lord Jim, the narrator
writes: "he, who had been too careful of it once, seemed to bear a charmed
life'' (XXIX), where Conrad is obviously less farcical than his predecessor
(in *Chuzzlewit*, XLVI) and inserts the words very elegantly and unobtrusively.
The other meeting ground is, so to speak, the milk of human kindness,
possibly *the* most hackneyed of all Shakespeare quotations. In *Chuzzlewit*,
and about Mr. Pecksniff, Dickens had turned it, or churned it, to comical
use, saying that it was not enough to assert that "he looked at this moment
as if butter wouldn't melt in his mouth. He rather looked as if any quantity
of butter might have been made out of him, by churning the milk of human
kindness, as it spouted upwards from his heart'' (III). Joseph Conrad, in
*Chance*, refers to a stranger casually encountered, and possessing "a species
of good nature; which, unlike the milk of human kindness, was never in
danger of turning sour'' (I, iii). Here, though the farcical intent is common
to both writers, it is more pronounced and more inventive in Dickens than
in Conrad. Besides, in Conrad it is exceptional, in Dickens habitual.

A few of Conrad's Shakespeare references are insignificant. Speaking of
"A world of inflammable lovers of the Romeo and Juliet type'' (again in
*Chance*, I, vii) is what one might call degree zero of allusiveness, in the sense
that it implies no familiarity whatever with the text of Shakespeare's play.
Then come the bulk of Conrad's quotations, characterized by being rather
commonplace in choice, but neatly fitted into the narrative context. Thus, the
"stuff of dreams'' is found in "The Planter of Malata'' (*Within the Tides*,
X) and one reads again in *The Shadow Line* (II) of something "less substantial
than the stuff dreams are made of.'' In *Victory* two short words are enough
to make up an allusion in "one doesn't argue against thin air'' (III, iv), or
(from *The Shadow Line*) "Having thrown off the mortal coil of shore affairs''
(III). A little more elaborate, but on unoriginal ground, we find this in *Victory*:
"Schomberg walked about swearing and fuming for the purpose of screwing
his courage up to the sticking point'' (II, v), which, once again, is not deficient
in neatness (and, in its context, adequacy); a slight alteration of the original

Shakespearian text is achieved with elegance in "there's some sort of method in his raving" (*Lord Jim*, V); perhaps because of my own past, I am rather fond of the description in *Chance* of Flora and her father on the beach at Brighton: "these two walking hand in hand the observed of all eyes by the sea" (I, v; what begins to emerge is the perfect fusion of a few Shakespearian words into a Conradian sentence). A similar effect will be found as early as *The Nigger of the "Narcissus"* with "in fooling him thus to the top of his bent" (V), and, later, in "Because of the Dollars" (I, *Within the Tides*), with "despair, like misfortune, makes us acquainted with strange bedfellows," where, in spite of two inaccuracies (*misfortune* instead of *misery*, and "makes us acquainted" for "acquaints us"), the reference is recognizable without being obtrusive. A phrase like "toil and trouble" is as neatly slipped into another passage of the *Nigger* (III). And the list may be closed with another elegant phrase from *Lord Jim*: "in the hot quest of the Ever-undiscovered country" (XXXVI) and no more.

Having by now, I hope, acquired some idea of Conrad's own way with the great Will, we may turn to three more specific procedures which are perhaps slightly more literary than anything Dickens ever did along those lines. I am not implying that literariness is an intrinsic merit, but perhaps it should not be regarded as an unpardonable sin either. One of the procedures is the epigraph, to which Dickens never became addicted. Conrad used one for his *Tales of Unrest*, at the head of which one reads, " 'Be it thy course to busy giddy minds / With foreign quarrels' SHAKESPEARE," which seems cleverly, though indirectly, appropriate to tales of *unrest*. And *Within the Tides*, also a collection of short, or relatively short, stories belongs to a genre that is often lacking in unity, so that its unifying principle has to be emphasized by the title, and reinforced by the epigraph; but the one chosen by Conrad for *Within the Tides* is simply, " '. . . Go, make you ready' Hamlet to the players." That is definitely less pungent, for one does not very well see in what way it applies to any of the stories in the collection, or to the series of four; on the other hand, one does not very well see what book could be wholly incompatible with such an introduction.

The second unusual procedure characterizing Conrad's way with Will is the double dose, or combined quotation, to be found in *The Shadow Line*, where the narrator-hero speaks of "this stale, unprofitable world of my discontent" (I; "stale and unprofitable" alludes to one Shakespeare quotation, and "of my discontent" clearly refers to a celebrated Shakespearian winter).

And finally, there is another thing that Conrad did which Dickens does not seem to have tried his hand at: that is having a Shakespeare phrase spoken by a foreign character, Mr. Stein in *Lord Jim*, who says "In general, adapting the words of your great poet: That is the question . . ." (XX). Mr. Stein's choice of quotation is not sensational, and his definition of Shakespeare as "your great poet" is not strikingly inventive either, but the point is that Conrad was in a particularly favorable position for that kind of amusement, and also that Dickens, unlike Conrad and Stein, could never have spoken of Will as "your great poet"; to him Shakespeare was of course, and preeminently, "our great poet."

Having hinted earlier that I found myself in a position more similar to Conrad's than to Shakespeare's, I would like now, briefly, to illustrate the case, with the help of three items only, two of which show the difficulties to which non-natives are exposed. The third example can be held over for the conclusion of this essay. The other two have to do with the experiences of a French innocent among the Dickensians. When an article was written for *The Dickensian* about the battle between the printer's men and Dickens over the text of *Bleak House*, the idea occurred to me of calling it "When the battle's lost and won . . ."[10] I had duly inserted a note giving the Shakespearian reference. The reference was canceled by the then editor of the magazine, who pointed out, no doubt rightly, that the phrase was far too well known to need the reference. Well and good; far too well known to native English speakers, at least. Then, in an essay about the character of Mr. Bevan in *Martin Chuzzlewit*, I had referred to him in Shakespearian terms familiar to Dickens, saying that Bevan "with all his manliness and other perfections on his head" was not beyond reproach. I recently received the proofs of that article, from the printer of *Dickens Studies Annual 15*, and I found that my poor little sentence had been editorially shorn of the words "on his head," so that it has lost whatever Shakespearianity—Dickensian Shakespearianity I would like to call it—it ever possessed. I seem to have survived the shock and the loss. But that is clearly one of the thousand natural shocks that flesh—especially foreign flesh—is heir to.

To summarize the difference, it might be claimed that Conrad's way is made up of two methods, both of which are intensely literary, traditional, and unattractive to Dickens: one is the epigraph, refined, drawing attention to itself, detached, and meaningful (in principle); and the other is the trite phrase neatly fused with the narrative sentence, apposite and elegant. By contrast, the Dickens way appears to be mainly theatrical, based on gestures and facial expressions, and mainly used for comic purposes (the comedy being, incidentally, two-edged, since fun is made both of the bad actors and of the characters who resemble them). The integration of the quotations and references into the Dickensian text is usually complete; the quotations are very rarely signalled as such (except in *Edwin Drood*, or by being placed on the lips of gentlemanly and cultivated characters). Finally, Dickens uses Shakespeare, in ways inaccessible to Conrad, in that he takes the reader behind the scenes and describes performances at some length. The difference, not surprisingly, is therefore largely that between Boz, the native writer for whom Shakespeare *is* the Theater, and the amazing foreigner.

One query that may be worth raising at this point is, why does one quote other authors at all? I found from one of the books I was also reviewing during that period that there are erudite explanations of the phenomenon as there are no doubt of every other human activity. Janet L. Larson, author of *Dickens and the Broken Scripture*, asserts that "A literary allusion is a medium of vision" and she quotes Herman Meyer (author of the highly relevant *The Poetics of Quotation in the European Novel*) as saying that literary allusion permits "another world to radiate into the self-contained world of the novel"[11]; that seems beautifully said and thought, but perhaps it is a little optimistic, at least in part. It may be feared that the use of extraneous and glamorous phrases has something to do with borrowing plumes, to put it brutally, that one uses them as one uses foreign words occasionally, for purposes of decoration, and as a manner of dropping names, exhibiting one's range of acquaintances; and that is how I put it, Shakespearianly, in connection with Conrad and foreign languages, in a paper that was later printed intact: "A few words of German, Italian, or Spanish sprinkled here and there may have an ornamental function in great part, though they also lay to the author's soul a flattering unction."[12] Yet most of all it seems that writers quote their predecessors without any such purpose in mind, without thinking about it at all, naturally, and mainly because what they wish to say has been said before, unsurpassably, definitively.

In Dickens' case—admittedly Conrad's is more complex, and Conrad does not merely quote or refer, he often borrows—it is clear that the novelist did not need borrowed phrases, and there were mighty few writers who could add glamor to his writings; I think the motivation was above all the joy of being at unison with Shakespeare and with his own readers as fellow-admirers of Shakespeare, and as fellow playgoers. There was an affinity between Dickens and the theater, and between Dickens and Shakespeare, and it was the source of emotions he shared with his audience at large.

## NOTES

1. *Edwin Drood*, IX. As there are many editions of Dickens' novels, references to his works are given by chapter only, and they are inserted parenthetically in the text whenever there can be no ambiguity as to which novel is quoted.

2. *Tales*, I, i.
3. Letter of October 1907 to Edward Garnett, in *Letters from Joseph Conrad 1895–1924*, ed. Edward Garnett (New York: Charter Books, 1962), p. 205.
4. See *Scenes*, XIII.
5. See *Chuzzlewit*, LII.
6. See *Chuzzlewit*, XXXII.
7. See *Our Mutual Friend*, II, viii.
8. *Edwin Drood*, XIV (chapter heading).
9. *Sketches by Boz*, *Tales*, X, i.
10. *The Dickensian* 79–3, No. 401, Autumn 1973.
11. See Janet L. Larson, *Dickens and the Broken Scripture*, Athens, The University of Georgia Press, 1985, p. 33; Larson quotes from p. 4 of Herman Meyer's *The Poetics of Quotation in the European Novel* (Princeton, 1968).
12. S. Monod, "On Translating Conrad into French", *The Conradian* IX–2, November 1984, p. 76.

# Dickens in Poland

*Daniela Bielecka*

## 1. THE NOVELS

The first records of the recognition of Dickens' genius in Poland can be traced in Polish magazines as early as the 1840s. They start a process of a steady growth of popularity of the English writer reflected in the increasing number of translations of his works into Polish and critical comments on them. The pattern of development of scholarly and critical interest in Dickens in Poland appears to be, on the whole, not much affected by the drastic changes in the critical attitudes to the writer in his own country. The opinions of Polish critics are more clearly shaped by the intellectual climate and the cultural and literary tendencies characterizing particular periods of Polish history. In effect, the history of the reception of Dickens in Poland is original and impressive in some of its manifestations, though on investigation, it turns out to be chaotically and sometimes poorly documented. The reasons for this are many, some of them connected with Polish history.

For example, it is virtually impossible at present to identify many Polish translations of Dickens' works, the existence of which were recorded in the past, because they were published in relatively obscure and quickly discontinued journals and magazines. The other difficulty is that, especially in the nineteenth century, many translators preferred to remain anonymous. In addition, even some identified books are at present hard to find and compare because the nineteenth-century copies were either worn out by their eager readers or destroyed in the course of the two World Wars, so that they cannot be traced in any major Polish library. Nevertheless, the material which can and has been documented and described makes it possible to recognize two distinct periods in the nineteenth-century reception of Dickens followed by a series of increases and declines of critical interest in the twentieth century, culminating in the peak of popularity enjoyed by Dickens' works after the Second World War.

The first period of the recognition and criticism of Dickens in Poland starts about 1840 and lasts till 1862.[1] The first translations of Dickens' works into Polish were preceded by some highly favorable reviews appearing in Polish literary journals. The earliest critical review of any importance, entitled "Boz," appeared as early as the year 1839 in the literary weekly *Tygodnik Literacki* published in Poznan. The anonymous reviewer praises, characteristically, Dickens' humor, noting that it can even reach the tragic tone, and foretells for Dickens in fiction a popularity comparable to that of Shakespeare in drama. He mentions *Nicholas Nickleby* and *Oliver Twist* but reserves a special admiration for *Pickwick Papers*, heralding it as a revival of the "form of comic romance."

When the first translations were actually presented to the Polish reading public, they created the image of Dickens as a story writer rather than a novelist since the earliest to be translated were some stories from *Sketches by Boz*, published in England in 1836 and in a Cracow journal *Rozrywki Umyslowe* in 1841. The choice of stories seems to suggest what elements in Dickens' writing were considered then most characteristic for him and most likely to win readers' enthusiasm, namely a sensational plot ("The Black Veil"), terrifying images ("The Drunkard's Death") and humor ("The Great Winglebury Duel"). When Dickens' novels started to be translated, they were offered first in fragmented versions. The opening passages (chapters 1 and 2) of *Pickwick Papers* were first published in 1843 by a Polish emigré, Felicjan A. Wolski, living in Glasgow. It is doubtful whether they ever reached readers in Poland, since the Scottish journal for Polish emigrants, *Rozmaitosci Szkockie*, in which they were published was soon discontinued. The 1840s produced more such excerpts and shortened forms—for example, *Nicholas Nickleby* in 1844 and *Martin Chuzzlewit* in 1845. It has been recorded that the full text of *Oliver Twist* was published in Polish in Leipzig in 1846 but it seems impossible now to obtain a copy of it. In the same year one Christmas tale, *The Chimes*, was published in Poland in an anonymous translation.

In the 1850s the situation remained basically unchanged. Translations continued to appear in literary journals and magazines, accompanied by a thin trickle of critical reviews and commentaries. For example, a number of stories from *Household Words* was published by a Warsaw daily, *Dziennik Warszawski*, and many stories for or about children were published in various magazines for children. As for the novels, the first translation of *Bleak House* appeared in 1856 and *David Copperfield* in 1857, though no copy of the latter can be found now in any major Polish library.

In general, when the first two decades of the reception of Dickens are considered, it appears that the task of translating his work into Polish had started early but the quantity and quality of the resulting production may often raise doubts: though the very number of translated works may seem to be large, when it is compared, for example, to the number of some second-rate French novels published in the same period, the effect is sobering. It becomes even more so when one takes into consideration that in this period Dickens wrote almost all his works (after 1860 he wrote only two more complete novels) and was widely translated in other European countries. In Poland in this time not one of his best known novels, such as *Pickwick Papers* or *Little Dorrit*, was accessible to the average reader. Besides, the quality of the translation often left much to be desired, which can be partly explained by the fact that not many translators could use the English original. It was a common practice to use French or Russian texts for translation.

The mere record, though, of translations in the 1840s and 1850s does not convey a full picture of Dickens' recognition and popularity among Polish literary critics—if not among a larger reading public. Indeed, the English master is evoked again and again in the course of long and heated controversies started in the 1840s concerning the future of the novel in Poland. The occasional statement that the novel is dying, that "beside Madame Sand there is no great novelist in Europe. . . . Neither the English Dickens, the Italian Manzone nor the crowd of Balzacs are geniuses," should be considered as isolated. It was generally accepted that the "romance" was the genre best suited to the needs of the times and Dickens was often mentioned as its most outstanding representative.

Dickens' reputation was undoubtedly strengthened by the fact that among his first admirers were the leading Polish novelists of the time, such as Jósef I. Kraszewski, Eliza Orzeszkowa, and Henryk Sienkiewicz, who joined a polemical battle in the Polish press to replace the French model in Polish novel writing by an English one. Kraszewski announced that "Dickens in England, Balzac in France and Gogol in Russia opened a new epoch, a new school of novel writing based on the depiction of reality."[2] He went on to lament that the English inspiration was not strong enough to counterbalance the French influence. Dickens was praised by Polish novelists and critics for avoiding the traps of an excessive imagination on the one hand and a reductive naturalism on the other. Kraszewski's opinion that Dickens was an ideal to be followed by Polish novelists was by no means exceptional. Polish critics frequently referred to his artistic merits in their discussions, especially in order to criticize the shortcomings of the Polish novelists of their time.[3]

Before this enthusiastic image of Dickens formed by Polish critics and writers could be fully absorbed into Polish culture through effective translations, Dickens was widely plagiarized.[4] The bizarre stories published under his name (mostly in various magazines for women and children) suggest what "Dickensian" meant in Poland before the novelist's work was made accessible. The list of fifteen such stories, collected by Marie Bachman, published in the years 1852–78, seems to confirm the reputation of Dickens as a writer of, first of all, short fiction. It appears that the most exploited Dickensian feature is humor. The second is the use of the supernatural. In four stories, children are protagonists, and two stories are directed to child readers. The most striking feature of all the stories attributed to but not by Dickens is the triumph of goodness and justice over evil and crime. Needless to say, when the canon of Dickens' fiction was established in the late 1870s, in the second period of his reception in Poland, plagiarism ceased to appear.

. The second period of Dickens' reception starts exactly in the year 1863. It was affected, no doubt, by the universally accepted position of Dickens as a supreme novelist but perhaps even more by the change in the political and literary situation in Poland. The Romantic movement, with its intense belief in the superiority of poetry as a literary form of expression, lasted in Poland until 1860. Eventually it was the failure of the January Uprising in 1863, dashing the nation's hopes and aspirations, which marked a definite break with this tradition both in life and literature. In an attempt to adjust to the new conditions in the country and to join the European Positivist approach to art, major Polish writers and critics turned to Western Europe for the theories and techniques of social realism. No wonder that they centered their attention on Dickens—the most popular representative of this trend.

The sudden growth of interest in the English writer was reflected most spectacularly in the increasing number and improved quality of translations. In fact, most of Dickens' works appeared in translation in Poland between 1863 and 1887. In this period almost all his novels were translated and published (some of them in installments) together with numerous sketches and stories from *Household Words* and *All the Year Round*. Two translations of *A Tale of Two Cities* appeared in 1863, one in Vilno and one in Warsaw, and a serial publication of *Great Expectations* in a newspaper, *Gazeta Polska*. It was in this newspaper that in 1866–67 the father of Joseph Conrad, Apollo Nałęcz Korzeniowski, published his translation of *Hard Times*. This imaginative translation shows such a good command of English that it was used (with only slight corrections) for editions in 1955 and 1957. The quick response of Polish translators and publishers to Dickens' continued productivity may be exemplified by the fact that *Our Mutual Friend* (the third complete novel translated into Polish) was published in Poland only a year after it had appeared in England (1866).

As Janina Kulczycka-Saloni has pointed out,[5] for the generation of Polish literary critics starting their professional careers in the late 1860s Dickens united the past with the present; they witnessed the publication of his last works, and when he died they commemorated him as one of the creators of the Golden Age in European novel writing. It is clear from numerous articles and reviews appearing in Polish literary magazines that Dickens was the favorite writer of the time, accepted as a great teacher and appreciated as a creative artist by major Polish critics and writers such as Antoni Nowosielski, Julian Klaczko, Feliks Bogacki, Kazimierz Kaszewski, Eliza Orzeszkowa, and Henryk Sienkiewicz. Their response to Dickens was often emotional, colored by the recollection of the impression made by his stories when read at a young age.

There was also a good deal of intellectual criticism when Dickens' artistic merits were used as an argument in a fierce struggle to create the modern Polish novel. For example, Dickens was favorably compared with Emile Zola and the Naturalistic movement as the writer whose fictional mirror reveals "perversities but shows them in the proper perspective and does not gloat over them" by Henryk Sienkiewicz.[6] He was praised for his power to create types and for the depth of his psychological insight. Understandably, several articles on Dickens were published in the year of his death, some of them dealing not only with a general assessment but also with certain selected features of his writing. It is interesting that though, on the whole, the Positivist critics emphasized, in the first place, the power of realistic observation in Dickens' works, some of them did not quite overlook the importance of his artistic "intuition" turning the English writer into a "universal historian of hearts and minds" (Kazimierz Kaszewski).

In general, Polish critics never separated the achievement of Dickens as an artist from what he had to say about the state of contemporary society and the need for reform in many areas of social life. Especially his humanitarian ideas were treated very seriously in Poland. Some of them even became the subject of public lectures. For example, in 1882 Wladyslaw Seredynski delivered a lecture in Warsaw "On the pedagogical concepts of Charles Dickens." Though Dickens' diagnosis of English society did not apply to Polish reality, he satisfied the severe criteria of social and national significance of literature established by Polish Positivists. As a result, they recommended and popularized his image as a progressive and a reformer, a great humanitarian. This approach prevailed till the end of the Positivist period in Poland, that is to the late 1880s. It is possible to use exact dates while discussing later new turns in the reception of Dickens, especially as they coincide with the changes taking place in Polish political and cultural life. A fresh and different approach to Dickens started in the year 1887. It was developed and continued till 1914.[7] According to Andrzej Weseliński, within this period it is possible to notice an increase of critical interest in Dickens on three occasions, namely the fiftieth anniversary of the publication of *Pickwick Papers* in 1887, the twenty-fifth anniversary of Dickens' death in 1895, and the centenary of Dickens' birth in 1912.[8] Each occasion, widely celebrated in England, was echoed in Polish journals in the form of lengthy reports. Each time it stirred fresh interest in Dickens' work among Polish publishers, critics, and readers.

The first date, 1887, coincides in Poland with the vigorous return to the Romantic spirit of experiment and revolt after several decades of the Positivist confidence in utilitarian ideals and scientific progress. The generation of leading Polish artists and critics that emerged around 1890 began to question recognized art and literature, announcing the end of naturalism in prose writing. The emerging movement, described by the term "Young Poland" and at first represented only by small groups of Bohemians and experimenters, started what is now considered the modern tradition in Polish literature. Naturally, great writers of the past were reinterpreted and the order of their importance was put into question. Dickens' position remained, by and large, unchallenged, but there was a significant shift in critical perspective. The critical reviews of the time make it clear that their authors were familiar with the opinions of their Western European contemporaries. This is not surprising as the foreign publications on Dickens were reprinted or reported in Polish and echoed by the Polish critics (for example, on Dickens' solidarity with the lower classes and his use of caricature and humor) but it was not uncommon for some of them to defend Dickens against English or French criticism (e.g., Edgar Mścisław Trepka in 1887). However, the most remarkable piece of criticism sprang from the desire to bring Dickens closer to the Modernist concept of art by pointing to the symbolic and irrational in his work. In 1888 Henryk Biegeleisen emphasized the irrational element ("feeling and fantasy") in Dickens' novels and argued that the writer's special feeling for the pure world of childhood confirms the suggestion that he felt unhappy in his married life.[9] Besides, in his comments on Dickens' art of character drawing, Biegeleisen mentioned what was later noticed by D. W. Griffith and Sergei Eisenstein,[10] namely, the cinematographic nature of Dickens' characterization. For the first time in Polish criticism Dickens' fascination with crime and the criminal was widely discussed and the presence of Gothic elements was fully acknowledged in his fiction, most explicitly in the preface to *David Copperfield* (1889) by Willa Zyndram-Kośialkowska.

Attempts to reinterpret Dickens according to the Modernist spirit were intensified between 1895 and 1904. In 1895 Waleria Marrené Morzkowska published an article entitled "Neoromanticism," demonstrating that, in spite of the triumph of realists like Flaubert and Zola, the Romantic tradition never lost its vitality and appeal to Polish readers. Concentrating on Dickens' sensitivity and compassion, she found in his works the underlying "neoromantic quality in Christian spirit."[11] It is possible that she and other Polish critics were inspired by Leo Tolstoy, whose ideas were regarded with interest and respect in Poland. Tolstoy himself explicitly mentioned Dickens' *A Tale of Two Cities* as a modern example of religious art.[12]

A significant turning point in the critical study of Dickens occurred in 1901 and was caused by a preface to *A Tale of Two Cities* written by Hajota (a pseudonym of Helena Pajzderska-Rogozińska). So far, some irrational elements had been occasionally noticed in Dickens' works and variously described as the "element of feeling and fantasy" (Biegeleisen), or "romanticism, horror, nightmares," or "neoromanticism in Christian spirit." Hajota was the first to approach Dickens from a consistently Modernist position and to find dark decadent elements in his characters.[13] As might be expected, Hajota's preface led to a heated controversy between Modernists and their supporting a more traditional image of Dickens as a typically Victorian man and artist. For example, the Modernist magazine *Chimera* strongly opposed Hajota's interpretation, insisting on the basically Philistine character of Dickens' work.

Besides this polemic about the "darker" sides of Dickens' writing, some more traditional elements were being analyzed, such as the structure of his novels. It was pointed out for the first time in 1898 that the installment form had a negative effect on Dickens' novels, becoming the main source of their structural weakness (Leon Winiarski).[14] Another approach placed Dickens more fully in the European context, linking him with the Puritan tradition (Biegeleisen, Zymdram-Kościalkowska).[15] Also, in 1887-94 parallels were drawn for the first time between Dickens and some Polish novelists, especially by Bolesław Prus (e.g., Józef Tretiak on the influence of Dickens on some characters in Prus's novels), starting the tradition, however slight, of comparative studies.[16]

As to the impact of Dickens on the leading Polish novelists of the time it is useful to examine the letters and interviews of Eliza Orzeszkowa, Henryk Sienkiewicz, and Boleslaw Prus. They provide clear and convincing evidence of their authors' admiration for the English master. Here is Sienkiewicz in an interview given to a translator of his works into English: "Among English novelists I like Dickens best. His *David Copperfield* seems to come closest to human nature. Of all English works of the century Dickens delights in the people he describes and has a sincere and deeply felt respect for his unusual character."[17] Dickens' characters were by this time so popular that they passed into the range of quotations and references in Polish fiction. They appeared as personifications of some attitudes (in Orzoszkowa) or were referred to by fictional characters (in Jan Lam).

As regards the sales of Dickens' novels in Poland, till the end of the nineteenth century the most popular were *David Copperfield, Pickwick Papers, Oliver Twist, A Christmas Carol*, and *The Cricket on the Hearth*. The translated works, adaptations, and condensed versions of Dickens' works were sold all over the country. They were published not only in major cultural centers, such as Warsaw, Cracow, and Lvov or Poznan, but also in smaller towns. Polish translations of Dickens' works were also published abroad, for example in Leipzig and St. Petersburg. The oldest Polish encyclopaedia, edited by S. Orgelbrand (1859-68), contains a comprehensive essay on Dickens full of exhaustive and, on the whole, correct information. Since then, Dickens has been present in all Polish encyclopaedias and school textbooks.

In the twentieth century, after a decade of decrease of interest in Dickens' work, there was a noticeable increase in 1912, the year of the anniversary of the writer's birth, resulting in several monographic articles. The most substantial of them, by Andrzej Tretiak, takes into consideration the cultural and social context.[18] The critic defends Dickens against the common charge of sentimentality, arguing that his ethical code was a faithful reflection of English religious culture and his melodramatic convention was influenced by the Bible. Dealing with the question of crime in Dickens' work, Tretiak comes close, in fact, in his interpretation to the ideas expressed much later by Edmund Wilson.

Dickens was also evoked in the discussions concerning the works of Boleslaw Prus, especially his early novels and short stories, after his death in 1912. Dickens' influence on Prus had been noticed in the Polish writer's lifetime. There was one obvious parallel between the two writers: they had both started as contributors of articles and short sketches to newspapers and magazines. They both become members of editorial staffs and their popularity as novelists was supported by that of journalists. Polish critics, however, emphasized that Prus, compared to Dickens, often came closer to a deeper knowledge of life. It was partly so because his personality was markedly different from that of his English master and favorite author: Prus had none of the childish simplicity which allowed Dickens to be more optimistic.

The idea of publishing Dickens' complete works was also born in the anniversary year 1912. The first attempt to realize it was made in 1914 when the first volume of the *Selected Works by Charles Dickens* was published in Poznan by the St. Adalbert Printing-house. The editor, Antoni Mazanowski, provided informative prefaces together with biographic and bibliographic information. Mazanowski's continued interest in Dickens resulted four years later in a highly original article on the structure of Dickens' novels. Contrary to the prevailing opinion, Masanowski argued that the large number of episodes and characters in Dickens' novels is not a sin against their organic unity. Foreshadowing the opinions of some English critics, (W. Axston and A. C. Coolidge), he suggested the concept of the polyphonic effect in Dickens' works.

The outbreak of the First World War meant a break in Dickens scholarship and the two interwar decades of independent Poland did not renew it.[19] The marked decrease of interest in Dickens can be explained by the change in the political and cultural climate of the period. The joy that followed the recovery of independence by Poland in 1918 gradually faded. Around 1930 it was replaced by a feeling of impotence and apprehension, as the economic crisis and the violation of the Constitution coincided with the emergence of Fascism in neighboring Germany. No wonder that the prevailing tone of the period was apocalyptic or humorously macabre. There was a marked change in literary tastes and fashions in favor of the visionary, the utopian, and the metaphysical. Besides, the Polish book market was limited and, as for translations, it absorbed, first of all, French authors. English fiction was represented by A. Huxley and D. H. Lawrence. Dickens appeared even less appealing and relevant to the Polish reading public than in the period of Young Poland.

His real triumph came after the Second World War. Of all the English writers whose works were published in Poland after 1945, Dickens reached the highest number of editions (over 60) and the highest estimated sale of copies (over 1.8 million). In this respect, he comes first even before Shakespeare and Joseph Conrad. The most popular novel by Dickens so far has been *David Copperfield* (three editions in the nineteenth century and fourteen in this century).[20] It might be mentioned that the editions of Dickens' works have usually been illustrated by the original drawings of Phiz, Doré, Cruik-shank, Landseer, and others.

The exceptional acclaim and accessibility of Dickens' works in Poland after the Second World War can be explained partly by the fact that, illustrating George Orwell's remark, Dickens proved worth stealing by the supporters of different doctrines and tendencies prevailing in Polish post-war literary criticism. Ideologically liberal writers and critics, such as Zygmunt Szweykowski (1947),[21] Janina Kulczycka (1947),[22] and Stefan Papée (1948),[23] dealt with the relations between the works of Dickens and those of, respectively, Sienkiewicz, Prus, and Sienkiewicz. In 1949 Socialist Realism was imposed on Poland. Works not satisfying the simplistic criteria of realism had no chance of publication or popularization. Since the official tendency was to return to the techniques of the second half of the nineteenth century and to avoid more experimental modes of writing, Dickens was easily fitted into the pattern of a "progressive," realistically depicting excesses and perversities of the capitalistic system.

Nevertheless, the critics applying Marxist criteria but trying, at the same time, to promote the idea of a "broad" realism, as opposed to narrow orthodoxies, found Dickens more attractive than other Victorian novelists. A good illustration of such special treatment of Dickens is provided in an essay by Jan Kott entitled "The Menacing Dickens," included in his book *The School of Classics* (1949). Dickens is admitted as an exception into the company of the recommended eighteenth-century writers as a faithful historian of his time, whose greatness makes the critic forgive even his sentimentality and naivete.[24] Not surprisingly, the only biography of Dickens chosen for translation in this period was that of the English Marxist critic T. A. Jackson (*Charles Dickens*, 1955). In its preface Grzegorz Sinko expresses the approach generally taken by Polish critics of the time: "Dickens as well as the whole of English critical realism, sees the sad truth of the epoch through Victorian spectacles. Tears and the grotesque help the writer, or at least the contemporary readers, to preserve illusions which are pleasant while they last. It would be even possible to state that the collapse and readiness to compromise of English critical realism were the sources of the melodramatic and sentimental elements in Dickens' works."[25]

Jackson's interpretation influenced the first book on Dickens to appear in Poland after the Second World War, *Charles Dickens—a Great English Writer of the Nineteenth Century*, by Stanislaw Helsztyński.[26] The Polish scholar also presented Dickens as a typical representative of the lower middle class, criticizing him for his belief that "improvement can be obtained by the internal metamorphosis of the propertied and ruling classes.'' He also fought the belief that the dejection of Dickens' last period was caused by his psychic exhaustion and personal problems. Instead, he maintained that the later novels simply expressed Dickens' indignation with the materialistic Victorian society. Soon another contribution was made in the area of biography when Roman Dyboski included a study on Dickens in his history of English literature, *A Hundred Years of English Literature* (1957).[27] He based his Dickens on Chesterton and was duly rebuffed for following the author who was ''idealistic, reactionary and witty in a journalistic way.''

A more original and scholarly discussion of Dickens was made possible in Poland in the 1960s when the dogmatic approach was rejected and Marxist criteria reappraised. Dickens emerged again as the novelist not simply ideologically safe and acceptable but also artistically satisfying and illuminating in his approach to problems and people. The subject of his reception in Poland was taken up by Miroslawa Kociecka (1962) and later by Maria Bachman (1974), Wanda Krajewska (1972), Andrzej Weseliński (1974), and Stefan Makowiecki (1984).[28] Kulczycka-Saloni returned to the subject of Dickens' influence on Polish novelists to produce in the anniversary year (1970) the fullest study so far of the influence of Dickens on Jan Lam and Boleslaw Prus, *Dickens in Poland*.

The most up-to-date discussion of Dickens so far has been provided by Irena Dobrzycka in her book *Charles Dickens* (1972). Her presentation is both highly informative and illuminating; the book is a biography but because of its preoccupation with the problems of Dickens' mastery of his art it may also be considered a critical study. It has been the most recent expression of the long-standing and well established tradition of scholarly interest in Dickens' work in Poland. At the same time, it conveys the author's sense of delight in Dickens which, it can be safely assumed on the evidence of Polish publishers and librarians, has been widely shared by Polish readers.

## 2. STAGE ADAPTATIONS

The origin of the first Polish stage adaptation of Dickens' works can be traced to an artistic experiment carried out outside the borders of the Polish territories shortly before and during the First World War, that is, on the eve of Poland's recovery of independence. This particular instance presents an exceptional departure from a deeply ingrained and politically motivated resistance of Polish artists and their audiences against any unmediated influence emanating from the cultural centers of the neighboring occupying powers. The artist whose personal integrity and powerful vision managed to overcome, to a significant extent, the barriers of Polish distrust of anything Russian was Constantin Stanislavski (1863–1938). His experiments in the Moscow Art Theatre since the turn of the nineteenth century continued to attract serious attention and, eventually, the secret or open admiration of several Polish artists. But the work which became a turning point in the reception of the Russian artist's working methods in Poland happened to be his experimental staging of *Cricket on the Hearth* at the First Moscow Studio in 1914. Its significance for the development of the Russian and later Soviet theater has been generally accepted.[29] Stanislavski himself acknowledged an almost symbolic place of the play in the modern theatrical experiment, comparing its role to that of *The Seagull* by Chekhov staged at the Moscow Art Theater.[30]

It may be useful to recall the basic facts and specific atmosphere surrounding the production of the play. It originated in Stanislavski's growing disillusionment with the way his naturalistic "method" had been applied and developed in the Moscow Art Theater after its enthusiastic introduction eight years before. The artist was especially anxious to preserve the freshness of his initial inspiration and to protect it against turning into another mechanical routine. In order to recover the experimental vigor he decided to turn away from the Moscow Art Theater and to offer his method to a younger generation by collecting a group of enthusiastic students and forming the First Moscow Studio in 1913. The aesthetic formula worked out by Stanislavski for his new stage aimed at the maximum of psychic concentration by the actors on the one hand and at an unusual degree of contact between them and the audience on the other. The contact was to result from a strong identification of the spectators with the actors—a process touching on and releasing their subconscious responses (in fact, Stanislavski uses the concept of "superconscious" in the sense of "subconscious" for the first time in the context of the discussion of the play). In order to put his intentions into practice Stanislavski had to find material which would successfully combine instant popular appeal of the subject with an intense and convincing emotional experience. The idea of looking for such material among the works of Dickens was suggested to Stanislavski by his talented stage director, the "soul" of the First Moscow Studio—L. A. Sulerjitsky. This ex-revolutionary and humanist in the Tolstoyan tradition was a great admirer of Dickens. He easily persuaded first Stanislavski and then the entire Studio that their opening production should be a dramatization of one of Dickens' creations. Considering the special attractiveness of *Cricket on the Hearth* to dramatists from the time of its first appearance in print at Christmas 1845 (in London alone as many as eleven versions were staged within months of its publication), the choice made by Stanislavski and Sulerjitsky turns out to be less of a surprise than it may have seemed at first sight.

Like many earlier English dramatists and readers of Dickens, they felt that "the images in his novels and stories seem to be created for the stage."[31] The preparation of a script based on the novel, considered an easy task, was undertaken by one of the actors, Boris Suszkiewicz. According to Stanislavski's account, the work on the play was a collective labor of love that resulted in its innovative artistic shape and its immediate success. Beginning with its premier on December 7, 1914, in the course of the next eight years the play broke the record of popularity in the history of the Russian and later Soviet theater at the beginning of the twentieth century. It was performed 509 times to sold out houses.

Because Stanislavski was strongly concerned with his own artistic imperatives, his treatment of Dickens' story was highly and consciously interpretive. First of all, the Studio broke with the melodramatic penchant of the theater in the treatment of Dickens in general and his Christmas stories in particular. The plot of *Cricket on the Hearth* was handled as a truthful drama of family happiness temporarily threatened by the misunderstanding of facts by the husband, resulting in his destructive suspicion of his wife's infidelity. The disturbing element of the story was personified by Tackleton, the villain of the piece (impressively acted by E. Wachtangow), who introduced the only sharp and sarcastic tone in the play. Otherwise, its critical social implications were toned down and its satirical elements eliminated to produce a clear-cut and unified story of a happy family reunion. Such interpretation best served Stanislavski's purpose of renewing the capacity of the theater audience for strong and fresh sensations. Since he aimed at furthering the psychological experiment which had started with the famous "method," he was interested in a narrative structure based not on some intellectual idea but rather on deeply felt truth, which would be acted out with the highest possible degree of psychological realism.

The interpretive strategies used in the play opened up new perspectives not only for the treatment of Dickens but also for the development of the Russian theater. First of all, the First Moscow Studio version of *Cricket on the Hearth* stressed, very much in the spirit of the Russian Formalist critics of the same period, the sheer fictiveness of the drama. It was made patent not only by the actual absence of traditional barriers between the audience and the stage (no footlights, and the stage at the same level as the audience), but also, and especially, by the absence of realistic setting. There was only one multi-purpose set and only a few stylized props were used, such as a dish closet painted on a wooden board and then cut out, or shelves with some objects. They were hand-made by the actors themselves as a spontaneous expression of their sense of the mood of the scene.

Critical discussions have concentrated mainly on the innovative attempts of the Studio at defamiliarization of the domestic reality in *Cricket on the Hearth*.[32] In doing so they have tended to overlook one obvious reason for the popularity of the play, indicated by Stanislavski in his autobiography. The play was such a success with the mass audience basically because it was produced by a group of people (mostly young non-professionals) who deeply sympathized with what Dickens wrote in his works and who came to share his humanistic aspirations for a decent society in which the individual would be able to claim his right to happiness. In a sense Dickens himself became the subject of the play almost as much as the story presented on the stage. This realization emerges quite clearly from some accounts of the play's reception. One author vividly described his initial disbelief in the popularity of the naive nineteenth-century English story in the Moscow of the first year of the "imperialistic" war.[33] When he went to see it, however, during his short leave of absence from the front, his disbelief immediately turned into a grateful acceptance of the theatrical experience. For one thing, it came as a relief after the chauvinistic rhetoric of the day, and, for another, it offered a comforting image of ordinary family happiness in a world of gathering gloom and mounting violence. The embittered Moscow theatre-goers of 1915 were moved to tears not because they fell victim to a nostalgic invocation of the past, but because the performance opened up Dickens' vision of virtue and goodness to their war-time present.

Among the spell-bound Russian audience there were also present some Polish artists whose personal impressions were to be translated into artistic experiments of their own. The most creative response came from Stanislatea Wysocka, an outstanding theater director and, at the same time, a great actress of the period, next only to Helena Modrzejewska (Modjeska) in terms of the range of her talent and popularity. Wysocka's interest in Stanislavski's art did not start with his staging of *Cricket on the Hearth*; in fact, she had known him personally since 1907 (in her eagerness to watch his artistic progress she was not above travelling from Warsaw to Moscow under an assumed identity and with a fake passport).[34] It was, however, the experience of watching the first play of the First Moscow Studio in February 1915 that became a turning point in Wysocka's own career.

In her book of reminiscences, Wysocka described the profound effect of the performance (which she could only compare to watching Eleonora Duse) followed by a meeting with the members of the Studio during which Stanislavski encouraged her to repeat his experimental formula in the independent Poland of the future.[35] By this time Wysocka had come to live in Kiev for family reasons. It was there that she started the most extraordinary Polish theater (named Studya as a tribute to Stanislavski) at a time when Poland did not exist as a country and Russia was on the brink of the October Revolution. In February 1916, Wysocka opened the Studio with her own version of *Cricket on the Hearth*, based on the Polish translation of the script used by Stanislavski. The Polish Studio quite openly took over the main elements of Stanislavski's form: the same physical intimacy with the audience (a small room, no foot-lights, no prompter, even no applause), the same simple and stylized setting, and the ingenious device of sheets of white cotton suspended on a wire-net spread over the stage in order to modify the stage space. As in the First Moscow Studio, the actors were predominantly young students not conditioned by any theatrical routine or preconceptions, and ready to enter the magic world of drama with open minds.

The formal similarities with the Moscow version were so striking that some Polish theater critics in Kiev, disregarding the enthusiastic reception of the play, immediately accused Wysocka of turning to "strange gods" (the Russian enemy) and wondered why she should choose, of all things, the same unambitious literary material as the Russian artist for her experimental theater.[36] The answer to this question remains uncertain; the choice could be interpreted as Wysocka's desire to follow or compete with Stanislavski. It is also possible that she treated the story and the script simply as available material fully satisfying her aesthetic aims. What the nationalistically-minded critics overlooked was Wysocka's original reading of the story, considerably different from that of Stanislavski. In her response to the critics she referred to the different "spirit" of her production, pointing out that even changing the actors' nationality necessarily modified the cultural meaning of the performance.[37] Besides Wysocka's own remarks and several reviews of the play there exists an account of the two-year history of the Kiev Studio by the outstanding Polish poet and novelist Jaroslaw Iwaszkiewicz (1894–1980), who first witnessed and later participated in the activities of the theater.[38] This makes it possible to reconstruct the theatrical shape and the meaning given to the story of *Cricket on the Hearth* in the paradoxical Kiev-based Polish theater.

The most important shift in the approach to the story was announced in the opening scene, which created, as in Stanislavski's version, a mood of heightened and intensified life, which emphasized the elements of poetic fantasy. The effect was achieved in this scene and maintained throughout the entire play largely by the use of music and sound effects (including, of course, the boiling of the kettle and the chirping of the crickets). The music provided a strongly emotional background, steering the imaginative responses of the audience beyond the visible and actual. Wysocka carefully controlled the use of music and, though she did not act in the play, she contributed to the musical background, for example, by playing the violin with great vigor in the final scene of polka dancing. The combined effect of the music, the special sounds, and the manipulation of soft lighting manifested a transition from the world of the domestic drama created by Stanislavski into a realm of poetic moral drama. The basic emotions of the characters were convincingly revealed and evoked in the course of the action, but psychological dimensions were not explored in the manner demonstrated by Stanislavski. The persuasiveness of Wysocka's version was of a different kind. By creating a dream-like atmosphere it appealed, first of all, to the audience's imagination, inviting them to go beyond what they could actually see or hear. In this respect Wysocka's reaction against Stanislavski's interpretation was most striking; she allowed her actors a greater imaginative freedom and, like no other Polish theater director of the time, she strongly relied on the imaginative contribution of the audience. It may be mentioned that, in a sense, Wysocka came closer to the spirit of Dickens, who strongly objected to the limitation of naturalism in art, considering it a "dreary, arithmetical dustyness that is powerfully depressing."[39]

The reading of *Cricket on the Hearth* presented by the Kiev Studio strongly emphasized a Christian vision of the struggle between good and evil in human nature. In the story of John Peerybingle the element of free will was emphasized. Faced with a painful situation, he has to choose between a corrupting desire for revenge and a saving grace of selfless affection. The sub-plot connected with the transformation of Tackleton was treated as a demonstration of the serious spiritual possibility of the miracle of repentance; though it may come late, it would still offer a chance for genuine repentance and atonement. Wysocka's treatment of the story was probably influenced by the prevailing tradition of Polish romantic and post-romantic drama: strongly poetic, highly spiritual, and grappling with moral and even supernatural matters. No wonder that the Polish audience in Kiev (consisting mostly of émigrées) responded with unqualified enthusiasm; they easily accepted any formal innovations as long as they could recognize in Dickens' romance the familiar poetic truth about the eternal struggle for goodness and virtue. It transcended the reality of the drama itself and, significantly, one of the impressions recorded by Iwaszkiewicz (who acted in the play) was that this essentially theatrical rendering of *Cricket on the Hearth* came, paradoxically, closer to literature than to drama.[40]

Wysocka was not the only Polish stage director responding to Stanislavski's adaptation of *Cricket on the Hearth*. Another woman, Regina Zanowska, decided to bring the first Moscow Studio version to a larger Polish audience by staging it in Warsaw according to Stanislavski's interpretation.[41] Zanowska was more strongly and directly influenced by Stanislavski's method than Wysocka (she had worked with the Russian artist in his Moscow theater for some time) and her interpretation was much less original. Like Wysocka, she started her own studio theater. Though situated in an attic, it was ambitiously called the Teatr Artystyczny (Artistic Theater). Wartime economic difficulties soon put a stop to its existence. Opening in November 1915, it continued to stage *Cricket on the Hearth* for three weeks (sometimes twice a day because of the play's popularity) and it returned to this play before its closing in January 1916. Zanowska's interpretation of Dickens' story was determined by her desire to transmit Stanislavski's artistic methods to the Polish theater, so she concentrated her attention on the modernist economy of expression on the one hand and on the psychological effects of naturalistic acting on the other. The spirit of the Dickensian world of romance, however, was neither convincingly preserved nor given a new interpretation, as happened in the Kiev Studio. Nevertheless, Zanowska's short-lived but memorable experiment not only delighted the artistic elite but also demonstrated for the first time in a Warsaw theater the possibility of a modernist treatment of a work by Dickens.

In Poland, reborn as a country after the First World War, this possibility was almost forgotten in the face of the more pressing need of the Polish theater for a repertoire which would attract and re-educate the culturally undernourished audiences. By this time, however, Dickens' image as a popular writer as well as a great educator propagating valid models of behavior was firmly established in Polish literary criticism and popular imagination. Thus it is not surprising that, after a few years, the adaptations of his works started to appear in all larger Polish towns but most frequently in Warsaw, where ten professional theaters functioned in the interwar period.[42] Of all Dickens' works, *Cricket on the Hearth* continued to enjoy the greatest popularity in the Warsaw theaters. It was staged first in 1924 in the Teatr Maly (Little Theater), which was affiliated with the leading Teatr Polski (Polish Theater), by one of the best stage directors of the time, Aleksander Węgierko

(1893–1941). His interpretation was an obvious answer to the need for moralizing entertainment. The story was treated as a clear-cut comedy in four acts, complete with singing, dancing, and musical background (provided by Rogowski). Węgierko solved the problem of showing the edifying tale of goodness and virtue in a convincing and attractive way by removing it from the realities of the present and turning it into a historical play. He was efficiently helped by a talented stage designer, Karol Frycz, who created a "rhetoric" of the whole period meant to evoke the spirit of the Victorian age by the use of costumes and settings marked by period details claiming "authenticity." The old-fashioned style served the purpose of historical distancing, making it easier to accept the moral lesson of the play. It was tacitly understood that things were simpler in the past and people more virtuous. Defending the consciously traditional and even naive concept of the play, staged amid a violent anti-realistic campaign in the Polish theater, one reviewer pointed on this occasion to a serious difficulty facing anybody attempting to translate Dickens' works into theatrical form.[43] It consisted in conveying the moral message of the "subtle poet of goodness" in a powerful and attractive manner without falling, at the same time, into the trap of sentimental naivete or overexaggerated caricature. According to the reviewer, this somewhat delicate task was reasonably accomplished in the Little Theater by reverting to old-fashioned methods of staging *Cricket on the Hearth*.

Poland was seriously afflicted by the American crisis of 1929 and economic difficulties were painfully experienced in all areas of life, including the theater. The crisis in the Warsaw theaters took the form of a prolonged and spectacular conflict between the actors and the theater managers.[44] The actors, a traditionally strong professional group, fought to defend their hard-won right to financial security, while the managers attempted to cut it down in order to avoid the financial ruin of the whole enterprise. The culminating point in the controversy came in 1931 when, after a number of short strikes, the actors started a general strike and on September 1 (the opening of the theater season) all theaters in Warsaw were closed. In the meantime, groups of actors were looking for places to give independent performances. One such place was found by the actors of the Little Theater in the working-class district (Wola), situated in the heart of the city. The local audience welcomed the performances enthusiastically. When the conflict was resolved after a few weeks, the actors realized that they had found not only a new place but also, by accident, a new audience who wanted to have a theater of their own. In this way the theater "Na Chlodnej" (At Chlodna Street) was established as a part of the social "revolutionary" experiment; it started its official existence by staging *Cricket on the Hearth* in November 1931.

This time Aleksander Węgierko "rewrote" the comedy in new terms, stressing its distinct social implications. It became not a comfortably distant costume play but a much more contemporary story about deprivation and wealth, not only in a moral or psychological but also in a material sense. Tackleton was exposed as a capitalist whose "surplus value" turned, in the end, into useless fiction. At the end of the play he bitterly realized that all his money could buy was the admiration of fools and all he really gained was boredom and emptiness. By contrast, the main plot demonstrated that goodness was the best commodity; John profited most because he relied on real capital, his own virtue. Tackleton, the capitalist, was turned into such a villain that the director could not accommodate him in the happy ending and stopped short of marrying him to Bertha. The play demonstrated that, as one reviewer put it, "in Dickens goodness is almost a social program."[45] Some features of Dickens' writing deplored by serious literary critics, like the excessive use of caricature, exaggeration, and melodramatic effects, were successfully explored and, in fact, turned into main attractions in performances directed at working-class audiences. Dickens' popularity among the Polish working classes could be measured by the fact that the poster of the play did not provide any of the usual information, such as the name of the author of the stage adaptation or of its translator, creating almost an impression of the folk anonymity of the production. Apparently it was sufficient to state that the play was a "story taken from Dickens" to guarantee a good entertainment.

The idea of a modernist treatment of Dickens originated by Stanislavski seemed to be forgotten by the Polish artists engaged in the task of "bringing culture to the masses." There was, however, at least one attempt to combine the two possibilities. It was made by Iwo Gall (1890–1959), one of the outstanding practitioners of avant-garde experiments in the Polish theater. Prompted by a desire to create a social revolutionary theater based on high artistic principles, he became involved for a time in a unique experiment with an itinerant theater in Warsaw. He periodically visited the five most culturally deprived districts with serious plays staged in places adapted for the purpose (usually schoolrooms). The enterprise was subsidized by the Municipal Board, which provided, among other things, a horsecart for carrying costumes and decorations. In 1935 Iwo Gall gathered together twenty-seven well-known and enthusiastic actors ready to endure almost medieval hardships in the name of New Art. They started the Teatr Powszechny (Popular Theater) by staging a Polish romantic drama *Balladyna* alternatively with *Cricket on the Hearth*.

Both performances were clearly inspired by the spirit of the European reform of the theater on the one hand, and by Gall's highly individual concept of the theater (in many ways foreshadowing the idea of the Polish "poor theater" practiced later by Jerzy Grotowski) on the other. Schematized scenography and simultaneous staging produced the stark modernistic effect of a stylized poetic tale, while the expressive but strongly controlled acting strengthened the impression of an almost classic dignity. In *Cricket on the Hearth*, a highly expressionistic effect was achieved by Gall's favorite device, a carefully designed manipulation of lighting. It became an integral element of the play as the interplay of light and darkness accentuated rhythmical pauses in the action and changes in the intensity of light coincided with dramatic movements of emotionally charged scenes. The plot and message were given a serious treatment and no attempt was made to satirize the characters or provoke laughter in general. The response of the audience was mixed, depending on their expectations and cultural background. More sophisticated viewers appreciated the efforts and effects, but the working-class audience brought face to face (no curtains, no barriers in a small room) with a familiar story presented in a strikingly unfamiliar style were too puzzled to be moved. School children were disappointed by the lack of fun expected from a story by Dickens. According to an enthusiastic reviewer,[46] its relative, and regrettable, failure with the audience was caused by the fact that the very concept of "popular" theater was confused. It tried to function as an elitist studio for ambitious artists such as Iwo Gall, as well as an educational theater supplying the masses with respectable entertainment.

The latter aim was consciously and successfully pursued in the adaptation of *Pickwick Papers* staged in the Teatr Polski (Polish Theater) in Warsaw in September 1936. The play was directed by Aleksander Węgierko and designed by Wladyslaw Daszewski (1902—), who shaped the production in a way equivalent to the ingenuity of the director. As happened in the case of *Cricket on the Hearth*, the script was a Polish translation (by J. Brodzki) of the Russian original (by N. Wegstern), preserving its division of the drama into two parts composed of eleven scenes, or "pictures," as they were called. The weaknesses of the stage version were indicated by one reviewer who recognized the attractiveness of Dickens' style to the theater but noted, at the same time, special difficulties confronting anybody adapting this particular novel for the stage.[47] First of all, it was necessary to find a way of translating into dramatic terms the crowded materiality and richness of characters typical of the picaresque manner of *Pickwick Papers*. The other difficulty was to preserve a gradual change of the mood and the transformation of Mr. Pickwick

play has been considered an important event in the history of Polish stage design and a remarkable contribution to the reform of the Polish theater.[48] One source of the play's originality can be traced to the tradition of Polish satirical cabaret. Modelled on the French examples, it functioned as a vigorous counterbalance to the poetic "monumental" style prevailing in the Polish theater. As in a cabaret, a variety of comic and farcical situations, often bordering on the absurd, reduced the audience to a state of constant laughter. In fact, the single break in the performance was welcomed as a chance to recover and get some rest. It may be suggested, especially in view of the recent criticism of Dickens, that this version of *Pickwick Papers* was, in some way, very close to the spirit of its author. In spite of the concreteness of his physical descriptions, Dickens easily enters into the realm of the unimaginable, even subverting conventional modes of perception. His realistic descriptions tend to move unexpectedly in the direction of the unfamiliar and the grotesque. The Polish producer of *Pickwick Papers* echoed this tendency by creating a new visual territory which had an air of familiarity but, at the same time, was patently unconventional and even "unnatural." It also managed to stay thematically and stylistically unified and outrageously funny.

The last adaptation of Dickens' work to appear on the Warsaw stage before the Second World War was *Little Dorrit*. The play under this title was first staged in February 1938 in the same leading Polish Theater as *Pickwick Papers*, but it was directed and designed by another famous team, Edmund Wierciński (1899–1955) and Stanislaw Sliwiński (1893–1940). It was also turned into a comedy, this time based on a script by an Austrian, Franz Schönthan (translated by W. Rapacki). It departed from the literary original even further than the stage version of *Pickwick Papers*, eliminating not only the social elements but also anything that was oppressive or depressing in the novel. As a result, the plot was changed beyond recognition and all that was left was the child-heroine presented as an embodiment of an ideal, full of loving kindness to everybody and wholly devoted to her father. The character of William Dorrit was given a thoroughly comic treatment and his difficulties became a source of harmless amusement. Even the Marshalsea prison was turned into something resembling a spacious palace room. This comedy in three acts evoked the world of pure and essentially happy childhood in a manner anticipating a musical comedy. Though music was not actually used in it, according to one reviewer, the play "asked for it."[49] It enjoyed a great popularity with the audience, who welcomed the transfer from the real world of the Depression and gathering threats of destruction to a happy and entertaining world of pure fantasy. The escapist nature of this entertainment was

"Klub Pickwicka" *(Pickwick Papers)* Teatr Polski (Polish Theatre), Warsaw, September, 1936.

"Klub Pickwicka" (*Pickwick Papers*) Teatr Polski (Polish Theatre), Warsaw, September, 1936.

realized by some reviewers, and at least in one review a reference was made to Witold Gombrowicz (1904–69), a Polish novelist fascinated with the ways in which adults tend to impose simplified and false masks or concepts on others, especially on still "unformed" adolescents.[50] The critic was right in that the play reduced Dickens' vision of childhood to an infantile paradise, a tendency severely ridiculed by Gombrowicz, especially in his *Ferdydurke* (1937). The reference to the Polish writer also pointed to the area explored much later in Dickens criticism, namely the way in which Dickens anticipated the modern interest in psychological defense mechanisms used to integrate conflicting and ambiguous attitudes.

*Little Dorrit* was the last interesting and popular adaptation of Dickens' work staged in Warsaw before the outbreak of the Second World War, and it expressed an extreme tendency in an otherwise extended range of interpretations employed by Polish theater artists dealing with the English author during a troubled period. But the spirit of Dickens was never far away from the Polish theater. It assumed different, sometimes puzzling, shapes modified by time and circumstances, but each of them tried to capture, more or less successfully, some element of this welcome "indomitable" spirit.

## NOTES

1. The first period of Dickens' reception in Poland was discussed by M. Kociecke in her article "Z dziejów recepeji Dickensa w Polsce 19 wie" ("On the reception of Dickens in 19th century Poland"), *Przeglad Humanistyczny* 6 (1962), 141–158.
2. Quoted by P. Chmielowski in *Dzieje krytyki literackiej w Polsce* (*A history of literary criticism in Poland*), Warsaw, 1902, p. 293.
3. The opinions of J. I. Kraszewski and other Polish novelists and critics concerning Dickens were discussed by J. Kulczycka-Saloni in her article "Dickens w Polsce" (Dickens in Poland), *Przeglad Humanistyczny* 5 (1970), 27–40.
4. The subject of Dickens plagiarism was presented by M. Bachman in her article "Dickens Plagiarism in Poland," *Kwartalnik Neofilologiczny* 2 (1974), 227–230.
5. Cf. J. Kulczacka-Saloni, "Dickens w Polsce," *op. cit.*, 38–40.
6. Quoted in *Polska krytyka literacka (1800–1918) Material* (*Polish literary criticism [1800–1918] Materials*), Warsaw, 1959–66, vol. 3, p. 228.
7. This period of the reception was characterized first by W. Krajewska in *Recepcja literatury angielskiej w Polsce w okresie modernismu, 1887–1918* (*Reception of English literature in the period of Modernism*), Ossolineum, Wroclaw, 1972, pp. 130–134, and next by A. Weseliński in his article "Closy polskiej krytyki literackiej o twórczości K. Dickensa w okresie modernizmu, 1887–1918" ("Polish literary criticism on Ch. Dickens in the period of Modernism, 1887–1918"), *Acta Philologica* 6 (1974), 261–281.
8. Cf. A. Weseliński, *op. cit.*, p. 261.
9. H. Biegeleisen, "Karol Dickens," *Zycie* (1888), 32–34.

10. S. Eisenstein, "Dickens, Griffith i my" ("Dickens, Griffith and the film today"), in *Wybór pism*, ed. R. Dreyer, Warsaw, 1939.
11. M. Marreñe Morzkowska, "Neoromantyzm" ("Neoromanticism"), *Przeglad Poznaski* (1905), 34–35.
12. Lew Tolstoi, *Co to jest sztuka (What is art?)*, trans. A. J. Cohn, Warsaw, 1900.
13. Hajola [Helena Pajzderska-Rogoziśka] in the preface to Ch. Dickens, *Opeurecé o dwéch miastach (A Tale of Two Cities)*, Biblioteka Dziel, Wyporowych, Warsaw, 1901, pp. 5–12.
14. L. Winiarski "Literatura angielska" ("English literature"), *Prawda* 24 (1898), 284–285. For a more recent discussion of the problem cf. A. Weseliński, "Structure powieśi Karola Dickensa w świetle seryjnej formy publikacji" ("The structure of Charles Dickens' novels as a serial publication"), *Acta Philologica* 4 (1972), 59–87.
15. In her preface to *David Copperfield*, S. Leweltal, Warsaw, 1888, pp. 5–59.
16. J. Tretiak, "Powieść ludowa" ("The popular novel"), *Gazeta Narodowa*, Lvov (1887), 119–120.
17. Quoted by J. Krzyzanowski in *Kalendarz zycia i twórczości Henryke Sienkiewicza (A Chronical presentation of Henryk Sienkiewicz's life and work)*, Warsaw, 1954, p. 314.
18. A. Pretiak, "Z powodu setnej rocznicy urodzin Dickensa" ("On the occasion of the centenary of Dickens' birth"), *Przeglad Powszechny* 10 (1913), 16–32.
19. Probably the most original contribution to Dickens scholarship was made in this period by A. Tretiak in his work *Na marginesie lektury Dickensa. O dramatycznej postawie Anglika (Some remarks on the reading of Dickens. On a dramatic attitude of the Englishman)*, Lvov, 1939.
20. The information concerning the number of the editions of Dickens' novels in Poland is provided by Irena Dobrzycka in her book *Charles Dickens*, Wiedza Powszechna, Warsaw, 1972, p. 311.
21. Z. Szwejkowski, *Boleslaw Prus*, Posnań, 1947.
22. J. Kulczycka, *Z dziejów Dickensa w Polsce: Emancypantki a Bleak House (From the history of Dickens' reception in Poland: Emanzypantki and Bleak House)*, Zodz, 1947.
23. S. Papée, "Pokrewieństwo Dickensa z Sienkiewiczem" ("Similarities between Dickens and Sienkiewicz") Cracow, 1948, p. 84.
24. J. Kott, "Greźny Dickens" ("The Menacing Dickens") in *Szkola klasyków*, Czytelnik, Warsaw, 1949, 1955, pp. 241–254.
25. G. Sinko in his preface to T. A. Jackson's *Charles Dickens*, Czytelnik, Warsaw, 1955, p. 10.
26. S. Helsztyński, *Karol Dickens—wielki pisarz angielski 19 wieku*, Czytelnik, Warsaw, 1955.
27. R. Dyboski, *Sto lat literatury angielskiej*, Pax, Warsaw, 1957.
28. St. Makowiecki, "The American experience: Charles Dickens and Henryk Sienkiewicz" (an unpublished manuscript presented at the Dickens conference organized by University of California, Santa Cruz, August 9–12, 1984).
29. *Teatralnaja Enciklopedija (An encyclopedia of theater)*, 6 vols., Sovetskaja Enciklopedija, Moscow, 1965, vol. 3, p. 970.
30. Konstantin Stanislawski, *Moje zycie w sztuce (My Life in Art)*, trans. Z. Petersowa, Ksiazka i Wiedza, Warsaw, 1951, p. 389.
31. Constantin Stanislavski, *My Life in Art*, trans. J. J. Robbins (New York: Meridian Books, 1956), p. 539.

32. A. D. Popov, *Vospominanija i razmyslenija o teatre* (*Reminiscences and reflections on the theater*), Moscow, n.d., 1963.
33. A. D. Dikij, *Povest' o teatralnoj junosti* (*An account of the theatrical youth*), Moscow, n.d., 1957, pp. 271–274.
34. Cf. Irena Schiller, *Stanislawski a teatr polski* (*Stanislavski and the Polish theater*), PIW, Warsaw, 1965. Also Zbigniew Wilski, *Wielka tragiczka* (*A great tragic actress*), Wydawnictwo Literackie, Cracow, 1982; Kazimierz Braun, *Wielka reforma teatru w Europie* (*The great reform of the theater in Europe*), Ossolineum, Wroclaw, 1984, p. 277.
35. Stanislawa Wysocka, *Teatr przyszłości* (*Theater of the future*), Wydawnictwa Artystyczne i Filmowe, Warsaw, 1973, pp. 199–200.
36. Hanna Zahorska, pseud. Savitri, *Kłosy Ukrainy*, Kiev (1916):15–18.
37. Stanislawa Wysocka, "O teatrze Studya" ("About the Studya theater"), *Kłosy Ukrainy* (1916):19–22.
38. Jaroslaw Iwaszkiewicz, *Stanisława Wysocka i jej kijowski teatr Studya* (*Stanisława Wysocka and her Kiev Studya theater*).
39. Quoted in G. H. Ford, *Dickens and His Readers: Aspects of Novel-Criticism since 1836* (Princeton, N.J.: Princeton University Press, 1955), pp. 134–135.
40. Iwaszkiewicz, p. 40.
41. Schiller, p. 196.
42. Cf. Edward Krasiński, *Warszawskie sceny: 1918–39* (*The Warsaw theaters: 1918–39*), PIW, Warsaw, 1976.
43. Tadeusz Boy-Zeleński, *Flirt z Melpomena* (*Flirting with Melopmene*), 10 vols., Gebethner i Wolf, Warsaw, 1925, vol. 5, pp. 23–26.
44. Cf. Stanislaw Marczak-Oborski, *Teatr w Polsce: 1918–1939* (*The theater in Poland: 1918–1939*) PIW, Warsaw, 1984, pp. 27–30; also in Krasiński, pp. 76–81.
45. Tadeusz Boy-Zeleński, *Pisma* (*Collected works*), 28 vols. PIW, Warsaw, 1966, vol. 24, p. 618.
46. Boy-Zeleński, *Pisma* (1969), vol. 26, pp. 229–231.
47. Tadeusz Boy-Zeleński, *Krótkie spiecie* (*Short-circuit*), Rój, Warsaw, 1938, pp. 229–231.
48. Zenobiusz Strzelecki, *Polska plastyka teatralna* (*The Polish stage design*), 3 vols., PIW, Warsaw, 1963, vol. 3, pp. 409–410.
49. Tadeusz Boy-Zeleński, "Chlopie jestem" ("I am a little boy"), *Kurier Poranny*, February 6, 1938.
50. Boy-Zeleński, "Chlopie."

# Barmecide Feasts:
# Ritual, Narrative,
# and the Victorian Novel

### Sarah Gilead

Much nineteenth-century fiction seeks to describe the muddle and shapeless-ness of modern deracinated life, and also to differentiate itself from the muddle by entering social discourse as a textual agent capable of reascribing meaning to individual life-histories and indeed to history itself. Peter Brooks comments on the lack in the nineteenth century of a sense of "a central, organizing Sacred myth." As the sense of Providence in history becomes more tenuous the burden of narrative to engender meaning becomes greater. "With the decline in belief in a sacred masterplot, the life-history of societies, institu-tions, and individuals assumed new importance. The interpretation of human plots, especially the understanding and justification of their generalizable patterns, became a task of prime urgency" ("Fictions," 74). Victorian an-alysts of culture and society think of history as a vast-scaled rite of passage in which a prior epoch of coherence and stability (an "organic," "feudal," "natural," or "concentrated" epoch) is superseded by a liminal phase (the clichéd "age of transition") which in turn will yield the next, higher period of cultural coherence. That literature is supposed to reveal and even to catalyze this teleological process is frequently asserted, both directly and implicitly. Fictions and autobiographies like *Sartor Resartus* and Mill's *Autobiography*, novels like *David Copperfield, Jane Eyre*, and *The Mill on the Floss* trace their subjects' personal rites of passage, which in turn represent the spiritual ills and likely cures of humanity in an age of transition.

In this light, Victor Turner's view of narrative as social drama seems particularly apt for investigating the nineteenth-century novel. Turner defines social drama as a matrix producing the many genres and cultural performances from ritual to oral and literary narratives ("Social Dramas," 158). That much nineteenth-century poetry, fiction, and autobiography portrays individual processes of social accommodation as a rite (or rites) of passage is apparent; how such portrayals function (or fail to function, or question their power to function) as social drama is somewhat less apparent. The terminologies and concepts developed by Turner and others may enable greater precision in thinking and writing about the ways in which ritual and narrative interact in the themes, structures, and purposes of nineteenth-century literature.

Ritual is commonly understood as preserving traditional meanings, social structures and categories; but it functions as a model for change as well as a model of behaviors and beliefs (Turner, "Social Dramas," 163). Such doubleness of function is surely present in the Victorian novel and indeed the Victorian sensibility: the desire to preserve still usable traditions and values, coupled with the felt need to revise them. The multiple purposes of ritual are reflected in the Victorian novel's analyses of the deficits of modern culture. Typically, the Victorian novel deplores the breakdown of the power of social drama to enact and thus defuse conflicts within social structures;[1] to inscribe cultural codes on the individual;[2] to derive the meaning of human enterprise in history from super-historical forces or realms of being;[3] to establish modes of interpersonal communication.[4] But, just as typically, the narrative traces a boldly reconstructed ritual derived from what comes to appear in the course of the novel as a shared cultural heritage inhabiting a generative ritual form. The orphan comes to represent the power of ritual transformation in which unleashed antisocial energies fuel a "liminal" experience that paradoxically becomes a necessary stage in an orderly symbolic affirmation or revision of the fundamental conceptual categories of culture and society.[5]

Oliver Twist, Jane Eyre, David Copperfield, Dorothea Brooke, Henry Esmond—each encounters or temporarily plays the role of anti-structural outsider before becoming domesticated or domesticating such an outsider, who is in any case typically a double. However, the fulfillment of the orphan quest for accommodation takes place not in the realm of the liminal (the transforming role-generating processes derived from religious or social tradition) but in the realm of what Turner calls the "liminoid": the liminoid "represents . . . the dismembering, the sparagmos of the liminal" and is its modern replacement, seen in various forms of art and social behavior ("Variations," 43). As fictional narratives, the orphan-quests are liminoid—are individualistic, idiosyncratic, and original, even as they invoke and validate themselves upon the cyclical, collective, and community-generated—upon the liminal.[6] Narratives that displace ritual and seek to function as its replacement encounter the Carlylean paradox: that the symbolic enactment or revision of values and modes of belief must be both deliberate, a recognized and assented-to cultural project; and unconscious, welling up spontaneously from the world-historical spirit into human imagination and its artifacts.

The feast is a genre or aspect of ritual which implicitly comments on the force or efficacy of rituals both communal and fictional. Arnold van Gennep regards the feast as comprising the third, post-liminal phase of rite of passage, that of incorporation or reaggregation (29). The feast normally signals successful completion of a prior ritual or phase of ritual. It emphasizes the integrative aspects or purposes of ritual, and in itself forms a primary social drama that ameliorates the strains, abuses, or rigidity of social structure; that counters the experience of society as aggressor against or represser of individual psyche. Like gift-giving, feast-giving is a dynamic, self-perpetuating reciprocal exchange constituting a social and sometimes an economic flow of goods, obligations, and interpersonal bonds—thus, a microcosm of the processes that maintain social interactions through time.

Given Victorian literature's obsessive interest in failed feasts, a virtual taxonomy could be constructed including feasts characterized by gluttony, starvation, solitude, exploitation, metaphoric cannibalism, and eating non-food or poison. The steam-vapor bath dinner of *Our Mutual Friend*, the Lotos eating in Tennyson's poem, the fruit-gobbling in Christina Rossetti's "Goblin Market," Alice's Mad Tea Party, Melmotte's disastrous dinner for the emperor of China in Trollope's *The Way We Live Now*, Sairy Gamp's quarrelsome tea with Betsey Prig (*Martin Chuzzlewit*)—the failed feasts in their exuberant variety attest to an entire range of psychical, sexual, social, political ills. But the failed feast also figures in the formation of successful literary rites of passage, the feast becoming itself liminal—a Nay to society's false or deluded assertions of ritual efficacy which is transformed into an affirmation of liminoid-force as adequate substitute for that failure.

In the following discussions of three Victorian novels, *Orley Farm, Great Expectations*, and *Adam Bede*, failed feasts do generate or complete compensatory rites of passage but also comment adversely on them. A central character creates or asserts a social identity which in turn valorizes traditional moral beliefs or values; yet social grievances and conflicts remain unredressed and unreformed. The conflicting functions and meanings of the failed feasts point to the novels' structural as well as thematic tensions—for example, at once providing closure but undermining the putative moral or psychological contents of such closure. In the three narratives, falsely imitative or parodic rituals and genuinely imitative reconstructed rituals are extremely difficult to distinguish, not simply because ritual in modern desacralized society cannot be authentic and not because narrative discourse tends to undermine itself, but rather because the great Victorian novels perpetually seek to define their relation to the larger discourses of history. The following readings of three very different novels investigate the ramifying idea of ritual in the Victorian novel: as thematic and structural organizing principle, and as means of raising self-referential implications concerning the complex and conflicting purposes of nineteenth-century fiction.

### *Orley Farm*: Feast and the failure of Social Drama

Feasts as rituals, parts of rituals, and meta-rituals in Trollope's *Orley Farm* reveal a social world characterized by meanness, frustration, and uncontrolled displays of aggression; that is, a world whose redressive mechanisms have failed. These failures form the background against which Lady Mason's crime, confessions, and expiation emerge as a rite of passage seeking to restore some sense of moral significance and individual value. The title *Orley Farm*, like *Great Expectations*, virtually trnslates into "Barmecide Feast"; Orley Farm, itself a lovely, fertile property, finally brings nobody satisfaction or pleasure. In the world of *Orley Farm*, plans, goals, and contracts are unfulfilled; energy, desire, and ambition consume themselves. Lady Mason's bold crime of forgery seeks to defend her son's property and social status, but Lucius as adult repudiates the crime and the property together. Joseph Mason is obsessed with vengeful hatred for Lady Mason's robbery of the estate which should have become his, but when it finally does, it fails to satisfy him after all; in fact, he is deprived of the pleasure of his chief grievance. The lawyer Dockwrath, a former tenant of Lady Mason, is outraged at her and Lucius because Lucius, upon coming of age, had insisted that he vacate the rented acres. Dockwrath, a virtual personification of aggression ("wrath"), successfully re-opens the original Orley Farm inheritance case to further his career and revenge himself on Lady Mason, but he is only "docked" for his efforts, frustrated, professionally ruined, and forced to leave town and his family.

Whether manifest as greed or as self-deprivation, a constant state of "hunger" prevails, a sense of unassuageable deprivation. Scenes, characters, descriptions in the secondary plots image and comment on the novel's central themes; Lady Mason's narrative constitutes itself as, on one level, counter-plot; on another level, as repetition.

Dockwrath's bullying of his family is repeatedly imaged in terms of food: he expresses his fury at the loss of the Orley fields by threatening his wife with food deprivation: " 'Where are you to get milk for all those children, do you think, when the fields are gone?' " In fact, he is himself a food depriver: Miriam Dockwrath complains that he hardly allows her enough money for bread, though he buys various small properties with money he has squirrelled away—that is, he feeds his ambition while half-starving his family, and does so under the pretext of fulfilling the traditional male role of provider. And though he has meals and drinks at a local pub, and even treats others if he has something to gain by such generosity, his wife reports, " 'I can't get a pint of beer—not regular—betwixt breakfast and bedtime' " (vol. II, ch. 2). There is something particularly cruel in this denial of nourishment to a perpetually breeding and nursing mother. It is as though Dockwrath has fathered such a large family so as to enjoy depriving them.

Dockwrath's contempt for his wife and rage at Lady Mason (who in fact had tried to dissuade her son from removing Dockwrath as tenant) suggest that part of his aggressiveness derives from an unfocussed and unacknow-ledged hatred of women. Lady Mason represents a "bad breast," a woman who is not consistently nurturing; he punishes the potential food-depriver in all women by enslaving his wife as breeder and nurser of infants.[7] Dockwrath uses his rage against Lady Mason as depriving female to advance male-bonding activities, but such bondings are characterized by exclusivity, jeal-ousy, and defensive conservation of class boundaries. In a time of unpre-dictable change in social arrangements (change not regulated by ritual or law), those either rising or wishing to rise in the social hierarchy and those fearful of invasion are anxious and insecure. Dockwrath the irascible bully is also an intruder on the feast, seeking approval and acceptance by males higher in the social power structure. Dockwrath's representative social hunger is ex-pressed as two-fold oral aggressiveness: in his characteristically rude speech; and in a brilliantly contrived scene of Barmecide feasting (ch. 9, "A Convivial Meeting"), in which Dockwrath invades the "Commercial Room" of an inn—a room to which he has legal right but not the right of custom. A traditional dinner for the commercial gentlemen reveals group subdivisions but within a larger homogeneity: all are male, and all (with the secret exception of Dockwrath) are engaged in trade. But Dockwrath refuses to join in the ceremonial mid-repast wine-drinking (if he did, he would later have to share the cost of the wine bill). Dockwrath's conflicting impulses—to enjoy male-bonding behaviors fostered by tradition and to fear erosion of his individuality and independence—reflect a larger conflict between law and custom. Thinks lawyer Dockwrath, "his pocket was guarded by the law of the land and not by the laws of any special room in which he might chance to find himself." But law has not fully replaced ritual as a social organizing principle. Dockwrath's breaching the solidarity of the feast raises the question of social identity in the new commercial world. Dockwrath as a lawyer is technically not "commercial," but, as he points out, in a commercial age, who is not? In a competitive society with a fluid class structure, subgroups of a single class are rivals. Festal solidarity among the members of a single subgroup is thus undermined by conflict over social terrains and boundaries, and reveals but without mitigating social straining at traditional divisions among professional and class subgroups. Confusion and hostility result; Dockwrath tries to appropriate privileges that accrue to male-bonding traditions, but he cannot perform the gestures, ceremonies, and transactions that create such bonding.

Similar patterns of deprivation and disinheriting are seen in the Joseph Masons of Groby Park. The eldest son and heir of the patriarch Sir Joseph Mason (Lady Mason's long-dead husband and denier of Lucius' claim to Orley Farm), Joseph Mason is the legitimate but deprived heir to Orley Farm. In effect, Groby Park is Orley Farm's inelegant and parodic replacement ("Groby" implying grab, grope, gross; and the German *grob*, rude, thick, rough). Groby Park is a microcosm of an uncongenial society; Joseph, its master, is hard, contentious, vengeful, and perpetually dissatisfied. He deeply desires to be a gentleman, just as Dockwrath desires to be professionally successful, but his playing at gentleman is inept, lacking the inner conviction of legitimacy and the awareness of the appropriate behaviors and attitudes. Like Dockwrath and Lady Mason, Joseph's social identity is undermined by unresolved and never fully comprehended conflict between the two notions of social order based on law or on custom. Cash and legal nexuses lack the bonding reciprocities established by ritual or custom, and generate monstrous or unstable versions of traditional social identities. Mason is infected with a vague but constant sense of suspicion and possessiveness: regarding Lady Mason, "The dreadful thing at which he shuddered was his own ill usage. As for her:—pity her! Did a man ever pity a rat that had eaten into his choicest dainties?" (ch. 8). Joseph, like Dockwrath, is much like an infuriated suckler deprived of the breast.

Mrs. Mason, Joseph Mason's wife, is in fact what Dockwrath and Mason subconsciously think Lady Mason to be, a bad breast, a denier-depriver of food. In the allegorical scene of life in a Barmecide society lacking psychosocial integrative dramas (ch. 8, "Mrs. Mason's Hot Luncheon"), Dockwrath fittingly appears as a bewildered and hungry guest (this chapter immediately precedes "A Convivial Meeting," discussed above). The large luncheon table "might have borne a noble banquet; as it was the promise was not bad, for there were three large plated covers concealing hot viands." When the covers are removed, "there reposed three scraps, as to the nature of which Mr. Dockwrath, though he looked hard at them, was unable to enlighten himself." Mrs. Mason, a solitary feeder and compulsive food-hoarder as well as a food-depriver, obtains sincere pleasure in starving others, but "nevertheless she would feed herself in the middle of the day, having a roast fowl with bread sauce in her own room." Her husband writhes in impotent anger at her meanness but collaborates with it: in the absence of good or plentiful food, and gentlemanly pride in open hospitality, Mr. Mason endeavors "to get the lunch out of his head, and to redirect his whole mind to Lady Mason and his hopes of vengeance" (ch. 8), thus using his food-deprivation at home to nourish his anger at property loss and his desire for vengeance.

In the main plot, Lady Mason's twenty-year-old crimes (forgery and per-jury), her private confessions of guilt, her public trial and acquittal reveal as they rebel against the meaning-deprived conditions of commercial society, and simultaneously dramatize the complex though nonfunctional relationship between law and ritual. Her confessions are ritualistic in that they formalize her idiosyncratic self-mythification (as Rebecca, heroic self-sacrificer, and penitent) and, more specifically, are liminoid, forming a self-contrived rite of passage from ordinary social identity to the more precarious but more emotion-laden role of martyr. Her enactment of a private ritual seeks to compensate for the dearth of effective social dramas, the dearth represented by the failed feasts. But her modelling herself on the biblical Rebecca, who stole the paternal blessing for her son Jacob, is parodic, self-serving and inauthentic.[8] Similarly, her trial takes the form of public ritual performance in such a way as to function properly neither as ritual nor as law. Her evasion of the law reveals its weakness as a culture-preserving force, its incapacity to compensate for ritual as a means of regulating social processes and conflicts. The prosecution and trial of Lady Mason reveal profound breaches between class structure and traditional values, but fail to provide redress for these breaches. Lady Mason's trial draws together as actors and spectators a virtual cross-section of society. But while ritual may indeed dramatize the rivalry and hostility between the subgroups of the community (Christian and Jew, gentry and nouveaux riches, rich and poor) here there is no larger drama enacting common goals, values, or beliefs.

The mood of the novel at closing is the same as at the beginning, char-acterized by nonsatisfaction of debts social, moral, sexual, and economic; by non- or miscompletion of transitions in status, such as coming of age and marriage. Lady Mason does not pay her debt to society for the crimes of forgery and perjury because society's ethical notions are at variance with its principles of social organization and class structure. Structure and antistructure are in a state of permanent tension, with no ritual to transform the tension into the energy that fuels social process. The result is badly muddled behavior. Lady Mason seeks for her son the benefits of social legitimacy by transgressing the law; that transgression effectively makes her the social equal of honorable old Sir Peregrine Orme, who later rejects her as fiancée because of the immoral way in which she obtained that equality; had she not committed the crime, she would have been morally but not socially worthy of Sir Peregrine. The aftermath of the crime—that is, the entire novel—reveals profound rifts between different professional subgroups (e.g., lawyers like Dockwrath vs. lawyers like the Rounds), different sectors of the middle class, old landed gentry and newly wealthy tradesmen, between generations, and between the genders.

Lady Mason's illegitimacy—to what class does she properly belong?—mirrors many others'; even the most legitimate Sir Peregrine comes to represent a class vitiated by anachronism, impotence, and inaction, as evidenced in his self-stymieing and conflicting moral and social ideals and by his grandson Perry's self-exiling. The newly powerful classes reveal self-doubt, greed, uncertainty (the Furnivals, Dockwraths, Joseph Masons). A society that has lost its patrimony of social dramas capable of renewing or revising its basic goals and values is a society whose energies, at certain levels, are exhausted (the Ormes); at others, misapplied or self-wounding (Dockwraths, Joseph Masons, Lady Mason). For different reasons, both Perry Orme and Lucius Mason exile themselves, relinquishing their patrimony and failing to fulfill their "coming of age" potentialities. The engagements of Lady Mason and Sir Peregrine and of Lucius Mason and Sophia Furnival remain unfulfilled. The Dockwraths are separated, as is Perry from Sir Peregrine and Edith. With the breakdown of the mechanisms for healing or making manageable the antagonisms that any social structure produces, the only stable personal relationships are those that operate at drastically reduced levels of expectation: the Moulders, the Joseph Masons, Lucius and Lady Mason, Sir Peregrine and Edith.

The pattern of narrative compensation for ritual dearth is present parodically in the martyr-transformation of Lady Mason and ironically in the comic-romance transformation of Felix Graham from potential malcontent to accepter of the status quo. Both Lady Mason's main plot and the Felix subplot may be read as wry Trollopian comments on the Victorian enterprise of cultural reconstruction by revised myths and rituals. Destined to become a double of the honorable, tolerant Judge Stavely, Felix embarks on a career of upper-middle-class compromise (the embarkation occurs at the successful Stavely Christmas feast), a career which in the context of the novel as a whole is so separated from the devastatingly detailed examination of an uncongenial society as to be negligible as an antidote to it. Felix's and Lady Mason's narratives turn out to be inversely parallel; the comic resolution of Felix's story, like the tragic one of Lady Mason's, is as much an escape from the intolerable realities around him as Perry's or Lucius's foreign journeyings in the wake of their failures.

### *Great Expectations*: Mourning, Debt, Ontogeny

In *Great Expectations* Dickens examines the psychical consequences of ritual incompletion, fragmentation, and vitiation; because of their ritual-deprived condition, characters struggle on their own to complete the psychological project of ritual: internal psychical integration brought about by structuring the psyche in accordance with the symbolic order of culture. In her essay on the figure of the orphan in eighteenth- and nineteenth-century fiction, Nina Auerbach sees in *Great Expectations* Dickens' most honest confrontation with the theme of orphanhood, recapitulating and commenting on previous orphan novels, and showing "why the myth of the orphan—which at its high point practically constituted orphan-worship—was losing its efficacy as the century drew to a close" (411). Pip's story is, as Auerbach implies, a parody of successful orphan-narratives, thus, a parody of novels that recreate or compensate for ritual dearth; but it is a parody that keeps seeking to turn the sham into the genuine, often by means of a sacrifice or series of sacrifices; to transform the deprived condition of orphanhood into the potent ritual phase of liminality.

Hunger and orphans form a frequent conjunction in Dickens. "Hunger" is deprivation in the realms of the physical, familial, and social; is failure in family and social economies to perpetuate or, when necessary, revise social arrangements.[9] Focussing on Dickens' comedy in general and in *Martin Chuzzlewit* in particular, Robert Polhemus perceives that oral excessiveness is aggressive; gustatory or verbal, open mouths strive to ingest the external world or to impose self on the world. Eating, though, like language, mediates between individual flesh and the world; food "proves that the self and the not-self do connect'' (113). But *Great Expectations* is a world of perpetual hunger, as Angus Wilson has pointed out (531). Connections between self and non-self remain tenuous and unfixed by ritual, whose completion would be manifest in feast; such ritual completion is perpetually sought and ever-further deferred.

As René Girard has observed, the liminal condition of being ''in passage'' is akin to the undifferentiation that characterizes generative, reciprocal violence—violence, that is, that has not been ''fixed'' by the symbolism of sacrifice. The liminal passenger in effect becomes innoculated with symbolic doses of violence, and will be immune to the disease of generative violence (283–285). Pip's is the reverse case: because he is uninscribed in cultural discourse, he breeds violence which in turn demands either revenge or purification by further violence but never attains to a stable ritual process whose completion integrates individual and society and transforms generative violence into usable social energy. Instead, Pip's initial lack of social identity inaugurates a narrative that vainly quests for the directedness, the shapeliness, the meaning-ascribing force of ritual. Feasts in *Great Expectations* are travesties of sacramental communion, of individual incorporation into cultural order, intrapsychic reconciliation of warring drives, and sacrificial-redemptive processes. The feasts mourn but without compensating for the loss of psycho-cultural binding mechanisms.

At the novel's beginning, Magwitch, like shivering, small Pip, is a victim of raw elements because he has not been ''cooked'' by culture, has not been ''clothed'' with social value. Magwitch wears broken shoes, an old rag tied around his head, and has no hat; he is ''a man who had been soaked in water, and smothered in mud, and stung by nettles, and torn by briars; who limped and shivered and glared, and growled, and whose teeth chattered in his head.'' The combined motifs of death, starvation, and cannibalism are synecdochal for his and for Pip's cultural deprivation. But he and Pip recreate, in miniature, the social contracts and the cultural order which have been denied them.[10] Pip swears to do Magwitch's bidding and not to betray him; implicitly, Magwitch agrees to leave him unharmed. But this contract, rather than defining a social relationship, creates a dangerous state of unregulated indebtedness to the past.[11] Magwitch translates his gratitude to Pip into a plot against a society which has betrayed him; yet he collaborates with that society. Pip is equally indebted for life, by his misplaced loyalty to Miss Havisham, by the fantasied future as gentleman, by responsibility felt as disgusting burden when he learns of Magwitch, by guilt at that disgust. ''Debt'' defines a guilty existence tormented by obligations that are illusory or that never can be met.

The Pip/Magwitch contract is not culturally sanctioned, and does not produce a bond assimilable to social structure. What is charity from the Christian-liminal perspective is crime from the structural-legal. Two conflicting narratives are thus set in motion: one, a liminoid ritual of moral transformation in which Pip ultimately integrates the fluid and egalitarian values of liminality with the requirements of social structure and thus achieves a stable social identity; the second, the story of Pip's mere reiteration of social and cultural impotence and of his failure to transform himself or his world.[12]

In his lecture/essay, "Desire and the Interpretation of Desire in *Hamlet*" (especially the section 'Desire and Mourning'), Jacques Lacan extends Freud's thinking on mourning. The work of mourning results from loss which leaves a gap or hole in the real, a hole which calls forth mourning on the part of the subject. By means of the hole, the signifier is set in motion. "This hole provides the place for the projection of the missing signifier" which, as in psychosis, produces swarms of images (38). "The work of mourning is accomplished at the level of the *logos*: I say *logos* rather than group or community, although group and community, being organized culturally, are its mainstays. The work of mourning is first of all performed to satisfy the disorder that is produced by the inadequacy of signifying elements to cope with the hole that has been created in existence." Lacan uses "mourning" in two ways, both as revealing and as filling the gap in the cultural-symbolic order, but we have seen that, indeed, the paradoxes of ritual include precisely such double vectors.[13]

In *Great Expectations*, crime seeks to generate the order of the law, the "nom [non] du père," the symbolic order of culture and community; but without ritual completion of the work of mourning, such a symbolic order fails to manifest itself—no form exists within which it may be actualized. What is foreclosed in the realm of the symbolic reappears in the real; denied symbolic substitution for what is lost, the subject is condemned to act out the terms of solution. Instead of ritually established symbolic sacrifice, castration, killing of the past, and rebirth, both Hamlet and Pip act out these processes with full, with literal violence. In *Great Expectations*, unresolved aspects of the past—secrets, fragments of self, guilt—seek composition but keep decomposing into ritual detritus, into mere parts, or into doubles which are parody-doubles of ritually consecrated substitutes. Unable to exorcise the past or assimilate it to the symbolic order of culture, Pip spends the novel, like Magwitch, "eluding the hands of the dead people stretching up cautiously out of their graves to get a twist upon his ankle and pull him in."

Rather than demonstrating familial/social interrelationships and symbolizing the power of ritual to integrate individual with socio-cultural economies, feasts in *Great Expectations* are part and representative of overall failure of ritual. Pip's theft and Magwitch's solitary feast occur on Christmas, and are immediately followed by a worse festal travesty, the family Christmas dinner. The Christmas feast at the forge fails to forge links between individual and family, family and community, past and present, secular and divine. Instead of integrating disparate cultural elements, the feast is itself mutilated (some of the food stolen for the convict); and the good quality and large amount of food are negated by overwhelming meanness. Pip at the feast is in a false and uncomfortable position, an unwelcome guest expected to pay his debt of gratitude towards his hostess in the coin of guilt and self-abasement. Inverting the Christian feast as celebration of Christ's birth, the birth of myth and credo, Pip's feast initiates a long, painfully protracted laboring at a rebirth whose deferred completion forms not a redressive social drama but an ambiguous, self-conflicting narrative. The efficacious sacrifice of Christ, reiterated in the cannibalistic symbolism of the mass, is here parodied in the sadistic cannibalizing of Pip. The guests verbally jab him, taunting his helplessness as if in preparation for sacrifice. "I might have been an unfortunate little bull in a Spanish arena, I got so smartingly touched up by these moral goads." Instead of liminal/festal equality among the feasters, social cleavages are emphasized. The powerful assert themselves against the powerless: adult versus child, many against one, the established versus the outsider, the named against the orphan. Pip is scapegoat but with no capacity to transform conflict into symbolic resolution; instead he embodies a vague sense of threat. Without these resolutions, nothing obviates the need for such overt expressions of hostility and covert expression of fear and insecurity as the feasters display when they dine off Pip.

Satis House is a microcosm of a society bereft of the mechanisms that create reciprocal relationships and integrate the individual into a symbolic order. A necropolitan, barren structure, Satis House is, again, virtually "Barmecide Feast," sufficing and satisfaction present only in its name and external form. At the site of the house is a large brewery in which nothing has been brewed for years. Estella offers Pip a Barmecide beverage: " 'You could drink without hurt all the strong beer that's brewed there now, boy.' " And, " 'Better not try to brew beer there now, or it would turn out sour, boy,' " an apt metaphor for inefficacy or corruption of the social processes that "cook" (or "ferment") the "raw" individual, that create culture from nature. The presiding spirit of Satis House is a failed liminal figure trapped in a liminoid world of her own devising. In typical liminoid fashion, Miss

Havisham has tried to reliminalize her ritual failure, and indeed has led a totally ritualized life; but her private rituals only reflect her obsessive-compulsive neuroses. The revenge-drama rituals she constructs for Estella, Pip, and her family further reveal her own and the others' imprisonment in time and circumstance, and their unmitigated indebtedness to the past. The rotting wedding cake images her failed effort to mourn a past which remains hideously present, not "digested" by any adequate ceremony. Miss Havisham is indeed out-of-time, as is proper for the liminal state, but not as part of a process that, upon completion, asserts a measure of human control over time by ascribing cultural meanings to it. Instead, she is permanently liminoid, the stopped watch and clock representing the defeat of culturally-organized time and human helplessness to stay its flow or make it meaningful.

Her corpse-like appearance parodies the liminal symbolism of death, burial, night, darkness;[14] dressed in white, arrayed as a bride, she is literally stuck in the middle of an incomplete marriage ritual, in the middle of an act of socio-cultural inscription on the temporarily blanked-out surface of identity. Its failure in turn has failed to be mourned. Frozen in a state that should be fluid, she can only repeat the betrayals of class consciousness, snobbery, materialism, and ruthlessness that led to her abandonment by her scheming lover. Like Mrs. Mason of Groby, Miss Havisham is a solitary feeder (described in chapter 29). A glutton for vengeance, she is never satisfied; in this, she is a double for Magwitch as well as Compeyson. Vengeance is self-generative, like violence, and is of course closely associated with it, here in such figures as Bentley Drummle, Orlick, Compeyson, Magwitch, and Molly (Estella's mother). Vengeance is both a form of indebtedness to the past and evidence that no symbolic structure exists to drain it off into safer forms.

Does Pip's narrative ultimately enact a compensatory, "recomposed" ritual that counters the overall decomposition of ritual in the novel?[15] Estella's development into ice-blooded lady, Pip's unwilling indenturing as blacksmith, then his illusory expectations, Miss Havisham's and Magwitch's false assumings of the patron's role—these failed or perverse transformations form the very stuff of Pip's own redemptive history; in a reading of the novel as successful if costly and prolonged rite of passage, the false transformations are themselves transformed by the alchemy of liminality into the necessary preliminary stages in the rite; in an alternate reading, the failure of the early transformations sets the pattern for the inauthenticity of Pip's final change. The cost of recomposition is high: the sacrificial deaths of Miss Havisham and Magwitch, the monitory corruption and abuse of Estella, the violent surrogate-murder of Mrs. Joe. Pip survives a plethora of ritual ordeals, Carlylean "baphometic fire-baptisms," the "rescuing" of Miss Havisham and burning himself, being nearly murdered and dissolved in lime, near-death by illness, impoverishment by literal debt, a baptismal river-journey. But Pip still does not free himself from his indebtedness to the past. Messy residues remain of regret, longing, and guilt because no systematic regulation of indebtedness exists; only violence has been able to transform vengeance and aggressive desire into the "softer" forms of guilt and nostalgia.

In the idea of "great expectations," the present is mortgaged to the future; the value of the present diminished. Pip's moral regeneration only exacerbates his sense of haunting and hauntedness; he remains a ghost, unable to live fully in present or future. In this novel, nearly every event, image, and gesture eventually (sometimes immediately) turns into food for nostalgia, vengeance, guilt, or grief; and everybody returns—Herbert, Estella, Magwitch, Compeyson, Biddy, Joe, Orlick. In the story of the loss of great expectations as the loss of cultural endowments, everything and everyone returns to the realm of the real because they find no place in a symbolic order. Thus, *Great Expectations* is a novel of repetition, but here the repetitions are, as it were, incestuous, repetitions of other or of prior repetitions, never attaining the longed-for, elusive authenticity of a dimly felt original.[16] Repetition in *Great Expectations* is a vertiginous multiplication of doubles[17] and of ritual symbols of purification, sacrifice, rebirth; but the symbols are excessive in number and in violence, excessive because seeking to fill an unfillable cultural gap, to pay an unpayable debt.[18]

### *Adam Bede*: Coming of Age in Loamshire

Offering a particularly clear case of a novel organized by ritual doubleness, *Adam Bede* portrays a community threatened with unredressed exposure of economic, social and moral breaches;[19] then dramatizes a cluster of compensatory personal and communal rituals that restore communal coherence, individual self-worth, and moral order. The following discussion will center on Arthur's coming of age celebration and its aftermath as the focus of threat to the community; then on the sacrifice of Hetty as compensatory-restorative ritual which is efficacious and ritually generative (enabling the others' rites of passage) but which vitiates the very moral order it effects. Adam, Arthur, Dinah, and the community as a whole experience a vicarious liminoid rite of passage through their association with Hetty, and in furtherance of which Hetty must play two contradictory roles. She is evidence for and object of the primacy of deep human sympathy as a theodicy for a secular world; she is also the sacrifice whose unmitigated expulsion from community is needed because she symbolizes in her person all that threatens the community's moral image and stability. This doubleness bespeaks the community's strength of ritual imagination, which recreates a spontaneous ritual solution to the threat offered by both Arthur's and Hetty's behavior (but symbolized in the person of Hetty alone).[20] Hetty simultaneously represents the uncontrollable, negative forces of accident, sexuality, and time; but also tolerance, compassion, sharing of suffering as binding moral-affective forces holding the community together. It is Hetty's task to act out the former but thereafter to be spoken of within the latter frame of reference. Hetty's ritual doubleness is at odds with a central aspect of the ontogenic rites at the novel's end, self-realization and deeper self-understanding, for it creates a kind of communal cognitive dissonance in the form of a refusal on the part of her ritual beneficiaries to see Hetty's sacrifice as sacrifice.

Arthur Donnithorne is to come of age at hay-harvesting time by means of a secular ritual which invests time with human significance and thus creates the necessary illusion of human control over time, change, and nature. It is to be a ritual particularly rich with meanings, combining birthday (a biological event, birth, is inscribed in culture); coming of age (the biological process of physical maturation is imbued with specific social significance, including the assumption of legal-social obligations and privileges); natural processes (seasonal change, the understanding of which makes possible both this particular hay harvest and the economic basis of this agrarian community). Such control is at best only partial; as the narrator, Dinah Morris, and Mrs. Poyser note at various times, nature is never fully understood or controlled by human will. Indeed, much ritual acknowledges this while simultaneously asserting the contrary. Arthur's coming of age fails to encompass this ritual double vector. Mortality, contingency, and uncertainty are excluded from the ceremony—Arthur in particular indulges in the dangerous illusion that he can shape future events according to his willed destiny and self-image. But in his secret sexual relationship with Hetty, the other vector is being acted out in full.

When Mrs. Poyser complains that farming is " 'raising victual for other folks, and just getting a mouthful for yourself and your children as you go along' " (ch. 5), she unconsciously images in a deflatingly realistic and unappetizing description of the farmhouse a social hierarchy so unjust as to threaten to topple: " 'this house—it's my opinion the floors up-stairs are very rotten, and the rats in the cellar are beyond anything'." The old Squire's niggardliness is responsible for the undermining rot behind the appearance of prosperity, order and fertility; Arthur plans to make repairs and improvements in both the house and the social hierarchy, putting both on a firmer base and cleaning away the "rot" "upstairs" (the selfishness and power-abuses of the gentry). But the rot is more pervasive than either Mrs. Poyser or Arthur realizes. The social edifice will be more seriously undermined by Arthur's naively arrogant sense of his privilege than it was by the old Squire's meanness. Arthur's "rot" is the inability to see Hetty as fully human, as like himself a being with a significant and fragile social identity. In fact, Arthur reveals and widens the potential lines of conflict in the community between labor and gentry, reveals and exacerbates the fragility of the social structure and the tenuousness of the personal and social bonds that underlie that structure. Arthur's biological paternity, of which he is culpably unaware, concurs with and undermines his supposed assumption of communal paternalism; the irreversible effect of the coming to light of his biological paternity is to negate his coming of age as communal father.

The feasting and festivity at Arthur's birthday mark a successfully completed transition in individual life-cycle, in the life of the community, and in the agricultural season; they function as aspects of a completing, integrative ritual for the participants, inscribing the cultural codes of the community on social, biological, and agricultural processes. Festal and ceremonial aspects include ringing of church bells, band music, and dancing. Class and age differences are marked in the seating, feasting, dancing, and other arrangements, but so is an underlying harmony of communal spirit and purpose. Differences exist but are made tolerable for the time being: structure is preserved by being temporarily and only in a measure superseded. But from the perspective of the narrative as a whole, the chapters on the feast initiate a risky liminoid period, rather than completion of ritual. July is a critical period in agriculture, as the narrator points out; it is between the time of promise and early growth, and before the final harvest of wheat: "we tremble at the possible storms that may ruin the precious fruit in the moment of its ripeness" (ch. 22, "Going to the Birthday Feast"). We fear, that is, the Barmecide feast that Hetty and her baby, and in some senses Arthur too, become, each blighted at her or his moment of ripeness, Hetty as marriageable young woman, her child as newborn baby, Arthur as young Squire. "If only the corn were not ripe enough to be blown out of the husk and scattered as untimely seed!" (ch. 27)—an apt description of Arthur's sexual misbehavior and its results.

Breach necessitates redress, traditionally, in the form of ritual capable of regenerating a perennially threatened human order. Hetty's pregnancy, child-murder, trial, transportation, and death form an unrecognized and unofficial liminoid ritual process for the community, which had been deprived of the effects of Arthur's earlier rite of passage. Hetty is initially the symbol of the failure of ritual in the face of indeterminacy, both Barmecide feaster and feast: "her short poisonous delights had spoiled for ever all the little joys that had once made the sweetness of her life" (ch. 31). But ritual juxtaposes contraries through the mechanism of transition: poison, rot, and bitterness are not only the contraries to nourishment, cooking, and sweetness, they are also their necessary precedents; they are purgative, medicinal, transformative. Hetty traverses "the borders of a . . . wilderness where no goal lay before her" (ch. 37) in her journey in a landscape of accident and mistiming (she misses both Arthur and Dinah by inches). But the narrative regulates this descent to chaos and death by assimilating it to rite of passage. Hetty's destruction is itself curative, though not, of course, to herself.

Adam, Arthur, and Dinah take in small, attenuated doses the bitterness that Hetty swallows to the last dregs; each is rewarded with rebirth of a sort, with humanizing "softening" of moral-judgmental "hardness" (Adam), of class pride and selfishness (Arthur), of sexual repressions (Dinah). Adam's ordeal mourns the irrevocable loss of Hetty but also of his former hard self: "Adam seated listlessly on the bench, pale, unwashed, with sunken blank eyes, almost like a drunkard in the morning" (ch. 38). His "drunken" disorientation will eventually become reorientation, as he gains in self-insight, tolerance, and human sympathy. But his rejection of Hetty, like that of the Poysers, is absolute, however grief-stricken: " 'My poor Hetty . . . she can never be my sweet Hetty again' " (ch. 41). Adam's "deep, unspeakable suffering," unlike Hetty's, becomes "a baptism, a regeneration, the initiation into a new state"—a clichéd rehearsal of liminal terms popularized by Carlyle—"we may come out from that baptism of fire with a soul full of new awe and new pity" (ch. 41). Dinah heroically offers to stay with Hetty to the last, until her death by hanging; and so acts, as she so often had, as Hetty's double. But when the postponed death takes place (as the far less dramatic result of the hardships of exile), Dinah is busy playing another role, that of virtuously passionate matron, wife of Hetty's former fiancé, inheritor of the feathers and linen that Mrs. Poyser had thriftily saved for Hetty, and, most strikingly, inheritor of Hetty's sexuality; but of course Dinah's sexuality is ripened, matured, well-timed; culturally and socially usable. In exchange she sacrifices her preaching. Arthur exiles himself, giving up his dreams of a pleasant life as adored Squire; that is, he does voluntarily and as a sign of his moral regeneration what Hetty is forced to do without that compensation. After eight years of military service, illness, and, presumably, loneliness and guilt, he returns cleansed and chastened to the sympathy of the Irwines and the Bedes.

The survivors enjoy a harvest feast together, not only without Hetty but by means of her absence. The earliest manifestation of reconciling communion is in the form of a mourning meal, with strong penitential-sacramental overtones, that Adam and Bartle Massey share during Hetty's trial. Vowing, " 'I'll never be hard again'," Adam accedes to Bartle's " 'Take a bit, then, and another sup, Adam, for the love of me. See, I must stop and eat a morsel. Now, you take some' . . . Adam took a morsel of bread, and drank some wine.''[21] After Hetty is gone, Adam says to Mr. Poyser, " 'Trouble's made us kin' " (ch. 48). Mr. Irwine joins Adam in convincing the Poysers to stay. Adam had firmly rejected Bartle Massey's platitudes about good coming out of evil, but in chapter 53, "The Harvest Supper," he expresses a similar moral economy, musing on Dinah, " 'I should never ha' come to know that her love 'ud be the greatest o' blessings to me, if what I counted a blessing hadn't been wrenched and torn away from me, and left me with a greater need, so as I could crave and hunger for a greater and a better comfort'." The Poysers, Bartle, Mr. Craig the gardener (another of Hetty's former admirers), Adam, and the farm-workers eat hot roast beef, drink fresh-drawn ale, and sing ceremonial harvest-songs in which all the men join. That November, the conclusion of the harvest is celebrated as Mr. Irwine, Bartle, the Poysers, and the Bedes rejoice at Adam's and Dinah's wedding. Mr. Irwine thinks, "what better harvest from that painful seed-time could there be than this?" (ch. 55). Hetty's sexual crime planted the seed of this harvest; her dead baby and she herself have fertilized that harvest, and promoted solidarity among the central families of the community, the Irwines, Bedes, and Poysers, who together form, symbolically, a complete community composed of gentry, clerisy, farmers, artisans, and peasants. By Hetty's sacrifice, her and Arthur's misplaced and mistimed sexual energies are converted to the uses of social structure: deepened friendship, communal solidarity, the founding of a new family complete with children. By the reverse logic of ritual, the social breaches that were barely visible threats at the time of Arthur's failed birthday feast become far less dangerous after being dramatized. Hetty's crime dramatizes the community's dependence on an immature, inadequate paternal leader who has furthermore betrayed that community's fundamental moral, social and sexual codes; but the discovery of that structural weakness functions as a sort of communal ordeal which ultimately proves that community's resilience and strength; and which completes the communal and personal rites of passage left incomplete by the flawed birthday feast. But that strength derives from the relentlessness of its social, moral, sexual codes, a relentlessness of which Hetty is aware. Her refusal, or rather inability, to nurture or protect her infant is an anticipation of and results from her fear of her family's and community's more deliberate refusal to shelter her. They reject her for shaming them; she rejects the child for shaming her. Like the child, Hetty is left to die of exposure, she being as unequipped to cope with the rigors of transported life as her baby was to survive deprivation of food, warmth, and air.

The acting out of Hetty's fate teaches Adam and Arthur the universal value of deep human sympathy but in fact more closely reflects Bartle's bitter misogyny: " 'I think the sooner such women are put out o' the world the better. . . . What good will you do by keeping such vermin alive? eating the victual that 'ud feed rational beings' " (ch. 40). Hunger demands feeding; feeding, often demands sacrifice. Mrs. Stone, who had helped Hetty at the birth, recounts her last sight of her: " 'I left the prisoner sitting up by the fire in the kitchen with the baby on her lap' " (ch. 43). The laborer who found the dead, buried child returns to the same site next day and sees Hetty sitting there: " 'She'd got a big piece of bread on her lap'." The consequence of Arthur's failed feast is Hetty sitting alone in the wood with a big piece of bread in her lap instead of a baby. Symbolically, she has eaten the child; depriving her or him of life gives Hetty a chance (she naively thinks) to save her own. But if Hetty eats her baby, her family and community eat her, depriving her of affection, social place, and shelter so that they may nourish the recuperative process that preserves their collective life. Not only does her anticipation of her community's and family's rejection of her cause, in large part, the child-murder; knowing how unforgivingly the Poysers have rejected her undoubtedly adds to her grief in exile and hastens her death—another child murder. *Adam Bede* universalizes and humanizes the Evangelical "spontaneous conversion" paradigm; but the secularization of the ritual dynamic of sacrifice-transformation-redemption also necessitates, apparently, the demythification and thus the literalization of sacrifice; the Christian dying god myth is transmuted into a modern version of the equally ancient ritual of the communal scapegoat, but in the modern version the community cannot afford to recognize or admit the price it pays for its solidarity. As in *Orley Farm* and *Great Expectations*, the narrative of *Adam Bede* traces the form of a liminoid monster: like Frankenstein's, made up of dead fragments of traditional ritual motifs, symbols, and processes; functional, but violent and parodic. The reintegrating, reconciling, redressive feasts and festivals compensate for prior failed rituals, but are inscribed with the record of those failures, inscriptions of necessity illegible to the hungry feasters.

## NOTES

1. Victor Turner ("Social Dramas") sees social dramas as having four phases: "breach, crisis, redress, and *either* reintegration *or* recognition of schism" (149).
2. As Turner phrases this idea (*The Ritual Process*), "the neophyte in liminality must be a *tabula rasa* . . . on which is inscribed the knowledge and wisdom of the group" (103).
3. Mircea Eliade characterizes "archaic societies" as being in revolt against "concrete historical time," in quest of "a periodical return to the mythical time of the beginning of things, to the 'Great Time' " (ix).
4. Turner (*Forms of Symbolic Action*) sees all rituals, including everyday ones, as exhibiting a triple function, "communication, control of aggression and bond-formation" (17).
5. Turner defines liminality as un- or anti-structure which is ultimately structure-generating. For basic definitions of his concepts, see Appendix A, *Image and Pilgrimage in Christian Culture*. Liminality is, in Turner's Carlylean phrasing, "the Nay to all positive structural assertions" but "in some sense the source of them all" and even "a realm of pure possibility whence novel configurations of ideas and relations may arise" (*The Forest of Symbols*, 97). This precedes and parallels his notion of liminality as "model of" and as "model for" ("Social Dramas," 163). The concept of liminality originated with van Gennep. I gratefully acknowledge the influence on my work of Nina Auerbach's explorations of the transforming powers of the orphan in nineteenth-century English literature.
6. In "Liminality, Anti-Liminality, and the Victorian Novel," I propose a taxonomy of "liminal" and "anti-liminal" novels: "liminal" novels anatomize the failure of ritual in Victorian culture, but then transform failed ritual into successful rites of passage; "anti-liminal" novels question or deny (often by parodying) the possibility of such transformations.
7. See Dorothy Dinnerstein's analysis of the gender arrangements by which women come to embody frustration and deprivation, and to evoke in males possessiveness, antagonism, general mistrust of life, and the drive to male-bonding activities. Many of the characters of *Orley Farm* exhibit the classical symptoms of food anxiety. Peter Farb and George Armelagos describe these symptoms among the Gurage, a horticultural people of southwestern Ethiopia (77).
8. For a detailed analysis of Lady Mason as a parody-liminal figure, see Sarah Gilead's "Trollope's Orphans and 'The Power of Adequate Performance'."
9. See James E. Marlowe for a related view of cannibalism in Dickens as exploration of English culture, especially the social chasms resulting from assertions of class differences. See Ian Watt for an overview of food and eating in Dickens as means of dramatizing a variety of moral, social, and psychological issues.
10. Barbara Hardy observes that Pip treats Magwitch as a guest, and evokes a guest response, so that "the rudest meal in the novel" becomes "an introductory model of ceremony" (353–354).
11. Norman Brown cites and develops Nietzsche's notion of guilt as that which generates debt and history; guilt tries to overcome mortality; but refusing to accept

death creates a civilization permeated by morbidity—an apt description of the narrative and ambiance of *Great Expectations* (242–243).

12. Dianne Sadoff argues that "two systematic metaphors mediate the father-son economic in this novel: Pip as George Barnwell and Pip as viewer of Hamlet" (32–33). Pip tries "to make amends for what he defines as his guilt for desiring revenge against a figurative father" (38)—to commit parricide and also engender the self in writing.

13. See John P. Muller for an explication of Lacan's text, and especially for succinct and clear explanations of the Lacanian Other, signifier, symbolic order, the imaginary, and foreclosure. For Lacan's development of the Freudian concept of foreclosure (*Verwerfung*) see his *Ecrits: A Selection*.

14. Turner (*The Ritual Process*) points out that liminal entities are "likened to death, to being in the womb, to invisibility, to darkness, to bisexuality, to the wilderness, and to an eclipse of the sun and moon" (95).

15. For affirmations of this view see especially Karl Wintersdorf and G. R. Stange.

16. Eliade's central argument is that ritual valorizes human experience by symbolically repeating primordial, divine, creative acts (5).

17. See Moynahan and Stone on doubles in *Great Expectations*.

18. See Peter Brooks ("Repetition, Repression and Return: *Great Expectations* and the Study of Plot") for a more rigorously neo-Freudian "psychotextual" view of the novel.

19. John Goode argues, "at the beginning the massively established world of Hayslope is threatened by three major possibilities of change, Methodism, the death of Thias Bede, and the affair between Arthur and Hetty, suggesting religious upheaval for Hayslope as a whole, familial disruption for the Bedes, and social exploitation of the Poysers" (25). At the birthday feast, "the separate orders of society confront one another so that from class distinction we turn to class relationship. . . . Arthur dramatizes the paternalistic ideal (liberality and order in the feudal ceremony of Adam's promotion. At the same time, we are conscious that the class-gap is being closed by exploitation: the public liberality which goes with order is undermined by the private liberality of the locket and earrings that will disrupt that order" (23–24).

20. Mary Douglas speculates that communities obsessed with their own fragility, or with external threats, may foster a cult of virginity in which the violation of the body serves as metaphor for the violability of the community as a whole.

21. See Reva Stump's discussion of Bartle's and Adam's communion scene as rite of confirmation following baptism (48–50). U. C. Knoepflmacher discerns a series of "symbolic suppers" that lead Adam to a Feuerbachian conversion (56–59), and identifies the Poysers' Harvest Feast as "a true fertility ritual" (p. 59, note 60).

## WORKS CITED

Auerbach, Nina. "Incarnations of the Orphan." *ELH* 42 (1975): 395–419.

Brooks, Peter. "Fictions of the Wolfman: Freud and Narrative Understanding." *Diacritics* 9 (1979): 72–81.

———. "Repetition, Repression, and Return: *Great Expectations* and the Study of Plot." *New Literary History* 113 (1980): 503–526.

Brown, Norman. *Life Against Death: The Psychoanalytical Meaning of History.* London: Sphere Books, 1959.

Dinnerstein, Dorothy. *The Mermaid and the Minotaur: Sexual Arrangements and Human Malaise.* New York: Harper and Row, 1976.

Douglas, Mary. *Purity and Danger: An Analysis of Concepts of Pollution and Taboo.* London: Routledge and Kegan Paul, 1966.

Eliade, Mircea. *The Myth of the Eternal Return.* Trans. Willard R. Trask. New York: Pantheon Books, Bollinger Series XLVI, 1954.

Farb, Peter, and George Armelagos. *Consuming Passions: The Anthropology of Eating.* Boston: Houghton Mifflin, 1980.

Gilead, Sarah. "Liminality, Anti-Liminality and the Victorian Novel." *ELH* 53 (1986): 183–197.

_____. "Trollope's Orphans and 'The Power of Adequate Performance'." *Texas Studies in Literature and Language* 27 (Spring 1985): 86–105.

Girard, René. *Violence and the Sacred.* Trans. Patrick Gregory. Baltimore and London: Johns Hopkins University Press, 1977.

Goode, John. "'Adam Bede.'" In *Critical Essays on George Eliot*, ed. Barbara Hardy. London: Routledge and Kegan Paul, 1970, 19–41.

Hardy, Barbara. *Forms of Feeling in Victorian Fiction.* Athens, Ohio: Ohio University Press, 1985.

Knoepflmacher, U. C. *Religious Humanism and the Victorian Novel: George Eliot, Walter Pater, and Samuel Butler.* Princeton, N.J.: Princeton University Press, 1965.

Lacan, Jacques. "Desire and the Interpretation of Desire in *Hamlet*." Yale French Studies 55–56 (1977): 11–52.

_____. *Ecrits: A Selection.* Trans. Alan Sheridan. New York and London: Norton, 1977.

Levi-Strauss, Claude. *The Raw and the Cooked.* Trans. J. and P. Weightman. London: Jonathan Cape, 1970.

Marlowe, James E. "English Cannibalism: Dickens after 1859." *SEL* 23 (1983): 647–666.

Moynahan, Julian. "The Hero's Guilt: The Case of *Great Expectations*." *Essays in Criticism* 10 (1960): 60–79.

Muller, John P. "Psychosis and Mourning in Lacan's *Hamlet*." *New Literary History* 12 (1980): 147–165.

Polhemus, Robert. *Comic Faith: The Great Tradition from Austen to Joyce.* Chicago and London: University of Chicago Press, 1980.

Sadoff, Dianne. *Monsters of Affection: Dickens, Eliot and Brontë on Fatherhood.* Baltimore and London: The Johns Hopkins University Press, 1982.

Stange, G. R. "Expectations Well Lost: Dickens' Fable for His Time." In *The Dickens Critics*, eds. George H. Ford and Lauriat Lane, Jr. Ithaca, N.Y.: Cornell University Press, 1961, 294–308.

Stone, Harry. "Fire, Hand, and Gate: Dickens' *Great Expectations.*" *The Kenyon Review* 24 (1962): 662–691.

Stump, Reva. *Movement and Vision in George Eliot's Novels.* New York: Russell and Russell, 1959.

Turner, Victor. *The Forest of Symbols: Aspects of Ndembu Ritual.* Ithaca, N.Y.: Cornell University Press, 1967.

————. Introduction to *Forms of Symbolic Action*, ed. Robert F. Spencer. Seattle and London: Proceedings of the 1969 Annual Spring Meeting of the American Ethnological Society, pp. 3–25.

————. *The Ritual Process: Structure and Anti-Structure.* Chicago: Aldine, 1969.

————. "Social Dramas and Stories about Them." *Critical Inquiry* (Autumn 1980): 141–168.

————. "Variations on a Theme of Liminality." In *Secular Ritual*, eds. Sally F. Moore and Barbara A. Myerhoff. Assen, Netherlands: Von Gorcum, 1977, pp. 36–52.

Turner, Victor, and Edith Turner. *Image and Pilgrimage in Christian Culture: Anthropological Perspectives.* New York: Columbia University Press, 1978.

van Gennep, Arnold. *The Rites of Passage.* Trans. Monika B. Vizedom and Gabrielle L. Caffee. Chicago: University of Chicago Press, 1960.

Watt, Ian. "Oral Dickens." *Dickens Studies Annual*, 3, ed. Robert B. Partlow, Jr. (Carbondale and Edwardsville: Southern Illinois University Press, 1974), pp. 164–181.

Wilson, Angus. Afterword. *Great Expectations.* New York: Signet, 1963.

Wintersdorf, Karl. "Mirror Images in *Great Expectations.*" *Nineteenth-Century Fiction* 21 (1966): 203–224.

# Recent Studies
# in Thomas Hardy's Fiction:
# 1980–86

## *Dale Kramer*

Book-length work on Thomas Hardy's fiction has in the period 1980–86 made some decided advances. It is no exaggeration to suggest that studies of Hardy's work have achieved maturity and that they are in a good condition for a new phase of critical interpretation. In neither respect do Hardy studies differ significantly from the situation in recent years regarding many other Victorian writers such as Dickens, Tennyson, Browning, Arnold, and the Carlyles. Studies in the Victorian period taken as a whole have been reaching a high level of accomplishment and scope, to an extent that would have appeared astonishing a scant twenty years ago, when there was fear that all the important work had been done and there was nothing more to say. What seems to account for this "golden age in the present" is a kind of ambitiousness that is Victorian in itself, seen in its most grandiose in the ongoing new editions of letters of the Carlyles and of the Brownings, from the university presses in the one instance of Edinburgh and Duke, from the personal commitment of Philip Kelley and Ronald Hudson in the other (who formed the Wedgestone Press specifically to publish all of the Browning letters). In other words, the materials for serious renewed study of the great Victorian writers are well in way of being available to us, and a commentary on other writers could take much the same line as I am taking here with Hardy.

To be specific, Hardy studies have been placed on a sounder footing in recent years through the publication of most of his letters and many of his notebooks, through the fairly secure establishment of the facts of his life (though the facts have been interpreted sensationally as often as reliably), and through the preparation and publication of critical editions of his shorter poems and several of his novels. To what extent the understanding of his works relies upon such textual and biographical matters can be debated, but unlike the case previously we can be relatively confident that a very great proportion of such biographical and textual material as has survived is now known to us. The reinterpreters who have yet to do their work can at least proceed with a fair degree of confidence in the facts (although it is the nature of things that vastly less is known than will be always unknown).

Of course not all of this factual work has been done in the 1980s. Much of it is being published during this time; but naturally it has been in progress for many years previously. The edition of the *Collected Letters*, edited by Richard Little Purdy and Michael Millgate, had its origin early in the 1970s or even earlier, the first volume appearing in 1978. Millgate's commanding biography appeared in 1982, but as long ago as 1971 his *Thomas Hardy: His Career as a Novelist* presented as many factually founded ideas about Hardy and his works as any previous study. And what ranks not too far behind Millgate's biography as the most important study of Hardy's ideas, Lennart Björk's edition of the *Literary Notebooks*, was published in part in 1974. Although I know little about the gestation period of the edition of the *Notebooks* it seems reasonable to believe that it must have been begun in the 1960s. Similarly, my edition of the Clarendon Edition of *The Woodlanders*, published in 1981, was initiated as a doctoral thesis in 1962; the research for the doctoral dissertations of Juliet Grindle and Simon Gatrell, completed as dissertations in 1974 and 1973 and published as a Clarendon edition (*Tess of the d'Urbervilles* [co-edited in this format by Juliet Grindle and Simon Gatrell]) and as a World's Classics edition (*Under the Greenwood Tree*, edited by Simon Gatrell) in 1983 and 1985, was also begun in the 1960s. But while it was fortuitous that these works were made available to readers and critics within a fairly brief span of years, the fact of their appearing in close conjunction with each other nonetheless imparts to this half-decade a distinctive scholarly tinge.

Because I have reviewed many of these works of scholarship and criticism elsewhere,[1] I want to concentrate in this essay on those works I have not judged previously.[2] In particular, I have written at great length on Lennart Björk's massive and invaluable (*The Literary Notebooks of Thomas Hardy* (London: Macmillan; New York: New York University Press, 1985) in *Review* (8 [1986], 1–19) and so offer here only the short but strong encomium that this ambitious work of scholarship is in itself an indispensable tool for other scholarship. In printing Hardy's notebooks of jottings and the passages he copied from philosophers, journalists, scientists, historians, and other authors, and identifying the original sources, *The Literary Notebooks* makes available much information bearing on Hardy's relationship to the ideas of his times.

Scholarship can both liberate and restrict the thoughts of critics and interpreters. It provides material to be reflected upon; and it can modify the free-form development of critics' theories and perceptions. If, for example, it has become nearly impossible to give credence to the Tryphena Sparks theory of biographical impact, we now know in more detail than before that Hardy loved a variety of women, mostly young, several related to him (none in an incestuous degree, however, as has been suggested turned out to be frustratingly revealed to him during his courtship of Tryphena), and that he may have proposed marriage with at least one of them before meeting Emma.

What stands out during these few years are the large projects on which Michael Millgate has been engaged. At this writing the final volume of *Collected Letters* has yet to appear, although I understand that most of the work is completed; *Thomas Hardy: A Biography* (London: Oxford University Press; New York: Random House) appeared in 1982, superseding in detail, scope, and balance the interesting two-volume study of Hardy's life by Robert Gittings in the 1970s; and his edition of Hardy's autobiography appeared in 1985 under Hardy's title, *The Life and Work of Thomas Hardy* (London: Macmillan; Athens: University of Georgia Press).

Publishing the *Letters* of great writers invaluably contributes to the study of their literary works even when as with Hardy an author may look upon letter-writing as a task to be got through for the sake of an—ordinarily—mundane communication, and even when as again with Hardy the author has gone to some trouble and time to destroy great amounts of correspondence and other papers. Some of the most interesting material in Hardy's letters makes clear that however much his reputation rests on readers' confidence in his possession of rural wisdom, he also made himself familiar with current thought. (Some letters suggest he maintained his currency through essays in popular literary and cultural journals as much as through reading the philosophers themselves.) The *Letters* contain several reminders that Hardy disliked being thought miserable because he was a pessimist ("'Pessimism' . . . leads to a mental quietude that tends rather upward than downwards" [III. 308]). Hardy's comments on matters of art do not present strikingly new views, but amplify ideas one would expect of him; for example, in a letter to Edward Garnett he defends plotted fiction as being more skillful and demanding than the sort of unplotted novel for which Garnett had expressed admiration (Richard Jefferies' *Amaryllis at the Fair*), and in others he objects to slice-of-life impressionism. Although one of the great writers of tragedy in the nineteenth century, he gives no particular honorific to the word: several allusions to "tragedy" in the fourth volume indicate that Hardy applied the term generally to moments of unhappiness or frustration, nothing discriminating. References to individual works, or problems he was having in writing them, are quite infrequent in these volumes. In relation to his career these are the letters of a businessman-author. He writes to ascertain an editor's interest in a novel or to permit the reprinting of a poem, not to think through in a different medium difficulties in drawing a character or in getting a plot into final form. This disinclination to discuss problems of creativity is marked even in relation to *The Dynasts*, the project which nearly totally absorbed his attentions far longer than any other single work, but which is seldom referred to in these letters, and rarely in a manner reflecting ideas either aesthetic or historical in the great verse-drama.

That Hardy looked upon letters as obligatory acts of writing seems demonstrated convincingly in those written after the deaths of his mother and his first wife Emma. Although Hardy declared in other contexts the importance to him of his mother, the letters in which he felt the need to express his grief (because the recipients knew of his loss) are written in a perfunctory and even forced manner. One letter about his mother that seems to express something of himself is that to Edward Clodd (III. 119–120), which gives details, expresses feeling, and concludes with resignation ("However, she suffered latterly, & wished to go, so that there is really nothing for commonsense to regret"). Jemima's death did not cripple the pace of Hardy's work—twenty-four days after she died he was in London for research on *The Dynasts*. After the death of Emma references to her in his letters are restrained and repetitive (perhaps reflecting that he was obliged to write so many), qualities notably lacking in the *Poems of 1912–13*, which manifest the depth and range of his distress. The truth is (a phrase Hardy was fond of using) that Hardy's medium for expressing emotions was not personal—unless one accepts that Hardy's art is more personal than such direct communications as letters. That Hardy was able to *imagine* emotions is clear from such moments as Clym's reaction to the death of Mrs. Yeobright in *The Return of the Native*; but it is also clear that to ascribe Clym's emotions as Hardy's own imaginative response to a projected similar grief of his own, and that he felt such emotions when the historical moment arrived, would be foolish and illogical reductivism. The *Letters* also indicate that away from his pen and study Hardy was more of an ordinary householder than a sensitive artist (new-born kittens were matter-of-factly drowned, Hardy accepting that the action made house-servants sad), and that when other people's griefs were in question, on, say, the death of a correspondent's ten-year-old son, Hardy could give quite remarkably cold comfort ("Tell [your wife] . . . how deeply our sympathy was with you both in your bereavement. Though, to be candid, I think the death of a child is never really to be regretted, when one reflects on what he has escaped" (I. 235).

While there is, then, a gap between the deeply moving use of language in Hardy's creative work and the general avoidance of emotion in his letters, and thus an ambivalent value in the letters as far as gaining a better understanding of the works is concerned, what Millgate has made of the letters—along with all the other "hard" evidence he has uncovered—in his *Thomas Hardy: A Biography* creates not only an impressive narrative biography in itself but constitutes a major commentary on the created works, quite in keeping with his more ostensibly critical study *Thomas Hardy: His Career as a Novelist* of a decade earlier. As there he had studied newspaper files to trace Hardy's use of them in the 1880s (*The Mayor of Casterbridge*), in the biography Millgate has identified the originals of many of his characters, and has disproved some previous suggestions (such as that the Mary Head arrested in 1797 for theft and threatened with hanging might be a relative of Hardy, and thus possibly a family predecessor of Tess). Millgate exploits a considerable amount of fresh evidence to advance new conjectures about Hardy's emotional life—for instance, that from 1863 to 1867 Hardy was engaged to an Eliza Nicholls, who inspired such poems as "Neutral Tones" and possibly served as model for Cytherea in *Desperate Remedies*. The evidence also adds to our knowledge about aspects of Hardy's life previously known. For instance, surviving letters reveal that Hardy knew Florence Dugdale, who became his second wife, for years before Emma's death, arranged for her to attend the opera *Tess* with Edward Clodd while discouraging Emma from coming to London for the opera that night, stayed at Clodd's while Florence was also staying there, and went with outings with her (including a tour of cathedrals in 1911, accompanied by his brother Henry and Florence's sister). On the basis of these sorts of references Millgate could have erected a dramatic story of illicit relations, but in fact he concludes from the evidence that the precise nature of Thomas and Florence's pre-marital relationship cannot be deduced but most likely was not that of lover and mistress. Throughout, Millgate's story of Hardy's life is similarly reserved in conclusions although the evidence is straightforwardly presented. Only in one or two situations does Millgate seem to extrapolate adventurously, for example in suggesting

Emma got Thomas to marry her by pretending she was pregnant (a device later employed in fiction by Arabella).

However circumspect Millgate may be in his biography, Hardy himself had been even more cautious in telling the story of his life in such a form that after his death it could be published as the work of his second wife Florence. In this format, Hardy implies many youthful flirtations with or "losing his heart to" this girl or woman and that; but no reference is made to Tryphena Sparks by name, and Florence Henniker is presented only as a social acquaintance, without any reference even to their collaborative writing. The ruse which allowed him to write his own autobiography and thus to impart his slant to details of his life was never secure; and by now everyone knows that Florence had little part in writing it except for the final four chapters, put together after Hardy's death. It has not been so generally known, however, that when she prepared the typescript for the printers after Hardy's death she was given advice by Sir Sydney Cockerell (Director of the Fitzwilliam Library, Cambridge; and the co-executor with Florence of Hardy's estate), nor that she solicited the advice of Sir James Barrie and E. M. Forster. Their advice affected the published version in material ways. Possibly to compensate for self-consciousness at his lowly social origins, or as Millgate suggests to add a measure of interest to the account of his own life (which he considered dull) as much as to reflect his enjoyment of good living and good food (which he did not have at Max Gate), Hardy had larded his own version with lists of his social engagements in London with titled and well-connected acquaintances. Barrie suggested to Florence that these lists gave a poor impression of the Great Writer; and Florence dutifully pared her husband's detailing of his success as a social lion. Her advisers also suggested deletion of several passages revealing how the thin-skinned Hardy frequently flinched at and responded viperishly to criticism. In addition, Florence fleshed out several passages in Hardy's typescript with material in letters Hardy had written to his sister Kate during his early years in London, and to Edmund Gosse after the publication of *Jude the Obscure*, and with anecdotes she had herself told Cockerell and had forgotten until he reminded her of them and urged their interest for the biography. Among these are the story of Louisa Harding (Hardy spoke to her but once in his life, but the romantic feeling she inspired lasted a lifetime and resulted in "Louisa in the Lane," written not long before his death), the story of his desolation at reading the *Spectator*'s review of *Desperate Remedies*, and the account of how the wheel-barrow episode of *Tess of the d'Urbervilles* came to be written. Presumably these stories are all true; but, the point is, they were not intended by Hardy to form part of his life in the eyes of posterity. Perhaps the most understandable type of alteration Florence made in Hardy's *Life*, however, is the deletion of Hardy's references to his first wife Emma. Clearly Florence resented so many reminders that Thomas' affection for Emma had re-bloomed after Emma's death in 1912, a late affection that resulted in many fine and several great poems in contrast to her husband's near-total poetic silence about *her*. Because of the way Florence prepared Hardy's life-story for Macmillan in 1928 (*The Early Life of Thomas Hardy, 1840–1891*) and 1930 (*The Later Years of Thomas Hardy, 1892–1928*), readers have never had the version that Hardy expected them to have. Michael Millgate's edition presents Hardy's own story according to modern editorial practice, removing material inserted by Florence (but printing the most interesting passages in an appendix, "Selected Post-Hardyan Revisions in *Early Life* and *Later Years*") and restoring those passages cut by Florence as advised by Cockerell and Forster and Barrie. The book is titled, as Hardy intended it, *The Life and Work of Thomas Hardy* (London: Macmillan; Athens: University of Georgia Press, 1985).

Despite the obvious relevance and interest of studies in Hardy's life, and although Millgate has been the dominant scholar during the period covered by this review, a different branch of scholarship has provided factual information equally as significant as details about his treatment of his two wives and his participation in London social events. Copyright protection of Hardy's works lapsed in 1978, and since that date they have steadily appeared in fresh editions. Here I shall not treat of the various reprints of the Wessex Edition, although I grant that the introductory material often is of critical (as opposed to scholarly) interest. Here I want to evaluate only those editions whose texts have been critically established. All but one of these have come from Oxford University Press, two in the form of expensive Clarendon Editions, five in the far cheaper World's Classics format.

The first true critical editions of Hardy were of his poetry, edited by James Gibson, in 1976 and 1978, and therefore out of the time-span covered in this review. The first critical edition of one of his novels is my edition of *The Woodlanders* (Clarendon Press, 1981), the second was that of *Tess of the d'Urbervilles*, edited by Juliet Grindle and Simon Gatrell (Clarendon Press, 1983). Although these editions were prepared separately—in their initial stages their editors were ignorant of the progress being made on the other volume—they follow essentially the same editorial practices, in accepting the manuscripts as the most appropriate source for the accidentals (punctuation, paragraphing, spelling, and the like) and the Wessex Edition as the best form of the words. The governing decisions were based on work done during the

1960s and 1970s (much of it by the three editors themselves, the results published in articles and embedded in their doctoral dissertations as mentioned above). Differences between these two editions lie more in the apparatus than in the editing practices: I employ such apparatus as appendices giving substantive and accidentals emendations, Textual Notes, and the full historical accidentals record of only two chapters, while Grindle and Gatrell give their substantive emendations in several places in their introductory matter, provide no Textual Notes discussing problematical passages, and provide a full historical record of accidentals for the entire novel.

A prime benefit of these editions is that they prove beyond doubt (if any doubt still remained) that Hardy took his novels far more seriously than he let on during his life (particularly during his years as a poet). There were eight clearly distinct periods during which Hardy shaped *The Woodlanders*, ten for *Tess of the d'Urbervilles*, from the manuscript through American and English serial versions, first editions, first cheap editions, and then the Wessex Novels edition of 1895–96 and the Wessex Edition of 1912. There were often sharp differences between the manuscript, serial, and first edition versions, usually brought about by Hardy's difficulty in getting his vision of sexual relationships accepted by the magazines' editors and publishers. But equally of interest in considering Hardy's methods of creating is that he gave painstaking attention to many small matters—especially phrasing of incidental passages and, in the collected Wessex versions, altering references to distance and direction in fitting his plots into the actual landscape of Dorset—while leaving alone larger matters of inconsistency. In a similarly peculiar fashion, several of the revisions were obviously only partial—that is, Hardy would leaf through the printer's copy or the proofs and stop to deliberate over a passage only—or so it would seem—randomly.

Each of the freshly edited novels in the World's Classics format—*Under the Greenwood Tree*, edited by Simon Gatrell (1985), *Jude the Obscure*, edited by Patricia Ingham (1986), *A Pair of Blue Eyes*, edited by Alan Manford (1985), *The Well-Beloved*, edited by Tom Hetherington (1986), and *The Mayor of Casterbridge*, edited by me (1987, which I can include in this survey only because I know its production schedule)—represents a critical text prepared in much the same manner as were the Clarendon Editions discussed above but lacking accompanying appendices, and costing a great deal less. These are among the better bargains in Hardy scholarship, especially useful because it may be some time before the supporting documentation will be made available in their to-be-hoped-for Clarendon versions. Their explanatory notes include some of the more interesting substantive variants, and thus they have in limited respects a value for criticism (exceeded of course by the vastly more detailed Clarendon Editions).

I cannot discuss all of these World's Classics editions in detail; but comparative observations might be in order. Patricia Ingham, perhaps owing to her having so much knowledge about changes and patterns, is not clear on all relevant aspects of a textual explanation in the four pages allotted to "A Note on the Text" of *Jude the Obscure*. For instance, she notes that the German Tauchnitz Edition of 1896 has variants most likely directed by Hardy, but she does not indicate whether these variants were inserted into the text during the re-setting and re-plating done for the English 1903 Uniform Edition. If they were not so inserted, the Tauchnitz variants would have fallen out of the line of transmission of the text, because it was a copy of the Uniform Edition Hardy used to prepare printer's copy for the following edition (the 1912 Wessex Edition). Thus, it is of some moment that she does not say whether the Tauchnitz variants were "lost," nor, if they were, whether these Tauchnitz variants are incorporated into her text as emendations. Indeed, comparing the introductory comment on the Tauchnitz Edition (the "Note on the Text," p. xxv) and the textual changes made on page 35 ("Explanatory Notes," p. 435) leaves a reader uncertain whether the pig's-pizzle scene was revised for the Tauchnitz Edition or for the 1903 Uniform Edition. Similarly, Ingham mentions that the American Autograph Edition of 1915 was re-set from sheets of the British Wessex Edition of 1912 and contains some fifty differences "clearly Hardy's," and says that "use has been made of" the Autograph Edition, but she does not indicate how many (if not all) of these differences were incorporated into her text. In contrast to the indefiniteness of some of the detail in Ingham's introduction, Alan Manford's equally brief "Note on the Text" compresses a most complicated account of the interrelationships among the texts of *A Pair of Blue Eyes*. This is a model for the explanation of texts to a (most likely) academic student audience, and raises great expectations for the Clarendon Edition of this novel, the one that Hardy continued to deal with after he had finished with the others (details of the scene of this novel, he felt, could be made more explicit after the death of Emma). The textual notes for the two novels I have prepared for the World's Classics Edition, *The Woodlanders* and *The Mayor of Casterbridge*, contain a substantial number of the readings Hardy rejected; and Hardy's thorough overhaul of *The Well-Beloved* after its initial, serial publication created a dual-text situation, which is well managed by Hetherington by means of a separate textual appendix. Such textual materials both underscore that the World's Classics Edition presents fresh texts of classic novels and, that being the case, that these World's Classics editions represent a practical advance over previous paperback editions of Hardy's novels.

The fresh edition coming from a publisher other than Oxford University Press is that of *Far from the Madding Crowd*, edited by Robert C. Schweik, as a Norton Critical Edition (New York: W. W. Norton, 1986). This edition, Hetherington's edition of *The Well-Beloved*, and Manford's edition of *A Pair of Blue Eyes* accept the Wessex Edition both in accidentals and substantives (Schweik using a 1920 printing of the Wessex Edition). Schweik's reasoning has to do with the relatively inadequate pointing of the manuscript of "his" novel, Manford's with the incomplete state of the manuscript of "his"; and both believe that Hardy's tacit approval of the alterations made to the texts by compositors gives the later texts a significant standing. Additionally, Manford and Hetherington believe that the survival of Hardy's printer's-copy for *The Woodlanders*, whose markings indicate clearly Hardy's deletion of hundreds of commas for the Wessex Edition, is sufficient evidence to argue that Hardy gave the accidentals for this edition as close a scrutiny as he did the substantives, thereby making the Wessex Edition a logical choice as copy-text of the critical edition of a Hardy novel. Schweik's edition, like the World's Classics volumes, presents a critically edited text; also, he offers somewhat more in the way of apparatus than do most of the editors of Oxford's paperback editions. He has a particularly interesting discussion of the dilemma faced by the editor of *Far from the Madding Crowd* owing to the fact that the 1901 Harper and Brothers "sixpenny" edition does not form part of the linear transmission of the text from the 1895 Osgood McIlvaine "Wessex Novels" edition to the 1912 Macmillan "Wessex Edition"; thus, the revisions Hardy made for this 1901 edition were in a very few instances repeated and in others modified in the later edition, and still others were abandoned in the 1901 edition. (While preparing printer's copy for the 1912 Wessex Edition Hardy did not have access to the revisions he had made for the 1901 edition.) The question, then, was whether Schweik should accept all of the 1901 changes under the assertion that surely Hardy would have preferred them to the 1895 readings had he been able to remember them, to stay with the 1912 readings as the last ones he read over and "approved," or to accept those of the 1901 readings which are clear improvements over 1895. Schweik's decision is to consider the Wessex Edition the primary authority, which means that passages revised identically for the 1901 and 1912 editions are retained, those revised slightly differently for 1901 and 1912 are judged individually, and those revised only for 1901 are rejected. The decision is a responsible one, but it is to be hoped that an edition of this novel with a complete apparatus can find a publisher. As with the similar situation with the 1900 sixpenny edition of *Tess of the d'Urbervilles*, a revision that escapes the chain of transmission offers wonderful opportunities for further understanding of a writer's procedures.

The advantage of true (as opposed to reprint) editions of Hardy's novels is that they give us texts closer to—at least according to a major line of modern editing theory—a version that the author would have wanted had he or she had full control over the production process (or a full memory of their different revisions). Schweik and Manford hypothesize that the author shares responsibility for compositorial and editorial alterations if they are permitted to remain unchanged in subsequent editions over which he or she has the power to make changes. In the case of Hardy, this means an essential perpetuation of the 1912 Wessex Edition. The majority of the modern editors of Hardy, however, resist this perpetuation, conceding that the words of the 1912 Wessex Edition represent in most passages the most authoritative readings, but reluctant to believe that the perception of those passages should be affected by an imposed punctuation, forced onto Hardy's texts by the compositors hired by the magazines which first published his stories. These editors insist that readers' perception should be guided by the punctuation of the manuscripts, which is characterized in all cases I know of by—in contrast to the Wessex Edition—substantially less internal punctuation such as commas and increased use of dashes, very much lower use of exclamation marks (great numbers were added to *The Mayor of Casterbridge* in the Osgood McIlvaine edition), and paragraphs either quite a bit longer than those of the Wessex Edition or broken into several rhetorical units. Hardy prepared his manuscripts carefully: much punctuation and paragraphing is altered within the manuscript, so the frequent argument that the author was indifferent to accidentals and expected the compositors to straighten things out rarely applies to Hardy. He may have acquiesced in what the compositors did, but he clearly would not have thought they were doing something he was incapable of.

Critical editions are thought to be of value because they represent a (presumably) experienced editor's judgments upon the innumerable textual cruxes of a literary text. The only better scholarly tool than a critical edition is one of the versions itself upon which a critical edition is based. The Garland Press has begun to bring out The Thomas Hardy Archive, facsimiles of the original manuscripts, under the direction of Kristin Brady and Michael Millgate. The first two facsimiles are of the manuscripts of *Tess of the d'Urbervilles*, in two volumes, and *The Return of the Native*, both edited by Simon Gatrell (New York, 1986). The text of the manuscripts is clear in these facsimiles, although naturally many of the erasures and passages crossed out are illegible. What reproduces best are passages written in black ink; fortunately, Gatrell provides lists of the relatively few locations of passages written in blue ink and pencil, as well as of erasures. Of particular interest to students studying the relationship between Hardy's manuscripts and the printed versions are Gatrell's lists marking the various compositors' stints, which will enable a study of individual compositors' alterations of the manuscript pointing by comparing the pointing in their stints with that of the first serial versions.

Although this review concentrates on Hardy's fiction, it seems excusable in this discussion of editions (it being editions of Hardy that distinguish particularly the years covered by this review) to mention if only in passing the editorial work on his poems in the on-going Clarendon Edition in five volumes (three of which have appeared) edited by Samuel Hynes. Hynes provides a goodly amount of rejected readings accompanying the text that he establishes. Some rejected passages are compositorial alterations, but most of them are of course earlier versions by Hardy. Even more so than with the fiction, Hardy could not rest content with an existing version. As Hynes says, "he was a lifelong reviser of his poems" (I, xx). A poem he revised for different editions within days of each other will have different readings. Making the editorial task more problematic is that there are two main lines of development, one dating from the volumes of poems in the Wessex Edition and the other from the poems in *Collected Poems* (set in 1909 but not published until 1919), both revised alternately at times of reprintings. It is scarcely surprising that Hardy never achieved his intention to "See how corrections stand in respect of each edition: get a set properly corrected: & destroy useless proofs in cupboard" (I, xx); as a result, says Hynes, "there is no *final* text" (I, xx) and editors can responsibly make different choices as to which text to use as copy-text. It is interesting that during most of his revisions of his fiction Hardy gave only sporadic attention to accidentals, thus the Wessex Edition volumes of his fiction—unmistakably the last version of his novels he saw through the press in all its stages—are not "definitive," while with his poetry he paid such close attention to accidentals as well as to substantives that a scholar is unable to ascertain which Hardy might judge to be his "best" version.

Most of the books of criticism published during this period on Hardy's fiction—like the majority of books written in any recent period on most writers—do not reflect findings made by this recent scholarship. Naturally, the time-lag between writing and publication date is the principal reason behind the general absence in critical books of theories based on knowledge recently made available. But I am not confident this scholarship will soon be used to any great extent. Most critics who deal with Hardy are drawn to him by his powerful and basic manner, by issues essentially psychological or philosophical which seldom need appeal to facts of recent revelation. Why this should be the case may have special implications for the practitioners of scholarship, but it has little to do with this review. Quite simply, I am discussing on the one hand what new has come to be known, perhaps even to be proved, about Hardy; on the other I am discussing various critical explorations of Hardy's works. By and large, current criticism engages well-established issues rather than explore innovatively matters that can be developed from the mass of new detail, although the best critical book produced during this period is bolstered by a detailed knowledge of many of the facts that have become available through the scholarship I have discussed, and through other scholarship produced earlier than the '80s—as well as by the writer's own significant discoveries.

My comments are structured in categories, and I begin with the books characterized by a strong thesis. That's a vague category in itself, and the first to be dealt with is perversely the least classifiable critical book of the period, unless it's to be seen as "anti-criticism, pro-literature." C. H. Salter's *Good Little Thomas Hardy* (Totowa, N.J.: Barnes & Noble, 1981) offers a brisk approach that is initially attractive, to the effect that all modern academic critics have either misread or distorted Hardy in setting him up as a significant social critic and purveyor of intellectual ideas, and that to get to the essential Hardy one needs only to read him with an open mind. Given that most academic critics are trained to extract finely shaded dimensions of complex ideas of the sort that most readers don't recognize as they read the original novels, at least for the first time, Salter's view is refreshing. He is very good in finding absurd claims or statements in the writing of conventional academic critics, and could be an aggravating questioner after a lecture. Unfortunately, from the very first paragraph his own writing reveals the pot-holes into which an over-literal critic can fall. He argues that Hardy's novels are historical, for example setting *The Mayor of Casterbridge* "about 1850." According to the footnote (this must be the most heavily documented study of Hardy ever), this ascription is based on Prince Albert's visit to Portland in 1849, which appears in the novel as the brief appearance in Casterbridge of a "Royal Personage" passing through the town. But the matter is more complicated than Salter notices. First, Prince Albert arrived by train, and while the novel makes explicit that the railway is yet several miles from Casterbridge, in reality the railway reached Dorchester in 1847; second, the dominant historical situation employed in this novel is not this incidental visit but the effect of the Corn Laws (repealed, as everyone knows, in 1846) upon Henchard's grain speculations. The point is not the minor discrepancy in date so much as Salter's failure to notice and honor the irrelevance to Hardy's imagination of historical punctiliousness. Certainly Hardy was aware of history and economic conditions, and from his "research" in the library of the Dorset County Museum he knew specific dates of long-ago local events; but he was seeking *effect* within his fictional context, not a reflection of reality.

One difficulty in resting content with Salter's positions throughout his book has to do with his indefatigable listing of all relevant passages followed by an assertion of a general principle that is supposedly cohering but more often simply lies atop all the evidence spread-eagled by Salter's inability to make his point clearly. This pattern is illustrated on page 19's dogmatic assertions one after the other regarding nature and law in *Jude the Obscure* and the equally cross insistence that in order to term a passage in Hardy "Darwinian" it must echo verbally as well as in general sentiment a passage in Darwin. This tactic may be useful in criticizing critics; but it is not of much value as a foundation for a critical perspective of Salter's own.

Salter's thrust is that no one has got right several theses about Hardy—not other critics and, sometimes, not even Hardy. He has a very lively way of attacking other critics (including this reviewer), which makes reading his book modestly ego-stimulating for the particular critic being attacked. But his attack on other critics is too thinly assertive and non-analytical to lead to reassessment of the criticism under seige. The basic indequacy of Salter's book is not that he may be wrong on many of his points; in fact, he is correct as often as he is wrong, but there is no continuity among his arguments: he simply quotes massively, states without argumentation that the interpretation by one other critic (or critics in general) is an error, or many errors, and states, again without argumentation, his own interpretation. Thus, even though I agree with his "reading" of many given passages in Hardy, I can see no general value to be gained from the book, no method of reading, only a testiness and pickiness not much in keeping with Hardy's own tolerance and commitment to relativity.

Peter J. Casagrande, *Unity in Hardy's Novels: "Repetitive Symmetries"* (Lawrence: Regents Press of Kansas, 1982) has the sort of unifying perspective that Salter lacks. One might even say he has two; but they are closely inter-woven. First, the symmetries of his title refer to characteristic patterns in Hardy's novels, one of "return" (*Under the Greenwood Tree, The Hand of*

*Ethelberta, The Return of the Native, The Woodlanders,* and *The Well-Beloved*) and the other of "restoration" (all the other novels); second, the element giving the novels their peculiar tone is Hardy's principal philosophical position, which Casagrande calls "deteriorism"—"The view that time, history and consciousness are caught up in an irreversible process of decline or decay" (p. 62). These controlling ideas sponsor the development of many categories, the drawing of many parallels and cross-influences between novels, and the reading of all of Hardy's novels in relation to these definitions, a reading which arranges them along a continuum. Although Casagrande rides a thesis, it's an enriching rather than constrictive one.

Frank R. Giordano's *"I'd have my life unbe": Thomas Hardy's Self-destructive Characters* (University: University of Alabama Press, 1984) is dominated by its thesis, that Hardy's characters trace his long obsession with the idea of suicide, prompted, Giordano speculates (as do others), by the 1873 suicide of his close friend Horace Moule. Although Giordano considers the ideas about suicide held by Sigmund Freud and Karl Menninger, Emile Durkheim's typology of suicide types is to such an extent the focus that he organizes his study along the lines of Durkheim's theories. Thus, one section is given to "egoistic" suicides (Eustacia Vye and Michael Henchard), a second to "anomic" suicides (Farmer Boldwood and Jude Fawley), and a third to "altruistic" suicides (Giles Winterborne and Tess Durbeyfield). Of course, all these men's public writing on the subject of self-destructiveness appeared after Hardy had completed his career in fiction, so what Giordano is dealing with is Hardy's *anticipation* of their thoughts. It is all too easy to find great theories "anticipated" by creative artists, so this aspect of his book is fairly predictable; but fortunately Giordano is a close and sympathetic reader of the novels themselves.

Rosemary Sumner's *Thomas Hardy: Psychological Novelist* (London: Macmillan, 1981) is like Giordano's in its premise that Hardy "anticipated" later thinkers—according to *her* thesis such psychological theorists as Freud, Jung, Adler, Konrad Lorenz, and R. D. Laing. There is a certain catch-as-catch-can aspect to Sumner's approach, as she takes a bit from one modern theory, another bit from another theory, sometimes drawing on as many as six theories to elucidate Hardy's anticipatory presentation of one character, with the oft-repeated intention to show the twentieth-century "modernity" of Hardy. Identifying these points of anticipation is used by Sumner as a theoretical starting-point in preference to the indications in Hardy's literary notebooks (referred to and quoted by Sumner on pages 5–7 and thereafter ignored) that he had deliberately studied Charles Fourier's *Passions of the Human Soul* and

Auguste Comte's *Social Dynamics*, which might have been more challenging to explore and more revealing of the imaginative act in Hardy. The intelligence with which Sumner elicits parallels between scene after scene in Hardy with passages and contexts in post-Hardyan theory (e.g., "Barbara of the House of Grebe" and aversion therapy) justifies the exercise; but it would have been better put to work tracing the consequences residual within Hardy's stories of his conscientious parsing and annotating of antecedent efforts to codify concepts of personality. To invert the process—to suggest, as Sumner does, that B. F. Skinner (had he read "Barbara") might have taken part of his theory of operant conditioning from Hardy—is to divert oneself with intellectual lexicon unless one takes the trouble to learn whether in fact Skinner *had* read the story. Still, it is wiser to appreciate what has been done than to lament what hasn't; and Sumner, in adhering to the topic she has chosen, offers several cogent analyses of Hardy's anticipatory psychology. Boldwood as a study of repression (whether his madness merits reprieve from the executioner remaining in doubt) draws upon an imagery of bulwarks and stagnant rivers; Henchard as a study in aggression and depression is highlighted by his rapid actions, susceptibility to gloom, and precarious self-control and self-esteem always threatened by challenges to his self-important need to maintain his absolute centrality in others' lives; Grace Melbury as a schizoid is deprived of a sense of identity—these and other characters are presented as detailed "case-studies"; and the latter part of the book offers extensive character analyses of such as Angel, Jude, and Sue in relation to "the psychological problems of modern men and women," posing correlations with Freud and Jung primarily. Granted that her theoretical approach is inherently reductive, Sumner's views of Hardy's characters are consistently sensible and balanced. None the less, in valorizing modern theory over the state of thinking contemporary with the imaginative act, implying that Hardy's understanding of human nature needs this updated buttressing if we are to hold it in respect, this type of literary criticism has little bearing either upon the development of psychological thought or upon the nature of Hardy's accomplishment.

Jagdish Chandra Dave, *The Human Predicament in Hardy's Novels* (Atlantic Highlands, N.J.: Humanities Press International, 1985) observes Hardy from a broad perspective. To Dave, Hardy is a philosopher in the same existentialist sense as Gide, Malraux, Saint-Exupéry, and Sartre, artists who offer their "passionate message of revolt and reconstruction" in literary form as opposed to well-reasoned treatises. More specifically, Hardy is an atheist and an anti-determinism humanist whose way of viewing experience closely parallels that of the Buddha. Hardy's mysticism is not happily "extrovertive" (his loss of faith made this impossible to him) but "introvertive": "A profound inner peace is its characteristic feeling," a tranquillity arising "from renunciation of all wishes as the root cause of sorrow" (pp. 28–29). Dave's study from this perspective of *The Return of the Native, Far from the Madding Crowd*, and *The Mayor of Casterbridge* is rich in suggestions, such as—in contrast to many critics' preconception—that there is no "sinister Intelligence" to punish Henchard and that the novel gives no endorsement of Elizabeth-Jane's confidence that Farfrae shares her views about the worth of life and about the "wretched humours of Christopher Coney and his tribe." These are relevant observations, even if one does not agree with them (and Dave doesn't argue his cases as much as present them). Dave's book has many things to recommend it, including discussions of Hardy and Camus, Schopenhauer and Hardy, and Hardy's ideas about guilt in sex; but most of these are too short to allow Dave to develop their issues beyond common knowledge, and the analyses of such points as Tess as a "pure woman" are carried out in the absence of any reference to the considerable amount of more sophisticated commentary. A more vitiating characteristic is Dave's essentially tunnel-visioned approach. Surely the most famous and most widely familiar instance of what most people would call mysticism in Hardy is the description of Tess walking through the unruly, fecund garden patch while listening to Angel's harp music. This passage does not form part of Dave's discussion. I can understand why it doesn't. He is centrally concerned with questions of morality—that is, with the guilt of Tess, with the religion of Mr. Clare, with compassion and sympathy, and these are unquestionably central issues in the novel. But a reader goes to a book with an approach like Dave's with the expectation or hope that passages problematic according to other methods of reading will be elucidated by the fresh perspective, particularly when that perspective would seem to be so deeply appropriate for the problematic passages. Dave provides numerous quotations from other philosophers and religious scholars; but Hardy's own portrayal of the complexity of mystical vision in the garden scene is richer than anything that Dave's supplementary critics say. In short, Dave presents a case that can be made about Hardy and Eastern philosophy, but the substantiation of it that will convince—with more relevant passages from the novels and with more extended analyses—has yet to appear.

Noorul Hasan, *Thomas Hardy: The Sociological Imagination* (London: Macmillan, 1982) offers another broadly based thesis. Hasan contends that Hardy, no annalist or analytic historian himself, was "averse to documentation and historical scientism" (p. 6) and presented his locales as visions of "an irreplaceable cultural past, and not naturalistically as a fact to be faced'' (p. 159). Placing himself specifically in opposition to Raymond Williams, whose approach Hasan conceives to stress economic forces solely, Hasan prefers to deal with characters' ''deeper emotions and responses'' to the ''community of feeling''—their ''collective moral and emotional identity'' (p. 5). Whether Raymond Williams deals so narrowly in facts as Hasan implies is questionable; in any case, Hasan develops his own ideas in chapters devoted to individual novels along fairly conventional lines in senses familiar to readers of Hardy criticism, such as the identification of the reddleman as ''a product of . . . a certain rhythm of life which is still active in *The Return of the Native*'' (p. 56). This is not to say that with some novels Hasan does not raise interesting points; for example, in considering the concept of progress in *The Mayor of Casterbridge*'s he suggests that Hardy has a ''strong regressive instinct'' that makes him anxious about ''any movement forward in history'' (p. 63), a view which though at variance with such characters as Jude and Sue living a life fifty years ahead of their time is not invalidated through this quite characteristic Hardyan ability to seem to favor both poles of an opposition. Hasan alludes to Ferdinant Toennies's *Gemeinschaft und Gesellschaft (Community and Association)*, nearly contemporary with *The Mayor of Casterbridge*, for some of his orientation, and so there is a measure of theoretical substructure. While on most points Hasan argues the standard judgment, he insists that in *Tess of the d'Urbervilles* ''Tess herself evinces no moral hesitancy or confusion'' (p. 137). Nonetheless, overall Hasan's approach does not sponsor particularly evocative insights into any of the novels.

Another batch of the books on Hardy I have been reading have their origin in a selection by the author of a special or limited area of Hardy's achievement. As the title of his work indicates, Richard H. Taylor (*The Neglected Hardy: Thomas Hardy's Lesser Novels* [New York: St. Martin's Press, 1982]) deliberately puts to one side the great novels, wondering whether there is much new to be said about them, concentrating instead on the minor novels, which he believes need ''rehabilitation.'' Taylor's deprecatory approach to these novels is perhaps unnecessarily defensive, in that even the most inconsequential of Hardy's novels has a wider *popular* readership (in England at least) than comparable books by Thackeray, Meredith, or Conrad, and Taylor has been criticized on this ground; but surely to concede that a great writer can also work in a low key raises a critic's credibility. To suggest there are parallels between *A Pair of Blue Eyes* and *Tess of the d'Urbervilles* is one thing; it is to suggest the former warrants or can sustain the same kind of frequent and unremitting attention as the latter that would be parochial. Although special pleading is inherent in literary criticism, Taylor's approach manages to avoid strained pleading. His modest introductory plan—"to discover the nature of each novel's deficiencies and (in so far as such things are discoverable) the circumstances which may have contributed to their lesser stature, and to validate what is good in them" (p. 5)—is expanded in the chapters into a background sketch of a novel's creation followed by detailed evaluations of Hardy's handling of the novel's substantive themes and its artistry, drawing in not merely Taylor's impressionistic reactions but reflections on issues raised by Victorian periodical criticism, and also events and ideas of the times. In short, Taylor's effort is to "place" these novels, and it is a bonus that his sensitivity and tact pepper the book with observations that keep a sense of Hardy's entire oeuvre in the reader's mind (*"Two on a Tower* remains a more pleasing, though less challenging novel than *A Laodicean"* [p. 176]). At a time when, as Taylor predicts, Hardy's lesser novels are being paid more and more attention by major critics, this book will hold its place, and not merely because it's the first book exclusively about the novels which time has lowered from the first rank. (Several of these novels—e.g., *A Pair of Blue Eyes*—were more appreciated in Hardy's lifetime than some of the masterpieces—e.g., *The Mayor of Casterbridge*.)

Hardy's short stories seldom attract critical attention. While not a master and only occasionally an innovator in the form, Hardy does achieve in his shorter fiction an economy of effect and message unmistakably by the same hand that deals more sweeping truths in the novels. Kristin Brady has noticed the absence of critical studies of the tales, and in *The Short Stories of Thomas Hardy* (New York: St. Martin's Press, 1982) she has produced a classic study of what might be thought a special subject. She believes that Hardy's acts of collecting stories into the separate volumes have a heuristic function. *Wessex Tales* "represents Hardy's most comprehensive single depiction of the fictional world that he called Wessex. The very discontinuity and disjointedness of the short-story volume—its varied settings, unchronological sequence, diversity of style and subject matter, and seeming haphazardness of arrangement—make it, when considered as a unit, a more complete portrayal of Wessex life than one novel could be." Her treatment of this volume is structured by her concept of *pastoral*, which in its classical neatness makes an instructive contrast with Bruce Johnson's phenomenological scrutiny (see below). Although a material place, Wessex to Brady is a symbol. "This strategy of subordinating realistic details to a symbolic pattern places *Wessex Tales* firmly in the tradition of pastoral"; the idea of contrast, the opposition of simple and complex, "leads to other contrasts: rural versus urban, regional

versus non-regional, past versus present,'' forcing "the reader to see his own
world by comparing it not to an ideal place but to another fully realized world,
one as fraught with suffering and difficulty as his own'' (pp. 4–5). From this
standpoint, Brady develops excellent analyses of such stories as "The Three
Strangers,'' noting how changes in social classes (village craftsmen losing
status; the non-local hangman being held simultaneously in contempt and
"peculiar esteem'') dramatize the story's situation in pastoral terms. Similarly, Brady discusses the stories in *A Group of Noble Dames* in relation to
the mutual contradiction in the moral perspectives of the convention-bound
narrators and the reader (who makes judgments "unfettered by the prejudices
of class'' [p. 54]) and those in *Life's Little Ironies* as "Tragedies of Circumstance,'' characterized by an ironic tone instead of either the pastoralism of
*Wessex Tales* or the ambivalence of *A Group of Noble Dames*. Among several
smaller observations, Brady notes that "Hardy's view of contemporary fiction
as a new form of tragedy contributes to the structure, tone, and narrative
technique of the stories in *Life's Little Ironies*, in which small episodes are
seen as tragic, and in which social conventions play a major role in working
out the destiny of the characters. . . . As he set down in a notebook in 1889:
'That which, socially, is a great tragedy, may be in Nature no alarming
circumstance' (*EL*, 286).'' Hardy's purpose differs "from that of the satirist,
who exposes inconsistencies in order to evoke ridicule and contempt. Here
a recognition of human foibles inspires sympathy and a deepened understanding of the tyranny of social conventions'' (pp. 97–98). In contrast to Hardy's
planning and selecting stories with a unified theme for his first three volumes
of short fiction, his fourth and final volume in 1913 denotes by its very
title—*A Changed Man, The Waiting Supper, and other Tales, Concluding
with The Romantic Adventures of a Milkmaid*—"the absence of a thematic
concept, his admission that the book has no coherent unifying principle'' (p.
157). Brady's ideas while not often striking can be measured not only in tact
and comprehensiveness but in a general validity that is enhanced by a graceful
style. Hers is an instance of what might be called "sufficient'' literary criticism, of the same quality as Joseph Warren Beach's book, whose ideas
continue to be cited because they state the essence of a matter.

    An extended consideration of Hardy's use of allusions has long been
needed. Hardy is one of the most self-conscious users of the classics, the
Bible, painting, and other areas of commonality who has written in recent
decades. Marlene Springer in *Hardy's Use of Allusion* (Lawrence: University
Press of Kansas, 1983) restricts her range of investigation to the first six
novels, with an "Aftercourse'' chapter to consider *Tess of the d'Urbervilles*

and *Jude the Obscure*. This organization inevitably makes the book the tracing of a predictable increase in skill, although Springer also explores Hardy's ironic use of his allusions. From his first novel, *Desperate Remedies*, Hardy was able to employ allusions both predictively and ironically, as when the base Manston is linked to the noble Curius (who was not interested in personal gain) and the deep-feeling King David (who had responded to Absalom's death quite differently than Manston does to news of his wife's). By the time of *Far from the Madding Crowd* Hardy was uneven in using allusions in treatments of animals (e.g., he is "unintentionally comic" in comparing Oak's guilty dog to Napoleon on St. Helena in contrast to the subtle humor in comparing the newly shorn sheep to Botticelli's painting of Aphrodite rising from the sea), but in evoking "the atmosphere of a particular location, he is now a master" (p. 59), and was scarcely less effective in allusive touches upon characterization. Springer believes that Hardy reached his stylistic maturity in *The Return of the Native*, with a richer and more varied use of allusions in more contexts than in the previous novels. All of the major characters are rounded through numerous allusions except Thomasin, "one of [Hardy's] few failures in feminine character development," who acquires only one allusion, the "martyred saint, St. Sebastian" (p. 107); and the characters are tied to their environment through particularly telling allusions, as with Eustacia and Egdon, and to the ideas they "represent," as with Clym and Hellenism.

Springer conceives the capstone of her approach to be the discussion of *Tess of the d'Urbervilles* and *Jude the Obscure*, as she "sets out to prove Hardy's perfection of these [allusive] techniques" (p. 6). The method of this chapter, however, is indistinguishable from that of the others; and given that Springer mentions much allusiveness that she sees as inadequate or flaccid it is not clear how Hardy's skill is better deployed in these novels than in—to mention only the moment of achieving mastery—*The Return of the Native*. Springer notes and categorizes the allusions in these late novels sharply and clearly; the brief but pointed discussion of how allusions to "nature's holy plan" (Wordsworth), Shakespeare's *The Rape of Lucrece*, Ascham's *The Schoolmaster*, and Augustine's *The City of God* amplify Tess's essential innocence despite her sexual experience is but one instance by which Springer clarifies Hardy's deliberate and doubtlessly painstakingly achieved command of emotions and ideas embodied in his culture's literary heritage. But in the absence of a more fluxuous and inspiriting prose style her sharp eye as a reader does not alter the truth of most readers' sense that Hardy's allusions are imposed onto his texts in sometimes gawky positionings and obtuse signpointings. Our understanding of Hardy's remarkable aesthetic effectiveness is not significantly advanced by Springer's methods.

If allusions can be classed as a "special" or limited area of study, surely even more appropriately placed in this category is a book that examines clarifications of Hardy's novels made by the illustrations which accompanied several of the serial versions. Although Hardy often suggested scenes and specific details for the illustrators to work with, by and large the illustrations are at best secondary evidence of Hardy's intentions and interests. Hardy's works appeared with engravings by artists well-known at the time. Hardy himself said that "the best illustrator I ever had" was Helen Paterson, who drew *Far from the Madding Crowd* (although this may have reflected his old-age reflections on the possibility that had they not married others in course of the novel's appearance he might have wanted to marry the artist); the extremely well-done illustrations by Robert Barnes of *The Mayor of Casterbridge* enhance the novel's verbal presentation of their scenes; and a few of the illustrations drawn by Hubert Herkomer for *Tess of the d'Urbervilles* and by William Hatherell for *Jude the Obscure* approach the level of free-standing art characteristic of Victorian narrative painting. The subject, then, is a potentially valuable one. Arlene M. Jackson, *Illustrations and the Novels of Thomas Hardy* (Totowa, New Jersey: Rowman and Littlefield, 1981) has prepared a book convenient for having in one place its seventy-three well-reproduced illustrations. Jackson divides Victorian book illustration into three periods: 1830–55, marked by the Cruikshank-Phiz caricatures we associate with Dickens' illustrators; 1855–70, the "Millais era" in which the representational illustration of Trollope is characteristic; and 1870–95, which is distinguished by no individual artist but remains linked to representational art. This is sound information but available elsewhere, namely in the standard works Jackson cites; the same is true with most of the chapter "Hardy and His Illustrators," which is no less interesting for its familiarity, and useful for its bringing together relevant passages from letters by Hardy and by the illustrators.

In her interpretive comments on the relationship between the illustrations and the stories in the long chapter on this subject, Jackson points out many details and qualities of the illustrations. Naturally she is primarily concerned with the manner in which the artists responded to verbal cues in the stories to attempt to create a complementary art, and does this well in explaining, for example, William Hatherell's use of a gray scale, grim interiors, weather conditions, and the rugged quality of his drawings to emphasize the grimness of *Jude the Obscure*. Her work does not provide much amplification of the fiction itself. It is of course to the point to have it noticed that Bathsheba's caprice is lacking in some of Helen Paterson's illustrations of *Far from the Madding Crowd*, but this is a criticism of the adequacy of the graphic artist, irrelevant to the study of the fiction. While the first parts of the book seem reliably researched and written, this analytical chapter has many inaccuracies. For example, Jackson seems wrong in attributing "pride" to Henchard's posture and demeanor in the first illustration of *The Mayor of Casterbridge*, which depicts him asking information of the turnip-hoer; she clearly errs in saying Henchard "cuts" Lucetta on the streets of Casterbridge in the illustration for 10 April 1886 (instead of cutting her, he is tipping his hat sarcastically as she looks in at him working as a hay-trusser in her husband Farfrae's barn) (both on p. 98). Occasionally one wonders about Jackson's familiarity with the novels themselves: she thinks that in the illustration of Henchard's last interview with Elizabeth-Jane he "seeks to explain his actions" (p. 99; again on p. 100), although Hardy in the novel emphasizes Henchard's proud resistance to that temptation. It is hard to word a final evaluation of this book. As the first book on Hardy's illustrations it has interest. But there is much more (one hopes!) to be done.

Another group of studies can be classified roughly but not inaccurately as written along lines of topical orientations, or, perhaps more fairly, according to contemporary critical issues. As might be expected, among such volumes we find some of the most stimulating books on Hardy during these years. Phenomenology may be too general an approach to literature to be classified as "special." It approaches literature on the same terms as it was written—one mind, aware of itself and its environs, attempting to grasp an inner core of meaning from those environs. Still, J. Hillis Miller (among others) a decade and more ago brought the concepts of phenomenology explicitly to Dickens and Hardy; and Bruce Johnson employs the method concretely rather than abstractly in *True Correspondence: A Phenomenology of Thomas Hardy's Novels* (Gainesville: University Presses of Florida, 1983). In fact, after an early discussion of Husserl, phenomenology fades from the center of attention in favor of a narrowly focused study of the pastoral. Johnson sees the pastoral as the mood that allows Hardy to make the phenomenological epiphany, to "see the nonhuman in the human, the sunlight in the depths of the hazel copse producing literally the same effect as the sun striking Elizabeth-Jane's loose hair" (p. 7), an epiphany which allows Johnson himself to see Hardy as "less the ranter against fate and more the quiet student of these tenuous filaments that lead not only to other people but to the earth and nonhuman life itself" (p. 8). As all too often occurs with critics employing tools bright with the latest theory, Johnson employs a heavy vocabulary of encompassing but flattening words, which instead of contributing to the message about Hardy provides a message in itself about criticism. Johnson likes "allotropy" although the old reliable "animism" would serve equally well in most of his contexts; "otium" is massively employed although occasional substitution of such ordinary language synonyms as "leisure" or "rural ease" or "repose" would make for more varied as well as more humane discourse. Other similarly strained terms used less redolently are "uncarnation" and "aletheia," although why Johnson did not rest content with the definitions (which he evidently felt compelled to supply) and scuttle the terms is not clear.

But perhaps this sort of vocabulary is inevitable. The book is essentially about the idea of pastoral, not about phenomenology. Johnson suggests that the basic quality of pastoral—the "meaning"—is that of built-in conflict (e.g., between otium and aspiration, between rural peace and activity). Not only is this idea not particularly fresh, but too mundane a vocabulary would prevent the critic from expressing aspects of the idea which are suggestive rather than explicit. Quite often Johnson's terms *do* seem to define features of Hardy's works that have been looked at often before but respond well to the new terminology. The description of the almost featureless snow falling outside Troy's barracks during Fanny's first call to him to fulfill his promises is an instance where the quasi- or pseudo-scientific term employed by Johnson creates philosophical as well as lexiconal resonances. As Johnson puts it, "Hardy begins to assert the involvement of the nonhuman and the psychological in the same ontology" (p. 23).

Johnson's approach has uneven rewards. To say that Henchard has abandoned a pastoral-like world for the opponent of otium, the "aspiring mind" or ambition, does not seem to contribute much to the understanding of this non-intimate of nature; but Johnson provides a quite good analysis of Fitzpiers's and Hardy's idealisms (p. 88), and has the good notion that the advance made in *The Woodlanders* does not concern aspiration but "the deepening complexity of the otium" at the core of the novel, in Hardy's perception that the Unfulfilled Intention is in mankind as well as in nature. "Hardy's theory of the Unfulfilled Intention is another form of the interest in a meeting point between the material and the ideal, since the intent is the ideal whose frustration has produced the blighted material nature" (p. 93). Johnson's perspective is clearly valuable when it is drawn on to demonstrate Hardy's Darwinism in seeing Tess as the "ideal" product of evolution —containing the health and energy of the d'Urbervilles, with essential connections to nature via the rural rituals—who had it not been for Angel's perverted "naturalism" (p. 119) would have been able to achieve Darwin's "happiness" ("symbiosis with the environment" [p. 118]). That is, Tess relates the past and the present and in her being does not find d'Urberville violence strange; instead, in her is an evolutionary connection among all life (i.e., different species). Angel, in contrast, "sees Tess as something of a sexual threat (as in the snake's mouth image), but primarily as a threat to his immaculate etherealizing process whereby the sensuous and emotional reality of Tess is made the abstract essence of a mythologized nature" (p. 109). Angel thus cannot perceive the perpetual renewing of nature's cycle nor Darwinian "sympathy for all truly natural behavior" (p. 120). Johnson's method equally clarifies the nature of the contrast between Jude and Sue: Jude's intuition of "larger harmonies involving both the past and a capacious Nature may be more important than seizing every chance for individual spontaneity" (p. 136), while "Sue has no access to the pastoral state of mind, which she mistakes as being simply beyond all but natural physical law," and further "mistakes the pastoral condition as 'freedom from' rather than 'sympathy for' " (p. 141). Moreover, Sue suggests the antipastoral, while Jude's response to and rejection of Arabella at least are rooted in a "natural taste that Sue constantly etherealizes out of existence" (p. 142). Sue indeed is the "spiritual mother of Little Father Time" (p. 145). And it is she and Oxford who "finally draw [Jude] from those primal sympathies which lie at the basis of 'community' understood in the largest pastoral sense. . . . Severed from the emotions and sexuality that Sue would etherealize, her intelligence can only see Nature's law as 'mutual butchery' " (p. 148). She is separated from the "great irrational substratum of all existence—deprived above all of those great ontological channels between the human and the nonhuman worlds" (p. 148).

Johnson's conclusion is that the keystone of Hardy's art is "this continuity of consciousness with 'lower' forms of life and finally with matter itself (in its most dynamic and evolutionary aspect)." The entire human race and consciousness are linked through "community" (p. 153). Again, one can claim that these ideas are not particularly fresh (unsurprisingly, they stir memories of J. Hillis Miller's basic postulates in *The Form of Victorian Fiction*); but despite the forcing of the issue in his use of special terms and in a degree of circularity in his arguments, Johnson's vocabulary (along with his sympathy for Hardy and his characters) allows him to rise often to eloquence in his teasing forth basic human needs treated in Hardy's stories. Johnson's sophistication makes a good match with the increasing intellectualization of Hardy's last three great novels.

Two frequently intertwined contemporary approaches, feminism and Marxism, help focus Penny Boumelha's *Thomas Hardy and Women: Sexual Ideology and Narrative Form* (Brighton: Harvester Press, 1982). Marxism occasionally leads Boumelha to decline into jargon; but overall the writing overcomes the given lexicon. Two survey chapters, one on contemporary views on female sexuality, the second on the "New Fiction" or "New Woman" novel of the 1880–90s, are excellent introductions both to Hardy's women and to the interrelationships of bourgeois ideology, feminism, and developments in the novel in the latter part of the nineteenth century. Hardy was responsive to the ambivalence of his peers about chastity and the double standard, and probably shared their ideas of the relative weakness and vulnerability of women, and other, similar views that earlier and later eras might think of as blinkered. He seems to have accepted "the Ruskinian polarity of man as culture, woman as nature" (p. 49). Boumelha's discussion of *Tess of the d'Urbervilles* from this perspective is a cogent exploration of a heroine's individual but still generic sexuality (esp. pp. 122–126). But Hardy came to make variations on this assumption. *Jude the Obscure* is the first novel in which Hardy bases the man's tragedy equally in his sexual nature as he does the woman's (pp. 140–141). Although Sue's tragedy is based nearly as equally in her intellectual nature as is Jude's, Sue "is made the instrument of Jude's tragedy, rather than the subject of her own" (p. 148). Moreover, by the time of *Jude the Obscure* marriage rather than sexuality has come to be the object of Hardy's ideological focus.

Hardy, then, was not merely a repository of received opinions. A sensitivity to the extensive reach of gender differentiation is clearly revealed in Bathsheba's perception that "language . . . is chiefly made by men to express their feelings" (quoted by Boumelha, p. 32). Nor is Boumelha's association of Hardy with New Fiction anomalous: numerous surviving remarks indicate that he always made a point of keeping aware of what was going on in contemporary fiction; and if no other of his remarks on the matter had survived, the Preface to *Jude the Obscure* underscores his consciousness of the problems of altered social-sexual roles (although Boumelha points out that "Sue is in no way representative of any discernible movement" [p. 135]). Lacking the determination of the other writers adduced by Boumelha—including Grant Allen, W. T. Stead, Sarah Grand, and William Platt—to stake out dogmatic positions in his fiction, Hardy was able to evade the boundaries and to see beyond the biases that characterized the immediate situation.

Because Hardy's novels portray individual dilemmas so powerfully it has become important to many people to ascertain whether Hardy is a feminist, or someone content with the patriarchal status quo. One resolution might be that Hardy could *perceive* the roles that social expectation forces people into, and that instead of claiming he was "approving" or "criticizing" the roles and the way they shaped (deformed) human emotion it is more to the point to note that he was simply portraying both the positive and negative sides of role-existence. Thus, Henchard is not simply "strong" and Bathsheba "weak," as Virginia Woolf (quoted by Boumelha, p. 2) put it, but they are both at once, and alternately. This is, after all, the way of life; and if art has any significance it is—let its ideology be what it will—its way of communicating something about "life." From page 7—"the radicalism of Hardy's representation of women resides . . . in their resistance to reduction to a single and uniform ideological position"—I would gather that Boumelha would agree with my simplistic resolution of the question; but, appropriately, her book demonstrates the manifestation, in fiction, of the ideology she has quite acutely identified, and the demonstration certainly enriches the resolution, whether or not Boumelha would explicitly accept my formulation of it. Boumelha's evocative book rewards re-readings.

So does, for different reasons, George Wotton's *Thomas Hardy: Towards a Materialist Criticism* (Dublin: Gill and Macmillan, 1985), which like Boumelha's is a Marxist reading of Hardy spurred by a personal commitment to the political ideas behind the method, although its orientation is more academic. Wotton's project is unexceptionable in conventional Marxist terms: "The object of study for a materialist criticism, however, is not, as with Leavis, 'Literature', but the relations between history, ideology, and criticism. And the aim of a materialist criticism is not evaluation or the discovery of meaning or significance in the 'literary text' but an understanding of the historical conditions of the production of writing and the ways in which literature operates in the process of reproducing the relations of production of class society." From the premises that writing is not creation, and that language and ideology are not determined by the author but are "materials upon which . . . labour [writing] is expended" to produce an artifact which thus has existence independent of the author', Wotton observes that "the nature of the relation between writers and what they produce is changed from one of private ownership to one of social process" (p. 2). Hardy's writing is "rooted in, and emerges out of, the contradiction between an historical process and an historical moment[—that is,] the contradiction between the long process of the separation of the producer from the means of production, which constituted the basis of the development of capitalism in Britain, and the effects of the Great Depression on the economic and social structure of the counties of south-west England in the last quarter of the nineteenth century.'' This does not mean that ''Hardy's writing 'reflects' history'' in the conventional, solipsistic way this idea is ordinarily held; rather, his primary materials are ''the ideological forms in which people become conscious of'' historical conflict—in Hardy's case, these ideological forms are ''those of his class of origin and those of the intellectual grouping to which he gave the name 'the thinking world' '' (pp. 5–6). Or, in somewhat different terms (but terms Wotton sees as parallel), Hardy's writings are shaped by problems of a transitional class whose unstable existence is dependent upon ''a compromise between the antagonistic classes between which it is uneasily situated'' and by problems raised by radical differences among such intellectual discourses of the day as ''an idealist philosophy, an empiricist theory of knowledge, an altruistic ethics, an undogmatic theology and a reformist politics'' (p. 6).

Wotton attributes the coherence in Hardy studies to a homology between the forces determining Hardy's works and those determining the critical discourses in the last hundred years—''between the contradictory modes of perception in Hardy's writing and the conflicting 'critical' perceptions in the discourses of aesthetic ideology, that is, between the writing's aesthetic project and the ideological intentions of criticism'' (pp. 7–8). But the coherence has not been an *identity* because ''Whereas writing puts the ideological into contradiction, the discourse of criticism effaces contradiction by excluding it'' (p. 8). While not explicitly declaring he intends to bring about a greater degree of identity between the writing of Hardy and the work of theory or criticism, in employing Marxist theory and taking into account the nature of critical discourse Wotton explores the relationship between Hardy's own production of his works and the social production of what is known as ''Thomas Hardy.''

Early points are that the idea of Wessex represents neither a timeless order nor a nostalgia for ''organic community'' but alludes instead to ''a classic case of uneven development in the history of British capitalism'' (p. 25), and that Hardy's autobiography is most remarkable not for its accuracy/inaccuracy or for its screening facts about his life that he wished not known but for its being ''the production of a world-view'' (p. 35) ''in which the real contradictions of his position are reconstituted on an imaginary level, presented as a coherent discourse which excludes those contradictions'' (p. 37). The early part of Wotton's book is—as I hope this paraphrase conveys—a straightforward and cogent exposition of a central Marxist approach. And subsequently most of the book's comments about Hardy are on this fairly general level of near-formulaic Marxist reactions. While the nature of Marxist analysis elides individualistic qualities (which Wotton acknowledges), it becomes increasingly disappointing that Wotton's determinedly ideological approach turns up few comments on Hardy not predicated by the approach itself or already well-known from other approaches. Wotton insists that his "theoretical concept can be used to say something about Hardy's writing which is not simply a repetition of what the writing itself is saying" (p. 82), just before he paraphrases Hardy's obvious intention in a section of *Desperate Remedies* (p. 83) and notes that what the writing itself does not say is that it " 'cannot see' . . . its own place and function in the class structure it is at such pains to reveal" (p. 84). In other words, it turns out that what Hardy's writing didn't itself say is twentieth-century Marxist insight, a scarcely surprising but nonetheless stunningly reductive "discovery" by Wotton. (A better justified observation of what writing "cannot see" because of Hardy's own subjection to views of his time is that "when Cytherea, or any other woman, 'fetishises' her appearance she acts not instinctively but ideologically, surveying in her appearance the image men have of her" [p. 130]. Indeed, the two chapters on Hardy and the women in his fiction are Wotton's clearest contribution, suggesting, as does Boumelha's book, that gender ideology is a good topic for Marxist analysis.)

There is a good deal of iteration of such basic premises as that a novel reflects not *history* but a *perception* of history, which (to this non-Marxist) doesn't seem all that marked an advance in thinking. And Wotton's own observation that "Wessex has its own mode of reality" (p. 44) has a distinctly New (i.e., Old) Critical ring, nor apart from its political dimension does it signally differ from the simple idea of organic expressiveness. Declaring that the origins of this observation are not in an author's (i.e., his own) consciousness but in "the contradiction between the aesthetic project and the conflicting ideological formations" (p. 44) is merely to insist on his formulations without advancing our knowledge of Hardy. Whatever may be the ultimate value of the application of Marxist terminology to literary study, it seems heavy-handed to paraphrase the significance of Melbury's statement to his daughter Grace "But if you do cost as much as they [the horses and wagons and corn she has just compared herself with], never mind. You'll yield a better return" into "The individual woodlander has been 'fetishised' into an object. Transformed into an investment, Grace is the living embodiment of the radical separation where the direct social relations between the individuals of the community of labour are transformed into material relations between them and social relations between the marketable commodities they produce" (pp. 54–55). And in a Marxist study it seems disingenuous or careless to the point of being modestly fraudulent to give the modern-day eleven pence as the equivalent of the Victorian two shillings and threepence Marty earns during her night's work in producing fifteen hundred thatching spars (p. 55), especially since Wotton has earlier (pp. 20, 21) cited Victorian authorities that in Hardy's time a Dorset farm laborer was paid only five shillings a week in 1850 and ten shillings a week in 1892.

Wotton's knowledge of the latter decades of the nineteenth century in both historical and literary detail is impressive, and a reader not already familiar with Hardy but conversant with Marxist terminology can learn a good deal about Hardy here; but apart from modest realignments of details he or she won't be discovering anything that earlier, non-Marxist students have been shielded from. There are numerous *aperçus*, as can be expected in a book by an intelligent reader, such as that although the initial description of Oak is as a parody of "Hodge," gradually "the essential diversity [of agricultural labourers] behind appearance" is revealed (p. 42); and some of the chapters ("The Sovereignty of the Subject and the World of the Workfolk" [pp. 60–73]) provide excellent applications of contemporary terminology (Bakhtin's concept of grotesque realism as a degradation of the idea of the collectivity of the community) to traditional aspects of Hardy's work (the ideology of what Hardy calls "the thinking world"). The entire chapter 8 ("The Radical Separation and the Conflict of Perceptions" [pp. 112–121]) is a fascinating study of *The Return of the Native* "as a structure of perceptions [intuitive insight vs. idealizing vision]" (p. 112) but Wotton's reading depends upon his Marxist orientation no more than upon conventional (if excellent) insights.

But the dominant impression this study very quickly imparts (and maintains) is, unfortunately, one of repetition of broad generalizations in context after context, an impression which does not reduce the genuine value of reading this analysis of Hardy but one which makes the effort quite noticeable. For example, the entire third part of his study ("Aesthetic Ideology and the Production of Thomas Hardy" [pp. 145–207]) sketches relationships between temporal shifts in ideology (to mention only two: Chance and its bearing upon Fate or tragedy; the idea of organic community [stemming from the work of George Sturt] and its relationship to change) and evolutions in criticism about Hardy; and Wotton makes some amusing comments whose drift is that all methods of criticism over the past century have resulted in the same judgments of Hardy, such as that his rural simplicity contributes both his ultimate strength and his stylistic crudeness. This section can be educative for students of literary theory and corrective for Hardy students persuaded they hold an "objective" judgment of Hardy; but its focus is even further from Hardy's own writing than the generalizations of the earlier portions of the book.

It is no doubt evident that I do not feel particularly at ease in trying to convey the qualities of Wotton's book. Not only may it be over my head, but I dislike iteration without accretive insight. However, I should point out that Hardy himself—the reader and admirer of Fourier and Comte—would almost certainly have approved Wotton's idealist, abstraction-making project. He might not have anticipated the terms used by Wotton to lay bare the connections between himself and his environs, but a goodly share of the philosophical musings in his autobiography and in the readings he made notes of participate in similar terminology, although that of his own time. But Hardy has another (at least putated) political dimension which Wotton's aspersions about O- and A-level study of literature does not approximate. The intellectual Marxism of Wotton's discourse has indistinct connections to the direct socialist and revolutionist sympathies Hardy claimed to have revealed in *The Poor Man and the Lady*, although the difference between the experiential and the intellected in literature is precisely the iterated center of Wotton's study. Thus there is an aridity about Wotton's work that's disappointing in view of his presumed political commitment, especially from the perspective of Hardy's deeply felt alienation from the ruling ideologies of his earlier years. Hardy was an intellectual, too (albeit of the autodidact variety), but he never for long lost touch with his instincts and inner self.

Although the relationship between scholarship and literature is often—like many issues within criticism itself—indeterminate, most scholars intend that their labors result in (someone else's, perhaps) better criticism. Although the books of criticism I have been discussing are by and large of fine quality, only occasionally does scholarship play a large role. More often, the critic is applying his or her perceptiveness and ability of expression to a general idea to be teased forth from Hardy's own works, or to a general proposition stemming from philosophy or life and literary conditions during Hardy's lifetime. Most often, the scholarship in these books is what one can fairly and non-pejoratively call "second-hand"—that is, the pioneering work of investigating the background facts has been done by someone else, and the critic is using that work as a corollary text to elucidate the point being made about Hardy's own text. An exception to this generalization is J. B. Bullen, *The Expressive Eye: Fiction and Perception in the Work of Thomas Hardy* (Oxford: Clarendon Press; New York: Oxford University Press, 1986), the strongest of the critical books I am noticing here. That Hardy was early and permanently interested in the visual arts is scarcely Bullen's discovery. References to art abound in the novels and in Hardy's autobiography; and Springer's book explains many of his allusions to specific artists and art-works. The publication of Hardy's "Schools of Painting" notebook by Richard H. Taylor in *The Personal Notebooks of Thomas Hardy* (London, 1979) provides evidence about the kinds of note-takings and jottings (evidently derived ca. 1863 from a yet-to-be-identified primer in art history) which Hardy when he was thinking of training to be an art critic thought relevant for a grasp of essential movements and developments. Bullen had all these sources ready to hand, of course; he more than any other critic I've read has benefitted from the "hard research" conducted by Lennart Björk and published in Hardy's *Literary Notebooks*. But he also makes original forays into the facts of his subject. He has a command of other material Hardy had available to him in contemporary metaphysics, evolutionary theory, mythology, art theory, anthropology, and ethnology and to which he refers in letters and elsewhere. Bullen identifies paintings not named by Hardy but which he evidently had in mind, and by reproducing them in excellent black-and-white plates allows his ascriptions to be measured by the reader. (He also reproduces several paintings Hardy did name.) Bullen's strength in pointing out in the paintings the qualities that Hardy could have been responding to is matched by a memory of incidental lines in Hardy which clearly allude to quite specific details in the paintings; and so even when he is discussing the more general features of particular novels his command of detail is secondary evidence of the solidity of his generalizations. With the exception of an extended (and richly suggestive) chapter on the combined impact of Ruskin, Turner, and Pater upon Hardy's use of light in *Tess of the d'Urbervilles*, Bullen discusses none of these materials extensively, but always with pinpointed relevance to the text of the novel at hand.

Bullen's large point is that Hardy had a visual orientation and founded the aesthetic structures of his novels upon concepts of "insight." To complement these structures Hardy drew upon his conscious study of paintings and art books (e.g., Ruskin's writings) to find expressive images for his instinctive, or artist's, sense of the need for a correspondence between image and idea. Hardy's aim is to employ imagery not as decoration but as polemical reinforcement. It has been many years since anyone seriously proposed that Hardy was a crude artist, but Bullen raises the case for Hardy's conscious artistry to new levels of subtlety which yet seem astonishingly evident once they are pointed out. For example, details of clothing and appearance dominate the presentation of *The Mayor of Casterbridge*, in which a solid and stable world resists historical change as it presents a moment of stasis; in contrast, in

Hardy's next novel, *The Woodlanders*, such details are vague even when they are present, for in this novel the characters' mental attitudes are characteristic of the different "universes" which each inhabits, mental attitudes "intimately bound up with the author's own modes of perception" (p. 172). In other words, from the solidness and stability of Casterbridge the novelist moves into a world of flux, a world governed by ideas more than characterization, in particular the idea that society is not "an aggregate of separate individuals but as 'one great network or tissue' which 'quivers in every part when one point is shaken, like a spider's web' " (*Early Life*, p. 232; Bullen, p. 172). Bullen's work, then, contributes to the awareness that has become dominant, that whatever Hardy's status as a philosopher in fiction, he refuses commitment to any fixed point, just as he always said he did.

One of the more interesting fresh perspectives that Bullen's approach provides is that *Jude the Obscure* is a deliberate "farewell to novel-writing" (p. 234), pointed up by the fact that in essential contrast with his other novels, in *Jude the Obscure* the characters do not find delight in visual experience. This observation dovetails well with a more widely noticed aspect of the novel, its abandonment of the role of Wessex as a repository of traditional beliefs and attitudes sustaining one against the stress of modern life; and as a summary of Hardy's career such an observation binds Bullen's portrayal of Hardy's visual imagination and his psychic and intellectual growth.

Bullen's book is criticism deeply enriched by scholarship. Another book published during this period cannot be placed in either of the simple categories I have used to structure this review. Ralph W. V. Elliott's *Thomas Hardy's English* (Oxford: Basil Blackwell, 1984) contains not only a dialect glossary, and in various portions of the book precise and non-interpretive material on derivations, classical and mythic allusions, intellectual indebtednesses, levels of diction, and parts of speech such as participial adjectives and phrasal verbs, sentence length, and cognate words; it also employs these kinds of solid evidence to make critical points about Hardy, such as pinpointing intended locations in novels from localized dialect usages, the use of syntax for adjectival emphasis, and the effect of passive contructions on the character of the narrator and characters. (And of course many details and readings of poems are strongly affected by such matters.) The benefits of such linguistic study may seem minor or even trivial to a reader or critic accustomed to settling philosophical issues, but aspects of linguistics permeate investigations of Hardy more grandiose and less skillfully presented than Elliott's. His book has some of the qualities of a compendium rather than those of a sequentially argued proposition, but such an observation is more in the way of a description than of a criticism. Arguing that Hardy's mixtures of diction and of dialect and standard English, along with his "syntactic idiosyncrasies" and "grammatical quirks" and coinages, "represent a deliberate forging of a linguistic instrument suited to Hardy's purposes as storyteller and poet" (p. 20), Elliott notes that Hardy drew upon historical English and was receptive "to linguistic promptings from . . . dialect, literature, science, painting, music, architecture, even jargon and slang" (p. 21). Many of Elliott's evidences are drawn from the frame of Hardy's life, always with a view toward the kinds of language used in the individual work (such as scholarly and architectural usages in *Desperate Remedies*, the influence of his parents and William Barnes upon Hardy's own use of dialect). Elliott's knowledge of Hardy's works seems encyclopedic, allowing him to choose unfailingly an appropriate passage in the novels and poems to illustrate a usage; and while he does not overturn any customary readings of Hardy it is clear that from now this is the text students will consult when dealing with Hardy's language. Regrettably, to assist a reader's search for a specific feature there is an adequate index only for dialect and unusual words, and an alphabetical arrangement of dialect words with illustrative passages. The general index contains many subject entries, but a book so full of detail constituting so authoritative a contribution to the century-long dispute about Hardy's skill (or clumsiness) with language was worth the pains of a fuller, perhaps analytical, index.

Fitting problematically into the frame I have constructed here are books of essays, some of which are "scholarly" and others "interpretive." A flurry of collections of essays of divers hands appeared in the 1970s, prepared by a range of editors; so far the only similar collections seen in the '80s have been edited by Norman Page. In 1980 appeared *Thomas Hardy: The Writer and his Background* (Bell & Hyman: London), distinguished by essays by Merryn and Raymond Williams (social class), Philip Collins (education), Lennart A. Björk (Hardy's notebooks), Norman Page himself (Hardy's language), Samuel Hynes ("The Hardy Tradition in Modern English Poetry"), and James Gibson (Grundyism). Beginning in 1982 has been appearing the *Thomas Hardy Annual* (London: Macmillan) under the editorship of Page. Although this production is a commercial affair, the essays taken all in all meet a high standard. Several eminent critics have published here, including John Bayley, Samuel Hynes, and Robert Langbaum, as well as Norman Page himself and several persons whose longer work I have cited here. Particularly noteworthy among these is Simon Gatrell, whose "Middling Hardy" in the fourth volume addresses the issue of Hardy's minor novels from a different perspective and more aggressively than does Richard H. Taylor. Taylor, incidentally, contributes to Page's 1980 collection a history of Hardy scholarship and criticism up to that time, and to each of the *Annual* volumes a sane assessment of "Recent Hardy Studies"—that is, of a year's work on Hardy, in bibliography, topography, biography, and criticism.

And finally there are the chapters in books written on larger topics. I have made no effort to systematically survey such books, since Hardy has become one of those classics whom modern literary criticism has seized upon for elucidative chapters, and to adequately explicate the orientation of these studies in order to "place" within them the use their authors make of Hardy would take a considerably longer space than I have given to those books specifically devoted to Hardy. I would like to mention only Roger Ebbatson's *The Evolutionary Self: Hardy, Forster, Lawrence* (Brighton: Harvester Press, 1982), which takes Hardy and his views toward evolution as a starting point for a significant literary-scientific tradition. I am also deliberately overlooking another kind of commentary on Hardy, "ordinary" essays in periodicals. The better essays published during these years are of a high standard, and I want to make clear that by the term "better essays" I do not intend a negative judgment of the minor essays. Hardy attracts the sort of interest, in fact, which makes tolerable even trivial explorations. But it would be misleading to suggest that more than a half dozen specialized essays each year fall in the "need to read" category; and in keeping with my intention to survey only books I do not cite even the thirty or so essays I think the most useful. I would only point out two trends: a spate of good essays on *Tess of the d'Urbervilles* ca. 1982 and a number of essays enriched by a feminist perspective published throughout this half-decade. All in all, Hardy scholarship is at a peak both of activity and accomplishment; Hardy criticism is plentiful and even fecund. As is usually the case in contrasts of scholarship and criticism, any given piece of scholarship is likely to "last" longer than a chance-chosen critical study; but at least three and perhaps four of the works of criticism I've surveyed will hold their place for the foreseeable future in selective bibliographies of works on Hardy that will need to be consulted by other critics of the topics.

## NOTES

1. I have reviewed volumes of Hardy's *Collected Letters* in the *University of Toronto Quarterly* 48 (1978), 92–94, and in *English Literature in Transition* 26 (1983), 200–202, and 27 (1984), 331–333; the Thomas Hardy Archive facsimile editions

of the manuscripts of *Tess of the d'Urbervilles* and *The Return of the Native* also in *English Literature in Transition* 30 (1987), 224–227; Millgate's biography of Hardy in *Nineteenth-Century Fiction* 37 (1983), 604–608; the Clarendon Edition of *Tess of the d'Urbervilles* in *Papers of the Bibliographical Society of America* 78 (1984), 363–367; Casagrande's study of Hardy's unity in the *South Atlantic Quarterly* 83 (1984), 234–236; Giordano's book on Hardy's suicidal characters in *Choice*, November 1984, p. 171; Millgate's edition of Hardy's autobiography also in *Choice*, November 1985, p. 125; Taylor's *The Neglected Hardy* and the first volume of the *Thomas Hardy Annual* in *Victorian Studies* 27 (1984), 393–394; and Bullen's *The Expressive Eye* in *Victorian Periodicals Review* 21 (1988), 40–41. I here re-use several passages from those reviews, almost always in recast form.

2. Owing both to this essay's concentration upon scholarship and criticism and to the space required to discuss these areas, I do not mention a number of books relevant to Hardy published during the period the essay covers. Among these are numerous Wessex topographies; *Thomas Hardy: An Annotated Bibliography of Writings about Him*, eds. W. Eugene Davis and Helmut E. Gerber (DeKalb: Northern Illinois University Press, 1983); and Emma Hardy's *Diaries*, ed. Richard Taylor (New York: Carcanet, 1985). These books are not without interest, especially the *Diaries*; and the *Annotated Bibliography* is useful particularly for contemporary references to Hardy. I have reviewed the *Diaries* in *Choice*, December 1985, p. 174. I have not been able to locate a copy of *A Thomas Hardy Dictionary* (Tokyo: Meicho Fukyukai, 1984), which would appear to contain useful etymological and dialect materials.

# Contemporary Biographers of Nineteenth-Century Subjects: The Novelists

## Frederick R. Karl

The problems confronting the contemporary biographer of the major nine-teenth-century novelists are of several kinds. Biographers, in the main, have been frightened off from writing lives of the most important Victorian novelists because of the majesterial biographies already existent: Edgar Johnson's two-volume *Dickens*, Gordon Haight's *Eliot*, and Gordon Ray's two-volume *Thackeray*, the most obvious among several examples. Only Ray's *Thackeray* seems impregnable, whereas the others, while still commanding the field in several respects, need replacement, either because of the emergence of new material or development of different ways of handling biography. Only Mi-chael Millgate in his *Hardy* has attempted a full-dress biography using the latest materials (Millgate is also co-editing the letters), although critically one would have liked to see a more intense psychological and post-structural critique. Even Ray's *Thackeray* is not completely protected against this charge of insufficient interpretation. His practical, empirical biographical study needs more critical equipment, more diverse approaches than a purely historical-critical one, more interesting readings of the writer's work; and then a folding back of those readings into the life.

Yet the problems for the biographer are even broader, intensifying in the last decades; and while these problems are endemic to biography in general, they are especially vital for earlier subjects which require "redoing." Criti-cism, the new glamorous genre, has mounted an attack on biography as a genre: those theories which emphasize the work, beginning with the New Criticism but becoming an onslaught with hermeneutics, semiotics, post-structuralism, and reader-response criticism; and which, as a corollary, depreciate the author or his relationship to the work. This problem, however, can be finessed, but a subsidiary issue raised is to what extent the biographer will respond to the tools revealed to him or her by these very critics. We perceive a paradox: that while critical theory tries to diminish biographical studies, biography can co-opt such theories to its advantage. Yet just as an earlier generation of biographers was wary of psychological probing (a wariness still not dissipated), now the present generation, as we shall see, hesitates to use more recent critical tools.

None of this is a plea for any particular approach, except perhaps some psychological astuteness. But the biographer must at least confront his subjects and the works with a nonpartisan, theoretical net, not an assumed neutrality. In previous generations, as noted, psychology and psychoanalysis were begrudged or ridiculed, and we still find biographers of Victorian subjects (Halperin on Austen and Gissing, Millgate on Hardy, Hennessy on Trollope, for example) hesitating to use, judiciously and sensitively, such tools. Another biographer, now writing on Lewis Carroll, stated at a recent biographical seminar that Carroll lived before Freud and in a pre-Freudian environment, we should eschew such analytic tools: this for a subject who posed little girls nude and did this in an age of severe sexual dislocation and eccentricity. Not all biographers are so oblivious to developments now over seventy-five years old, but we see even a recent generation avoiding what criticism, psychological or more contemporary ideas, can tell it.

Another, but related, problem is still our uncertainty about how much of the subject's work should be utilized as itself "true" biography. Where does the life lie?—in the chronology as supported by data or in the vastly intricate workings of the fiction, made all the more intricate and complex in the greatest writers? Without analytic tools, the biographer is fearful of gaffes and, therefore, hews to data (chronologies, letters, diaries or memoirs, manuscript and typescript revisions, contemporary witnesses, public statements, et al.); but neglects the full run of a primary source of biographical material, the subject's own work. If attempted, this procedure must be accomplished with considerable tact, taste, and strategical skill, for while obviously the work is not quite the life, in a sense it *is* the life, the sole justification for our doing the biography. Unlike historical figures, literary subjects have little meaning except for the work, 'little" in the sense that their lives are not much different from other lives; and it is only because of the work that the literary figure becomes an interesting subject. When in a previous generation, Edgar Johnson separated his splendidly researched and readable "life" from the work, he

was writing a particular kind of biography. Although he succeeded in communicating what Dickens was about, that type of biographical writing should
not any longer be possible; for too many other disciplines have been validated
as part of the biographer's art and world. Yet many biographers now, although
they do not physically divide the life and the work, insufficiently interweave
them: the life stops when the work is introduced, and then resumes after
discussion and analysis. This is not what we have in mind.

When we attempt to determine how the present group of biographers has
handled nineteenth-century subjects as differentiated from their predecessors'
treatment of often the same subjects, we note an increase in the quality of
scholarship, but not a much greater critical advance. But before taking up
this point in detail, we should examine what contemporary biography has
become. The very validation of the genre is further confused by the fact that
it has become such a mixed business. The biographer finds himself (herself)
in a maelstrom of excessive information and uncertain of the genre's direction.
A corollary of this is how much of that information is applicable.

Often, the biographer still looks backward. Although Lytton Strachey certainly opened up aspects of biography which needed airing, his own practices
must be eschewed—he cannot be a model, as he still seems to be for many
academic or narrow practitioners of the genre. Biography is, today, in the
problematical position of taking a stand outside literary criticism and yet
desperately in need of critical tools. Although certain critical methodology
which draws on linguistics, deconstruction, hermeneutics (Derrida), and
Freudian revisionism (Lacan) suggests that biography is beside the point,
biographers must respond by assimilating these critical tools to some degree.
A life as well as its works can be deconstructed, be subjected to hermeneutics
and/or Freudian revisionism. Biography has intermittently incorporated history, psychology, anthropology, and sociology—Edel in his *James*, Painter
in his *Proust* come readily to mind—and to this it must add literary criticism.

One reason for the great length of recent biographies, of earlier as well as
of contemporaneous figures, is the felt need to establish cultural contexts for
the subject. Such contexts have become, and should be, multifold. As we
shall note below, some recent biographies of nineteenth-century novelists fail
to be satisfactory because of the paucity of context and the lack of deeper
literary criticism. John Halperin's *Jane Austen* fails to be a meaningful biographical study because the cultural context is introduced like so many slabs
of meat, and most of that from a single study, J. H. Plumb's *Georgian
Delights*. His *Gissing*, likewise, lacks sufficient backgrounding; whereas

Hennessy's *Trollope* has the context, but no theoretical underpinning, no ideas.

The biographer must venture beyond the usual expectations, especially as he redoes or retouches familiar subjects from the past. This does not mean the introduction of technical terms from hermeneutics or psychoanalysis, but the assimilation of psychological, linguistic, or other techniques which can be used when needed. The day has passed when these disciplines can be ignored or finessed, no matter how uneasy one may be when trying to explore the mind of someone dead for a hundred years or more. Here, the work is often a better guide than the life, although the good biographer will find ways of blending life and work. Biographers of nineteenth-century subjects have not mastered these methods as well as have biographers of later figures.

Whatever the degree of analysis, however, it is clear that biography has become the great assimilator. It is more than history since it incorporates more than data or statistics; it provides interpretation, and if anything we are in an age of interpretation. The interest in biography cannot be separated from the interest in nonfiction as a whole. The growth of biography, in fact, parallels almost exactly the surge in popularity of the new journalism and the nonfiction novel. We all awaited, for example, the late Richard Ellmann's study of Oscar Wilde: not only for our expectations of Professor Ellmann's elegant presentation of biographical data, but for the historical context, for some good gossip about Wilde and his circle, for the reverberations that would carry us out into late Victorian culture as a whole. We expect some of the excitement that we obtain from a first-rate nonfiction novel.

It may be fair to say the surge in interest in biography is connected less to what is occurring in our literary genres and more to people's concerns outside of literature itself. If we want to discover the reasons for biography's popularity and for its quasi-psychological basing, then we must seek it in the larger culture. If there is a sense of *deja vu* about what I will say—if Lytton Strachey and the kind of biography he wrote to counter Victorian monuments seem analogous—it is probably because our own era parallels cultural changes that began to take place almost one hundred years ago. It is not that we have moved from the large, inclusive novel, rather that such a novel no longer expresses what we feel about ourselves and our era. It is not the novel that is beginning to fail us, but that we have changed so that the inclusive novel no longer obtains. It has become an academic exercise, still strong, but for the few. When a vacuum results from such historical and cultural changes, something must rush in; and biography fulfills that function because it blends those elements which presently concern us.

A good deal of contemporary biography, of both past and present subjects, fulfills an even more primitive need, which is gossip—even when the biography is about a noncelebrity, an anti-celebrity, in fact, such as Kafka or Samuel Johnson (both subjects of recent, well-praised biographies). The influence of television and print journalism is acute here, in that they have accustomed us to fictional nonfiction, to broad areas of news and reporting where frontiers are blurred, to the "inside story" which is a little bit of this or that. To carry this over into biography and into our interest in how people live in our or another era does not take a great effort. It is impossible to disentangle the increased audience for biography and biographical study from somewhat baser interests, such as our avidity for information in story form which we gain from television and various news magazines. This may be less noble, but biography—even at its best—is moving parallel to communication areas we may have little cultural respect for.

The major issues in biography, nevertheless, do not lie in its length, nor in excessive use of psychological or other tools, nor in the proliferation of lives of secondary and tertiary figures, nor even in the breakdown in taste. The key issues lie, rather, in the refinement of biographical tools in serious lives; not simply more original research—we have achieved that—but a more profound assimilation of the multiplicity of tools in the biographer's hands. This means more subtle use of psychological analysis, better absorption of linguistic, historical, and philosophical backgrounds, more integration of the myriad critical elements which go into biography. There is, also, another point, and that is as both biographers and readers we must become accustomed to the use of novelistic strategies in the writing of biography. Johnson's great success with his two-volume *Dickens* in 1952 stemmed from his ability to turn Dickens into a great fictional character, however little our present survey reveals that practice. Although some achieve it—besides Johnson, Ruby Redinger with George Eliot, Michael Holroyd with Lytton Strachey, outside our purview—it is, admittedly, a mine field for the biographer.

To speak of literary biography alone, we emphasize that the crucial factor lies in the biographer getting at his or her subject's imagination. We must learn through biographical data how this subject came to write those novels, poems, plays. There must be integration of the life—its personal aspects, styles, tastes, reading, attitudes, relationships—with qualities of imagination and creative force or creative will; and if the biographer misses that dimension or fails to elucidate it, then greater or lesser length, detail, persistence, even large contexts, make little difference. This is the area where valid literary biography rests.

With these cautions in mind, we turn to several biographies of nineteenth-century English novelists written in the last decade or so. If ever a subject needed a different touch from that provided by her biographer, it is Jane Austen, whose most recent biographer is John Halperin (*The Life of Jane Austen*, Johns Hopkins University Press, 1984). Here we find an able research job almost completely subverted by commonplace, even vulgar, critical taste and, worse, by an egregious lack of knowledge of the fiction and larger culture preceding and contemporaneous with Austen. Further, Halperin's lack of psychological acumen, or even awareness of psychological dimensions, moves us back to Chapman and Garrod, a different era and a different set of biographical assumptions. It is true that Jane Austen sets a sharp problem for any critic/biographer even with psychological insight; but while the life does not have sufficient detail for clear resolutions, there are numerous elements in the fiction which psychological analysis can elucidate. Thirty-five years ago, Marvin Mudrick showed how a critic could bring forth materials which the biographer might reroute and use.

When Halperin (the Centennial Professor of English at Vanderbilt University) does attempt analysis, he comes up with the appreciatory type, rarely with any in-depth probe of literary meaning. He seems innocent of all critical theory, or how it might be applied to biography. But probably the most apparent omission is any substantial setting of Jane Austen in her culture. Halperin admits he has leaned heavily on J. H. Plumb's *Georgian Delights*, but he uses Plumb's material in bits and pieces, not integrated into Austen's life and way of thinking. Early on (p. 11*ff*), for example, Halperin gives a rapid run-through of what constituted this "age of elegance and taste—and of squalor and callousness beyond imagination." He cites the rise of newspapers, the interest in travel, the beauty of rural, pre-industrial England, the stress on etiquette and manners. He even writes of the age's love of dance, its practical realism, its manner of dress. But what of language—what was occurring in language, since, in several respects Jane Austen, like Dickens after her, was a creature of language: in her case, a sharp-edged, ironic, distanced language? What were people reading?—and not simply Gothic novels and novels of sentiment—and what role did theater play in the larger culture as well as in the novel? What could women expect from life? In a paragraph here and there, Halperin touches on this, but without any sustained sense of what it was like to be a woman, in Austen's class or otherwise.

Further, why does he validate points by bringing in other critics and biographers, instead of using primary sources? He is trying to supersede Elizabeth Jenkins's excellent biography, which dates from 1938 (new edition in 1949), and yet when he wants to substantiate a point of his own he cites Jenkins, or someone else. When he speaks of Austen's parents as being "traditionally Tory," why does he omit any explanation of what it meant to be Tory in the latter eighteenth century? More generally, where is any extended discussion of political matters, of Tory-Whig contexts, of what the political divisions meant in terms of class and caste, of how religion entered into politics and politics into religion? These are all formative matters on Jane Austen, since she grew up in a lively family, with many brothers, and political discussion could not have been absent from the table, however much she may herself have eschewed direct political argument in her novels. None of this would be definitive information, but it would provide still another way of getting at a writer who did not often tip her hand.

These absences of essential information lead to a biography which fails to set Jane Austen into her time and place. At no point in Halperin's biography do we enjoy that sense of ease in the writer's command of his subject, such as we feel with Haight's *Eliot* or Johnson's *Dickens*. We suspect an interloper who has read all the relevant material on Austen, but who has not digested it or used his resources fully. At the conclusion of this study, we lack any clear sense of what Austen thought, what her intellectual priorities were, how she fitted into the role of a woman in what was clearly still a difficult time for women. We need a biography of far stronger intellectual shaping.

There is, moreover, a good deal of overkill, the sign of critical flaccidity and a failure of a more disciplined point of view. For example, Halperin, discussing Austen's early "Lady Susan": "It is an astonishing, frightening performance by an eighteen-year-old girl—who somehow, within the confines of the Rectory at Steventon, acquired vision into the heart of darkness within man (or, more properly, woman) and learned to articulate her vision of that darkness with unerring conviction" (p. 49). Heart of darkness! That is another dimension altogether, as is the comparison with James's Madame Merle, still another order of darkness there. Overkill blends into simplistic statements: discussing Austen's interest in Tom Lefroy, who married in 1799 and never saw the novelist again, Halperin writes: "A major theme of *Persuasion* is that woman's love is more enduring than man's; it is likely that Jane Austen never entirely forgot Tom Lefroy" (p. 62). To equate a fleeting romance with the meaning of the novel is a critical reductionism we thought had long since disappeared. *Persuasion* is structured on far more complex materials.

More significant than these critical lapses is the lack of a point of view into which certain definite Austen attitudes can be placed. Commenting on her feelings toward her parents, Halperin writes: "one can perceive, from the distance of 175 years, only good feeling and affection between Jane Austen and her father. If parents in her novels are often bad parents, they stand in for her mother alone, with whom her relations were always less easy (pp. 144–145). How can Halperin come to this conclusion after citing a good number of weak or insufficient fathers and father figures? Any study of Austen cannot conclude she was on good terms with her father; it should, instead, explore why she presents fathers in such a bad light, what this meant in terms of her attitude toward her brothers, toward men. And then, once this has been surveyed, one moves on to the mother and mother figures, likewise either silly or insufficient to indifferent. Parental figures appear in sizable enough numbers to provide psychological clues to Austen's attitudes; and if we seize these clues along with an analysis of the language she uses, we have a wedge into a novelist who gives little away.

Halperin also tries historical or comparative criticism; i.e., "*Mansfield Park* is Jane Austen's *Vanity Fair*" (p. 234). What should we make of this, when the two novels are only superficially similar? On the primary level, they derive from completely different outlooks about life, well beyond male-female differences. Halperin speaks of Austen's characters as "selfish—self-absorbed, self-indulgent, and vain" (p. 234). But the entire thrust of *Mansfield Park* is how these qualities can be transcended, how a community of clever people can fall, while the lackluster Fanny triumphs. In Thackeray's novel, there is no triumph—the vain and self-indulgent win the day, and when Dobbin finally gains Amelia, his triumph gives shape to the meaning of a Pyrrhic victory. He gets the consolation prize, not the prize. Fanny Price, however, has brought things back to an even keel: the country virgin has triumphed over urban wiseacres. Whether we believe in her victory or not is another matter; in Thackeray, everyone, including the winners, loses.

Halperin attempts to equate real life people and novelistic characters: "Mr Woodhouse [of *Emma*], meanwhile, is probably a male version of Mrs Austen, though no one has noticed this before" (p. 269). No one has noticed it because the equation makes neither literary nor biographical sense. Why not say that Lady Bertram (in *Mansfield Park*) is an upper class version of Mrs. Austen and offer the same reasons? We all recall thinking Shakespeare must have been like Hamlet, or Hamlet like Shakespeare.

The more complicated novels such as *Mansfield Park* and *Emma* are not Halperin's forte. For example: "*Emma* is by far the most psychological of the novels, that book of Jane Austen's in which, more than anywhere else in her work, the human mind is so often caught in the process of thinking. . . . In *Emma* the dialogue brilliantly follows the associative processes of the thinking mind. This makes it one of the most 'scenic,' in Jamesian terms, of Jane Austen's novels, and may help to explain why it is such a favourite of modern readers'' (p. 274). Halperin cites the scene in chapter 5 of volume III in which Mr. Knightley watches others playing a game, and this reminds him of the scene in *The Golden Bowl* ''in which Maggie watches the others playing bridge'' (p. 274). Intermixed in this passage is Halperin's comment that ''Virginia Woolf was right to suggest that Jane Austen, had she lived another twenty years, would be considered now a forerunner of James and Proust.'' Criticism here is so haphazard, so flailing around for support, so indiscriminate in its reliance on James in one place, Woolf in another, that *Emma* and its psychological resonances become submerged. The lack of critical method in the handling of the more complicated novels hobbles the entire biography. If we believe the work is an integral part of biography, then the work must be handled with sensitivity so as to illuminate the life. Halperin does quite the contrary. He hops and skips, moves forward and backward, uses lateral comparisons, historical citations—none of which illuminates his very point, that *Emma* has psychological resonance.

When background, finally, is reintroduced in order to give some context to the year 1815 in Austen's life, it comes in like this: ''Spring and summer 1815 was an interesting time in the outside world too'' (p. 278). Then we get a brief glimpse of Napoleon—seven lines in all—and the reader is redirected to the Austen family, especially Charles, who was stationed in the Mediterranean. In a novelist who lived such a short time, every year is ''interesting,'' and if one wants to provide context, it must be accomplished with greater sophistication and far greater grasp of background. Whatever biographical detail Halperin supplies from previous biographers—and one gets the impression this is a life built out of other lives—he adds almost nothing of his own; and when it comes to critical assessments, he makes us realize that criticism as long ago as Mudrick's trenchant study is a far better guide to Jane Austen's biography than her current biographer.

At the other end of the century (although born only twenty-three years after Austen's death) is Thomas Hardy, and at the other end of the scale in accomplishment is Michael Millgate's *Thomas Hardy: A Biography* (Random House, 1982). Before his work on Hardy, including the co-editing of the Hardy letters with Richard L. Purdy, Millgate was best known for his careful scholarship on William Faulkner. His *The Achievement of William Faulkner* (in 1964) was quite possibly the best early study, before Joseph Blotner's two-volume biography in 1974. Millgate brings to Hardy that same attention to detail. From the first page, we know we are in the hands of a biographer who has been to the primary sources and is not writing a life based on others' studies. Further, we have the assurance the material has been fully digested—that the end is implicit in the beginning, and that the author is not working sequentially as he does his research.

Millgate (Professor of English at the University of Toronto) is of the hard-fact school of biography. If there is no direct evidence, he hesitates to take a leap. He eschews the novelistic, the imaginative creation of scenarios, the intimate reading of the mind which the works, as well as life, may provide. He prefers outward actions, documentation (which is awesome), the single fact to what it may more generally mean. In his assessment of a life, he is a pragmatist, and what you see through documentation and scholarship is what you have. This does not mean he cannot find in manuscripts and typescripts and their revisions ways to enter Hardy's mind; but it does mean he balks at scenarios which might prove speculative or a little distant from the data.

Millgate, nevertheless, attempts to maintain balance between the mere accumulation of data and interpretive readings. A critical area occurred in Hardy's relationship to his mother, upon whom from an early age he was overwhelmingly dependent. His early illnesses and frailty surely reinforced that dependency and turned him from his father, a mason. Millgate interprets that conflict: "But Hardy was at the same time damaged, like Clym Yeobright, by so extreme an emotional dependence upon his mother, by his early and perhaps inevitable surrender to her all-encompassing influence and direction. The tenacity of that material hold was to hamper him at all stages of his first marriage, and it was the primary cause, along with his early ill health, of that prolonged immaturity which left him, in his own estimation, a child till he was nearly fifty'' (pp. 22–23).

Once Millgate ventures on this compelling territory, however, he is obligated to follow it through, although it does lead into thickets that are virtually impenetrable. It is, perhaps, no coincidence that Millgate's other biographical subject, Faulkner, was likewise emotionally dependent from childhood on his mother, and it, too, hampered him in marriage and generally in his relationships with women. Yet to say it hampered Hardy is to lose sight of the fact that his life as lived is secondary to what he presented to the world. We do not really care about Hardy's immaturity or unhappiness unless it nourished his work; for it is the work, the novels and poetry, which give Hardy interest. If we recognize this, then we must take it to the next stage: how did the emotional dependence on his mother hinder Hardy's development as a writer, if it did? How did it subvert his novels and poetry?

We must, ultimately, relate his immaturity until he was nearly fifty to his ability to transcend that unhappiness in his fiction, to 1895, and to his poetry thereafter. If that connection between life and art cannot be established, then on what basis can we claim he was hampered or dependent? On what grounds can we assert it was harmful? If we do not or cannot—and Millgate does not carry through on this critical point—then any assessment of his early development must be qualified. Hardy, after all, became a great literary figure, deserving of the Nobel Prize far more than many who received it, and if this is the result of an emotional dependence on his mother, then whatever she did, worked. The only other argument might be that if he had been less emotionally dependent, he would have achieved more; but no biographer is willing to take up that position, not with Hardy, anyway.

Similarly, Hardy's emotional involvement with his wife—once more like Faulkner's with Estelle Oldham—went beyond unhappiness, shame, desire for relief, fantasies of abandonment and escape. He stuck until she died, when both were old; and he remained faithful, as far as we can tell, whether out of wish or circumstance. Millgate establishes very well the facts of the relationship—Emma's resentment of Hardy's growing fame, her delusions she was also a good writer, her attacks on his agnosticism, her vehement assertions of her own traditional Christianity, her ridicule of him in public. All of this is made part of the record.

Yet it does not appear to have harmed Hardy except to make him wish for a more peaceful partner. He still wrote what he intended to write, and his philosophical-ideological position did not change as a result of domestic infighting. And he stayed with her, although he spent less and less time in her company. As an author, anyway, he would normally have spent a good deal of time away from any wife, pleasant or otherwise. Millgate would have to demonstrate, somehow, that Hardy lost artistic or creative ground as a consequence of Emma's unpleasant presence. There is no evidence he did, or that he considered backing off. His novels, in fact, became increasingly outrageous in Victorian terms, bleaker, less giving, from *Tess* to *Jude*. When Hardy left fiction, it was not the result of Emma's onslaughts upon his pagan outlook, but brutal reviews and his own assessment of what he could still do in fiction. We would have to say Hardy's gloom, in his later fiction and then in his best poetry, if it resulted from Emma's influence, worked to the good, since it reinforced what was already potential in the writer. But we would not wish to make that statement unless we had more definitive evidence.

Millgate opened a Pandora's Box in the area of Hardy's relationship to women as the result of his dependence on his mother. Yet he cannot demonstrate that Hardy's immaturity—he would fall in love on sight of a lovely woman, someone seen from a carriage or bicycle—hampered his work or hobbled his creative imagination. Several passages throughout the biography cited Hardy's response to women who were the opposite of Emma: the rich and titled, the well-educated, the wives of friends and acquaintances who showed interest in him. He writes: "Hardy's emotional susceptibility was as naïve and adolescent as it had ever been, and he was readily charmed by physical and social graces which had been quite unknown to his early experience and which even since his marriage had scarcely become things of every day" (p. 243). Such graceful passages abound, but what do they mean? We must, once again, confront a man who had bound himself to a woman he possibly could not bear once the bloom had worn off, a woman with whom he very possibly had a frigid relationship, or at least an unsatisfactory one, or a woman with whom he was, possibly, impotent—all these scenarios are available to us—and yet he wrote steadily and at a high level throughout this unhappy marriage. Whatever she was, however silly, however pretentious, however hostile, Emma must have sparked something in her husband, or else he would have suffered blockage or simply given up. Instead, he churned out fiction and poetry, including four or five novels which have become part of the canon and dozens of poems which have made their entrance into literature.

The problem with a biography even as solid, well-researched and well-presented as Millgate's is the lack of any psychological organizing principle. We do not mean here that the biographer has to ride herd on a pet belief of mother worship or an Oedipal conflict or a penchant for self-punishment. What is involved is something subtler. Millgate does address Emma's role in Hardy's life, as a "living" quality; but it is necessary to demonstrate what the relationship meant in his artistic or imaginative life. A psychological analysis could, possibly, link Hardy's personal and professional lives or provide insight into the writer's willing of himself into a major novelist and then into a major poet, not because of an emotional dependence, not despite it, but as an integral part of it.

Unlike Halperin, who revealed little feel for Jane Austen or her times, James Pope Hennessy fitted himself into Trollope and his period. Nevertheless, his study (*Anthony Trollope*, Cape, 1971) offers no more of an understanding of Trollope than does an earlier life by Michael Sadleir in 1927 (or other earlier studies like A. O. J. Cockshut's *Anthony Trollope: A Critical*

*Study*, Bradford A. Booth's *Anthony Trollope: Aspects of His Life and Art*, or Robert M. Polhemus's *The Changing World of Anthony Trollope*). Although Hennessy has a keen sense of Trollope's England, and his book is packed with interesting observations, he fails to use the novels as ways of penetrating into Trollope himself. This is old-fashioned biography with a vengeance. While Halperin makes pitiful attempts at psychology, Hennessy knows his limitations and eschews any psychological analysis, even when the material means little without it. We are not suggesting here some kind of postmortem psychoanalysis of corpus Trollopus; but, rather, some recognition that that enormous output, that need to produce words, that energy which could produce thousands of words in repeated morning sessions all had some etiology which requires explanation. The explanation from poverty—since Trollope experienced extreme poverty at points in his childhood—is insufficient; the response went well beyond balancing out a deprived, miserable childhood. It requires another level of analysis, and only a psychological plan can work, some psychological hypothesis which remains flexible and elastic.

Surely, as with Dickens in some respects, the outpouring of words, the sudden rages, the acts of near violence, the inability to tolerate other people's opinions have some common etiology, whether sexual or otherwise. One suspects a sexual explanation, but some other might serve; yet Hennessy does not even attempt to get at a meaningful interpretation of Trollope's outpouring of words. Instead, the biography proceeds in a predictable way, through large chunks of background information, followed by plot summaries. Such summaries, moreover, contain no analytic material, no effort to link the novels to the writer, or to see in the novels dimensions of the writer which reflect on biographical elements. The summaries are just that, as though they were being offered as aids to examination questions. Most of these novels, except for the well-known Barchester series and the Palliser group, will remain unknown; so that their summaries can have no meaning for the reader unless such novels can be integrated with the life. But they are not used to ''explain'' Trollope; nor is Trollope used to explain them.

One area of potential exploration, which here goes by the wayside, is a comparison of Trollope's Barsetshire as a realm of the imagination with other such places. We think of Hardy's Wessex or Faulkner's Yoknapatawpha, each of them an invented area which contains strong personal, psychological, and emotional overtones. While Barsetshire is perhaps more ''objectified'' than any of these, it nevertheless has strong personal overtones for Trollope: Edenic, with intimations of the serpent; a place of control; an area permitting an exploration of institutions (the church, life in the surrounding villages, the workings of town governments); an idea of order. Some or all of these potential areas of exploration are worth looking into to try to seek some ideological positioning of Trollope; but Hennessy refuses or is unable to work through these possibilities.

In other areas, Trollope's attitude toward money is taken up. Hennessy remarks that the writer's "attitude to money was neither romantic nor, on the other hand, was it cynical" (p. 265). He then relates it directly to Trollope's childhood of "genteel poverty," a blight; and to his decidedly unromantic memories of his famous mother "quill-driving into the small hours by the light of a flickering tallow candle, keeping herself awake with green tea, rubbing her aching fingers in a cold room of that grim house in Bruges" (p. 265). All of this is undeniably true, and well put—one must stress how well written this study is. But it ignores important aspects of Trollope's psychology. Since Hennessy is speculating anyway about the etiology of the writer's need to compensate for his abject childhood, he might have carried speculation further and seen money as linked to emotional needs, to sexual fantasies, to other dimensions of the writer; as we must do with Dickens, where in later years, the desire to give readings and to pile up a fortune even while nearly killing himself in the act transcended any need to compensate for an abject childhood. It went far deeper, into a dissatisfaction with self, a sense of despair, a depression that overwhelmed the man, a need to find in money (power) compensation for a self that was falling into fragments. Trollope was, perhaps, a much simpler subject than Dickens, an easier read; but the basic needs were there, and they need exploration. Hennessy fails us here.

In other respects, the level of criticism falls to what we assumed was no longer viable in contemporary biography. For example: "I do not think that there can be much doubt that *The Prime Minister* is a pretty dull book, with a quantity of political scenes that are no longer stirring, and a heroine who, for once, fails to enchant the reader." This simply will not do. One needs far more sophisticated comment, some sense of structure, a critical terminology, ways of aligning commentary with biographical data. This is the language of pre-Lytton Strachey, and it demonstrates to us nothing except Hennessy's own feeling, which is not what we want.

Not unrelated to this paucity of critical acumen is the lack of notes. This biography, appearing as full dress, gives no sense of sources, no idea whether Hennessy has returned to primary materials, or is simply building his work on the research of others. New biographical material may no longer exist, but a serious flaw is Hennessy's failure to arrange existing material so as to gain the most from it in conjunction with the fiction. Even in the area of his expertise, his use of background contexts, we are not satisfied. He speaks of Trollope's friendship with George Eliot, and how Eliot was the only woman of intellect he saw regularly and became close to. Yet even here, the relationship is not examined in detail, only the surfaces, and those perfunctorily. The friendship of two such different people, both at such high levels of achievement, creates curiosity why and how it could continue; but here, as in so many other areas, we find only details, not substance.

In another area, touched on above, we wonder at Trollope's screaming, his inability to listen to others even when his own fortunes are on the line, his rudeness and crossness in dialogue with others, especially at the official level, his desire to create the conditions under which he might be expected to fail professionally. We have here a very interesting phenomenon, psychological, emotional, or otherwise; and yet Hennessy throws no light on it, nor does he try. There is, we sense, some linkage between this behavior and Trollope's need to produce words: in one case, he screams out words without regard for what the listener might think; in the other, he pours out thousands of words crafted toward some end. In each instance, words become the expression of his personality, and yet, we ask, where do the two streams meet, or how? It is in these areas that the biographer is expected to provide clues, make forays, establish scenarios of possibility.

By one fifth of the way through the book, we have no explanation of why Trollope turned out the way he did, no sense of his emotional and psychological development, not even any sense of his ideological positioning of himself in nineteenth-century England. Further, why cannot we have comparisons with other writers, someone like Dickens, who also grew up angry and deprived, frustrated by circumstance, and who, also, broke out with words. For both, language became the way they could respond to past anger and hurt; and even Trollope's organization of the postal system in Ireland is, not so indirectly, connected to words—letters, communication systems, people reaching other people. This, too, is part of biography: his obsession with the organization of the postal system, language as the key. How did he differ from Dickens in this respect, these two men of volubility, of incessant outpouring? How did the postal system affect Trollope's need to be close to his readers, to communicate directly with them? We leave Hennessy's life no more aware of these problems than when we entered.

We feel some hesitation in speaking about the revision and abridgment of Edgar Johnson's truly classic biography of Charles Dickens, published in two volumes in 1952, as *Charles Dickens: His Tragedy and Triumph*. The revision

(Viking, 1977) appeared exactly twenty-five years later, at about half the length of the original and with almost no commentary on the fiction itself. If we back up, first, to the two-volume edition, we find a wonderfully readable narrative of Dickens' life unbroken by discussions of individual fictions, which appeared in separate chapters, chronologically arranged. This was, in itself, problematic. The very format suggested that the life was the text, the work the subtext; that biographical detail was privileged, the work an addendum. This puts it a little stronger than it should be, but the method did detach man and work in ways that created problems. It meant, among other things, that the psychological tensions of the works remained unlinked to certain themes in Dickens' life. For one, the relationship of Dickens to his father, while indicating in the life segments some annoyance, involved tolerance and indulgence; whereas in the works, fathers (and often mothers) are handled with devastating, even murderous, criticism.

Another problem in the original edition was the absence of those thousands of letters, only some of them available by 1952, which have since surfaced and are being collected in the splendid Pilgrim Edition published by Oxford. Those letters provide an almost day-to-day, sometimes hour-to-hour, account of Dickens' life. Further, the writer's affair with Ellen Lawless Ternan did not assume its rightful place in his later life; and other possible affairs are barely suggested. As against this was the remarkable narrative pace Edgar Johnson was able to bring to the full life, his sense of drama, his rich prose which complemented Dickens' own. There was the apparent sympathy of biographer and subject—something we might take for granted but which, when missing, keeps a biography off-center.

Finally, still with the earlier edition in mind, was the absence of deeper analysis, which could have derived only from a deeper view of the fiction and the use of that fiction as an illumination of themes in the life. The emphasis on Dickens' social interests—rightfully expressed—distracted from areas in his emotional life which are extremely compelling: his angers, his penchant for violence in his work and then in his readings, his depressions and despair, his lavish life-style. These personal areas are surely not disconnected from the work, and yet they seemed curiously detached.

The 1977 revision and abridgment reveals the bare bones. The commentaries on the fiction have been removed, so that critical remarks are often no more than sentences, which perforce must state the obvious. The narrative remains rich, the prose still supple and eminently suitable for such a novelist. Nevertheless, the losses in this edition are apparent; and in some curious way they point up the failings of the earlier, fuller volumes. Whereas once we read the two volumes as possibly the last word on the life (although not on the work), now we perceive that the life was far more varied and intense in its heights and depths. Johnson tended to make Dickens reasonable; but that approach slighted those manic flights characteristic of so much of his life. In turn, the manic flights shaded the valleys of depression and despair, as well as the need for vicarious violence. Several dimensions to Dickens remain which we want to know more about and which can be reconstructed only from his fiction: a deeper analysis of his relationship to his wife, Catherine; his attitudes toward sex—how different from centrist Victorian ideas, how much the same; his response to radical movements, what Gissing tried to get at in his trenchant, but limiting, study and what we find in Dickens' own reaction to the Governor Eyre incident in Jamaica, where he aligned himself with the most reactionary forces; his response, overall, to real change, as apart from cosmetic change; his feeling about the institutions which he mocked and burlesqued, how ready he was to accept alteration of the English way of life in order to usher in reform.

Other areas include how he tried (or failed) to reconcile his own lavish life style with his evident sympathies for the poor and disadvantaged; how he confronted his distaste personally for marriage with his fictional endings, which exalted romantic, idealistic marriage; how he faced his sense of burnout, when he suddenly became fallow and enervated, and yet the desire to succeed was still present. Most of all, what we miss, as suggested above, are those deeper connections between the work and the life; how the two interpenetrate each other, so that Dickens, perhaps more than most novelists, becomes so deeply embedded in his work and his work in him, that the two are indistinguishable.

Johnson's biography of course confronts those points of contact between the life and the work, or between various extremes in Dickens' behavior apart from the work. But the fairly rigid chronological organization miscalculates how a writer like Dickens contained it all in his head before he started to write, and how the material which he used later in his career was already present in his earlier life. One point is the famous blacking factory episode, which Johnson rightly emphasizes. Yet the psychological ramifications of the episode, besides the obvious ones, are not explored: the personal shame and embarrassment, the overcompensation, the secrecy, the playing with the secret, the revelation of it in David Copperfield's experiences, the social shame, so that the episode contributed to Dickens' need to control and dominate everything he came into contact with. Another area: one wishes for a greater shading between what the episode actually was and how it was perceived.

If the episode was so significant in Dickens' emotional life, then it should recur, a subtext in his next forty-five years.

Another critical area is Dickens' obsessive feelings for Mary Hogarth, his sister-in-law, who lived with him and Catherine in the early part of their marriage. Dickens' worship of the young Mary projected her into a madonna figure, and it led to certain archetypes in his fiction. Once the specter of Mary is raised—whether worshipped as virgin, or desired as perfect wife, or perceived as unattainable and, therefore, as meta-sexual—it must be followed through into Dickens' attitudes toward women in his fiction. *Dombey and Son* would appear to be the best place to follow through on this—to learn a good deal about Dickens by reading back through the novel to the author. Yet we find none of this either in the two-volume edition or the abridged one. Florence is viewed as the "angel in the house"; but it is quite possible to see her as using her weakness as a means of triumphing, luring in her father by acquiescing and playing up to what will destroy him; or, in another sense, using her desire for masochistic submission as a way of gaining an ultimate triumph, a father who is beaten and humbled and who begs forgiveness while living out his life emotionally crippled. One thinks, in somewhat similar terms, of Jane Eyre and Rochester. If character is fate, as Dickens implies in most of his books, then Florence has used her character as a way of creating Dombey's fate—at least this is the direction the novel takes. But even if this view is rejected as too much of a present-day reading, one misses a suitable frame of reference for Dickens' attitudes toward women—certainly a subject of immense proportions in his own time and in his most important fiction.

In still another area, touched upon above, we find no effort to deal critically or psychologically with Dickens' manic behavior, which is, once again, linked to his work. The runs and trills of comedy in Dickens are often "manic" or supercharged manifestations—where the logical or rational faculty is let down, and the author allows himself to run on, his comic imagination unimpeded. The Boodles and Noodles episode is one such example; but they are legion. There must be some linkage between these comic riffs and the author's personality, and they would appear to be connected by the manic manifestations Dickens displayed in his life: the need to expend energy, the rise and fall of alternating depression and bursts of almost superhuman energy, the piling up of commitments, the inner compulsion to act out, first in amateur theatricals and then in the readings from his works. The latter, in particular, must be tied more intimately to central dimensions of Dickens' life, not made to appear aberrant. The entire question of alternations of depression and high energy needs investigation, both clinically and critically.

What the abridged *Dickens* ultimately lacks is a sense of adequate coordinates for his work in the public arena and his "hopeless despair" in the private. We were less critical of such omissions in the two-volume edition because of the profusion of detail, the sheer sweep of narrative, the "mighty torrent" Johnson created which well suited Dickens' own kind of torrent. In the sparer version, however, we sorely miss such coordinates, altogether lacking except for some extended discussion of his relationship with his wife. Yet even here, the analysis slides over key issues: the whole question of Dickens' sexual relationship with Catherine, which seemed to key in to pregnancy. Since she was pregnant most of the years of their marriage (either going to term or miscarrying), their sexual life was surely one of disruption. To what extent did Dickens deal with this, since he was equally responsible, of course, for the pregnancies, equally responsible for the inadequacies of their sexual life, if that was indeed so. Only the fiction can reveal clues into his feelings about this, a close, multi-dimensional reading of the work; since, obviously, we cannot expect letters or public statements about such private matters.

We are, once again, thrown back to the same problem: only the fiction can tell us what we need to know about the inner life. Letters, others' comments, confessional diaries or memoirs, whatever, will be inadequate or partial. The fiction, however, read psychologically, read delicately and carefully, reveals the author; and what Dickens demands is that kind of reading. Steven Marcus started such an analysis in his *From Pickwick to Dombey*, but did not go on; and in any event, that work would need sharp revision in the light of new material. The life of Dickens which approximates the personal and creative fullness of the author remains to be written.

Before turning to three studies which offer a good deal biographically —although all three are hybrids of sorts—we should take a look at another life by John Halperin, *Gissing: A Life in Books* (Oxford, 1982). As in his *Jane Austen*, Halperin is writing the type of biography which might have been acceptable several generations ago. Clearly his lack of psychological sophistication and his inability to sustain any kind of critical point of view vitiate what seems to be careful research. Halperin lacks the critical acuity of Gillian Tindall (*George Gissing: The Born Exile*, Harcourt, 1974) and the biographical authority of Pierre Coustillas and Jacob Korg. His book must be viewed as an interim life, a lackluster Gissing for the '80s which, nevertheless, strives mightily to seem important.

Although not a proper biography (nor does it intend to be), Tindall's study makes more trenchant biographical sense than does Halperin's, especially in the area of Gissing's attitude toward women, his positioning himself as an exile, his internal conflicts which perhaps kept him from developing even further as a novelist. Halperin pitches his level of discourse too low. To obtain his critical estimate, he depends on "rankings," and his rankings themselves make little sense. We meet this at the outset:

> It is my opinion that no less than a dozen of Gissing's novels—*The Unclassed, Demos, The Nether World, New Grub Street, Born in Exile, The Odd Women, In the Year of the Jubilee, Sleeping Fires, The Paying Guest, The Whirlpool, The Private Papers of Henry Ryecroft*, and *Will Warburton*—are first rate. To produce a dozen good novels is no common achievement; indeed, few novelists of any nationality have written so much passable fiction. Among Gissing's novels, as among Wordsworth's poems, there is a fair share of disasters, and certainly Gissing was no Chekhov when it came to the short story. But the amount [number?] of good novels is prodigious; and *New Grub Street*, which deservedly has been his most popular novel with modern readers, is in my opinion an unqualified masterpiece. Certainly it is better than any novel by Disraeli, Collins, Reade, Kingsley, or George Moore, better than any of Mrs Gaskell's novels with the possible exception of *Wives and Daughters*, better than any of Charlotte Brontë's novels with the possible exception of *Jane Eyre* [*Villette* is her masterpiece], better than any of Meredith's novels with the possible exceptions of *The Ordeal of Richard Feverel* and *The Egoist*; indeed it may well be a greater novel than any of those I have named (p. 2).

Halperin then makes a number of statements, offered as criticism, which are no less reductive than the rankings above. "One may ask: Whence cometh all this gloom? The answer to this question lies in the facts of Gissing's life and personality; no English novelist put more of himself into his novels than George Gissing. To read his books without a detailed knowledge of his biography is to read blindfolded" (p. 6). Such comments if derived from a student paper would be struck; in what purports to be a major biography, they are an embarrassment. Halperin proceeds: "It is the story of Gissing the novelist, the great neurotic whose books are so extraordinarily full of his own problems and prejudices, fears and fixations, that I wish to tell" (p. 7).

He does proceed to tell; but he makes little use of the fiction as *psychological* material to illuminate the very Gissing he wishes to reveal. His lack of sophistication in such matters seems worse here than in his *Austen* because Gissing is so much more a confessional writer. Halperin is quick to dismiss those who would apply critical apparatus (he scorns phenomenological and structuralist approaches); but while these may indeed be inadequate, he finds no substitute. His criticism is either ranking of the laudatory kind—he refers (p. 136) to *New Grub Street* as "one of the greatest novels in the English language''—or else comparisons which are, perhaps, entirely wrong; as "in Hardy's later novels there is the sense of a world out of control" (p. 112). What does that refer to? *Jude the Obscure, Tess, The Mayor of Casterbridge?* In those novels, surely the point is *not* that the world is out of control—if that were so, where would be the irony?—but that the main characters are out of step with the world and with themselves. There is a disproportion between expectation and actuality; but the world lies there neutral, neither for nor against, unless one makes a misstep.

Hardy as a whole is not Halperin's strength. When he comments on how Gissing dismissed *Jude the Obscure* as a "sad book" and Hardy as "utterly on the wrong tack" (p. 230), the Gissing evaluation cries out for explanation or interpretation. Hardy would appear to be mining territory close to Gissing's own, and yet the latter's dismissal is clear. Halperin simply passes it by, adding that Hardy "was to write no more novels though he lived until 1928," as if Gissing's assessment were correct and it, somehow, drove Hardy into early retirement.

The critical ineptness undermines what could be a useful book offering much significant data. But Halperin insists on gussing it up with comments: "I find it difficult to quarrel with any of Gissing's conclusions about Dickens" (p. 261). The assumption here is that Halperin's reinforcement of Gissing makes everything right. Gissing's study of Dickens is valuable, but it is also full of Gissing, not Dickens; and when that occurs, one must distinguish between them, as Halperin fails to do. One senses that the biographer with such comments is futilely trying to close the distance between Dickens and Gissing. There is a kind of desperation in this critical approach, for on the final page of the text proper, Halperin says: "At his best Gissing is as good as any novelist; at his worst, he is still interesting" (p. 362). No college sophomore would write that—good as "any novelist"? Another Tolstoy or Eliot?

Even these critical gaffes and embarrassments would not have completely defeated this life if Halperin had revealed an aptitude for some psychological (not psychoanalytic) penetration of Gissing. The novelist was a man of enormous interest in his rise from desperate poverty, his failure to make a living until the final years of his life, his need to associate with women who could drag him down to the nether world he wrote about, his desire for bourgeois comforts even while he aimed at self-destruction personally, his conservatism socially and politically when everything else about him made him a social and political misfit. There is plenty of fare here, almost on the scale of Dickens, although lacking Dickens' achievement. And the books surely deserve more than a retelling; they require an analysis, a psychological probing, an effort to read back through them to conflicts in the author. Instead, we get comments like: "Fate in *The Nether World* is up to no good" (p. 111); and "The waste-land motif that was so vital a part of *Demos* comes back with a vengeance in *The Nether World*" (p. 112). There are paragraphs (the fourth on p. 195, for example) which juxtapose material so that they make no sense. A book such as this, which has some careful scholarship at its base, makes one wonder why a reader at Oxford University Press did not catch the excesses. Editing and vetting might have made this study more respectable as criticism—but in its present state, it makes one hope for a reissue of the Korg or else a full-dress study by Coustillas.

The three works which follow move us into contemporary biography at its best, although none is a proper biography. Ruby V. Redinger's "life" of George Eliot (*George Eliot: The Emergent Self*, Knopf, 1975) has qualities in common with John Maynard's *Charlotte Brontë and Sexuality* and Ian Watt's *Conrad in the Nineteenth Century*. We identify here critical studies which tell us more about the biographical subject than a straightforward biography may. In several ways, they extract from a reading of the subject's work dimensions of his or her life which the biographer often passes by. These three books are in a sense, then, biographical hybrids, and they may be the harbinger of serious biography in the future: eliminating the chronological detail we associate with an older form of biographical study, emphasizing certain clusters in the life, possessing a strong theme. In all instances, they are explicitly or implicitly psychological documents; but not psychoanalytic, not overdetermining the subject, such as we find in Bernard Meyers' *Joseph Conrad: A Psychoanalytic Study*. The latter has a value of its own, but it rigidly enforces a pattern on Conrad's life which, in the long run, overdetermines or even distorts.

As her title indicates, Redinger (Professor of English at Baldwin-Wallace College) is interested in Eliot's development, her "emergent self." One can see it is an excellent choice of procedure, as is Maynard's with Brontë's "sexuality." Every major writer hides some central metaphor deeply embedded in the work; if the subject is to be "perceived," the biographer or critic must discover it. Redinger has this metaphor in emergence and a method which fits perfectly with the theme. She hovers, moves in and out, impacts on Eliot in one place, shifts to other grounds. As a consequence, her Eliot is not simply a figure going from year to year but developing on a multi-level scale, as if a Proustian character caught in time and memory. Proust, in fact, hangs heavily over the entire life. This is biography which contains its own conception of time. As early as the Prologue, we know we are going to have to deal with transformation, as we must do with Joseph Conrad. Who is George Eliot? When she emerges, what nominal identity does she have? Mary Ann Evans or Marian Evans becomes what: Marian Lewes? George Eliot? Mrs. John W. Cross? When she wished to identify herself legally, could she call herself Mrs. Lewes, when George Henry Lewes was still married to his first wife? Could she call herself George Eliot, a name she and Lewes concocted, using his first name and George Sand's? Was she still Miss Evans, ostracized under that name by her family? In her conflict with names, we have her need for various selves; as with Conrad, who suffered the slings and arrows of Polish critics for Anglicizing his name, writing in English, and becoming an English national. If we examine rosters of ships on which he sailed, we note a dozen spellings and misspellings of his name; and even his Anglicized name was a play on the original Polish—giving him a nominal identity halfway between. With Eliot, from naming alone, Redinger has her central metaphor of identity, emergence, transformation; the remaking of self into new forms, like some of those natural phenomena studied so ably by Lewes in his geological and botanical researches.

As a hybrid critical-biographical study, Redinger's *Eliot* comes in concentrated chunks, rather than in stretched-out episodic pieces. One cluster concerns Eliot's early depression and despair, and the struggle she had with her father, Robert Evans, over values, styles, ultimately ways of life. For her self to emerge in any meaningful way, she had to get past the father. Redinger is particularly sound on despair, which is, biographically speaking, a heavy part of most Victorian writers' secret equipment. Despair and depression are often the other side of achievement, and to explore the latter, the biographer must find the etiology of the former. Redinger is excellent on tracing depression as it played through Eliot's career, but less successful at finding its etiology. Perhaps more should have been made of Eliot's perception of herself, physically and sexually: depression or despair that, possibly, derived from uncertainties about herself, questions of identity, as well as those uncertainties which derived from her gradual breaking of many Victorian proprieties. Intermixed with the despair, we must repeat, was a steely quality which enabled her to break from the religion of her father, gave her the strength to join John Chapman's Woodstock-like household, reinforced her choice of Lewes as "husband," when his own uncertainties about his wife and her sexual peccadilloes made it impossible for him to gain a divorce.

In another area, Redinger makes it possible for us to see—as several of the biographies we have already examined fail to do—that this person wrote those books. Probably the most difficult task for any biographer is to link person and craft, subject and achievement. This is a multi-dimensional enterprise, requiring a deep understanding of the subject's emotional and psychological response to his or her experiences, and a critical sense on the biographer's part which can transform those experiences into the materials of the fiction. Then, in a reverse action, the biographer must be able to read back from the work and "recreate" the life from that, even providing experiential areas which the life does not directly yield. Redinger does not completely succeed in this respect, but she comes close by means of her clustering method; so close in fact that she reveals all the weaknesses of Gordon Haight's otherwise majesterial biography. As noted, Haight so commanded the Eliot field he frightened off other biographers; and while no one will exceed his grasp of detail, his knowledge of Eliot's life, his ability to marshall the materials, he lacks the critical acumen which can use the fiction as itself the major part of the life. The future biographer of Eliot—and the enterprise is by no means foreclosed—should combine the overall grasp of Haight with the hovering, almost obsessive quality of Redinger in wringing meaning out of a situation. That future biographer must also have a theme or pattern; must, especially with Eliot, avoid episodic treatment. A woman of her intellect moves, in her teens, beyond any treatment which insists on straightforward development; she must be perceived as advancing massively on several fronts simultaneously.

The method of hovering and clustering does have its disadvantages. The circling method inevitably scants several areas; and often one feels that the subjects chosen for the clustering are arbitrary, that others just as significant might have been selected. The method, however, works at close to its best in Redinger's discussion of Eliot's relationship to her father: "underlying her rebellion against her spiritual father lay the rebellion against her earthly father. Her real emotional struggle was over the latter. When that struggle with the real father was seemingly overcome (it was to reappear in different form) and her intellect free to take command, all friction was removed from the path which led inevitably to the second rejection. She might have abandoned only Evangelicalism; instead, she was driven to attack the very heart of Christian orthodoxy—her belief in God" (p. 113). While we may have suspected the linkage among these rejections, Redinger provides numerous coordinates; so that when she comes to emphasizing the point—and rejection is a significant part of Eliot's emergence into her self—we can accept it and the theoretical reasoning behind it. This is the method working well.

It reveals flaws, however, in the following statement: "There is little doubt that at the time George Eliot took the defiant step of refusing to attend church, she was totally unaware of the hostile aggressiveness implicit in it. She saw it, rather, as an act of conforming to the dictates of her own conscience" (p. 119). Here a method of hovering and clustering fails to penetrate to the deeper reaches, which only working from within can create. It was, indeed, the hostile aggressiveness of her rebellion, her desire to replace the father as authority figure, which was implicit in her rejection of church and orthodox faith. To say she was "totally unaware" of it turns the rejection into some kind of unconscious action, when in fact her rejection and rebellion were quite conscious—intellectual, emotional, willed. They involved a rejection of the father, since loss of faith meant loss of a seemingly god-like man. Eliot made a very conscious decision, and in an internalized reading, one must see her—despite her desire to maintain placid surfaces—as working, consciously, on a series of hostile rejections throughout her life. The most deep-seated rejection, apart from father, was that of the role expected of her as a traditional woman. She may have been in her rhetoric a lukewarm feminist, even rejecting feminist doctrines, but in her choices, she was nothing but a rebel. Unlike Maggie in *The Mill on the Floss*, she took final, decisive steps. She transformed herself, as Redinger so ably points out; but it was a conscious act of one rejection after another.

Another area we would like to know more about is the recurring presence of Eliot's debilitating headaches, which sound like some form of migraine. She was, on many occasions, laid low for days at a time. Were the headaches, which extended the full range of her life, linked to the strains of conflict she imposed on herself? Did her need to maintain the placid surface, while the subsurface was turmoil, rebellion, reshaping, create tensions which emerged in the headaches? Or were they the result of some other force, perhaps even organic or connected to her creative ability—the pain she had to suffer while she achieved something; a lower form of the artist's suffering, Dostoievsky's epilepsy, for example? Redinger merely lists headaches here and there, and yet in a major writer, any kind of illness is informative, and headaches are a biographer's gold mine.

But to return to the strengths of this life: the early works are used splendidly as biographical quarries, as are some poems. Redinger digs into the relationship with Lewes, also, touching Eliot's sensibility at every vital point, giving her the confidence and stability she needed to help her find her own self. Lewes was remarkable in his devotion to her needs, his recognition that of the two, she was the genius, he simply a master of many fields. Once he realized that, he made it possible for her to emerge, and I know of no other study of a Victorian relationship or marriage in which both partners are probed so thoroughly and so plausibly. True, few other Victorian relationships provided such a high level on both sides; but Lewes' response to her, after many acts on his part which make him seem somewhat flaky (especially in his married life), demonstrates a symbiosis which was all to Eliot's advantage. Would she have written without Lewes? Unquestionably, as we see from her translations and her articles for Chapman at *Westminster Review*. But would she have written fiction? She embodied in herself the deepest reaches of what fiction should be, but whether it could have emerged even after *she* had emerged we cannot answer with certainty. Redinger's method of clustering and hovering works perfectly here.

> What Chapman and the Brays could not have understood was that she was not an ordinary woman anxious over the faithfulness of her lover; she was also a child reawaiting the return of the mother-brother [Isaac] who had once abandoned her. Lewes had imperceptibly slipped into this role with her, the first side of it having begun in London early in their acquaintance when they gave no thought to the potential seriousness of their relationship; then his lighthearted companionship had revived in her the sense of fun which had been dormant ever since she lost Isaac as playfellow. Although their games were never to be childish, their ability to play took them without bitterness through their days of poverty and outside malice; and it survived into the affluent days and the solemnity of George Eliot's fame (p. 286).

As suggested above, this type of hybrid interpretive life serves as corrective to those biographies which forge ahead stolidly, month to month, year to year. It does not replace them, but it does provide alternatives, and it does give the reader linkages that the episodic, chronological study fails to do. One loses the narrative surge, of course—what Johnson does so well in his *Dickens*; but few biographers write with such fullness, as we see with Halperin in his *Austen* and *Gissing*. Of the old-fashioned studies, one finds Millgate's *Hardy* the most able; but one would like more of these hybrids.

Even though it does not take us through the life, nor does it provide the range of details we expect from a more formal life, John Maynard's study of Charlotte Brontë's novels (*Charlotte Brontë and Sexuality*, Cambridge University Press, 1984) is a type of biography. Such books are prolegomena to full-dress biographies, absolutely essential and, in recent times, forms of hybrid biography. By making close analyses of sexuality in Brontë—surely along with her feminine concerns, the most significant means of entering her work—Maynard suggests an internalized biography, where the books are essential as ways of understanding the life. We have a reversal in this form: whereas in more traditional lives, the biographer moves along the subject's life, bringing in the books at regular intervals (or, in some instances, hardly at all), in this hybrid biography, the critic discusses the books in such detail and with such intensity the life is illuminated from within the work. Such a method is extremely valuable, especially when, as here, it is done with taste and sensitivity.

In another respect, Maynard's book *is* biography: the biography of Brontë's sexual development. Since she contained intense pools of feeling which she successively revealed in her novels and poetry, everything in Charlotte Brontë is a matter of unfolding, emerging, transforming. The culmination of such revelations is *Villette*, where her preoccupation with sexual tensions is most artistically expressed, although *Jane Eyre* has assumed an archetypal position as an expression of a young woman's emotional life. *Villette*, however, perhaps because it is the expression of the older Lucy Snowe looking back over her younger years, is the more mature novel: the true book of Brontë's discovery of self. She was now so secure with her art that she could look back and chart it, not needing the "moment," as in *Jane Eyre*. By pursuing sexuality in Brontë, Maynard (Professor of English and chair at New York University) is able to deal with two other significant elements in her work, her concern with a young woman's fate in a male world and her craft itself. The theme of sexuality is interconnected, then, with both feminism and art; and, in Maynard's hands, each is handled fully. It is these very qualities, or their appropriate male equivalents, we vainly sought in the biographies of Austen, Gissing, Dickens, and Trollope.

Starting with sibling associations for Brontë, Maynard demonstrates that her "hopeless passion" for Constantin Heger at the Brussels pensionnat was by no means the sum total of her sexual life. At the same time, Maynard is fully aware of the dangers of what he calls, in chapter 2, "posthumous analysis." But since his analysis relies in the main on the stories, poems, and novels themselves, he stands on firm ground. One would, perhaps, like to have seen more examination of the alternating sadism and masochism which occur in the relationships of Brontë heroines with male figures. Although her young women—Jane Eyre and Lucy Snowe in particular—become steely when they must, they also demonstrate a strong desire for linkages which create personal pain and suffering. One says this with full cognizance that Brontë needed coordinates or metaphors for women's position in the nineteenth century and masochism served well. But even with this in mind, we can find in Lucy Snowe's masochism a way of manipulating M. Paul, whose excessive sadism, especially in the matter of the theatrical, when he locks Lucy in the attic, must be taken into account in any judgment of his character and role. In *Jane Eyre*, Jane of course rejects the outright masochism of Helen Burns, who chooses suffering and martyrdom as her form of "protest." Yet even here, Jane does not take into account, sufficiently, it would seem, Rochester's humiliation of her, his sadistic pleasure in toying with her, in her final evaluation of her character. There would appear to be in Charlotte Brontë some residue of acceptable masochism which possibly derived from her relationship to her father, Patrick, or her brother, Branwell; which, of course, she incorporated into her juvenilia, with its strong, fearsome males.

Maynard's close readings of *Jane Eyre* and especially *Villette* are as good as we will find anywhere. The discussion of *Villette* is a masterful presentation of Brontë's craft, her use of opposing metaphors and her structuring of the novel's scenes, as a means of saying something significant about her biographically. Here we have comments near the end of the chapter:

> De Hamal's nun exists simultaneously as a prank that symbolizes the inherent problems of both the prankster and the school he visits and as a version of the inner tensions of Lucy's lonely battles with desire, loss, suppression, and unconscious repression. The school becomes Lucy's psychic as well as physical environment, the place of her single solitude and her temptations into fuller life, the place from which she must finally escape. Without violation of the social realism of the setting and story, there is a patterning of relation between Lucy's psychological growth and the vivid symbols offered by the world in which she lives.

Brontë's intense sexual conflict as evidenced in her heroines is itself a form of social realism, certainly that as given extension by Richard Levine in his fine study of nineteenth-century realism. The sexual emergence of the heroine in Victorian fiction is itself a biographical tool of considerable magnitude; but, too often, biographers of Victorian novelists have accepted narrow definitions rather than the lived life of the character in a particular novel. As Peter Gay's studies open up Victorian sexuality (in his extended series under the rubric *The Bourgeois Experience: Victoria to Freud*, of which *Education of the Senses* and *The Tender Passion* have appeared) and reveal the provinciality of much previous scholarship, we can see Charlotte Brontë as far more deeply rooted in social realism than her critics have allowed her. All too frequently, she has been located as "outside," her novels falling more into a "Gothic" vein than a realistic one; or else she is placed in a "romantic" tradition, as a counterpoint (say) to George Eliot or Thackeray, who rest solidly in the realistic tradition. Maynard's study shows us a Charlotte Brontë much closer to George Eliot than we had considered; and it opens up the possibility of a study of Eliot along similar lines: picking up from Redinger's "emergent self" to an analysis of sexual themes, repression, suppression, masochism, sense of loss, triumph. One reason we can say such studies have powerful biographical dimensions is that they afford the biographer a psychological entree into the life; not a possibly inaccurate psychoanalysis, which psychobiography is prone to, but a more accurate psychological portrait. It is precisely the latter which so many biographical subjects lack.

Of all the books under discussion here, Ian Watt's *Conrad in the Nineteenth Century* (University of California Press, 1979) is the closest to a hybrid form; really less a biography than a critical study of Conrad's work before the turn of the twentieth century.[1] Watt's plan, to divide his work into two volumes, with the second to concern itself with the twentieth-century Conrad, is itself a solid critical act, inasmuch as Conrad was the only one of the great "moderns" to have a nineteenth-century career. Perhaps Hardy could be considered as sharing somewhat of a similar split, but despite his lean, ironic, whiplash poetry his fiction was clearly set in the nineteenth century. And because of the splitting of Conrad in this way, a felicitous design, Watt's very concept of biography had to undergo revision. As biographer, Watt (Professor of English at Stanford University) leans heavily on the research of others, and, in fact, one finds few areas indeed of any effort at original research. His sources, as of 1979, include Baines's previous (and unreliable) biography, the even more unreliable work of Jean-Aubry in his two-volume study of Conrad, the solid research of Norman Sherry, and several published volumes of letters, some well-edited, some not. In a very few instances, original manuscript letters are used. As biographer, then, Watt is not seeking new ground, although his ordering of the material is intelligent and sound.

Once we leave biography proper behind, we see Watt attempting something quite different: grafting onto somewhat perfunctory biographical data huge chunks of historical and critical material so that Conrad's early works—from *Almayer's Folly* through *The Nigger of the "Narcissus," Heart of Darkness,* and *Lord Jim*—are set very firmly into their nineteenth-century settings. Here Watt's gifts as a cultural commentator come into play, and we find that curious hybrid of biography and critical-historical matter. Yet even here a caveat: although Watt's idea of dividing Conrad into his two parts, with two faces, as it were, energizes his contexts, the conclusions he draws are not extraordinary.

They are, in fact, conclusions one would expect. In the segment on *Heart of Darkness*, perhaps one third of a long book, the substantial matter comes down to a conflict between the values of Marlow and Kurtz. Nothing unusual here. Watt, however, does provide a consummate synthesis of material, bringing to bear relevant (and some less relevant) texts on Conrad, and then showing how his work derives from such cultural contexts. On some occasions, Watt strains for linkages, saying that Conrad may have known this, or perhaps read that, or could have been acquainted with something else. This is criticism of the "as if" school, and it distracts us from Conrad's acts of imagination which pulled him from contexts available to everyone into areas which were his own.

One problem with even Watt's skill in handling contexts is overdetermination of the material. Too much is given to backgrounds (Nietzsche, Nordau, others), and too little to the individual writer's ability to leap beyond into imaginative acts of his own. In another area, even while the documentation is massive, the interpretations, as already suggested, remain what we have already assimilated. Watt's *Heart of Darkness*, for example, is close to J. Hillis Miller's in *Poets of Reality*. Consequently, while the synthesizing of material is all to the good, when it comes to extracting final meanings, Watt falls back on what we already know; and too little is given to Conrad's skill in transcending historical contexts, or transforming them into creative acts.

To return to an earlier comment: the hybrid biography may be a genre of the future, no longer the kind of work we associate with Ellmann's *Joyce*, Painter's *Proust*, or Edel's *James*. Such studies involved the author's complete immersion in the biographical detail of the writer, but in the latest biographies we begin to see less and less of that. There will, of course, be exceptions to this, but as biographical data become exhausted or recede into trivia, there may be an increasing number of such hybrids, where cultural contexts and critical approaches balance data. This does not necessarily mean a decline in biographical studies, especially when applied to major figures; yet it is, clearly, the biographical response to our immersion in several fields of study—history, sociology, psychology, anthropology, linguistics, criticism—and our desire to incorporate these forms of knowledge into biography. Increasingly, we may see earlier biographical data synthesized, rather than re-researched, while historical and cultural contexts are brought to bear.

Like all other fields of study, biography must become many things, and in this area we have the possibility of serious change. One danger, only alluded to above, is that the cultural or historical contexts become ends in themselves. In Watt's study, while he is balanced and tasteful, there does seem some tipping. One implication of this is that instead of seeking areas of intertextuality in Conrad—where his own works influence and interpenetrate each other—there is a determined effort to provide external materials which Conrad, for one, may not have been familiar with. In a weak study, like Halperin's *Austen*, such external material is introduced like dollops of plaster. Watt is a far more mature and intelligent critic, and his use of historical matter only barely tips the balance. But on occasion, the externals begin to take on a life of their own, as when he compares (and contrasts) Conrad with Freud, in that both saw "that culture was insecurely based on repression and restraint, and yet what seemed most worth their effort was to promote a greater understanding of man's destructive tendencies, and at the same time support the modest countertruths on which civilization depends" (p. 167).

The Freud here is the author of *Civilization and Its Discontents* and *The Future of an Illusion*, but in paralleling Freud and Conrad, Watt selects these works arbitrarily. How about the Freud of *Beyond the Pleasure Principle*, who moves completely from Conrad's orbit? And even in Watt's arbitrary selections, Freud is concerned with repression in terms of a sexual etiology—quite different in kind and degree from Conrad's measurement of human behavior. Further, no matter how Freud relented here or there, he was deterministic—man's battle was like that of Sisyphus, uphill, against fated characteristics. The very point about Conrad is that he played with ideas of determinism, without trying to resolve the matter. *Heart of Darkness*, the centerpiece of Watt's study, is itself a meditation on determinism. The method of Conrad's work, as apart from its point of view, can be perceived as deriving from the same kinds of dream material Freud codified in his *Interpretations of Dreams*; but Conrad's sense of dream material came, more likely, from his acquaintanceship with French symbolists and other *fin de siècle* and decadent literature, whereas Freud's sources were quite different.

All this is simply by way of being cautionary. As we note the increase of the hybrid biography, we must beware of contexts overwhelming the writer's own achievements, his or her crossings over, what we consider to be intertextuality; plus neglecting the ways in which the writer leaps beyond the contexts into self-defined creative acts, willed acts which have little to do with deterministic cultural or historical codes. Otherwise, one falls into insidious patterns of interpretation, as when Watt approves of Edward Said's overdetermined and historically distorted comments comparing Conrad to Nietzsche; when, in fact, Conrad's few comments on Nietzsche were disparaging, and the two diverged on so many questions any assignment of "influence" or "presence" of the German philosopher on or in Conrad is critical over-reach. Similarly, efforts to locate Conrad within a Burkean political tradition—Avrom Fleishman's concept, which Watt rightfully refutes—ignores the heavy presence of Polish politics on his thought. Watt himself does not work sufficiently with Conrad's Polish backgrounds. The English and French context for Conrad is by itself inadequate, and while the latter does not fit neatly into any pattern (whether Burkean, Nietzschean, or other), the Polish political and social context is essential.

All this said, Watt's study filled a distinct need, as of 1979. As we await the second volume, on Conrad in the twentieth century, we find almost no need for the biographical detail which Watt will perfunctorily supply; but we look forward eagerly to his discussion of Conrad amidst modernism and avant-gardeism (both of which he detested). Here, Watt's contribution can be distinctive and unique. The more hybrid the second volume, the better it should be. With these latter three "lives," biography has itself clearly found new life.

## NOTE

1. Although beyond our purview, another study of Conrad, Zdzisław Najder's *Joseph Conrad: A Chronicle* (Rutgers University Press, 1983) was labelled a biography by all reviewers, and catalogued as such; but it is a chronicle, not a biography—generically, a different item with a different purpose. A chronicle presents data as ends in themselves. Najder's book, in its emphasis on documentation, takes nearly all of the life out of the life and extrapolates only what is empirically viable. That experiential tissue which connects events, circumstances, imaginative acts—the very energies of biography—is missing. Furthermore, Najder's declared empiricism works at cross-purposes with his subject, and his very choice of a chronicle is an effort to impose on the Conrad "mystique" limiting historical interpretations. In its way, a chronicle is a restrictive biographical hybrid as much as an original critical study is an expansive one.

# Recent Dickens Studies: 1986

## David Paroissien

The challenge facing anyone writing a comprehensive review of the year's work in Dickens studies for 1986 brings to mind some remarks Mr. Venus made to Silas Wegg concerning the anatomist's flourishing trade in bones. On the moist raw evening of Wegg's visit to ask about the fate of his own amputated leg, Wegg's questions prompt Venus to rise above his "low" state and respond by echoing a comic variant of the boast of Georges Cuvier, the French osteologist, who claimed he could reconstruct the entire skeleton of any animal from its smallest bone. If Wegg had been brought to him "loose in a bag," an exuberant Venus notes, he could have articulated his bones blindfolded, picking them out and sorting them "in a manner that would equally surprise and charm you" (*Our Mutual Friend*, I, 7).

This year's "miscellaneous" equals any collection of bones that might have turned up in Venus's little dark greasy shop during a comparable period of the taxidermist's curious business. "I've as much to do as I can possibly do," Venus remarks of his present labors, a response I fully share. Books on Dickens, "warious." Studies of the Victorian novel, "warious." Monographs, articles, ditto. Dickens Companions, annotated editions of the novels, bibliographical studies. Everything within reach of your hand, assembled and sorted from the Dickens Checklist.[1] "Oh, dear me! That's the general panoramic view." There's material here to employ a team, let alone one individual attempting to move quickly by sorting and picking as fast as he can. To make this assignment manageable, I have excluded those items Alan Cohn lists under "Miscellaneous" and have ignored abstracts of theses, conference proceedings, study guides, essays in foreign languages, and versions of Dickens' novels variously adapted to electronic media. For reasons of propriety, I have made no reference to the essays published in Volume 15 of the *Annual*, other than to list them here in the order of their appearance without commentary: Gerhard Joseph, "The Labyrinth and the Library: A View from the Temple in *Martin Chuzzlewit*," Sylvère Monod, "Mr. Bevan," John Hildebidle, "Hail Columbia: Martin Chuzzlewit in America," David Parker, "Dickens and America: The Unflattering Glass," Ruth Glancy, "Dickens at Work on *The Haunted Man*," Chris R. Vanden Bossche, "Cookery, not Rookery: Family and Class in *David Copperfield*," Michael S. Kearns, "Associationism, the Heart, and the Life of the Mind in Dickens' Novels," Nicholas Coles, "The Politics of *Hard Times*: Dickens the Novelist versus Dickens the Reformer," Michael Cotsell, "Politics and Peeling Frescoes: Layard of Nineveh and *Little Dorrit*," Susan Schoenbauer Thurin, "The Seven Deadly Sins in *Great Expectations*," Stanley Friedman, "The Complex Origins of Pip and Magwitch," Eloise Knapp Hay, "Oberon and Prospero: The Art of Nathaniel Hawthorne and Charles Dickens," Hana Wirth-Nesher, "The Literary Orphan as National Hero: Huck and Pip," and Robert Tracy, "Stranger than Truth: Fictional Autobiography and Autobiographical Fiction." Readers will find at the end of this essay full bibliographical details of all other studies I mention. Whether they will be surprised or charmed in the manner Venus promises his visitor remains to be seen.

### Bibliographies and Reference Materials

This has been a good year for books published in each category which serve both broad and specialist interests. Brahma Chaudhuri's *Annual Bibliography of Victorian Studies 1984* makes the most wide-ranging contribution in the period under review by providing in a single volume over 4,800 references to books and articles published in 1984, together with items missed in earlier volumes in the same series. *The Annual Bibliography* is divided into two parts, with substantial sections on Dickens under Individual Authors (Part I) in which entries are arranged by novels, and on Dickens as a subject (Part II). This section of the bibliography also contains entries grouped under the titles of Dickens' works in addition to entries set out under sub-headings ranging from "Africa" to "Violence" (pp. 276–283). In addition, Chaudhuri devotes space in Part II to Author, Title and Review Indexes, a most useful feature. Chaudhuri's *Annual Bibliography*, compiled from the LITIR Database in Edmonton, Alberta, supplements Alan Cohn's Dickens Checklist in the *Dickens Quarterly*, so that these two resources jointly provide almost total bibliographical coverage of materials published annually on Dickens and Victorian Fiction.

Kevin Harris's *The Dickens House Classification* represents an achievement of a different sort, the first step of The Dickens House Library Project. This document, a Research Report published by the Polytechnic of North London, provides a design for the bibliographical control of the library of Dickens House in London, from which the cataloguing of the museum's important collection of printed texts and other materials will proceed. Harris uses *The Dickens House Classification* to establish his plan for arranging the library in five sections, two of which deserve notice for their utility beyond the immediate scope of the author's purpose. In section (i), "Common divisions," Harris includes a useful sub-section (pp. 27–32) covering the chronology of the life and writings of Dickens, while in section (ii), "Background to Dickens Studies" (pp. 39–49), the assembled list of topics offers a remarkably detailed overview of those aspects of nineteenth-century life most important to Dickens' interests. Students in search of a research topic on some aspect of Dickens' life or his culture might profit from the information Harris has assembled. A simplified index adds to the usefulness of this publication and helps users locate topics within the five sections. When personnel at the Dickens House Museum complete the second stage of this project by producing the Library's catalogue, scholars will have access to an outstanding collection of materials whose lack of organization has long deterred all but the most persistent researcher.

Two more Garland Bibliographies published this year bring the series to six completed volumes so far. George J. Worth and David Paroissien are the respective authors of *Great Expectations: An Annotated Bibliography* and *Oliver Twist: An Annotated Bibliography.* Clearly, I am in no position to offer detailed comparisons or evaluative assessments. Both authors provide accounts of the changing critical status of the novels in their Introductions and comment on the ebb and flow of critical studies since the appearance of each work. Worth notes how *Great Expectations* came into its own later in the twentieth century, when new critical attention began to focus on the novel's structure, a prelude to the apparently unending debate in more recent years about the merits of Dickens' revised ending. *Oliver Twist*'s fortunes follow a different course, one Paroissien traces through phases dominated by readers with specific concerns. These range from the early Newgate opponents of the novel, Jewish writers raising questions about the portrait of Fagin, partisan comments on Cruikshank's controversial claim, repeatedly and variously asserted, to have given Dickens essential elements of the novel's plot, to the many professional studies of the novel characteristic of the last few decades. Both volumes, I can report with detachment, will serve readers well

by providing useful guides through the extensive secondary material surrounding each novel. A glance at the tripartite division of each study and the
various subdivisions, used to impose order on the numerous entries, will
reveal their potential for a range of readers with specialized interests.

I have included Harry Stone's *Dickens' Working Notes for His Novels* in
this section to emphasize the book's indispensability as a reference work for
anyone interested in Dickens' artistic process and method of composition.
Stone's long awaited edition makes available all of the extant plans of the
notes that Dickens jotted down while working on a novel. His practice, as
readers know, was to allot a sheet of paper for each numbered installment
and divide the paper into two. On the left half Dickens recorded ideas that
pertained to the overall planning of the novel (injunctions to bring forward
or delay the action, ideas to develop, characters to introduce, and so on) and
on the right he outlined the substance of individual chapters (titles, events,
and motifs). Once the afflatus had taken hold, Dickens usually filled out each
sheet in succession as he worked his way through the novel. In some instances,
Dickens worked ahead of the plans and then would go back and note what
he had done after the fact.

Readers can now consult all the extant plans in a single handsome volume,
which presents on facing pages photographic facsimiles and typographic tran-
scriptions of each sheet of the notes. This side-by-side format no doubt adds
to the book's expense, but it serves a useful purpose because it allows readers
to judge for themselves the nuances of emphasis and afterthought implicit in
the way Dickens set out and arranged his thoughts. Stone's volume also has
a critical purpose as well: to convince us that, in his words, "Dickens was
a consummate artist and totally dedicated to his craft." It is a moot question,
I think, that the notes themselves will convince anyone who persists in arguing
that Dickens' novels lack artistry or form. But Stone has performed a genuine
service by transcribing them so accurately and painstakingly.

So far the reference works I have considered all have in common some
aspect of Dickens' literary significance and status. But Dickens was also (and
still is) a popular phenomenon, a writer known to hundreds of thousands not
through print but through versions of his novels first staged world-wide in
theaters, later filmed in numerous languages, and subsequently broadcast,
principally in Britain and North America, by radio and by television.

Literary scholars welcome the diverse means by which the Inimitable has
been spread as evidence of his universality, but generally they devote little
energy to a systematic study of this aspect of Dickens' fame, leaving scrutiny
of the technological diaspora of his novels and stories to enthusiastic amateurs

instead. I have in mind the work of Malcolm Morley (*The Dickensian*, 1946–56) and Dorothy Pierce (*Bulletin of Bibliography*, 1937), and studies by S. J. A. Fitz-gerald (1910), J. B. Van Amerongen (1927), and F. Dubrez Fawcett (1952), to name several representatives, individuals who have provided signposts to the study of Dickens on stage, screen, and the air but no definitive bibliography or guide. Set out to survey, for example, the apparently limited history of British and American stage versions of *Oliver Twist* from its first abortive adaptation at St. James's Theatre, London, on March 27, 1838, to the present and these names will furnish leads, only to open the door on a vast and uncharted territory. Just how extensive and uncharted I know from my own attempt to assemble a reasonably complete chronological listing of stage, film, musical, radio, and television adaptations of *Oliver Twist* in a section I devoted to the topic in my *Oliver Twist: An Annotated Bibliography*.

As a measure of my failure and another's success, let me refer readers to H. Philip Bolton's section on the same novel in his *Dickens Dramatized*. I thought I had done quite well to record nearly one hundred different versions; Bolton's total is 407. In self-defense, I should add that we both began with different objectives and that my task precluded separate notations for each version. At the same time, the difference in our results suggests the magnitude of Bolton's accomplishment, which takes into account every novel and story of Dickens known to him in adapted form, rather than the adaptation of a single novel. *Dickens Dramatized*, in fact, provides a massive record of Dickens' theatrical posterity and his enduring popular reputation as it spread through its successive mutations from *tableaux vivants*, plays burlettas, dramatic parodies, to silent films, thence to radio dramas and sketches, and finally to the modern cinema and to contemporary television serial productions.

With a mixture of shrewdness and modesty Bolton disclaims his study as complete, definitive, or even exhaustive. Any casual researcher, he observes, "with access to a local archive or library could find evidence of productions of plays that I have not noted." True enough, no doubt. But *extensive* this book most unquestionably is. *Dickens Dramatized* is also a most *readable* research source, for in addition to the twenty-nine sections of "Handlists" containing all the bibliographical data he has assembled on the adaptation of Dickens' novels and stories, Bolton supplies a good deal of well-written commentary. The "text" in fact comes in two principal forms: a descriptive introduction or "Headnote" to each of the twenty-nine bibliographical sections of adaptations, and five substantial essays Bolton contributes by way of establishing his focus. In these essays Bolton moves from a well-informed discussion of the history of stage versions of English novels to some suggestive hints for studying the influence of British pantomime on Dickens' works. Other related subjects include a survey of Dickens' dramatic fame and posterity and an essay treating the playwrights, actors and actresses who attached themselves to the rising star of Boz and in turn shed back on him the light they borrowed by lending their names to later adaptations. *Dickens Dramatized* is the fruit of many years of investigation profitably and judiciously spent. No research library will be complete that lacks a copy.

Tony Lynch's *Dickens's England* documents another aspect of Dickens' legacy: the enduring and harmless preoccupation his fiction has given rise to of inspiring numerous readers to track down scenes and places so prominently and evocatively described in the novels. Anyone whose interests lean this way will do well to buy a copy of *Dickens's England*, a reasonably complete gazeteer of the English locations associated with Dickens' life and his novels. Lynch has arranged the book alphabetically for easy reference. He has also provided over eighty attractive photographs showing how some of the places associated with the novels look today. London inevitably receives the major portion of his attention and the fullness of this section might prove a strong incentive to energetic pedestrians to slip into the past and walk around Dickens' London, much of which still survives, as Lynch's photographs show. On a more utilitarian note, this book will serve as a good source for instructors who use slide illustrations when they teach Dickens.

## The Dickens Companions

Comparisons between Dickens and Shakespeare have flourished ever since John Butt and Kathleen Tillotson linked the two writers in 1957. Speaking in their Preface to *Dickens at Work*, they noted the absence of reliable texts of the novels and lamented how Dickens scholarship had not passed beyond the early-nineteenth-century phase of Shakespeare studies. Butt and Tillotson made no reference on this occasion to the lack of annotated texts of Dickens' novels. Nor did they address this matter in their joint remarks introducing the first volume of the Clarendon Dickens (*Oliver Twist*), except to admit in 1965 that the "immense task of explanatory annotation" had not been attempted. Establishing a critical text free from corruption, one might assume, was all one could expect for the moment. Equate Dickens and Shakespeare, by all means, but do not look for comparable treatment in all professional matters.

Shakespeare, of course, has been well served by textual experts and by annotators, although we know that critics have often placed greater emphasis on establishing texts than they have on the need to elucidate obscurities. No less a figure than Dr. Johnson grudgingly admitted that notes are "often necessary, but they are necessary evils." The mind "is refrigerated by interruption," he contended in the Preface to his edition of Shakespeare's plays (1765). Notes might clarify particular passages but they diverted the reader's thoughts "from the principal subject," inducing a weariness that at last prompts him to throw away the book, "which he has too diligently studied." Perhaps Johnson deliberately overstated his case, although his views fitted with his neo-classical assumption that the appeal of great art lay in the truths it conveyed rather than in the evanescent advantages a writer might derive from "personal allusions, local customs, or temporary opinions."

Johnson's hostility to annotating the plays failed to win over subsequent Shakespearians, although, as I have noted, Dickens scholars seem to have shown a Johnsonian reluctance to begin a task even some of the novelist's own contemporaries recognized as inevitable. "So much has changed, both in manners and customs of the English people and in the scenes in which the adventures of Mr. Pickwick and his friends were laid" wrote Charles Dickens, Junior, in 1886, that allusions, once familiar enough, have become "obscure and doubtful" to new generations of readers. Thus for audiences today, the need for an annotated edition of Dickens' works has increased to the point Edward Guiliano and Philip Collins describe in the Preface to their *Annotated Dickens*: "It is a mere fact of the times that readers of Dickens, becoming like readers of Shakespeare, will doubtless rely more and more upon and benefit from notes."

Readers who have waited for someone to annotate Dickens' works with the precision Clarendon editors are bringing to Dickens' texts will be grateful to Susan Shatto and Michael Cotsell, respectively General Editor and Associate Editor of the new Dickens Companions series. The editors' goal, as they write in their General Preface, is to "provide the most comprehensive annotation of the works of Dickens ever undertaken." Cotsell's *Companion to Our Mutual Friend* and Wendy Jacobson's *Companion to the Mystery of Edwin Drood* launch the enterprise, a projected set of nineteen books, one for each of Dickens' fifteen novels, one apiece for *Sketches by Boz* and *The Uncommercial Traveller*, one for the five Christmas books, and a final General Index to the whole.

The Dickens Companions are an original undertaking in every respect, distinct and distant from the elliptical annotative materials students often find packed into the final pages of modern editions, a reluctant afterthought to the text itself. The Companions, for example, provide no text at all but devote their entire focus (each is the responsibility of an individual editor) to documenting the varied and imaginative ways Dickens responded to his culture. The annotations set out to identify allusions to current events and intellectual and religious issues. Editors also supply detailed information on social customs, topography, costume, clothing, furniture, transportation and so on. Literary allusions are included, borrowings identified, the 'originals' of characters described, biographical influences documented, and the work of Dickens' illustrators discussed. The editors supply no critical commentary or exegesis of stylistic matters, but their factual work will clearly facilitate further critical study of the novels.

Since novels lack numbered lines of text, unlike lines of poetry, and since Dickens' works exist in so many diverse editions, the general editors had to find an appropriate way to help the reader relate a note to its place in the novel and, conversely, to discover if something in the novel appears as a note. Shatto and Cotsell devised a solution both practical and aesthetically pleasing. Each Companion editor presents the opening phrase of the paragraph which includes the entry as a guide set off in italics. The phrase or word annotated appears below in bold-face type, following which is the explanatory annotation. Thus each Companion will serve any edition of its respective novel, since readers turning from the text in search of a note on a particular word or phrase need only consult the appropriate chapter in the Companion and locate the italicized phrase of the paragraph in which the sought information is set out.

The volumes by Cotsell and Jacobson demonstrate just how well the concept works and how indispensable the series will become to the professional study of Dickens' fiction. Take, for example, the occupational contexts Dickens chose when he conceived his last two works. *The Companion to 'Our Mutual Friend'* provides full information about the financial activities of Messrs. Veneering, Podsnap, Lammles and Fledgeby and documents with equal detail how those on society's margin survive as scavengers, mudlarks, Thames watermen, dollmakers, ballad-sellers, dustmen, and schoolmasters. Moving from the metropolis to the provincial southeast, the setting for much of *The Mystery of Edwin Drood*, we find Jacobson assembling comparably helpful information about the practices of the Church of England, as she elaborates on details embedded in the text that assume some familiarity with its history and the hierarchical structure of ecclesiastical officeholders. Both authors also treat authoritatively each novel's topographical aspects and help readers understand the importance of the geographical and social settings of the diverse groups populating the novels by providing illustrations and maps. In addition, readers will find comprehensive entries on characters which discuss the etymology of their names and set out what is known about character prototypes and analogues as they appear elsewhere in Dickens' writings.

Literary matters receive equal consideration. The authors provide transcripts of Dickens' working notes rationally placed among the notes to the first chapter of each monthly number. They also identify allusions, quotations and borrowings from a range of authors, an achievement which lays the ground for future studies by documenting the extraordinary degree to which Dickens' texts refract almost any aspect of Victorian culture one can name. There is, in short, something to interest almost every specialist reader in these two studies, companions in the fullest sense, subordinate to the texts they illuminate but autonomous intellectual achievements offering readable commentary rather than a glossary of gelid notations likely to congeal the liveliest mind.

This year also sees a second entry into the field of annotations, an enterprise of a different sort by Edward Guiliano and Philip Collins. *The Annotated Dickens* (two volumes) brings together six novels and one Christmas book, providing introductions and notes to the texts of *The Pickwick Papers, Oliver Twist, A Christmas Carol, David Copperfield, Hard Times*, and *Great Expectations*. Guiliano and Collins state in their Preface that the texts they reprint represent "the main phases" of Dickens' creative work as it evolves from the early works to the late, dark novels by way of one Christmas book and Dickens' own "favourite child." This seems like a tenuous rationale at best in view of several other works conventionally designated as representative of the chronological stages of Dickens' career as a novelist. With the exception of *The Pickwick Papers* and *David Copperfield*, the editors have assembled in two volumes Dickens' *shortest* works, a more likely explanation for this permutation of texts.

Whom do the editors have in mind as readers and why prepare a two-volume edition of six complete novels based on the Oxford Illustrated edition whose authority as a copy-text (the 1867 Charles Dickens edition) textual scholars have discredited? In their Preface, Guiliano and Collins make a convincing case for thoroughly annotated texts, but thoroughness not carefully defined can be an elusive goal. Because Guiliano and Collins provide the text of each novel they clearly cannot compete in annotative fullness with Cotsell and Jacobson. The format they choose, in fact, compels them to settle for much less, since they adopt one which requires them to place all annotations to the left or right of a three-and-a-half-inch column of text set out on a page measuring eight by eleven inches.

*The Annotated Dickens* offers much better coverage than either the Penguin texts or the notes in the paperback Clarendon editions of Dickens' novels, although the appearance of fullness in some instances proves illusory. Guiliano and Collins tend to gloss words and phrases that some might judge unnecessary (sincere, short commons, trivet, mealey, etc.) and on occasion, they even gloss the same word more than once ("kennel" in *Oliver Twist*, for example). The margins are also crowded with critical notes in which the editors cite critical opinions from secondary sources, and comment on standard literary or artistic effects, rather than provide cultural information the novels assume and which present-day readers lack. One might also question the editors' decision to pack the two volumes with illustrations from varied sources. We come across illustrations ranging from work by Cruikshank and Hablot K. Browne and their successors to stills from modern film and television adaptations of the novels. *The Annotated Dickens*, one suspects, misjudges its audience by combining limited erudition with popular appeal attractively packaged to meet the assumed interests of a non-academic readership.

## Editions

Readers will find full details of the republication of Dickens' works as they continue to appear, year by year, listed in Cohn's Checklists in *Dickens Quarterly*. Such editions, evanescent achievements, for the greater part, are of little interest to specialists, except as one more manifestation of Dickens' popularity. I shall comment in this section only on James Kinsley's edition of *The Pickwick Papers*, the seventh Clarendon Dickens to date. Kinsley's volume contains few textual surprises, providing for us the logical primary text (the 1836–37 first edition in nineteen monthly parts and in one volume), and relegating to the textual apparatus almost all the substantive variants Dickens later added. The later revisions are not inconsiderable numerically, totalling about one thousand, three quarters of which Dickens introduced when he looked over the sheets of the text for the Cheap Edition of 1847.

Kinsley characterizes the revisions Dickens made in 1847 and then later in 1867 as "casual and sporadic," a judgment he makes after collating the texts and classifying all the changes. In all, Kinsley specifies nine "main groups" of alterations, amongst which he lists "improvements" in grammar and expression, word-order, avoidance of repetition, and the removal of profanities, colloquialisms and vulgarisms. Following the Clarendon textual policies originally established by Kathleen Tillotson and John Butt, Kinsley adheres strictly to his chosen copy-text and records all substantive variants in the textual apparatus. There is no attempt here, as with the other Clarendon texts, to create the kind of eclectic text proposed by W. W. Greg in 1950 and put into practice by the Center for the Edition of American Authors under the leadership of Fredson Bowers.

A restored text of Dickens' first novel, error free and with the variant readings conveniently displayed at the foot of each page, represents no small achievement. Of equal importance is Kinsley's lengthy introduction, an interesting commentary on *The Pickwick Papers* in the course of its composition by monthly numbers. Once again, expect no major surprises: Kinsley rehearses a familiar story. But this account comes close to definitiveness in its masterly command of detail and facts as Kinsley traces *Pickwick*'s evolution from a series of miscellaneous "papers" collected by an "editor" into a coherent, sustained novel. Kinsley notes how the tension between the two contradictory impulses, each partially articulated by Dickens, reverberates from month to month, as continuity and coherence develop, only to be checked by seasonal distractions (the Christmas number, for example) before oscillating toward a more controlled and certain plot.

Other accomplishments worthy of note are the use Kinsley makes of contemporary reviews to document the serial's reception and the editor's knowledge of *Pickwick*'s literary contexts, which he employs to illuminate Dickens' sources and borrowings. James Kinsley died before he saw this edition through the press; the Clarendon *Pickwick Papers* forms a fitting monument to his work as a textual scholar and critic.

## Biography

Work in this area continues to produce fragmentary but useful mosaics contributing to the evolving composite of Dickens' life and times as scholars investigate peripheral events and people whose interest derives principally from their association with the novelist. Carol McLeod's essay, "Canadian Notes: Francis Dickens of the North West Mounted Police," falls into this category. McLeod uses State Military Records in the public archives of Canada to fill in some of the details relating to the years Francis Jeffrey Dickens (the novelist's third son) spent as a commissioned police officer in the north west of Canada from 1874 to his death in Moline, Illinois twelve years later.

Two other writers touch on some broader concerns. In "Dickens and Friends," Fred Kaplan reports briefly on the biography of Dickens he is currently writing and notes that Dickens' "preoccupation with friendship" forms a dominant motif of his study. Steven Marcus, by contrast, stands back from the book he completed on Dickens in 1966 to raise theoretical questions about the biographer's art. What factors determine one's critical orientation and lead individuals to engage with great passion all their force on a single figure? Marcus supplies candid and affirmative answers as he addresses these and other questions put to twelve biographers at an invitational conference held in 1981 on "The Psychology of Biography." Marcus's work in nineteenth-century British studies embraces interests that obviously extend beyond a focus on individual lives, but his books on Dickens, Engels and the anonymous author of *My Secret Life* all reveal, as Marcus duly notes, biographical interests and impulses none of which is "easily separable from autobiographical circumstances."

Readers interested in the constellation of factors behind *Dickens: From Pickwick to Dombey* will enjoy Marcus's essay. "A Biographical Inclination" is a short but insightful apologia pro scriptura sua, in which Marcus sets out his version of why he writes and what draws him to Dickens. Three factors strike him as especially significant: a conscious delight in Dickens' inexhaustible creativity and linguistic complexity, various personal resonances between events in Dickens' life and events located in the early matrix of Marcus's, and a commitment to reading Dickens' novels as they intersect with English history and culture. Marcus makes no attempt (and none is required) to arrange these three in any hierarchical order, but he left this reader impressed by the purposefulness that infuses Marcus's writing. To Marcus the instruments of literary criticism and literary authorship *matter*, a conviction less apparent among many prominent in the profession today, in whose work one detects an unsettling discrepancy between the ideals a society espouses and the way in which these ideals are implemented in critical or biographical works.

A brief reference to K. J. Fielding's *Studying Charles Dickens* will close this section. I make an exception to my announced policy of excluding handbooks (this one comes in the York series, edited by A. N. Jeffares) because Fielding's short study merits comment as an introduction to Dickens that looks at his works in relation to his life and his life in relation to his times. Fielding has in mind neophyte readers, for whom something basic is necessary. Thus the book's obvious merit—a chronologically arranged study which interweaves the texts and events in Dickens' life. *Studying Charles Dickens* is exactly the kind of guide one can recommend to beginning students with confidence.

## Victorian Fiction: Contextual Studies

Last year my predecessor noted in his comments on studies by Joseph Kestner and Catherine Gallagher that the social novel had come in for revisionist scrutiny. Contextual studies of Victorian fiction continue to draw attention, as the current yield of books received on a range of topics indicates. Under review in this section are works of varying scope and quality on the ills of capitalism, conceptions of beauty and the visual aspects of Victorian fiction, murder and sensation, and the novel's challenge to philosophy as a means of naming. I have also included in the following pages several works devoted to such conventional literary issues as the development of the Victorian short story, serialization, an anthology of Victorian essays on fiction and two useful studies of the nineteenth-century novel. This season, one might conclude, has loaded and blessed the reviewer with an ample supply of fruit.

Two books focus on money and on the financial aspects of Victorian life, Barbara Weiss's *The Hell of the English: Bankruptcy and the Victorian Novel* and Norman Russell's *The Novelist and Mammon*. The "Hell" in Weiss's title alludes to Carlyle's contention in *Past and Present* that the terror of "the modern English soul" was of not succeeding, "of not making money, fame, or some other figure in the world." This preoccupation, Weiss argues, inevitably surfaced in the novels of the period. Thus, assemble any group of texts, she proposes, and one can easily see how the Victorians tormented themselves with the fear of being judged legally insolvent.

Economic failure came to the Victorians in three principal forms. To the poor—rural and urban—financial ruin usually forced them into the dreaded workhouse. To the more affluent living in the vast range of the middle class, a gentleman's failure to pay his debts often led to prosecution under existing Insolvent Debtors' statutes, while to the trading or merchant class alone came the most ignominious public fate of all: bankruptcy.

Weiss uses her preliminary chapters to examine the nineteenth-century debate about the distinction, based primarily on class assumptions, between debtors and bankrupts. Gentlemen, she notes, could be arrested for debt and even thrown in jail, but only merchants and traders were sentenced under the Court of Bankruptcy, a stigma which lost its distinction under the Reform Act of 1861, which abolished the legal (and moral) difference between insolvency and bankruptcy.

The new legislation had a dramatic effect, for by rejecting the traditional distinction between traders and non-traders and by making all debtors liable to bankruptcy proceedings, the number of bankruptcy cases rose dramatically. Weiss notes that prosecutions in the 1860s increased eight and then fourteen times beyond those in the first quarter of the century. Not surprisingly, the novels of the period reflected both the typical preoccupations with economic destitution and changing assumptions about the social significance of failing one's creditors.

Weiss makes a case for a distinction between two broadly representative attitudes in the fiction of the period. Up to 1861, novelists tended to present bankruptcy as a metaphor for individual collapse, in which characters like Mr. Tulliver, Mr. Thornton, Robert Moore, and Mr. Dombey fell from prosperity, Victorian victims of fortune's wheel, that instrument of the Medieval world so adept at toppling the hubristic. In some instances, fictional falls prove fortunate and lead to moral and spiritual rebirth. Dickens makes this very point with Mr. Dombey, who, as a poor man loving and loved by Florence, ends the novel redeemed, exemplifying the traditional Christian view that money is evil and that the poor are full of grace. Weiss avoids suggesting that Dickens abandons this theme in *Little Dorrit*, but she makes the useful observation that Merdle's collapse functions quite differently as a metaphor to suggest not individual weakness but social collapse or even apocalypse.

Weiss seems to prefer the conclusion to Dickens' later novel in which he mutes the happy ending and appears less dogmatic than he does in *Dombey and Son*. On balance, *The Hell of the English* makes a useful contribution to its subject, despite occasional simplifications about Dickens' attitude toward money and despite her contentious and somewhat confusing agreement with Angus Wilson that Dickens ruined his novels by ending them happily.

Where Weiss errs on broad matters relating to Dickens and money Norman Russell treads with caution and proves better informed. For a start, Russell seems to understand the novelist's personal economic orientation: a hard working self-improver capable of enjoying without guilt the fruits of his labors. Russell also shows good judgment when he reminds twentieth-century readers that Victorians talked about capitalism without invoking either a socialist condemnation of the concept or an aggressive monetarist's defense. In a modest but sensible introduction to *The Novelist and Mammon*, Russell notes that concern with the poor and indignation about economic oppression did not put Victorian authors into the socialists' camp, no matter how hard armchair liberals and state-supported academics try. "Dickens, for instance," he writes, ''was an excellent man of business, investing throughout his career in steady Government, Russian, and Indian stock, railway paper and property (p. 8).'' When he died in 1870, he left £93,000, exceeding by £25,000 the fortune Anthony Trollope earned from his writings and described in his autobiography as ''comfortable, but not splendid.'' Comments Russell: ''One is not here trying to impute a kind of hypocrisy to these novelists in detailing their financial success. As sons of their age, they are openly proud of their success and, more important, their readers, too, would have shared their pride.'' To the novelists, money itself was free of moral reprobation: it was the moral limitation of amassing wealth with no care of others that the novelists condemned rather than the economic or political conditions that made wealth on a grand scale possible.

The remaining eight chapters of Russell's study examine some of the ways Disraeli, Catherine Gore, Thackeray, Trollope and Dickens reacted to the development of capitalism and its institutions in Victorian England. Two sections of *The Novelist and Mammon* center exclusively on Dickens: a detailed discussion of the practices of the fraudulent West Middlesex Free and Life Assurance Company and a close look at the activities of the financial swindler John Sadleir, whose public career and spectacular prosperity terminated in suicide in February 1856. Russell demonstrates Dickens' familiarity with each and shows how the novelist drew on the first for Tigg's Anglo-Bengalese Company in *Martin Chuzzlewit* and incorporated features of Sadleir's career into the portrait of Mr. Merdle in *Little Dorrit*.

Both sections of the book analyze intelligently the way Dickens interweaves factual material and fiction. Also worth reading is Russell's last chapter, a wide ranging discussion of the way Dickens and other novelists manipulated ''the everyday realities of commerce'' to suit the backgrounds they invented for their merchants and manufacturers. *Nicholas Nickleby, Martin Chuzzlewit, A Christmas Carol,* and *Dombey and Son* receive careful scrutiny, but oddly Russell makes no reference to *Our Mutual Friend*. Ignoring this novel is puzzling in view of Russell's focus on Mammon as the pursuit of money motivated more by selfish greed than by a sound business sense or laudable impulse to improve oneself and do well.

''Victorian fiction is rich in physical description, and heroes and heroines, who are usually the most fully described characters in a novel, invariably develop into standards of beauty.'' Lori Hope Lefkovitz opens her study, *The Character of Beauty in the Victorian Novel*, with these words, highlighting concerns that overlap with those of two other writers. Rhoda L. Flaxman describes her approach as "a generally semiotic" one in her *Victorian Word-Painting and Narrative: Toward the Blending of Genres*, in which she sets out to establish the distinctive features of Victorian word-painting. This phrase, she explains, refers "to extended passages of visually oriented description that are composed with attention to framing devices, recurrent iconographic motifs, and a carefully established, consistent perspective." By contrast, the third author to focus on the visual aspects of prose fiction, Alexander M. Ross, opts for a cultural and historical approach in his *Imprint of the Picturesque on Nineteenth-Century Fiction*.

Ross devotes a single chapter to Dickens, paying attention to the novelist as part of his overall thesis about the role picturesque theories played in the Victorian novel. Ross posits two eighteenth-century sources of the picturesque, which, in turn, emanate principally from aestheticians (Gilpin, Burke, Price) and painters (Constable, Turner, Salvator Rosa, Sandby). The interests of both groups in ruins, landscapes, and the play of light, he argues, led to an influential graphic tradition that subsequently made its impact on fiction through Scott. Ross catalogues the picturesque qualities of Dickens' novels and documents his sense of the tension between early Dickens fond of typically picturesque scenes (Mr. Pickwick's view from Rochester bridge, the exterior of the Maypole Inn in *Barnaby Rudge*), and a later, ironic writer. Picturesque scenes still continue to attract this Dickens, Ross maintains, but most frequently their introduction "serves as a premonition that all may not be well," which is the response Ross reads into the view of the Thames seen by Arthur Clennam at Twickenham on his visit to the Meagles family. Ross refers briefly to the impact of Dickens' American and Italian tours on the development of his views, but makes insufficient use of how foreign travel contributed to a changed perception of the picturesque. I suspect that one might make more of Dickens' knowledge of the aestheticians, too, despite the assertion by Ross that Dickens drew effectively but "rather seldom" upon the eighteenth-century theorists.

Flaxman's study inevitably touches on similar issues, although she allows Dickens more attention (he and Tennyson form the book's central focus) and covers *Barnaby Rudge, David Copperfield*, and *Little Dorrit* in detail. Flaxman also sets her sights more ambitiously than Ross, who confines his investigation to the picturesque rather than pursue, like Flaxman, a study of formal parallels between visually oriented poetic and fictional descriptions and a comparison of the techniques of painters with those of descriptive writers. Developing her argument, Flaxman also works toward a qualification of Lessing's distinction between poetry (a temporal and kinetic art) and painting (a spatial and static art) by suggesting that landscapes in both arts engage the reader/viewer in "a kind of metaphoric journey" through the natural world that tends to blur Lessing's formulation.

Preoccupation with these concerns, however, does little for the half of the book Flaxman devotes to Dickens. To call Dickens' imagination "visual" at this stage in Dickens studies seems to me somewhat lame. Equally hackneyed is the developmental thesis Flaxman advances based on the three novels she selects for intensive study. In summary form, Flaxman asserts a familiar progression in Dickens' fiction from early (simple visual effects) to late (complex effects). *Barnaby Rudge*, for example, she sees as a picturesque work full of Scott-like scene painting. *David Copperfield* follows as "a transitional novel" in which Dickens experiments with "alternate points of view to the picturesque," while in *Little Dorrit* he composes a late masterpiece noteworthy for its "sophisticated descriptive writing" and "generally symbolic overall technique." At this stage, word-painting prefigures changes in the sensibility of characters and "assumes an intimate relationship with its narrative."

Unlike Flaxman, Lefkovitz spends only a fraction of her time with Dickens, but her *Character of Beauty in the Victorian Novel*, in my judgment, proves the most interesting of these three visually oriented books. Lefkovitz's central premise is that beauty is culturally defined, despite our tendency to speak of it as if it were natural and universal. "Our culture teaches us what to value for its beauty and how to express that appreciation appropriately," she asserts.

Realistic novels in which characters are invested with materiality through detailed descriptions prove a fertile area for investigating how representations of beauty rely on conventional ideas or codes, which novelists both endorse and question. Beauty, Lefkovitz argues, may well be in the eye of the beholder, "but the beholder is a controlled subject," a viewer whose response is shaped and trained by the underlying structures current in any culture.

Much of the book's intellectual excitement occurs when Lefkovitz examines the tension between various cultural codes of beauty as they interact and collide in literary texts that incorporate contradictory impulses. For example, Lefkovitz isolates such culturally endorsed concepts of beauty as charm, grace and delicacy and notes how these aristocratic values confronted competing definitions of female and male beauty in the course of the nineteenth century. The challenge, she argues, came principally in the form of a new emphasis on health, vigor and strength, a set of values she associates with the middle class, whose voice the Victorian novel generally represented. Also worth noting is her discussion of the impact of Rousseau's notion of the "Noble

Savage'' and Itard's Wild Boy of Aveyron, twin interests she connects with the democratization of beauty and the development of the foundling tradition in the English novel. This last topic receives full consideration in her sixth chapter, "Grace: The Birth of Breeding," which analyzes changing conceptions of beauty as they evolve in *Wuthering Heights, Jane Eyre*, and *Great Expectations*. Dickens' novel, she argues, represents the culmination of a growing wish among writers to overturn the expectations of readers "long accustomed to romance plots," something he attempts by showing Pip reaching in Estella for a false conception of beauty. Lefkovitz thinks that the original ending in which Estella remarried someone else made it clear that Pip did not regret his loss of a false ideal, a point Dickens rethought in deference to Bulwer's warning that his readers would not tolerate such revisionism.

The remaining titles for inclusion merit no special grouping, so I shall proceed without introducing further sub-sections. "What's in a name?" asks Romeo, a question that fascinates Michael Ragussis in his *Acts of Naming: The Family Plot in Fiction*. In a deft introductory chapter, Ragussis sets up an original and exciting hypothesis: that fiction rivals philosophy in its preoccupation with naming as a central subject of inquiry. Ragussis points out that the novel emerged as a genre just as Western philosophy, represented by Locke's *Essay*, returned to the semiotic theories Plato explored in the Cratylus dialogue. This development also coincided with the Enlightenment, a period historians characterize as one that signals a new era of subjectivity and individualism. Ragussis exploits this conjunction of interests and proposes a definition of the novel as a genre that developed in opposition to the prevailing view of naming, which brought people into the cultural system (classifying, as Levi-Strauss argues) as fixed identities and tended to reduce individuals to a single, unchanging value. Fiction, by contrast, operated differently, undermining the workings of social forces by exposing the dangers of assigning "meaning" to a person. This endeavor, Ragussis suggests, was affirmed in the novel's tacit goal: "the telling of a complicated and varied individual life story."

This simplified summary does little justice to the subtlety of Ragussis's argument and the thoroughness with which he sets out his taxonomy of plots that typically discharge in different ways their essential naming function. In some works (*Clarissa* and *Huckleberry Finn*) characters invent names for themselves, perpetually rewriting and recharging their names with varying meanings, as if to suggest how difficult it is to fix one's identity and hold it still. Others (*Bleak House* and *Tess*) show characters with an equally full list of names, nomenclatures not chosen but bestowed or assigned by others.

*Oliver Twist* illustrates another important variant, in which false or fictitious names must be exposed or replaced in the course of the plot as Oliver struggles to outlive the names that threaten to annihilate him. To Ragussis, *Oliver Twist* defines itself as a fable illustrating how two hostile forces fight over names. One group, a combined set, which includes with the criminals those who threaten Oliver with the generic appellation of orphan or bastard, does battle with those attempting to rescue the workhouse child by conferring on him a socially acceptable identity. Oliver's inheritance, Ragussis suggests, signifies both monetary and genetic wealth, two important ways to define Oliver's ontological status and allow him to flourish by connecting him with his dead parents. Ragussis develops important variants of this theme in his essay on *Bleak House*, a version of which appeared in *Nineteenth-Century Fiction* in 1979.

Threats of a less philosophical sort interest Beth Kalikoff. *Murder and Moral Decay in Victorian Popular Literature* focuses on gallows writing and offers some broad generalizations drawn from street literature, melodrama and popular fiction published between 1830 and 1900. In the first part of the period, Kalikoff argues, the victims of most murders, muggings, and homicides were generally struck down by unknown aggressors—assailants who attack randomly, motivated primarily by economic impulses they cannot control. As the century developed, this pattern of crime for gain was replaced by one in which victims suffered more typically from violence done to them by someone within the family circle, by kin rather than anonymous attackers lurking in dark streets. So marked was this change, she concludes, crime writers in the final decades of Victoria's reign referred frequently to "the night-side of nature" to explain it, invoking the existence of an inner recess of the heart common to every man and woman, not exclusive to a wicked criminal class. In support of this argument, Kalikoff points out that writers spoke of the proliferation of "a degenerative and contagious criminality" which lay beyond the control of the police because it was increasingly distant "from recognizable human passions and motives."

*Murder and Moral Decay in Victorian Popular Literature* gives one the impression of an author trying too hard to impose a thesis on resistant, unruly material. Some difficulties occur, I think, by dividing the study into three twenty-year periods. In a chapter devoted to "Fiction, 1830–1850," she aligns *Eugene Aram, Oliver Twist, Catherine*, and *Mary Barton* in order to compare and contrast the shared concerns and individual interests of four writers. Another permutation of texts, one feels, might have produced quite different conclusions. For example, if she had considered *Paul Clifford* or reflected on John Forster's comments about Dickens' Newgate intentions in *Oliver Twist* to connect the high and the low, she might have modified her temptation to conclude the book with dubious assertions about the erosion of faith in justice late in the century and a new tendency to shrink to the minimum the difference between "good people and criminals."

A second problem arises from the author's reluctance to examine skeptically her thesis about degeneration. She provides no statistical or historical evidence to support her interpretation, and she accepts without question the assertions of late Victorian essayists that the police had become much less efficient as the century developed. Familiarity with the history of the police, the successes of the detective force, and reference to Victorian criminal statutes designed to check crime might anchor her discussion and provide empirical evidence to support her claims. One might also question her choice of literary texts. How usefully can one generalize about public and private crimes in *Bleak House* (Kalikoff's choice) and ignore Dickens' later version of the same issue in *Our Mutual Friend*?

The veteran observer of shock and sensation, R. D. Altick, covers an adjacent piece of territory in his *Deadly Encounters: Two Victorian Sensations*. His study provides an entertaining account, scrupulously based on contemporary press reports, of two mysterious and bloody assaults which occurred almost simultaneously in the second week of July 1861. This double-barrelled dose of horror, Altick contends, had much to do with the vogue for "sensation" melodrama and fiction characteristic of the 1860s. Altick's final chapter, "The Novel Experience," provides a concise overview of representative sensation writers (including Dickens), helpfully related to their journalistic context. Students who enjoy reading about murder as "one of the Fine Arts" will enjoy Altick's reflections.

Anthologies of Victorian essays on the novel continue to make their appearance and occasionally assemble identical materials. Ira Bruce Nadel's *Victorian Fiction: A Collection of Essays from the Period* gives us pieces by Eliot, Lewes, and Stevenson which Edwin M. Eigner and George J. Worth included in their selection reviewed last year, but otherwise ranges more broadly than *Victorian Criticism of the Novel*. The Nadel volume includes an additional nine essays and provides a selection which spans from 1836 to 1912. The essays chosen by Nadel also illustrate various threads of discourse about nineteenth-century fiction, as critics argue about the novel's value, the subversiveness of the genre, and its popularity. Unlike the well-produced volume from Cambridge edited by Eigner and Worth, Nadel's edition makes do with facsimile texts, an economic choice, but an unappealing one to the eye.

Over thirty years ago Kathleen Tillotson argued in the Preface to *Novels of the Eighteen-forties* that it was inappropriate to talk about "Victorian novels." She recommended instead that scholars work in manageable segments and concentrate upon a decade or so rather than treat fiction of the period under the loose designation of an eponymous label. Academics generally heeded her advice, by producing since her admonition books on multiple aspects of Victorian fiction carefully limited by chronology or subject. Two writers, however, have recently ignored Tillotson's caveat and attempted to cover in a single book the fiction of the entire Victorian period.

Michael Wheeler makes a convincing case that readers new to the study of the Victorian novel need a comprehensive survey of the kind he produces in *English Fiction of the Victorian Period 1830–1890*. Wheeler places appropriate emphasis on the introductory nature of his enterprise and keeps that qualification to the fore as he covers briefly fifty novelists and relates their work to its nineteenth-century context. Wheeler proceeds chronologically, dividing the main body of the book into four phases, each of which covers sub-genres of the novel, aspects of the novel's development, and its major themes, motifs, and conventions. Well-documented chapters and a helpful general bibliography sub-divided into various sections, notes on each of the fifty writers, and a detailed contextual chronology setting novels in relation to literary and non-literary events assist the reader Wheeler addresses.

Robin Gilmour in *The Novel in the Victorian Age: A Modern Introduction* conceives a different approach to help the novice. Aiming at more than a study "of a few selected novels," but avoiding the comprehensive survey undertaken by Wheeler, Gilmour provides a fine critical and contextual introduction to the work of the major writers and several minor ones. Gilmour's book concentrates on themes and groups writers topically under such rubrics as the aristocracy (Bulwer, Disraeli, Thackeray) and the ache of modernism (Hardy, Moore, Butler, Mary Ward). Only Dickens receives a full chapter to himself, a shrewd appraisal at once concise and illuminating as Gilmour manages to write gracefully about Dickens' achievement in thirty pages. Students seeking a limited but sound perspective on Dickens' contribution to the Victorian novel might well start with this chapter. Gilmour's select bibliography makes an equally valuable departure point for readers interested in a concise summary of the main contours of this overwhelming field.

Two slim and well-produced volumes from Cambridge University Press conclude this section. In *The Victorian Short Story: Development and Triumph of a Literary Genre*, Harold Orel devotes a chapter to Dickens as he sets out to investigate why the short story genre became so popular in nineteenth-century England. Wilkie Collins, Le Fanu, Trollope, Stevenson, Kipling, Conrad, and Wells also receive extended treatment. Orel writes informatively and marshals evidence carefully, providing readers new to the subject with pertinent facts about each writer. This study excludes American masters of the genre and makes no reference to minor British writers. Mary Hamer's introductory chapter to her *Writing by Numbers: Trollope's Serial Fiction* comments briefly on the historical conditions affecting the production of part-issue books from the beginning of the eighteenth century. She draws frequently on Robert L. Patten's *Charles Dickens and his Publishers* and uses Dickens as a useful reference point.

## Books on Dickens

The number of books received this year treating either a single novel or some aspect of Dickens' oeuvre attests to Badri Raina's comment that Dickens scholarship today "is a copious industry" and that one must have "a good reason" to add to it. Justifications for doing so range widely, from the high minded, to self-assertive claims of originality, to modestly phrased hopes that one can be "useful" to new readers of Dickens. Alternatively, one can hedge a little and combine reasons for writing and offer, like Raina himself in *Dickens and the Dialectic of Growth*, a "personal essay," an apt term for the book's slim 128 pages of text, yet hardly an adequate one for the developmental account of Dickens' writing Raina offers. "I see Dickens' work from the 1830s to the 1860s as one composite *Bildungsroman* that builds progressively superior insights as each succeeding novel deconstructs its predecessor(s) into a mounting historical graph. In current idiom, 'all [Dickens'] writing takes place in the light of [his] other writing' " (8).

A cautionary note about Raina's terminology lest his use of "deconstruct" in the passage above sets off verbal fireworks in the reader's mind that take shapes and colors suggested by Derridian usage. This essay, as Raina points out, is "critically old-fashioned" in that he sets out to write about Dickens as a single writer contained by specific biographical circumstances and by a continuous struggle to come to grips with himself and with the Victorian *Zeitgeist*. But *Dickens and the Dialectic of Growth* is new-fashioned in one respect: Raina's insistence that he "situate" himself in relation to contending theorists and make explicit his "habits of reading" and evaluatory comments. "These days it is hopeless to imagine that we shall not be found out" (3), he explains.

Readers of this book will discover Raina occupying the middle ground between Jacques Derrida and Frederic Jameson, a position from which he shuns "the personal-anarchic subjectivism" he associates with "the extreme poststructuralist formulations" and affirms "the reality of the perceiving subject" and the reality of historicity. In Raina's own words: "For a person from the Third World, such as the present writer, to declare a general skepticism about reality based upon the tenuous nature of linguistic signifieds is to immediately announce a stance of reaction. Hungry and sick populations must remain a fairly unmistakable text, and to the extent that such is the case, language has important uses" (7).

I draw attention to the self-consciousness with which Raina details his assumptions because the way he perceives himself—a privileged, well-to-do teacher of an alien literary tradition surrounded by illiterate fellow citizens living "below thinkable levels of subsistence"—necessarily influences the Dickens he sees and constructs. "Of the major intelligences engaged with the Victorian scene, Dickens, placed as he was, seemed the most closely to approximate the ambition, the self-doubt, and the guilt of many of us in India," who grew up socially advantaged but radical in the decade after independence from British colonial rule in 1947 (18–19).

Essentially, those three nouns—ambition, self-doubt, and guilt—define Raina's Dickens and convey in shorthand his basic thesis. Raina relies on the Autobiographical Fragment ("an intensely class-conscious document") to anchor his argument and chart his interpretation of "the one central contradiction" of Dickens' career. In Raina's view, this was Dickens' aspiration to succeed, because he was so uniquely talented, and win through hard work and self-discipline the fruits of a bourgeois civilization he simultaneously despised and longed for. This creative opposition of antithetical drives began in *Oliver Twist* and stretched throughout Dickens' works, carrying him with increasing subtlety through a series of "self-images" to Charley Hexam, Dickens' "total rejection" of his culture's callous self-seeking.

Raina offers a coherent and intelligent overview of Dickens' development, but his argument strikes me as myopic partly because he foregrounds only selective aspects of Victorian historicity and partly because his formulation is too neat. He takes due note of the effects of such material factors on Dickens as the culture's preoccupation with money-making, consuming, and the ethics of the market place only to diminish the importance of ideas, political or religious. Dickens' diagnoses of "the high-Victorian view of value," he writes, "are wholly those of Marx and Engels" (130), surely a conclusion that reveals more about Raina than about Dickens. Place less emphasis on guilt and more on a cultural affirmation of free will and personal salvation and a different Dickens emerges, recognizably closer to the tenets of Pelagian Christianity and the secular beliefs of Samuel Smiles than the systematic philosophy of Karl Marx.

Interpretations such as Raina's also tend to flatten the achievements of the Victorian middle class to their wholly disagreeable aspects, an act of simplification that obliterates that culture's emphasis on progress and on the need to plan and work for a better future. All that remains, in Raina's version, is a Podsnappian routine of getting up at eight, shaving at quarter-past, breakfasting at nine, going to the City at ten, coming home at five, and dining at seven, a mere caricature of English life and of seventy years of urban history. I have questions, too, about Raina's unverifiable developmental hypothesis. Laying out in linear fashion each novel and arguing that in each succeeding work Dickens catches "himself in each repeated act at a higher point of clarification" reduces the Dickens dialectic to a narrow form of self-preoccupation. Such an argument also allows little room for a writer whose novels provided a public conscience and frequently assumed positions at odds with the national consciousness.

A less personal sense of urgency shapes Kate Flint's *Dickens*, a comparably slim volume that belongs to the Harvester New Readings, a self-described "major new series" offering "important new critical introductions" to eleven canonical English writers (vi). In a book preoccupied with the "inevitably slippery, unreliable medium of written language" (7), the ambiguity of the phrase about "new critical introductions" indeed seems unfortunate. The series, of course, focuses on the "new bearings" generated by contemporary literary theory and uses recent developments in structuralist, deconstructive, Marxist, and Feminist approaches to understand the concerns of major writers ranging from Chaucer to T. S. Eliot. Thus Flint takes up her pen according to this prescription and examines Dickens' writing by discussing "various strategies of reading" to challenge "the more old-fashioned assumptions" made by some writers and to "call into question" their ingrained habits when analyzing fiction. An air of critical checkmate almost stifles her endeavor since Flint has so much to address and so little space in which to execute her moves. Pocket chess sets reduce one's spatial perspective, but they don't distort the game, unlike diminutive books such as this one which scale down territory as elusively large as fifteen novels by Dickens and the entire range of current critical theory.

Commendably, Flint states her determination to avoid any single strategy designed to answer and tie up neatly Dickens' writing. But she overworks her thesis about his novels being "full of contradictions" to the point of absurdity when she casts around for a single theorist to "explain" many well chosen and lucidly presented examples of contradiction in his works. Flint, for example, considers the complicated nature of his plots and points out how the narrative tone of a single work often shifts from description to satire, from the exhortatory to the sentimental. She also documents how divergent views on central ideas emerge, to be further modified by the "unsaid" of the text, the conscious or unconscious gaps an acute critic can reveal. Such "unresolvable contradictions," she asserts, permit no one way to see the novels, no one "unequivocal source of meaning" (7). But at this point, Flint changes her methodology and abandons the skepticism she used successfully on the texts. Rather than pursue further the implications of the interpretive difficulties she has illustrated, or question her own claim about the impossibility of finding a stable meaning, she calls Bahktin to her aid. The ahistorical polyphonic principle explains all, we learn, because the novel, in Bahktin's formulation, functions according to more than one scheme of logic and has more than one voice to be listened to within it (48).

By coupling Bahktin with vague generalizations about the nature of language as an unreliable medium, Flint puts a contemporary critical spin on her denial of intentionality and on statements such as this: "Esther [Summerson] . . . has no consistent voice herself and, one could argue, therefore is, in fact, no more stable a character than the constantly shifting omniscient narrator himself" (56). In short, Dickens seems to have had little control over his artistry in *Bleak House*. This uncertainty, in fact, operated so widely in his novels that disquiet and not knowing seem to emerge as their predominant mode. "The overriding characteristic of the dialogic imagination," Flint asserts, "is that it admits and presents unresolvable differences and points of view" (48).

Elsewhere in *Dickens* Flint offers different strategies. She is not unrelentingly hostile to biographical criticism and she makes some brief but insightful comments about Dickens' persona. She also reads well as a contextualist, providing several sharply etched observations and occasionally a longer, more sustained argument, of which her chapter on Asmodian revelations is perhaps the best example. Chapter 4, "Asmodeus Takes the Roofs Off: Narrative Point of View and Contemporary Society," intelligently exploits secondary sources and presents a convincing teleological account of Dickens' interest in revealing secrets, linking the phenomenon to literary, historical, and sociological sources. Yet overall, the brief she was given—to emphasize several different critical approaches and employ them side by side—works against the series' stated objective. The New Readings, we are told, are designed to help students understand "the full range and complexity" of major writers. Pious prose, and a good intention. That end, I suggest, can more likely be served by encouraging readers to engage and master the texts themselves rather than approach them through contradictory and challenging theories stretched out to accommodate the all-pervasive Bakhtinian blueprint provided by Flint.

Two other books this year also make a deliberate appeal to the presumed needs of new readers, as Cambridge University Press and G. K. Hall market simultaneously a pair of near clones: attractively designed studies of world classics, available in cloth and paper, and short enough to read in a single sitting. In addition, both books provide a chronology of the author's life, basic contextual details specific to each text, and brief accounts of the works' reception and critical fortunes, as Bert G. Hornback concentrates on *Great Expectations* in Twayne's Masterwork Studies and Graham Storey on *Bleak House* in Cambridge's Landmarks of World Literature. The decision to focus on a single work rather than on the output of a career makes the introductory task easier for Hornback and Storey than it was for Flint. So does the determination to avoid "critical jargon." The Landmark and Twayne series, in almost identical phrases, advertise their commitment to clear, conversational language, whereas Flint, following the injunction from Harvester, went out of her way to include what Hornback terms "all that stuff called theory of criticism."

Yet for everything Hornback and Storey share in intention and scope, their similar agendas offer two quite different approaches to the introductory format defining each series. Storey, for example, divides his study into four chapters, reserving most of his energy for a close reading of *Bleak House* that in five sub-sections examines the novel's structure, language, organization by social groups, irony, and use of set-scenes (the deaths of Nemo, Krook, Jo, and Lady Dedlock). Storey's efficient exposition of the novel's principal contexts (historical and intellectual) draws extensively on Butt and Tillotson's *Bleak House* chapter in their *Dickens at Work*; two remaining chapters treat the book's critical reception and its European context, with the latter giving Storey the chance to rehearse familiar links between Dickens and Dostoevsky.

Hornback, by contrast, follows a more idiosyncratic route, a clue to which is revealed in the full title of his essay: *Great Expectations: A Novel of Friendship*. As one might infer from the sub-title, Hornback takes a particular perspective and sets out to provide a reading of the novel, one that focuses on friendship as its major theme. Once a year, Hornback tells us, he teaches *Great Expectations* and during the twelve months in which he wrote this book he taught it three times. Familiarity, in this instance, has bred not contempt but conviction and insight. Reading the book, I had the sense of Hornback lecturing in a brisk, authoritative manner designed to make a student audience sit up and take notes. I can think of no better recommendation of the overall effect than to say that I would urge my own sophomore daughter, if she were a student at the University of Michigan, to enroll in Hornback's course.

Hornback sets the scene for his discourse on friendship by relating Dickens' assumptions about art to the theories of the English Romantic poets. He cites Coleridge's explanation of the imagination in the *Biographia Literaria* as a faculty that dissolves, diffuses, and dissipates in order to "recreate . . . to idealise and unify" and argues that Dickens held a similar view. To the novelist, the imagination allowed him to fabricate not lies but a vision of "the wholeness of the whole cloth." The imagination, Hornback continues, "is that wise faculty through which we comprehend the otherwise confusing world around us. . . . The imagination is what enables us to make meaning out of life" (16–17).

What kind of a world featured in Dickens' fiction and what special version of it does he present in *Great Expectations*? Hornback notes Dickens' peoccupation with corrupt social institutions in the novels that precede *Great Expectations* and asserts that in this penultimate complete novel, the major emphasis shifts to money, class, and property. Our concern with those features of the good material life, to paraphrase Hornback's argument, corrupts us and brings certain moral ruin. Unless, of course, we can learn to value true friendship and make a conscious effort to give it and receive it. Only such interpersonal engagement and a steady resolve to create and put forward the good self will bring happiness and mitigate the pervasive evil and corruption around us. By the late stage of Dickens' career, Hornback continues, the novelist had abandoned whatever revolutionary fervor he ever had for collective social action and put his hope for a better world in individual action as the only fitting agent for overall change. One can't escape one's involvement in this process, Hornback contends, so rather than deny the world (Jaggers, Wemmick, and Miss Havisham all opt for that course in various ways), one should follow Pip's example and learn to value true friendship. By the time Pip narrator has come to tell his life's story, he can offer his own experiences as an authentic model, one that shows his mistakes but presents them in such a way as to enlarge our sympathies and do something for us morally.

At times this insistence on the book's thesis ("The real lesson of *Great Expectations* is friendship") leads to oversimplification and a tendency to present this novel as Dickens' greatest single achievement on the grounds that it is more "subversive" than any other work. "*Great Expectations* attacks our idea of what is good, and what makes the good life: and money is at the center of that attack." And later, Hornback adds, "money is worthless in a *mortal* world: and that is Dickens' point. Happiness is the only thing that makes mortal life worthwhile. And happiness is a social pleasure, not a selfish one" (78). These statements trouble me not because I think they are false but because in the context of the argument Hornback makes for their validity they corroborate an earlier assertion that friendship *alone* became Dickens' overriding concern. Beginning with *A Tale of Two Cities*, Hornback suggests, Dickens' central characters "don't marry at the ends of their novels. Rather, they learn friendship, and the freedom that friendship brings" (60). This statement ignores *Our Mutual Friend* and overlooks the marriages which close that novel and the way in which dust is finally scattered and money, "after a long rust in the dark," can turn bright again and sparkle in the sunlight.

Other instances of unwary enthusiasm drive Hornback in a different direction and precipitate oracular statements: "Life is essentially a matter of relations, and relationships" (86); "If we use our minds . . . to make our lives meaningful, then we will justify human existence" (119) and so on. But generally, his long familiarity pays off, allowing Hornback to speak with commendable authority about Dickens' art and the art of this particular novel. "I have long used as a working rule in reading Dickens' novels that anything which is repeated must have some special meaning" (83), Hornback notes, as he introduces the subject of recurring motifs in Dickens' fiction preparatory to devoting two fine chapters to the use of repeated details and themes in *Great Expectations*.

To return now to Storey's measured introduction to *Bleak House* and his close reading of that equally artful novel: If Storey's study lacks what one might term Hornback's faults, it also fails, in my view, to exhibit Hornback's virtues. Storey examines a set of logically devised topics and treats each successfully. But he comes across as much less engaged with the text than Hornback and in that respect perhaps proves less helpful to the putative audience for these books. Storey and Hornback offer two models, one a compartmentalized, ostensibly objective and detached treatment of the text, the other an urgent and impassioned monologue which projects the persona of a teacher deeply committed to his task. Another reviewer might respond differently to the two styles; so might students. But whatever one's preference, we can enjoy the best of both and make our own choice.

Discussion of three books of different orientation will conclude this section. The Dickens universe Juliet McMaster explores in her *Dickens the Designer* assumes a consonance between appearance and essence, a world characterized by a reliable connection between the visible and a character's incarnate self. McMaster notes that the signs Dickens assembles often require a careful reading, calling for a reader with interpretive skills and ability to discriminate between the specious and the true. But most frequently, she argues, the narrator assembles information about characters helpfully arranged and coded in a verbal portrait leaving little room for indeterminacy.

What Dickens sees and how he perceives form the center of this study, whose dual signification of "designer" McMaster explains in her Preface. Dickens operates as a designer in the sense that he writes as a graphic delineator in a visual mode often shaped by Victorian theories of physiognomy and phrenology. He is also a designer in a second manner, an artist "who plans and arranges the materials of his vision into shapes of beauty and significance" (xi).

McMaster organizes her study around this double meaning of designer. In Part I, "The Value and Significance of Flesh," she concentrates on Dickens' ability to make characters visible, illustrating her thesis by providing a survey of his "iconography of physical appearance." This section surveys Dickens' works and often makes useful connections between his descriptive techniques and the observations of such authorities on physiognomy and phrenology as John Elliotson, George Combe, Johann Kaspar Lavater, Charles LeBrun, and Sir Charles Bell. McMaster has a good eye for detail herself, but her presentation of the evidence of Dickens' tacit kowledge of the leading theorists via selective categories runs the danger of degenerating into lists, as she furnishes data on heads, faces, bodies, hair, eyes, noses, and so on.

In Part II, "The Story-Weaver at his Loom," McMaster puts away her magnifying glass and stands back to explore the "large-scale visual effects" of six novels, works where mass and line, color and tone, and light and shade predominate and contribute to the design and meaning of the total work. Chapters in which McMaster sustains her interest in Dickens' visual orientation generally work well and yield insights, such as her analysis of lines of rotundity and erect lines in *The Pickwick Papers* or her discussion of *Bleak House* as a Turneresque exercise in modes of perception. On other occasions, we encounter brisk comments on works that offer little more than new critical commentaries on the texts.

"A collocation is a habitual juxtaposition of a particular word with other particular words" (87), write Knud Sørensen in the penultimate book before us. The effect of this stylistic device, one of several Dickens exploited to amuse and startle readers by confronting them with an unconventional verbal alignment, might also describe one's initial reaction to the prospect of a Danish linguist writing on Dickens' style. Doesn't Sørensen's *Charles Dickens: Linguistic Innovator* catch us off balance a little, similar to the way readers of *Great Expectations* feel when they come across Mr. Jaggers cross-examining not a witness but the "very wine" in the glass in his hand?

In the case of this scholarly monograph, I predict that Dickensians will overcome momentary amazement and recognize Sørensen's book as a significant contribution to the study of Dickens' language. "Up to now," Sørensen notes, "there has been limited documentation of the innovative aspects of Dickens's prose. This book presents the evidence I have found" (12).

An introduction and three chapters set out Sørensen's findings. He looks closely at numerous aspects of Dickens' vocabulary, studies his syntax and style, and finishes with an examination of the way Dickens handles narrative and speech, following lines similar to those of Norman Page in *Speech and the English Novel* (1973). An appendix on Dickens' neologisms closes the book.

The results of this inquiry are not earth-shattering, but Sørensen proves consistently interesting. Where do neologisms and stylistic oddities predominate in Dickens' works? *Sketches by Boz* and *The Pickwick Papers* win hands down. Of Dickens' later works, *Bleak House* leads the novels that follow, drawing keen competition only from *Our Mutual Friend*, an interesting refutation of those who argue that this last panoramic novel shows Dickens' talents in decline. Overall, however, Sørensen notes that Dickens was less inclined later in his career to create new prose patterns than he was to "pitch it strong," the one feature, with its multiple variants, that best summarizes the dominant characteristic of his style.

Commenting on his methodology in the introductory chapter, Sørensen underlines the need to proceed comparatively if one is to assess accurately the extent to which Dickens created innovative prose. *The Oxford English Dictionary* served as an essential instrument in this enterprise. Sørensen also admits to following hunches and that he was "much helped by serendipity." Readers looking into *Charles Dickens: Linguistic Innovator* might emulate the author. Open any page and you will find abundant evidence to confirm

Sørensen's own brief conclusion in his epilogue. What strikes the reader about Dickens' style, comments Sørensen, is a "wonderful linguistic facility," wielded with ease, care, elegance, and a gift for turning out happy phrases. What better testimony do we need to support Sørensen's contention that to study Dickens' prose is to confront "one of the makers of Modern English"?

### Studies of Individual Works

Of Dickens' fifteen novels, only five in the period under review received no attention as the sustained focal point of a single essay contributed either to a periodical or to a collection of essays. Three of the novels passed over this year are early works (*Nicholas Nickleby, The Old Curiosity Shop*, and *Barnaby Rudge*), an omission which will change soon as the *Dickens Quarterly* extends its special 150th anniversary issues to the six early novels. This series, from *Pickwick* to *Chuzzlewit*, began in March 1986 when the journal published a special number devoted exclusively to *The Pickwick Papers* to observe the sesquicentennial publication of Dickens' first novel.

To some extent, critical interest in the March issue of *Dickens Quarterly* centered on ways in which to read the novel. In *"The Pickwick Papers* and Travel: A Critical Diversion," Michael Cotsell argued for looking at the work in relation to a particular model of travel literature, one which, in Cotsell's words, was not "end-oriented" but circular, digressive, and subject to the diversionary impulses of curiosity. Mark M. Hennelly, Jr., and Joseph Rosenblum responded differently, with Hennelly proposing John Huizinga's model of play as the appropriate one for analyzing the novel's "glorious tomfoolery" and Rosenblum countering that a careful reading of *The Pickwick Papers* indicates that "in plot, character, and theme the novel owes much to Milton," whom Dickens evokes through repeated allusions to *Paradise Lost* to heighten the work's comic elements and deepen its moral vision. In this same anniversary issue, Robert L. Patten shows Dickens at work within two opposed traditions of character theory. From Robert Seymour he inherited the idea of static character types favored by graphic artists; as the novel progressed beyond the conception initially defined by the illustrator, Dickens found himself increasingly attracted to "the potentiality of character," a novelistic tradition which placed due emphasis on growth and development. Elliot D. Engel and Margaret F. King conclude the special number with a survey of the novel's critical reception from 1836 to 1986.

Two other writers comment on Dickens' first novel. Diane Keitt argues in

"Charles Dickens and Robert Seymour: The Battle of Wills" (*The Dickensian*) that Seymour's published designs of character types and humorous subjects provided the novelist with "a wealthy source for ideas." Keitt notes that during the early period of the novel's composition Dickens never made "slavish use" of Seymour's work, but she thinks that his sketches prove more significant as a source for some of the incidents in *Pickwick* than critics generally recognize. In "Muggleton and the Muggletonians" (*Dickens Quarterly*), Edward G. Preston proposes Ashford, Kent as a possible model for the fictional town Dickens wrote about in chapter 7 of *The Pickwick Papers*.

The 150th anniversary series in *Dickens Quarterly* also accounts for six essays on *Oliver Twist*. In "Benthamite Utilitarianism and *Oliver Twist*: A Novel of Ideas" and "Dickens, Oliver, and Boz," K. J. Fielding and Morris Golden explore, respectively, complementary versions of the novel's stable meanings. For Fielding, meaning is most appropriately sought in the vigor with which he sees Dickens taking on Bentham and plotting a strategy to combat the influential philosopher's conception of human nature based solely on the principle of self interest. Fielding makes a persuasive case for Dickens' "fabular design" and his use of the plot to dramatize duty and self-sacrifice, as Dickens constructs an alternative to Bentham's ethical system. In the course of his argument, Fielding effectively counters Humphry House's influential assertion that Dickens knew little about Bentham's theories. Quite the contrary. Long before *Hard Times*, as Fielding's essay shows, Dickens was familiar with Benthamite teaching and an ardent opponent of his ideas from the start of his career. For Golden, the overriding concerns prove biographical rather than philosophical. In Oliver's career, he suggests, we can see the operation of Dickens' personal recollections as well as his current sense of the world, a view which brings together twin sources, one flowing out of "private reveries" and the other taking its shape and meaning "from a variety of external events connected with the bitter winter of 1836–7."

By contrast, Iain Crawford and Brian Rosenberg concentrate on contradictions within the novel and on those elements of *Oliver Twist* which seem to destabilize the text. In " 'Shades of the Prison House': Religious Romanticism in *Oliver Twist*" Crawford looks at the conscious and unconscious use Dickens makes of Wordsworth's *Immorality Ode* as an intertext; in "The Language of Doubt in *Oliver Twist*," Rosenberg examines Dickens' methods of description, searching for evidence of hesitation, qualification, and ambivalence. Sylvia Manning and Robert A. Colby conclude the issue. In "Murder in Three Media: Adaptations of *Oliver Twist*," Manning focuses on two adaptations of the murder of Nancy (Dickens' own and David Lean's) "with a particular interest in what they tell us about the powers and limits" of the novel, the dramatic reading, and the film. Colby's essay, "Oliver's Progeny: Some Unfortunate Foundlings," is a companion piece to one he published in 1967. On this occasion, Colby looks at the books Dickens' novel inspired instead of at the foundling literature of the 1830s, which Dickens drew on when he composed his serial contribution to *Bentley's Miscellany*.

In 1970 Northrop Frye proposed reading Dickens' novels as analogues of "the New Comedy Structure" by aligning them with the works of Plautus and Greek romances. Such stories, Frye argued, employed stock devices, stressed the triumph of the young over the old, ended with festivities, and ignored the restrictions of realistic fiction by violently manipulating events. Roland F. Anderson's "Structure, Myth, and Rite in *Oliver Twist*" takes its departure from Frye's essay, "Dickens and the Comedy of Humors," and functions essentially as an extended gloss on Frye's argument, an attempt "to make sense" of the novel's "rather puzzling elements" through a relentless exposure of what he classifies as *Oliver Twist*'s "mythic heritage." Anderson rises to the challenge of tidying up an ostensibly loose, uncertain plot with the zeal of a fullback exploiting a five-foot hole in the opposing team's secondary defense. Literary strategies, however, require delicacy, an ability to respond with subtlety rather than with the speed and power necessary to success on the gridiron. Like Walter Payton, Anderson flattens the opposition as he knocks down every element of the novel by forcing the plot, structure, and almost every character in *Oliver Twist* to conform to his ritualistic-mythic reading. Particularly disturbing are the liberties Anderson takes with the novel's social and historical context, compelling even its slang to serve his Procrustean thesis. Oliver's "greeness," he contends, connects him with Dionysus and fertility rituals associated with a younger brother (summer, the New King) who challenges an elder brother (winter). Far more likely is the commonly held view that Dickens incorporated flash vocabulary to add to the novel's realism rather than to shape its mythic content.

The remaining pieces on *Oliver Twist* concentrate on influence studies of one kind or another. In "Cervantes, Dickens, and the World of the Juvenile Criminal," Constance Dowling proposes a new source for *Oliver Twist*: Cervantes' novella, *Riconete y Cortadillo*, English translations of which began to appear from 1741. Parallels between Dickens' work and the Spanish tale of the initiation of a pair of juvenile delinquents into the Sevillian underworld furnish evidence for Dowling's contention. In "Fagin, Effie Deans, and the Spectacle of the Courtroom," Daniel Whitmore makes a more limited claim, arguing for connections between Scott's *Heart of Midlothian* and the penultimate chapter of *Oliver Twist*. Effie Deans, accused of child-murder, is on trial for her life in Edinburgh in chapter 22. Her position, suggests Whitmore, closely parallels Fagin's in chapter 52, defeated, arraigned for murder, and awaiting his judgment in the courtroom.

Paul Davis pursues a source study of a different kind in his "Imaging *Oliver Twist*: Hogarth, Illustration, and the Part of Darkness." Davis posits Hogarth's "Progresses" as Dickens' starting point, remarkable instances of "urban realism" whose tales of apprentices, harlots, and rakes shaped the novelist's interests. But Davis thinks that Dickens quickly outgrew the narrative patterns ("linear moral dramas") that characterized Hogarth's world view, even in an early work like *Oliver Twist*, and developed a more complex vision. To define that sense of complexity, Davis borrows Sergio Eisenstein's vocabulary of montage, arguing that the dialectical collision of contradictions in the novel shows an expanded perspective whose development from a Hogarthian progress into a "novel of consciousness" anticipates Conrad. Davis mixes uneasily commentary on the graphic techniques of Cruikshank and Hogarth with film language, making the whole piece somewhat confusing and out of focus.

Different aspects of the language of *Martin Chuzzlewit* attract two essayists this year. Barrie Saywood has little to add that's fresh in his "*Martin Chuzzlewit*: Language as Disguise." Saywood offers an extended brief for wordplay as the principal "binding agent" of a seemingly disorganized novel. He wastes time on the organic unity issue and attacks straw opponents with a long series of examples from the text, mainly to establish the familiar point that in *Martin Chuzzlewit* Dickens "alerts the reader to the ambiguity of language." Readers will find more satisfying Carol Hanbery MacKay's Lacanian scrutiny of epistolary activity in the same novel. MacKay offers a taxonomy of the various kinds of letters that appear in the novel (public letters, personal missives, confessional letters, and secret, coded letters) and comments on their various functions. Characters write to reveal themselves, to keep secrets, and to make rhetorically hollow affirmations. The relation between what is known and what is secret consumes much of MacKay's attention, as does her search for a tripartite structure of the novel. In her formulation, insincerity and selfishness give way to hollowness and greed, to be succeeded, in the novel's final episodes, by a rejection of secrecy and a return to directness that signals the "triumph of good."

Appearance and reality and a Lacanian interest in the various meanings of "letter" clearly played no part in the way freshmen read the same novel in 1934, some of whom, Leslie A. Fiedler tells us, found *Martin Chuzzlewit* "funny, raucous, vulgar and mean-spirited." Writing impressionistically and anecdotally in *"Martin Chuzzlewit*—A Great Bad Book," Fiedler recounts how he and several classmates found Dickens confirming many of their own prejudices about American types who are still very much "in our midst." Fiedler remembers his own introduction to Dickens' American novel "with gratitude" and makes no attempt either to revise or to update his response. We should read it, he advises, "not as the first of Dickens' art novels but as the last of his pop romances, . . . which though a failure by elitist critical standards, somehow refuses to die."

Three other writers also focus their attention on Dickens' fiction of the 1840s. Philip V. Allingham's "The Naming of Names in *A Christmas Carol"* is self-explanatory, a succinct study of the connotations of the names of the principal characters in Dickens' first Christmas book. Roger D. Sell also clearly announces his interests in the title of his essay: "Dickens and the New Historicism: the Polyvocal Audience and Discourse of *Dombey and Son."* Sell endorses the tendency in some quarters to read Dickens' fiction as "social discourse," by which he means the tendency to stress how novelists capture the polyphonic clash of different voices present in any given culture at any given time. Sell subscribes to Bakhtin's argument that heteroglossia characterizes the novel as a genre in which "a diversity of social speech types . . . and a diversity of individual voices" find artistically organized expression.

*Dombey and Son* challenges Sell's interests because Dickens made a concerted effort in that novel to impose unity on his material through a metaphorical urge toward closure, shape, and significance. To show not so much that Dickens failed but that some degree of randomness and openness operates, Sell points to the novel's array of characters, in whose distinctive speech he sees a work "so alive with the counterpointings of heteroglossia that to think of it 'only' as a novel would be a mistake." Social discourse, one assumes, remains a better term.

Discourse in another more specific and controlled context attracts Judith Newton, whose "Making—and Remaking—History: Another Look at 'Patriarchy' " traces variations in the patriarchal tradition Sandra M. Gilbert and Susan Gubar constructed in *The Madwoman in the Attic* (1979). Newton moves from Wordsworth to Arnold via Dickens, focussing on the emphasis each placed on women as a refuge for men and on the cultural and ideological forces that shaped gender roles. Newton sees an important shift between Wordsworth and Arnold in which dependency on women intensifies, so much so, she argues, that *Dombey and Son* reflects an oddly split attitude.

On one level the novel affirms the power of women's moral influence, as the plot vindicates Florence's goodness and shows how she reformed her father. On another level, Dombey's fear of women and of their capacity to feel suggests a reaction, a horrific awareness that women have learned so effectively to use their influence and wield power. Florence is valued, she notes, but not needed, her angelic role undercut by the fact that Walter ''is already perfect'' and by the equally important fact ''that the real moral influences on his life have been male.'' Dickens' solution, Newton thinks, ''is represented by a group of economically marginal, poetically sensitive, 'old-fashioned' men,'' a self-sufficient male community that looks forward to a new notion of manliness later embodied in that powerful institution of male privilege, the Victorian public school for boys.

The number of essays on *Bleak House* this year clearly identifies that novel as the current Dickens favorite. At least two of the contributions under review deserve recognition as major pieces, essays that will earn a place in the vast body of scholarship that has already accumulated in the wake of the novel's glory. In the first of these, Suzanne Graver carefully selects her focal point in ''Writing in a 'Womanly' Way and the Double Vision of *Bleak House*.'' Less frequently remarked than the novel's unconventionally divided narrative, she notes, is the additional split in Esther's first-person voice. Graver sees in Esther's self-division two predominant modes, one a self-affirming, accommodating, benevolent self and the other a critical or ''desiring self'' whom she at once suppresses and obliquely expresses. Graver concedes the brilliance of Dickens' choosing to write obliquely when he writes as a powerless woman. But she also sees something disturbing in his fictional strategy, which he uses, unlike Victorian women writers, not to subvert cultural womanly ideals ''but to celebrate a dutifully willed acceptance of them.'' Esther's obliqueness, she argues, reveals a disorder ''that is at least as disabling as it is corrective,'' causing her narration ''to call into question the assurances Dickens would have it provide.'' Also worth noting about Graver's argument is her emphasis on the social rather than the psychological roots of Esther's disorder and on Dickens' uneasy response to female intelligence.

Paul Pickrel makes a contribution of a very different kind in his ''*Bleak House*: The Emergence of Theme,'' an essay remarkable for its vigor, intelligence, and the force of its good writing. Pickrel's is a broad-ranging piece that considers the novel's ''moral cosmology,'' the way characters run errands for the plot and advance its theme, and the significance of the dual narrators. As the title perhaps suggests, the essay also affirms the intentionality of the author. The novelist, Pickrel states in his introductory remarks, produces meaning by manipulating the concrete particularities of the narrative in such a way as to shape simultaneously a theme "that is both legible and abstract and general." In a novel we cannot easily trace how this is done, Pickrel contends, "but we can identify some of the effects."

Perhaps the most dramatic of those Pickrel examines is Dickens' division of the narrative as a means of advancing Esther to the center of the novel. Pickrel comments perceptively on the aspectual differences of the two voices of the narrator's (Esther's perfect or completive tense voice and the narrator's progressive or continuitive mode) and discusses the implications of the temporal perspectives employed by each in the telling of her or his story. The anonymous narrator, Pickrel points out, speaks in the voice of history, employing the present tense as if to suggest that orientation in time for him is irrelevant. Esther, by contrast, speaks in the completive voice, one that emphasizes how the process of growing up and living can be perfected or brought to an end. Private life, Pickrel concludes, is marked for tense, giving, therefore, time meaning, while the "voice of history" is continuitive. In the starkest terms, characters either opt, like Esther, to build a successful, constructive life or face, like Tulkinghorn, Carstone, Krook, and others, self-consuming destruction by refusing to recenter their lives and find "in the fullness of time a fullness of being."

Graham Hough inevitably touches on similar concerns in his "Language and Reality in *Bleak House*," when he examines the two voices responsible for narrating the novel. Hough provides a brief taxonomy of the different voices belonging to the omniscient narrator and contrasts his vision with the modest, gentle tones that characterize Esther's authenticity and her moral authority, pointing out that by juxtaposing her more limited narration with the greater complexity of the anonymous narrator Dickens gains a double advantage. He both affirms that things in the novel lie beyond her range and yet also demonstrates how effectively natural feeling and moral goodness serve an important role. The ultimate rationale of Esther's part in the book's dual structure, Hough concludes, "is to show that a simple and single-minded girl, with little experience and no knowledge, . . . can see *almost* all the truth about a complicated world." And in showing this in the novel, Dickens commits himself to another position. He confronts head-on any sense of social determinism in Esther's denial of what her birth, ancestry, and upbringing nearly make her—a psychopath. Concludes Hough: "She *chooses* herself as she is, as much as any Sartrean hero."

Two other writers examine various aspects of Dickens' knowledge. How much did the author of *Bleak House* know about the scientific theories of

Robert Chambers and Herbert Spencer, propounders of progressive evolutionary ethics in the 1850s? Enough, argues Karen Jahn, to invert their optimistic assertions and to use *Bleak House* to dramatize the destructive effects of misplaced confidence in a natural law working to ensure national progress. In "Fit to Survive: Christian Ethics in *Bleak House*," Jahn makes a convincing case for reading the novel's devolutionary imagery as a reminder of the folly of leaving institutions and the environment unattended, secure in the belief that improvement inevitably followed because Providence guaranteed it. To uphold Providential values, the world needed human intervention, through which society might be transformed if everyone joined the Christian community and worked, like Esther and Allan Woodcourt, to create an environment supportive of life, not hostile to it.

Research by G. S. Haight, Trevor Blount, and E. Gaskell has already documented several aspects of Dickens' public skirmish with G. H. Lewes over Krook's death through spontaneous combustion. Peter Denman in "Krook's Death and Dickens's Authorities" adds one further detail to this sensational episode: the extent to which Dickens was bluffing when he responded to Lewes that he had looked into "a number of books with great care" before writing his account of the rag and bone dealer's smoky demise. In fact, as Denman illustrates, Dickens evidently went no further in his search for scientific corroboration than Robert Macnish's *Anatomy of Drunkenness* (1827), a popular medical treatise on alcoholic intoxification owned by Dickens. Macnish's twelfth chapter, "Spontaneous Combustion of Drunkards," cited reports from earlier medical writers and outlined the more commonly reported cases. Denman argues that it was to this source Dickens turned for help when Lewes pressed him to level with his readers and furnish "proof." Denman also notes that Dickens made little effort to search further. He ignored standard works of medical jurisprudence skeptical about spontaneous combustion and relied almost exclusively on Macnish, whose name he withheld. Concludes Denman: "What emerges from a study of the background to the dispute is the alacrity with which [Dickens] takes up a position and the tenacity with which he defends it. His inclination was to contend rather than to concede, even though he cannot but have been aware that the foundation in which he based his side of the argument was shaky."

The remaining notes and an essay cover various points. In a "Note on *Bleak House* and *The Merchant of Venice*," R. D. Drexler traces allusions to the play in the novel and argues that they underscore Dickens' moral satire. Stanley Friedman also examines another borrowing, suggesting in "The *Bleak House* 'East Wind' and Pope's *Rape of the Lock*" that Pope's couplets about the Cave of Spleen indicate Dickens knew the mock-epic and drew details from it which he used in connection with the east wind, Esther, Krook, and high society.

John Jarndyce's meteorological complaint turns up again in two other notes. Michael G. Miller in "The *Bleak House* Number Cover: Which Way is the Wind Blowing?" is the first to observe contradictions in H. K. Browne's cover design. The drawing, Miller points out, illogically shows the E (ast) and W (est) letters on the weathervane reversed and the fox's posterior wrongly positioned, according to the wind's direction in the drawing. In "Another Note on the *Bleak House* Cover: East Wind and Foxes," Michael Steig offers his explanation for Browne's error. Anyone interested in the use of emblematic details should consult Steig's note.

Another pair of essays focus on pedagogy. G. L. Gibb's "Teaching *Bleak House*" is self-explanatory, the record of a British teacher's strategies to help sixth-formers struggle through "900 pages of close packed typeface" in fifteen weeks. In "Reading Long Stories on the Installment Plan," Michael Lund makes a case for using the original serial divisions to teach long novels. As evidence, he describes his own experience teaching *Bleak House* and other works in parts, spread out over the entire semester rather than crammed into one or two weeks.

Finally, in *The Gadfly Literary Supplement*, Duke Maskell spends more time attacking the premises and language of the Roskill Parliamentary Report on the siting of a third airport for London than he does on Dickens' novel, the ostensible focus of his essay, "Grubbing on—by System: Or Krook vs. Bucket." Maskell sees the fictional world of *Bleak House* as the epitome of a virus he associates with industrial bureaucracies: the tendency of people to define themselves solely in relation to the duties they have to perform. As a collection of separate, disjunctive 'I's, people (exceptions are those occasional individuals who get out) subordinate their individual sense of moral integrity or decency to the office, becoming corporate men or women devoid of human qualities. This essay strikes me as a therapeutic exercise with only tangential literary concerns.

What assumptions about language permeated Victorian culture and how do those assumptions differ from those that define our intellectual moment? Robert L. Caserio in "The Name of the Horse: *Hard Times*, Semiotics, and the Supernatural" explores these questions, an ambitious undertaking full of insight into Dickens' novel and remarkable for the use Caserio makes of Umberto Eco's theory of signs to illuminate a Victorian work rather than damn it for its own inadequacy. Caserio looks clearly at his enterprise and writes with candor about what we 'do' when we work in an environment awash with critical theory. Some critics ignore it altogether. Others apply a particular system to a work and in a dispassionate way unmask the author's or work's naivete in relation to the theory they advocate. Alternatively, they congratulate the author or the work for having confirmed what their adopted theory predicted.

Caserio avoids these particular pitfalls and undertakes something less frequently attempted: reading *Hard Times* through "a semiotic looking-glass" in order to engage in a cross-cultural dialogue between the Victorians and ourselves about language. Caserio sets about his task by juxtaposing *Hard Times* and *The Name of the Rose* and by using Econian ideas about language to examine such typical critical concerns as the novel's politics, Stephen Blackpool's sense of the world as a muddle, and his dialect. Viewing Dickens' work from this perspective, Caserio sees *Hard Times* as it unfolds as miming our knowledge about language. The novel, he argues, rejects the Gradgrindian assumption "of a non-arbitrary, strictly denotative relation between names and things or facts" and expands the definition of *horse* to show how meaning is both fixed and polysemous.

Patricia Ingham also looks at language in *Hard Times* but with different interests. Her scrutiny of Stephen Blackpool's speech in "Dialect as 'Realism': *Hard Times* and the Industrial Novel" reveals that Dickens relied heavily on his copy of *Tim Bobbin: View of the Lancashire Dialect, with Glossary* (1746), the primary source, she contends, for Blackpool's non-standard vocabulary and speech. Dickens also added some touches of local color, she notes, as he responded competitively to Elizabeth Gaskell's efforts in the same direction with John Barton in her industrial novel, *Mary Barton* (1848).

A third essay on *Hard Times* re-examines the importance of love or charity in the novel and connects this theme with St. Paul's First Epistle to the Corinthians, 13. The influence of this "Love Chapter," argues Joan E. Klingel in "Dickens's First Epistle to the Utilitarians," is so pervasive as to make Dickens' work a gloss on St. Paul's teaching and render *Hard Times* Dickens' First Epistle to the inhabitants of Coketown.

Dickens' two last panoramic novels attract fewer writers than one might expect. In "The Shifting Point of View in the Narrative Design of *Little Dorrit*," Adela Stycznska distinguishes three principal modes: that of the main narrator (controlled and ironic) and two perspectives divided between major characters (Arthur and Amy) and minor characters (Affrey and Miss Wade). The overall effect, Stycznska concludes, in which parts of the action are filtered through individual minds and parts through the viewpoint of the main narrator, conveys the complexity of human inter-relations in the novel. Its polyphonic voices, she adds, "anticipate the experiments in narrative technique of the 20th century novel."

Alison Booth, by contrast, sees Dickens, along with George Eliot, looking back into the century at Carlyle. Booth contends in "Little Dorrit and Dorothea Brooke: Interpreting the Heroines of History" that both novelists set out to revise Carlyle's notion that "Universal History" is made up of the "united biographies" of great men. In *Little Dorrit* and *Middlemarch* they proceed, she argues, by invoking figures "neither preeminent nor manly who yet redeem the common experience of a burdensome past."

Booth's essay, however, more consistently explores Eliot's revisions of Dickens' novel, which she sees as an attempt by Eliot to reverse aspects of Dickens' strategy and record "psychological shades" in her protagonist with "photographic realism rather than [with] fanciful precision." Booth then moves on to consider the common ground shared by Amy Dorrit and Dorothea, two saintly women, each imprisoned by social conventions, yet sources of strength in a world threatened by collapse. The difference in Eliot's "perhaps unconscious revision of Little Dorrit," Booth notes, is that Eliot's ambivalent feminism and meliorism make her discontented with Amy's "homely, inarticulate passivity." In an attempt to show Dorothea transcending the ministering role, Eliot permits her heroine to engage in various "manly activities," although Dorothea finally ends up enmeshed in the Middlemarch web, married to Ladislaw and far removed from cottage building, scholarship, and estate management. "The female idealist's story apparently could not be completed beyond the contingencies of the historical world," Booth concludes. In "The Stephen Family and Dickens's Circumlocution Office Satire," Michael Cotsell qualifies the familiar explanation for James Fitzjames Stephen's violent criticism of *Little Dorrit* in his 1857 essay, "The Licence of Modern Novelists," a retaliation for Dickens' assault on Sir James Stephen, his father. Cotsell notes that Fitzjames Stephen probably did think Dickens was satirizing his father in Book I, chapter 10 of *Little Dorrit*, but he was wrong to do so. Dickens' attack on civil service inefficiency was, in fact, second hand, derived from an earlier criticism of Sir James Stephen by Charles Buller, author of "Mr. Mothercountry, of the Colonial Office," which appeared in 1840 in Buller's *Responsible Government for the Colonies*.

In "Omniscience in *Our Mutual Friend*: On Taking the Reader by Surprise," Audrey Jaffe offers a modish explanation for the novel's apparently modernistic preoccupation with fragmentation and confusion. Surprise, or the rhetorical term peripeteia, operates in one of two ways, she suggests. Readers either experience a pleasant moment of recognition, in which they exclaim, "Just so! I never thought of that," or a disconcerting sense marked by uneasiness at the exposure of one's vulnerability and lack of knowledge of the unexpected. Readers of this review won't be surprised to learn which version Jaffe "valorizes."

The argument proceeds along predictable lines. *Our Mutual Friend* lacks a single presiding consciousness, largely because Dickens offers instead "a pattern of epistemological one-upmanship," in which multiple characters collect knowledge the way old Harmon accumulated dust. In this endeavor, she continues, the characters use knowledge to entrap others or to invent their own plots. Jaffe notes the presence of both positive and negative versions of this Asmodean figure, an individual who often shares his vision and knowledge but fails to function as a fixed center. This formulation reaches its epitome in Jaffe's interpretation of Boffin's revelation, a designed moment of surprise that engenders confusion rather than disappointment, an emotion some critics express who feel let down when they discover that Boffin was faking all along.

Mary Ann Kelly discusses the creative powers of the imagination in the same novel, focussing particularly on Lizie Hexam and Jenny Wren, two characters strengthened by adversity and able to dream or to imagine as a result of their early exposure to hardship. This power of the mind, Kelly argues in "From Nightmare to Reverie: Continuity in *Our Mutual Friend*," accounts for "the lingering hope" we detect in the novel, despite the often hopeless reality Dickens describes in his last completed work.

Catarina Ericsson's "A Child is a Child, You Know: The Inversion of Father and Daughter in Dickens's Novels" examines the exchange of roles between parents and children and suggests that Dickens attempts to come to terms with this reversal in *Our Mutual Friend*. The treatment of fathers and daughters in the novel, she thinks, differs from the presentation of idealized daughters in Dickens' early fiction by showing in Lizzie, Jenny, Pleasant Riderhood, and Bella young women who set themselves up against their fathers and rebel. In this respect, she argues, they resemble "many of Dickens's son figures." Readers should be aware that Ericsson's essay imperfectly fits into this section featuring periodical contributions since hers is a published version of her University of Stockholm dissertation. I include it here for want of a better category.

Reference to short pieces on *Great Expectations* and *The Mystery of Edwin Drood* bring this section to a close. George J. Worth sets out his conclusions about an 1861 adaptation of the novel after examining a rare copy of the play at Cambridge University. Worth's careful note supplies full bibliographical details about the adaptation and its distinctive features. Worth also corrects misinformation supplied about the same play by Malcolm Morley and S. J. Adair Fitz-gerald. Practical questions about the staging of another version of the novel by Barbara Field are answered by Matthew Kiell in "Dickens on Stage." Field's adaptation enjoyed a long run at the Guthrie Theater in Minneapolis. In "The 'Vulcanic dialect' of *Great Expectations*" Naomi Lightman makes some tentative connections between the novel's smith imagery and Carlyle's Gospel of Work, offering *Sartor Resartus* as a possible source for Dickens' references to blacksmiths and the importance of forging one's destiny.

In "The Sapsea Fragment—Fragment of What?" Charles Forsyte offers a new explanation for the five sheets Forster found placed within the leaves of Dickens' other manuscripts and later printed in his *Life* under the heading "How Mr Sapsea ceased to be a member of the Eight Club. *Told by himself.*" Forsyte challenges Forster's assumption that the fragment bore a direct relation to *The Mystery of Edwin Drood* and argues that it was the first version of the idea Dickens developed into *George Silverman's Explanation.* Forsyte assembles an array of evidence to build a convincing case, basing his analysis on a careful examination of the colors of Dickens' inks, names from the *Memoranda* book, and the literary features of the fragment.

### Dickens and . . .

One essay on Dickens' periodical writings this year merits special notice. In "The Uncommercial Traveller on the Commercial Road," Michael Cotsell examines Dickens' response to Limehouse and London's East End. When Dickens returned to this area, which he first knew from visits to his godfather Charles Huffam, and wrote about it in the last decade of his life, social realism predominates, a sharp contrast to the Limehouse of childhood featured in *Dombey and Son*, where "compensatory fancies" generally shaped the waterside scenes. In the essays Dickens contributed to *All the Year Round* and later collected and republished as *The Uncommercial Traveller*, the novelist airs his midnight thoughts about Wapping, Limehouse, and the adjacent slum districts. These essays, argues Cotsell, are great because "they articulate discomfort."

The more personal elements of that later lack of ease interest Deborah A. Thomas, whose essay "In the Meantime: Dickens's Concern with Doubling

and Secret Guilt between *A Tale of Two Cities* and *Great Expectations*''
covers similar literary territory. Thomas looks at the "short fiction" (stories
and sketches) Dickens produced between 1859 and 1860 and isolates the motif
of doubling and secret guilt. Both concerns appear in the two weekly novels
on either side of the period she highlights and both elements, Thomas thinks,
deserve consideration since they seem "part of his general thinking about
style at this point in his career." Doubling evidently emerges as a preoccupation as Dickens became increasingly interested in his own divided nature
and in a person's capacity to lead a double life. Allied concerns attract Henri
Justin, who focuses on "The Signal-Man," a short fictional piece that has
elicited several attempts by different scholars to interpret its apparently occult
or ghostly nature. In "The Signalman's Signal-Man," Justin argues that
Freudian hindsight enables us to see the figure haunting the railway employee
not as a specter but as a projection of the signal-man's death wish.

Other pieces about Dickens' later journalistic contributions are of a bibliographical nature. William F. Long presents evidence to suggest that Dickens
borrowed the name of his famous Cheap Jack, Dr. Marigold, from John Galt's
*Annals of the Parish* (1821), noting also the presence of a Pickwickian Mr.
Snodgrass in *The Ayrshire Legatees* (1820). R. M. Ross and A. G. Bagnall
identify one Reverend Robert Carter as the author of two stories published
in *All the Year Round* in 1862 and 1864. In "Parody and the Dickens-Collins
Collaboration in 'No Thoroughfare' " Jerome Bump uses an annotated copy
of *No Thoroughfare* as a play to correct the usual view that the two divided
equally the writing. Instead, argues Bump, working from notes originally
made by Richard Herne Shepherd (1842–95), Dickens' role was larger than
critics had thought.

Recent years have seen a steady growth of interest in comparative studies
of Anglo-American writers. Some books pair novelists; others take as their
subject a broad investigation of travel volumes written by English and American author-voyagers. Of the first, the Dickens-Melville link continues to
draw attention since the two were casually connected by Edward Rosenberg
in *Melville and the Comic Spirit* (1955) and later studied more systematically
by Pearl Chester Solomon (1975), Edwin M. Eigner (1978), and Jonathan
Arac (1978). Robert Weisbuch notes, however, that we still lack studies that
investigate texts intensively "to get at a characterization of Anglo-American
influence."

Weisbuch's ambitious *Atlantic Double-Cross: American Literature and
British Influence in the Age of Emerson* addresses such an agenda by combining the intensive textual studies he advocates with a focus on the broader

questions of influence. What makes American writing between 1830 and 1860 specifically "American"? How useful are theories of American literature that make claims for its uniqueness? What constitutes influence and how do we account for our current tendency to elevate the views of Walter Jackson Bate and Harold Bloom, two critics actively hostile to T. S. Eliot's version of the literary tradition as one likely to strengthen and nurture writers rather than fill them with anxiety?

We can leave to Americanists the big issues this book raises and isolate for our purpose Weisbuch's contribution to the Dickens-Melville connection. In "Melville's 'Bartleby' and the Dead Letter of Charles Dickens" Weisbuch argues that the American author pits himself against his English "burden" as an act of both personal and national affirmation, a kind of literary David who takes on no less a Goliath than *Bleak House* in order to show that he can do more to explore "life's sorrows" in a short story than Dickens can in a panoramic novel.

Dickensians might be forgiven for smiling at such an instance of literary hubris. Weisbuch, however, keeps a straight face and argues that slights to Melville in *Bleak House* and a conscious sense of patriotism prompted the American author to misread Dickens creatively. Adopting Bloom's test on matters of influence, Weisbuch contends that Melville successfully offers "Bartleby" as "an encyclopedic fiction," startling in its compactness, a new version of Dickens' traditional epic in which Melville presents an exhaustive portrait of society within the confines of a short story. In another Dickens-Melville connection, Edwin M. Eigner examines similar tendencies by each writer to assert how art becomes "the true moral and religious medium of the nineteenth century." Eigner's starting point is his comparison of over-lapping concerns expressed by Melville in "The Two Temples" and Dickens in "Two Views of the Cheap Theatre" (*The Uncommercial Traveller*).

Thomas C. Caramagno makes no reference to theories of influence when he brings together Dickens and Twain. Instead, he proposes reading *Bleak House* and *The Gilded Age: A Tale of Today* (1874) in tandem simply because the two address political corruption and social disorder and also focus on "the knotty problems of nationalism and Providential destiny" in a prophetic mode. "Bad Fictions and the Improvident Heart in *The Gilded Age* and *Bleak House*" seems to lack a clear objective. The essay falls into two sections (one on each novel) and airs in the *Bleak House* part faddish formulations about Dickens' novel as a meta-fiction enclosing itself and commenting on its own design "as an illusion." Caramagno also sets out to correct misperceptions of Esther as a neurotic failure by asserting that her narrative is "an attempt to locate a new, self-generated identity in terms of the providential blessings and curses she chronicles so carefully.'' Readers curious about the essay's title should note that ''bad'' fictions are those which propose ''personal solutions to . . . social chaos'' and the ''improvident'' hearts those of Dickens and Twain. Caramagno finds both authors pessimistic in their appraisal of human nature but committed to applying a brake to their imaginations by leavening the novel with a dose of optimism.

Other recent essays on Dickens and American authors focus on the more limited question of literary borrowings. In ''A Possible Source in Dickens for Poe's 'Imp of the Perverse','' Adeline R. Tintner proposes Sikes's injunction to Oliver, ''Drink it, you *perwerse imp*, drink it!'' of a glass of liquor he forces on the orphan before compelling him to break into Mrs. Maylie's house, as the original of the phrase Poe used as a title for his story published in 1845. Tintner also traces ''two definite references'' to *Oliver Twist* in Henry James's short story ''Julia Bride'' (1908), as well as several other less convincing echoes. Added together, continues Tintner, these references serve as testimony to the ''private altar'' to Dickens that James kept all his life. Tintner notes that if one includes the comments James made on Dickens in his critical writings, references to him are exceeded only by those to Balzac and Shakespeare.

George Lippard, minor novelist and nineteenth-century American radical, also took Dickens seriously. But as a nationalist, Lippard thought that the Boz fever that swept the eastern seaboard during the early part of Dickens' 1842 visit became too extravagant and got out of hand. Let us feed Dickens, he exhorted readers in a brief essay contributed to *The Spirit of the Times*, ''but do not let us lick his dish after he has eaten out of it.'' Lippard's essay is now available in a selection of his writings edited by David S. Reynolds. Readers interested in the details of Dickens' knowledge of the Parkman murder in 1849 will find them in Robert F. Fleissner's ''The Harvard Affair 'Proves' a Holmes Connection with *Edwin Drood*.'' Fleissner draws on an earlier essay by Jim Garner to argue that the case served as a source for some aspects of *The Mystery of Edwin Drood*.

Several other writers also contribute influence studies of various kinds. Dickens' knowledge of Charles Lamb serves as a starting point for Kathryn Sutherland, who examines various parallels between *The Old Curiosity Shop* and the *Essays of Elia*. Sutherland seems to be on firm ground when she compares Master Humphrey and Lamb's narrator as two noble and tender-hearted narrators of the shifting panorama of urban life. But she strains too hard when she moves beyond presenting specific echoes in an attempt to establish broader aspects of a Dickens-Lamb connection. In "Dickens, Ruskin and the City: Parallel or Influence," Charles Swann suggests that Dickens taught Ruskin how to see the city and shaped the art critic's presentations of "moralized landscapes," despite Ruskin's repudiation of the novelist in "Fiction, Fair and Foul."

In a modification of the borrowing formula, Karl Kroeber argues that Dickens resisted the work of another writer rather than adapted it. In a brief discussion of *Barnaby Rudge* and *The Heart of Midlothian*, Kroeber makes the case that Scott's novel epitomized a model of historical fiction Dickens rejected, opting in *Barnaby Rudge* for a drama of "timeless psychic patterns" as fathers and sons battle together. Scott, by contrast, located his action in historical specifications, which required a complex interweaving of the factual and the fictional and resulted in a more complex work than Dickens'. Kroeber concedes, however, that Dickens' greater freedom to ignore history proved beneficial because it allowed him to generate so much emotional heat, especially when he wrote about mobs.

Earlier in my remarks on Bolton's *Dickens Dramatized* I noted how stage versions of Dickens' novels often provided career opportunities for actors. Jim Davis's essay documents a typical instance, detailing how Dion Boucicault's adaptation of *The Cricket on the Hearth* offered J. L. Toole and Joseph Jefferson important openings at an early stage of their theatrical careers.

Neil Sinyard pursues a connection of a different sort: ways to use one discipline to learn about another. Sinyard writes as an aggressive proponent of cultural studies anxious to break through narrow academic boundaries and write about film from a context instead of from a vacuum. Sinyard calls prevailing attitudes to film in the academy "almost unbelievably reactionary," a response he hopes to correct by encouraging respect for each discipline and a habit of making "particular parallels between the two media." To advance his sense of the importance of the analogies between film and literature, Sinyard begins by discussing how frequently Dickens and Charlie Chaplin intersect. This topic might prove fruitful to someone knowledgeable about both figures, an indispensable qualification for anyone drawn to the interdisciplinary approach Sinyard advocates. But Sinyard quickly destroyed his credentials as a literary critic, as far as I was concerned, when he started on a tiresome recitation of Dickens' faults. These, he reminds us, primarily concern Dickens' inability to aspire to "the analytical complexity of a George Eliot or a Henry James."

Sinyard's case for the ideal study he advocates hardly improves when he turns to four specific adaptations of Dickens' novels, including David Lean's

1947 version of *Great Expectations*. He praises the film's opening—nothing new—faults its middle, and argues that Lean's ending, through its abrupt shift in tone from realism to melodrama, questions Dickens' revised ending. Sinyard's verdict: "This is still probably the best film treatment of Dickens to date."

Dickens abroad features in two short pieces. Yair Mazor argues that Dickens played an important role in the evolution of the 'Haskalah' novel popular in Eastern Europe between 1850 and 1890. His impact, Mazor thinks, was substantial, steering several Jewish writers toward social didacticism and to intricate plots populated by flat characters. Dmitri Urnov provides a brief survey of Dickens' popularity in Russia from the works of his first translator, Irinarkh Vvednesky, to recent editions of *Oliver Twist* and *The Old Curiosity Shop*, which flood the market in editions of one million copies. Soviet citizens read Dickens not only in Russian, Urnov adds, but in many languages of the Soviet Republics.

One can infer from this section that the "Dickens and . . ." formula is capable of almost infinite variation, including adaptation to an entirely non-literary field of discourse. Susan Addario and C. D. Webster, two members of the University of Toronto's Center of Criminology, urge child-care and youth workers to look to Dickens for advice about treating children. His novels, they argue, document many sound practices and usefully supplement twentieth-century textbooks devoted exclusively to matters of child care. "We feel that Dickens offers descriptions and ideas regarding the treatment of children, the relevance and keenness of which are undiminished by the passage of time." How Boz would have glowed with pride! And how he must have done when he read any of the extraordinary and varied dedications lavished upon him by contemporary authors. Readers interested in this manifestation of literary idolatory should consult Anne Lohrli's "To Charles Dickens, Esq." in which she assembles a comprehensive survey of dedications published between 1838 and 1870.

### In Closing

In quantitative terms, 1986 has been an extraordinarily productive year for Dickens studies. The number of books and journal articles compares favorably with figures in each category for Dickens' centennial year in 1970 and exceeds those for any year since 1979, when Robert Newsom wrote the first annual review essay for this journal. One major difference between the productions in 1970 and those in 1986, however, is that most of the books published during the centenary year came out by design as part of a concerted effort. Sixteen years later, current books and articles simply appeared, the result of uncoordinated individual efforts, publishers' schedules, and other arbitrary factors. Certainly future years might see this year's level equalled or even surpassed. But it seems safe to predict that in statistical terms 1986–87 will stand alone for some time.

Facts and figures, as Dickens reminds us in *Hard Times*, convey only a portion of reality and provide limited help in non-statistical matters. Has this year been a *good* one in Dickens studies, readers may well demand. To answer the question fully would take me beyond the scope of this essay. It would require assessment of the materials before us within the context of the current national debate about higher education and reference to those who argue that faculty interests shape the curriculum and facilitate the production of published research at the cost of educating undergraduates. Allan Bloom, William H. Bennett, and others turn this screw further and blame faculty members for the fragmentation all too frequently the hallmark of the undergraduate experience and for the tendency of academics to measure professionalism only in terms of quantifiable scholarship. Shouldn't professors, the critics ask, get back into the classroom and add less fuel to the voracious fires consuming more and more time spent in the solitary production of published research?

Does the present flourishing state of Dickens studies reflect one aspect of this larger national problem? Yes and no, I think. Some of the works I have read this year could have been written with greater brevity. Some, one might argue, shouldn't have been written at all. And others, valid pieces of research or argument, lacked elegance and passion. But I have also found many substantial contributions, notable in their intellectual engagement with the multiple aspects of Dickens' literary achievements and often concisely and indeed elegantly written.

In a recent editorial in *The New Republic* headed "The Case for Book Burning," the editors took a caustic look at scholarly over-production among sociologists, and argue that "the journal junkies, and not the researchers, are now in control." The writers go on to emphasize that they do not want to muzzle scholars, but advocate instead the imposition of some reasonable limits by the producers themselves. I can see no easy way to implement this suggestion, even if agreement prevailed about its need. But for all its impracticality, I find attractive a variation of this idea wittily expressed by A. Dwight Culler, who described his fantasy of "a SALT II treaty in the academic arms race," whereby scholars would have "a lifetime quota of 500 pages in which to record their thoughts.'' The occasion of Culler's remarks in *Dickens Quarterly* was his review of a book by a writer he much admired, John D. Rosenberg, whose study of Carlyle he praised for its conciseness and ''depth of feeling and freshness of imagination'' unusual among scholars. If these qualities characterized everything written during the period covered by this review, 1986 would indeed be an *annus mirabilis* in Dickens studies.

## NOTE

1. I want to thank Alan M. Cohn for sending me monthly computer printouts of the materials he collected for his quarterly Checklists. I also wish to thank Kalyani Pattel for her help as a research assistant and Wanda M. Bak for typing the final draft of this essay.

## WORKS MENTIONED

**Books**

Addario, Susan and C. D. Webster. ''Concepts of Child Care in the Novels of Charles Dickens.'' In *Adolescents, Literature, and Work with Youth*. Eds. J. Pamela Weiner and Ruth M. Stein. New York: The Haworth Press, 1985, pp. 59–67.

Altick, Richard D. *Deadly Encounters: Two Victorian Sensations*. Philadelphia: University of Pennsylvania Press, 1986.

Bolton, H. Philip. *Dickens Dramatized*. Volume 1 of *Novels on Stage*. Boston: G. K. Hall, 1987.

Chaudhuri, Brahma, Comp. and ed. *Annual Bibliography of Victorian Studies 1984*. Edmonton: LITIR Database, 1986.

Cotsell, Michael. *The Companion to 'Our Mutual Friend'*. London: Allen and Unwin, 1986.

Eigner, Edwin M. ''The Two Temples of Melville and Dickens.'' In *Mythos und Aufklärung in der Amerikanischen Literatur/Myth and Enlightenment in American Literature*. Eds. Deiter Meindl and Friedrich W. Horlacher. Erlanger: Universitätsbund Erlanger-Nörnberg, 1985, pp. 251–256.

Ericsson, Caterina. ''A Child is a Child, You Know: The Inversion of Father and Daughter in Dickens's Novels.'' *Acta Universitatis Stockholmiensis* (*Stockholm Studies in English* 61). Stockholm: Almqvist and Wiskell, 1986.

Fielding, K. J. *Studying Charles Dickens*. York Handbooks. Harlow, Essex: Longman, 1986.

Flaxman, Rhoda L. *Victorian Word-Painting and Narrative: Toward the Blending of Genres*. Michigan: UMI Research Press, 1987.

Flint, Kate. *Dickens*. Harvester New Readings. Atlantic Heights, N.J.: Humanities Press International, 1986.

Gilmour, Robin. *The Novel in the Victorian Age: A Modern Introduction*. London: Edward Arnold, 1986.

Guiliano, Edward, and Philip Collins, eds. *The Annotated Dickens*. Two volumes. New York: Clarkson N. Potter, 1986.

Hamer, Mary. *Writing by Numbers: Trollope's Serial Fiction*. Cambridge: Cambridge University Press, 1987.

Harris, Kevin. *The Dickens House Classification*. Research Report No. 18, School of Librarianship and Information Studies. London: The Polytechnic of North London, 1986.

Hornback, Bert G. *Great Expectations: A Novel of Friendship*. Twayne's Masterwork Studies. Boston: G. K. Hall, 1987.

Jacobson, Wendy S. *The Companion to 'The Mystery of Edwin Drood'*. London: Allen and Unwin, 1986.

Kalikoff, Beth. *Murder and Moral Decay in Victorian Popular Literature*. Ann Arbor: UMI Research Press, 1986.

Kinsley, James, ed. *The Pickwick Papers*. Oxford: Clarendon Press, 1986.

Kroeber, Karl. *British Romantic Art*. Berkeley and Los Angeles: University of California Press, 1986, pp. 132–135.

Lefkovitz, Lori Hope. *The Character of Beauty in the Victorian Novel*. Ann Arbor: UMI Research Press, 1987.

Lynch, Tony. *Dickens's England*. New York: Facts on File Publications, 1986.

Marcus, Steven. "A Biographical Inclination." In *Introspection in Biography: The Biographer's Quest for Self-Awareness*. Eds. Samuel H. Baron and Carl Pletsch. Hillsdale, N.J.: The Analytical Press, 1985.

McMaster, Juliet. *Dickens the Designer*. Totowa: Barnes and Noble, 1987.

Nadel, Ira Bruce, ed. *Victorian Fiction: A Collection of Essays from the Period*. New York: Garland, 1986.

Orel, Harold. *The Victorian Short Story: Development and Triumph of a Literary Genre*. Cambridge: Cambridge University Press, 1986.

Paroissien, David. *Oliver Twist: An Annotated Bibliography*. New York: Garland, 1986.

Raina, Badri. *Dickens and the Dialectic of Growth*. Madison: University of Wisconsin Press, 1986.

Ragussis, Michael. *Acts of Naming: The Family Plot in Fiction*. New York: Oxford University Press, 1986.

Ross, Alexander M. *The Imprint of the Picturesque on Nineteenth-Century Fiction*. Waterloo, Ontario: Wilfrid Laurier University Press, 1986.

Russell, Norman. *The Novelist and Mammon: Literary Responses to the World of Commerce in the Nineteenth Century*. Oxford: Clarendon Press, 1986.

Sinyard, Neil. *Filming Literature: The Art of Screen Adaptation*. London: Croom Helm, 1986, pp. 118–126.

Sørensen, Knud. *Charles Dickens: Linguistic Innovator*. Acta Jutlandica, 61. Humanistick serie 58. Arkona: Aarhus, 1985.

Stone, Harry, ed. *Dickens' Working Notes for His Novels*. Chicago: University of Chicago Press, 1987.

Storey, Graham. *Bleak House*. Landmarks of World Literature. Cambridge: Cambridge University Press, 1987.

Weisbuch, Robert. "Melville's 'Bartleby' and the Dead Letter of Charles Dickens." In his *Atlantic Double-Cross: American Literature and British Influence in the Age of Emerson*. Chicago: University of Chicago Press, 1986, pp. 36–54.

Weiss, Barbara. *The Hell of the English: Bankruptcy and the Victorian Novel*. Lewisburg: Bucknell University Press, 1986.

Wheeler, Michael. *English Fiction of the Victorian Period 1830–1890*. London: Longman, 1985.

Worth, George J. *Great Expectations: An Annotated Bibliography*. New York: Garland, 1986.

**Articles**

Allingham, Philip V. "The Naming of Names in *A Christmas Carol*." *Dickens Quarterly* 4 (March 1987): 15–20.

Anderson, Roland F. "Structure, Myth, and Rite in *Oliver Twist*." *Studies in the Novel* 18 (Fall 1986): 238–257.

Booth, Alison. "Little Dorrit and Dorothea Brooke: Interpreting the Heroines of History." *Nineteenth-Century Literature* 41 (September 1986): 190–216.

Bump, Jerome. "Parody and the Dickens-Collins Collaboration in 'No Thoroughfare'." *Library Chronicle of the University of Texas* 37 (1986): 38–53.

Caramagno, Thomas C. "Bad Fictions and the Improvident Heart in *The Gilded Age* and *Bleak House*." *College Literature* 14 (1987): 62–75.

Caserio, Robert L. "The Name of the Horse: *Hard Times*, Semiotics, and the Supernatural." *Novel* 20 (Fall 1986): 5–23.

Colby, Robert A. "Oliver's Progeny: Some Unfortunate Foundlings." *Dickens Quarterly* 4 (June 1987): 109–121.

Cotsell, Michael. "*The Pickwick Papers* and Travel: A Critical Diversion." *Dickens Quarterly* 3 (March 1986): 5–16.

————. "The Stephen Family and Dickens's Circumlocution Office Satire." *Dickens Quarterly* 3 (December 1986): 175–178.

————. "The Uncommercial Traveller on the Commercial Road: Dickens's East End." *Dickens Quarterly* 3 (June 1986): 75–82; and *DQ* 4 (September 1986): 115–122.

Crawford, Iain. " 'Shades of the prison house': Religious Romanticism in *Oliver Twist*." *Dickens Quarterly* 4 (June 1987): 78–90.

Davis, Jim. "The Importance of Being Caleb: The Influence of Boucicault's *Dot* on the Comic Styles of J. L. Toole and Joseph Jefferson." *The Dickensian* 82 (Spring 1986): 27–32.

Davis, Paul. "Imaging *Oliver Twist*: Hogarth, Illustration, and the Part of Darkness." *The Dickensian* 82 (Autumn 1986): 158–176.

Denman, Peter. "Krook's Death and Dickens's Authorities." *The Dickensian* 82 (Autumn 1986): 131–141.

Dowling, Constance. "Cervantes, Dickens, and the World of the Juvenile Criminal." *The Dickensian* 82 (Autumn 1986): 151–157.

Drexler, R. D. "Note on *Bleak House* and *The Merchant of Venice*." *The Dickensian* 82 (Autumn 1986): 149–150.

Engel, Elliot D. and Margaret F. King. "*Pickwick*'s Progress: The Critical Reception of *The Pickwick Papers* from 1836 to 1986." *Dickens Quarterly* 3 (March 1986): 56–66.

Fiedler, Leslie A. "*Martin Chuzzlewit*—A Great Bad Book." *Dutch Quarterly Review* 16 (1986): 16–21.

Fielding, K. J. "Benthamite Utilitarianism and *Oliver Twist*: A Novel of Ideas." *Dickens Quarterly* 4 (June 1987): 49–65.

Fleissner, Robert F. "The Harvard Affair 'Proves' a Holmes Connection with *Edwin Drood*." *Clues: A Journal of Detection* 7 (Fall/Winter 1986): 109–113.

Forsyte, Charles. "The Sapsea Fragment—Fragment of What?" *The Dickensian* 82 (Spring 1986): 12–26.

Friedman, Stanley. "The *Bleak House* 'East Wind' and Pope's *Rape of the Lock*." *Dickens Quarterly* 3 (June 1986): 90–92.

Gibbs, G. L. "Teaching *Bleak House*." *Uses of English* 38 (Autumn 1986): 63–71.

Golden, Morris. "Dickens, Oliver, and Boz." *Dickens Quarterly* 4 (June 1987): 65–77.

Graver, Suzanne. "Writing in a 'Womanly' Way and the Double Vision of *Bleak House*." *Dickens Quarterly* 4 (March 1987): 3–15.

Hennelly, Jr., Mark M. "Dickens's Praise of Folly: Play in *The Pickwick Papers*." *Dickens Quarterly* 3 (March 1986): 27–45.

Hough, Graham. "Language and Reality in *Bleak House*." In *Realism in European Literature: Essays in Honour of J. P. Stern*. Eds. Nicholas Boyle and Martin Swales. Cambridge: Cambridge University Press, 1986, pp. 50–67.

Ingham, Patricia. "Dialect as 'Realism': *Hard Times* and the Industrial Novel." *Review of English Studies* 37 (1986): 518–527.

Jaffe, Audrey. "Omniscience in *Our Mutual Friend*." *Journal of Narrative Technique* 17 (Winter 1987): 91–101.

Jahn, Karen. "Fit to Survive: Christian Ethics in *Bleak House.*" *Studies in the Novel* 18 (Winter 1986): 367–379.

Justin, Henri. "The Signalman's Signal-Man." *Les Cahiers de nouvelle* 7 (Autumn 1986): 9–16.

Kaplan, Fred. "Dickens and Friends." *Humanities* 7 (Nov.–Dec. 1986): 4–7.

Keitt, Diane. "Charles Dickens and Robert Seymour: The Battle of Wills." *The Dickensian* 82 (Spring 1986): 2–11.

Kelly, Mary Anne. "From Nightmare to Reverie: Continuity in *Our Mutual Friend.*" *Durham University Journal* 79 (December 1986): 45–50.

Kiell, Matthew. "Dickens on Stage." *Humanities* 7 (Nov.–Dec. 1986): 21–23.

Klingel, Joan E. "Dickens's First Epistle to the Utilitarians." *Dickens Quarterly* 3 (September 1986): 124–128.

Lightman, Naomi. "The 'Vulcanic dialect' of *Great Expectations.*" *The Dickensian* 82 (Spring 1986): 33–38.

Lippard, George. "The Spirit of the Times." February 1, 1842. Rpt. in *George Lippard Prophet of Protest: Writings of an American Radical, 1822–1854.* Ed. David S. Reynolds. New York: Peter Lang, 1986, pp. 227–230.

Lohrli, Anne. "To Charles Dickens, Esq." *Dickens Quarterly,* 3 (December 1986), 155–167.

Long, William F. "John Galt's Mr. Snodgrass and Dr. Marigold." *Dickens Quarterly* 3 (December 1986): 178–180.

Lund, Michael. "Reading Long Stories on the Installment Plan." *Humanities* 7 (Nov.–Dec. 1986): 17–20.

MacKay, Carol Hanbery. "The Letter-Writer and the Text in *Martin Chuzzlewit.*" *Studies in English Literature, 1500–1900* 26 (1986): 737–758.

Manning, Sylvia. "Murder in Three Media: Adaptations of *Oliver Twist.*" *Dickens Quarterly* 4 (June 1987): 99–108.

Maskell, Duke. "Grubbing on—by System: Krook vs Bucket." *The Gadfly Literary Supplement.* Retford, Notts.: Brynmill, 1983, pp. 23–48.

Mazor, Yair. "Traces of the English Victorian Novel in the Enlightenment Hebrew Novel: Between Dickens and Smolenskin." *Hebrew Studies* 25 (1984): 90–103.

McLeod, Carol. "Canadian Notes: Francis Dickens of the North West Mounted Police." *The Dickensian* 82 (Autumn 1986): 142–148.

Miller, Michael G. "The *Bleak House* Number Cover: Which Way is the Wind Blowing?" *Dickens Quarterly* 3 (June 1986): 93–94.

Newton, Judith. "Making—and Remaking—History: Another Look at 'Patriarchy'." *Tulsa Studies in Women's Literature* 3 (Spring-Fall 1984): 125–140.

Patten, Robert L. " 'I thought of Mr. Pickwick, and wrote the first number': Dickens and the Evolution of Character." *Dickens Quarterly* 3 (March 1986): 18–25.

Pickrel, Paul. "*Bleak House*: The Emergence of Theme." *Nineteenth-Century Literature* 42 (June 1987): 73–96.

Preston, Edward G. "Muggleton and the Muggletonians." *Dickens Quarterly* 3 (September 1986): 129–131.

Rosenberg, Brian. "The Language of Doubt in *Oliver Twist*." *Dickens Quarterly* 4 (June 1987): 91–98.

Rosenblum, Joseph. "*The Pickwick Papers* and *Paradise Lost*." *Dickens Quarterly* 3 (March 1986): 47–54.

Ross, R. M. and A. G. Bagnell. " 'From the Black Rocks on Friday': More than a Bibliographical Footnote." *Turnbull Library Record* 16 (May 1983): 43–53.

Saywood, Barrie. "*Martin Chuzzlewit*: Language as Disguise." *The Dickensian* 82 (Summer 1986): 86–97.

Sell, Roger D. "Dickens and the New Historicism: The Polyvocal Audience and Discourse of *Dombey and Son*." In *The Nineteenth-Century British Novel*. Ed. Jeremy Hawthorn. London: Edward Arnold, 1986, pp. 63–79.

Steig, Michael. "Another Note on the *Bleak House* Cover: East Wind and Foxes." *Dickens Quarterly* 4 (March 1987), 20–22.

Stycznska, Adela. "The Shifting Point of View in the Narrative Design of *Little Dorrit*." *The Dickensian* 82 (Spring 1986): 39–51.

Sutherland, Kathryn. "The Coming of Age of the Man of Feeling: Sentiment in Lamb and Dickens." *Charles Lamb Bulletin* 55 (July 1986): 196–210.

Swann, Charles. "Dickens, Ruskin and the City: Parallels or Influence?" *The Dickensian* 82 (Summer 1986): 67–81.

Thomas, Deborah A. "In the Meantime: Dickens's Concern with Doubling and Secret Guilt between *A Tale of Two Cities* and *Great Expectations*." *Dickens Quarterly* 3 (June 1986): 84–89.

Tintner, Adeline R. "The Charles Dickens Imprint on Henry James." *American Bookman* (11 August 1986): 453–455.

———. "A Possible Source in Dickens for Poe's 'Imp of the Perverse.' " *Poe Studies* 18 (December 1985): 25.

Urnov, Dmitri. "Dickens in Distant Siberia." *Soviet Literature*, no. 486 (March 1987): 174–177.

Whitmore, Daniel. "Fagin, Effie Deans, and the Spectacle of the Court Room." *Dickens Quarterly* 3 (September 1986): 132–134.

Worth, George J. "*Great Expectations*: A Drama in Three Stages." *Dickens Quarterly* 3 (December 1986): 168–175.

# Index

373

# Contents of Previous Volumes

## Volume 4 (1975)

## Volume 5 (1976)

## Volume 8 (1980)

## Volume 9 (1981)

## Volume 12 (1983)

# Volume 15 (1986)

\*  \*  \*